IRS Collection Solutions Handbook

The Comprehensive Guide to Resolving IRS Tax Debt and Enforcement Issues

2025-2026 VERSION
ISBN: 979-8-218-78004-3
www.TaxProblemsHandbook.com

First edition

Paperback ISBN: 979-8-218-78004-3

About the Authors

Jim Buttonow, CPA, CITP

Jim Buttonow, CPA, CITP, has been a leader in helping taxpayers and tax professionals resolve tax problems with the IRS.   He is the founder and principal at JL Buttonow CPA PLLC, a tax firm dedicated to resolving tax problems for clients and helping tax professionals and tax firms work better with the IRS.

For 19 years, Jim worked at the IRS in various compliance enforcement positions. Since 2006, Jim has been in private practice and tax and accounting software development. Jim consulting practice focuses on the areas of tax controversy and tax administration. Jim led product development and marketing for a successful software company that developed tax problem software for tax professionals and has developed and implemented post-filing tax services for large tax providers, including H&R Block and Jackson Hewitt. This software is currently being used by tens of thousands of tax professionals and businesses in the United States.

Jim has been an IRS partner in improving IRS operations and post-filing service to taxpayers. Jim served as chairperson of the IRS Electronic Tax Administration Advisory Committee (ETAAC) in 2015 and 2016 during which ETAAC played a central role in promoting the IRS digital strategy to develop transformative technology solutions to systemic challenges in tax administration. Jim also served as the North Carolina representative on the IRS' Taxpayer Advocacy Panel (TAP) from 2020-2022.

Jim regularly speaks on areas of tax administration and problem solving to national associations and has testified before Congress in areas of tax administration. He has also published many articles in industry publications. In his articles, Jim focuses on delivering practical insights, advocating for IRS transparency and efficiency, and proposing innovative large-scale solutions for taxpayers and tax professionals.

Jim currently authors the *Tax Problems and Solutions Handbook*, a publication aimed at helping tax pros work more effectively in post-filing matters and resolving their clients' most common tax problems. The book can be found online at TaxProblemsHandbook.com. Jim can be reached at Jim@buttonowcpa.com or at his website at ButtonowCPA.com.

Madison Whitfield, Enrolled Agent

Madison Whitfield is an Enrolled Agent at JL Buttonow CPA PLLC, where she specializes in resolving post-filing tax problems and working with the IRS. Madison represents clients in IRS and State tax issues such as audits, unfiled returns, penalties, business and payroll tax issues, tax debt solutions, and other areas of tax controversy. Madison uses her deep knowledge of IRS procedures to ensure clients receive effective, personal solutions to their tax challenges.

In addition to her hands on work with clients, Madison services the editor of the *Tax Problems and Solutions Handbook*, a leading resource that provides practical guidance on resolving tax controversies and issues. Her contributions keep tax professionals and taxpayers updated on the latest resolution strategies and IRS procedures.

Table of Contents

Introduction:
HOW TO USE THIS BOOK

The *IRS Collection Solutions Handbook* helps you resolve IRS tax debt issues. The *Handbook* provides practical guidance and resources for all IRS collection solutions, including extensions to pay, payment plans, and hardship options, including not-collectible status and the IRS offer in compromise program. The book is designed to be used by both taxpayers and tax professionals to resolve collection issues with the IRS.

Most IRS rules and collection procedures are not found in the Internal Revenue Code and its regulations- they are found in IRS announcements and most, in its Internal Revenue Manual ("IRM"). IRS employees must follow the rules in the IRM when enforcing collection issues and allowing IRS collection agreements. As such, many of the references in this Handbook refer to the appropriate rule in the IRM to guide the taxpayer and the tax professional in properly resolving a collection issue.

Use the following chart to help with collection issues and agreements:

If you want to:	Chapter
Understand the IRS collection process and collection options.	Chapter 1
Understand IRS collection alternatives.	Chapter 2
Learn the steps to address an IRS collection situation if the taxpayer does not know where to start.	Chapter 3
Obtain taxpayer and tax account information to evaluate collection alternatives.	Chapter 4
Evaluate which collection alternative is best.	Chapter 5
Obtain an extension to pay.	Chapter 6
Obtain a simplified installment agreement including guaranteed and simple installment agreements.	Chapter 7
Obtain a full- pay non-streamlined payment plan (owe between $50,000 and $250,000).	Chapter 8
Determine ability to pay for collection options (ATP IA, CNC, OIC).	Chapter 9
Obtain an installment agreement based on ability to pay analysis.	Chapter 10
Obtain currently not collectible status.	Chapter 11
Evaluate and apply for an offer in compromise.	Chapter 12
Evaluate and obtain OIC for Effective Tax Administration.	Chapter 13
Reinstate/renegotiate a defaulted installment agreement.	Chapter 14
Avoid/release a wage garnishment or levy.	Chapter 15
Avoid/relief from a federal tax lien.	Chapter 16
Avoid/remove passport restrictions.	Chapter 17
IRS Collection appeals options.	Chapter 18

Get IRS expense allowances and collection standards to help with evaluating collection options.	Appendix A
Get links to useful templates, forms, and worksheets to use for collection issues.	Appendix B
Get links to IRS forms to use with collection agreements.	Appendix C
Get links to read common IRS collection notices.	Appendix D
Get links to read IRS publications on collection issues.	Appendix E
Index	Appendix F

IRS Collection Solutions - Key Highlights:

- *Many owe and cannot pay*: over 20 million individuals owe the IRS at the end of 2023 – and more are added to this status annually as more taxpayers file or have additional adjustments (i.e., from IRS compliance activity such as audits) and cannot pay. Each year, millions file and cannot pay. Over 4 million businesses in 2023 owe the IRS back taxes. It is estimated that, as of 2025, approximately 26 million individuals and businesses owe the IRS. Of these 26 million individuals and businesses who owe the IRS, only 20% are in an agreement to pay. The other 80% are subject to IRS collection enforcement actions.
- *Cannot pay — get a collection alternative*: taxpayers who owe and cannot pay need a collection alternative or they will face IRS collection enforcement.
- *Collection statute*: the IRS has ten years from the date of assessment to collect back taxes.
- *The power to collect*: IRS enforcement tools are liens, levies, and passport restrictions. In egregious situations, the IRS may seize assets, but it rarely does so.
- *The alternatives to full payment*: the IRS has four categories of collection alternatives to full payment: extensions to pay, installment agreements, currently not collectible hardship status, and the tax settlement called an Offer in Compromise.
- *Most common solutions*: extensions to pay and installment agreements are most of the collection agreements executed with the IRS.
- *Most deal with IRS by phone or online*: most IRS collection activity is completed through automated collection notices, enforcement actions, and refund offsets. Most IRS interactions regarding complex collection solutions are done by phone. Business taxpayers and taxpayers with large balances owed are often sent to local IRS collection offices for collection. However, over 2/3rds of all payment plans are now completed online using the IRS's Online Payment Agreement (OPA) application.

Post-filing tax issue	Solution	Solution Explanation	Use Form
IRS Collection Issues	Extension to pay	Request up to 180 days to pay the balance and/or execute an IRS collection alternative	None; use IRS online payment agreement or call directly
	Simplified installment agreements	Request IRS payment plan to full pay amounts under $50,000; will avoid a financial disclosure and tax-lien filing Request IRS payment plan to full pay amounts between $50,000 and $200,000; will avoid a financial disclosure but a tax lien will be filed	Form 9465 Form 433D Online Payment Agreement
	Complex installment agreements	Request an installment agreement based on the taxpayer's ability to pay, normally past 72 months	Form 433D Form 9465 Forms 433F, 433A, 433B, 433H
	Currently not collectible status	Request a payment deferral status based on the taxpayer's ability to pay	Forms 433F, 433A, 433B
	Offer in compromise	Request a settlement for less than the taxpayer owes, based on the taxpayer's ability to pay and reasonable collection potential	Form 656, with Forms 433A-OIC or Form 433B-OIC
	Passport restriction restoration	Request a qualifying collection alternative that will decertify the taxpayer as having "seriously delinquent tax debt"	Expedite request to IRS Collection or to Taxpayer Advocate Service via Form 911
	Levy release	Request removal of wage garnishment, bank levy, or other levy, based on a collection agreement and/or hardship	Obtain levy release by phone
	Lien release and other relief	Request lien release, withdrawal, subordination, or other relief to remove or change the nature of a federal tax lien	Lien release obtained by phone Form 12277 (lien withdrawal) Form 14135 (Lien discharge) Form 14134 (Lien subordination)
	Collection appeals hearing	Appeal an IRS Collection determination, such as a lien, levy, or installment agreement term	Form 9423
	Collection Due Process (CDP) hearing	Appeal an IRS levy or lien with a collection alternative and/or dispute the taxes and penalties owed	Form 12153

What's New for 2025 and 2026?

- Updated collection financial standards and exemption amounts to determine ability to pay.
- Updated collection forms: including Form 656-B, *Offer in Compromise* Booklet.
- IRS restarts campus collection notices and enforcement through levies.
- IRS retires the Streamlined Installment Agreement and replaces it with the more favorable Simple Installment Agreement.
- Expansion of online accounts to allow for viewing of balances owed and executing Online Payment Agreements.

What's Covered in This *Handbook*?

- Step-by-step approach to resolving a collection issue.
- How to determine which collection alternative is best.
- How to compute a taxpayer's ability to pay through an installment agreement, currently not collectible, or an Offer in Compromise.
- How to obtain an IRS collection alternative for extensions to pay, installment agreements, currently not collectible, and Offer in Compromise.
- How to resolve collection enforcement actions.
- How to appeal an adverse collection determination.

What's Not Covered — and Why?

- *Bankruptcy options*: these options are legal remedies that require the expertise of a bankruptcy attorney. Few taxpayers utilize this option solely for tax debt resolution.
- *Evasion of payment situations*: taxpayers who have evaded payment by transferring assets or other means should consult an attorney for assistance and legal advice.

Most Common Actions Performed by Taxpayers and Tax Professionals When Addressing Collection Issues

- Evaluating which collection alternative is best.
- Contacting the IRS for tax history and to execute agreements.
- Simple installment agreements.
- Extensions to pay.
- Avoiding IRS collection enforcement (lien, levy, passport restrictions).
- Making payments.

When to Get an Expert Involved

- *Field collection*: collection enforcement by the Collection Field function (revenue officer).
- *Complicated solutions*: complex ability to pay collection alternatives (Ability to pay installment agreements, Offer in Compromise), especially for small business taxpayers.
- *Notice of Federal Tax Lien complications*: evaluating and executing lien relief options.
- *Bankruptcy*: contemplating bankruptcy to resolve back tax debt issues.
- *Potential criminal violations*: taxpayers who have wilfully evaded payment should always consult an attorney.

Professional Assistance Fees

- *Hourly*: range from $80-$500 an hour for an EA, CPA, or tax attorney representation.
- *Flat fee*: national firms can charge flat fees from $3,000-$25,000 depending on the amount owed and complexity of the issues involved.
- *No fee*: low-income taxpayer clinics can assist taxpayers free of charge.

Closely Related Issues

- *Unfiled returns:* taxpayers must have filed all returns to qualify for most IRS collection alternatives.
- *Penalties:* taxpayers who cannot pay incur penalties. Taxpayers should request penalty abatement if they qualify.
- *Trust Fund Recovery Penalty investigations*: IRS Collection has the authority investigate, assess, and collect the Trust Fund Recovery Penalty on unpaid employment taxes from any and all responsible persons.

Time Frame Estimates for Common Collection Solutions/Actions		
Collection Action	**Estimated Hours to Complete**	**Average Duration Estimate**
Obtaining tax history and transcripts from IRS	<1 hour (best to call IRS by phone)	1 day-3 weeks (if transcripts come by mail)
Extension to pay (non-hardship)	<1 hour (by phone or online)	1 day
Simple installment agreements	1-2 hours (by phone or online)	1 day (up to 6 weeks to finalize if paying by direct debit)
Complex ability to pay installment agreements involving production of Collection Information Statements	6-25 hours (self-employed taxpayers require more financial analysis)	1 day-3 months (quickest by contacting IRS by phone/fax)
Preparing and negotiating an OIC	15-40 hours	6-12 months
Post-agreement levy release	1 hour	1 day
Lien relief options	6-20 hours	1-3 months
Expedited passport restriction relief (post-agreement)	5-10 hours	14-30 days
Follow-up status check with IRS	<1 hour (by phone)	<1 day

Chapter 1:
UNDERSTANDING THE IRS COLLECTION PROCESS

This section provides a basic overview of the IRS collection process and conveys important information when working with the IRS on a collection issue.

Topic	Covers
Introduction to IRS Collection and U.S. Tax Debtors	How the IRS collects tax and the most likely situations taxpayers face when they have a balance with the IRS.
Basic IRS Collection Principles	Ten fundamental principles of IRS collection and how to attain a collection agreement.
Relevant IRS Internal Revenue Manual Sections	Highlights of the IRS collection manual that contains the procedures used in IRS collection alternatives, agreements, and enforcement.
Frequently Used IRS Collection Phone Numbers	IRS contact numbers used for IRS collection issues.
Useful IRS Website Resources and Online Tools	IRS resources to obtain tax account information and enter into collection agreements.
Key Terms and Definitions	IRS terms used in resolving a collection issue with the IRS.
Overview of IRS Collection Alternatives	Quick summary of IRS collection alternatives to full pay.
Overview of IRS Collection Enforcement	Quick summary of IRS Automated Collection System and Collection Field function.
IRS Collection Process: The Collection Notice Stream and the IRS Collection Roadmap	The IRS notice process used to collect back taxes owed and the process of collection.
IRS Collection Enforcement: Levies and Liens	Quick overview of IRS collection enforcement through levies and liens.
IRS Collection Enforcement: Passport Restrictions	Quick overview of IRS collection enforcement using passport restrictions.
Collection Statute of Limitations	Explanation of how long the IRS can collect on back balances owed.
Additions to Unpaid Taxes: Failure to Pay Penalty and Accrued Interest	Failure to pay penalty rates and interest rates on back balances.
Payments Methods	Various ways to pay the IRS. How and why to designate payments on specific balances owed.

Private Debt Collection	How the IRS's private debt collection process works.
Tax Debtors: Annual Notices of Balances Owed and Activity	Notices that taxpayers will receive each year when they have a balance with the IRS.

Key Highlights:

- There are approximately 26 million individual and business taxpayers in 2025 who have a balance with the IRS and need a collection alternative to be in good standing with the IRS.
- Taxpayers who are not in an agreement on their unpaid balances face IRS collection enforcement, including levies, liens, and passport restrictions.
- The IRS has a system of collecting through automated notices and systems as well as local collection officers. The rules for working with IRS collection are contained in the IRS's Internal Revenue Manual.
- The IRS has ten years from the date of assessment to collect on taxes owed. After the collection statute expires, the IRS writes off the remaining balances owed.

Chapter 1.01: Introduction to IRS Collection and U.S. Tax Debtors

Taxpayers who owe and cannot pay the IRS can enter into an agreement with the IRS to pay their taxes. This agreement allows them to get into good standing with the IRS; otherwise, they face possible enforced collection of their balances owed. These agreements can come in the form of:

- an extension to pay,
- one of the many types of IRS payment plans (called installment agreements),
- currently not collectible temporary hardship status, or
- an offer in compromise.

Taxpayers who do not achieve good standing with the IRS face potential enforced collection in the form of IRS levies, federal tax liens, and passport restrictions. It is essential for taxpayers who need a collection alternative to understand the options available to them and the required procedures to successfully execute an agreement with the IRS. Once the taxpayer has successfully executed an agreement on the back taxes owed, they will achieve good standing with the IRS and will avoid enforced collection as long as they abide by the terms of that agreement.

U.S. Tax Debtors

Each year, millions of taxpayers file their tax returns but are unable to pay the balance. Millions more have additional taxes that they cannot pay as a result of assessments from audits, return adjustments, and other additions to tax, such as penalties. As of September 2022, delinquent taxpayers owed the IRS $545 billion. The IRS enforcement resources could only collect approximately $72 billion of the outstanding amount. [TIGTA Report 2024-300-011, Trends in Compliance Activities Through Fiscal Year 2022, December 20, 2023]

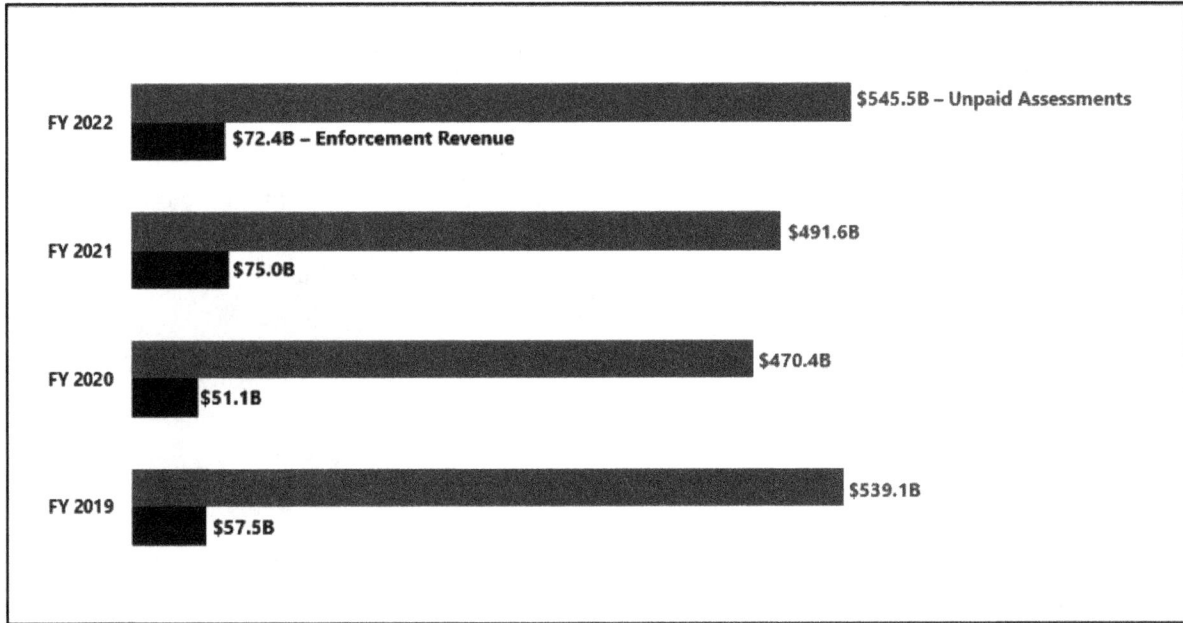

Source: Office of Research, Applied Analytics, and Statistics for the enforcement revenue, and the Chief Financial Officer for the unpaid assessment data.

In 2023, the IRS reported that there were 24 million individuals and businesses that owed back taxes and could not pay them. Of those individuals, 95% owed less than $50,000 to the IRS. [IRS FOIA Response #2024-05289, February 2024] For businesses, 94.1% owe less than $50,000. The median amount owed is far less than $5,000 for both individual and business taxpayers.

Tax Debtors (Individual and business/specialty) as of 9/30/2023 (by amount owed)

Tax Debt Owed	Individual taxpayers						Business and Specialty taxpayers (EIN)					
	# of taxpayers	%	Cumulative	Amount owed	%	Cumulative	# of taxpayers	%	Cumulative	Amount owed	%	Cumulative
<$500	3,494,441	17.5%	17.5%	$ 687,046,428	0.2%	0.2%	1,102,877	27.6%	27.6%	$ 195,798,732	0.2%	0.2%
$500 - <$1K	1,967,691	9.8%	27.3%	$ 1,442,959,157	0.4%	0.6%	459,574	11.5%	39.1%	$ 337,370,060	0.3%	0.4%
$1K - <$5K	6,779,390	33.9%	61.1%	$ 17,417,666,348	5.3%	5.9%	1,245,862	31.2%	70.3%	$ 3,088,878,746	2.5%	3.0%
$5K - <$10K	2,925,157	14.6%	75.8%	$ 20,906,594,782	6.3%	12.2%	433,228	10.8%	81.1%	$ 3,028,826,861	2.5%	5.5%
$10K - <$25K	2,755,691	13.8%	89.5%	$ 43,083,878,178	13.0%	25.2%	356,840	8.9%	90.0%	$ 5,560,936,929	4.6%	10.0%
$25K - <$50K	1,105,420	5.5%	95.0%	$ 38,490,359,516	11.6%	36.9%	160,395	4.0%	94.1%	$ 5,583,678,663	4.6%	14.6%
$50K - <$100K	534,833	2.7%	97.7%	$ 36,941,538,723	11.2%	48.0%	100,642	2.5%	96.6%	$ 763,556,408	0.6%	15.3%
$100K - <$500K	397,571	2.0%	99.7%	$ 78,742,052,493	23.8%	71.8%	106,950	2.7%	99.3%	$ 22,289,152,899	18.3%	33.6%
$500K - <$1M	38,287	0.2%	99.9%	$ 26,149,355,858	7.9%	79.7%	15,520	0.4%	99.6%	$ 10,782,701,469	8.9%	42.4%
$1M - <$10M	19,948	0.1%	100.0%	$ 42,246,409,914	12.8%	92.5%	13,492	0.3%	100.0%	$ 33,587,589,074	27.6%	70.0%
$10M - <$50M	666	0.0%	100.0%	$ 12,645,358,323	3.8%	96.3%	833	0.0%	100.0%	$ 15,779,210,591	13.0%	83.0%
$50 - <$100M	53	0.0%	100.0%	$ 3,719,979,600	1.1%	97.4%	63	0.0%	100.0%	$ 4,478,655,180	3.7%	86.7%
$100M+	30	0.0%	100.0%	$ 8,611,166,806	2.6%	100.0%	60	0.0%	100.0%	$ 16,220,805,049	13.3%	100.0%
TOTAL	20,019,178	100.0%		$ 331,084,366,126	100.0%		3,996,336	100.0%		$ 121,697,160,661	100.0%	
Averages				Average amount owed $ 16,538						Average amount owed $ 30,452		
				Median amount owed $ 3,686						Median amount owed $ 2,397		
				Average amount owed for those who owe <$100M $ 16,108						Average amount owed for those who owe <$100M $ 26,394		
				Average amount owed for those who owe >$1M $ 3,247,955						Average amount owed for those who owe >$1M $ 4,849,547		
				Average amount owed for those who owe <$1M $ 13,194						Average amount owed for those who owe <$1M $ 12,966		
				Average amount owed for those who owe <$50K $ 6,413						Average amount owed for those who owe <$50K $ 4,734		

Although data is not yet available for 2024, it is estimated that 26 million taxpayers now the IRS.

The majority of these taxpayers could enter into a simple installment agreement that would satisfy their liability and allow them to achieve good standing with the IRS.

Despite this, many taxpayers fail to seek a collection alternative.

As of September 30, 2024, approximately 20% of taxpayers were not in one of the available IRS collection agreements – and are subject to enforced collection actions.

80% of Taxpayers are NOT in an IRS Collection Agreement

Options:

- Extension to pay
- Payment Plan (installment agreement)
- Hardship agreements
  - Not collectible
  - Partial Pay Installment Agreement
  - Offer in compromise

TAX DEBTORS AND IRS AGREEMENTS: 2024

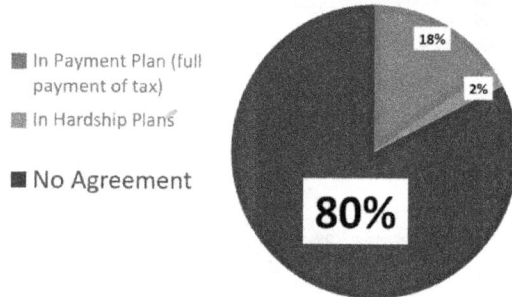

■ In Payment Plan (full payment of tax)
■ In Hardship Plans
■ No Agreement

18%
2%
80%

Tax Debtors and Collection Agreements	#	% of Total	% in IRS Agreement
Total Tax Debtors (estimated)	26,000,000		
In Payment Plan (full payment of tax)	4,642,420	17.86%	
In Hardship Plans: (not full payment of tax)			19.63%
Currently not collectible status	421,125	1.62%	
Partial Pay Installment Agreement	32,388	0.12%	
Approved Offer in Compromise	7,199	0.03%	

As of September 2024, the IRS had over 14.9 million delinquent taxpayer accounts in collections with the IRS. [IRS Data Book, 2024, Table 27] Out of the more than 163 million individual filers for the 2023 tax year, 41.6 million filed with a balance due to the IRS. [IRS Filing Season Statistics for 2024 Filing Season, December 27, 2024] Ultimately, several million of these taxpayers will not be able to pay the IRS immediately and will join the population of taxpayers who will require a collection alternative.

Taxpayers who owe back taxes, penalties, and/or interest to the IRS can face IRS collection enforcement if they do not pay the balances owed or come to an agreement with the IRS, called a collection alternative. The IRS can enforce collection of back taxes through levies and federal tax liens that can seize their income and assets to pay the outstanding balances. [IRC sections 6331(a) and 6321] Beginning in 2018, the IRS began to certify seriously delinquent tax debtors, providing their information to the State Department for purposes of restricting their passport use. [IRC §7345]

Taxpayers who are unable to pay have alternatives to facing collections by the IRS. The IRS routinely allows taxpayers extensions of time to pay and payment plans that allow the taxpayer to meet the payment obligations. For taxpayers facing financial hardship, the IRS has temporary hardship relief, referred to as "currently not collectible." The IRS also has a settlement option called an "offer in compromise" that allows for a satisfactory settlement with taxpayers who do not possess the capability to pay in full with their current assets or future income. Each year, millions of taxpayers enter into extensions to pay, installment agreements, and currently not collectible status. 7,199 taxpayers in 2024 successfully secured an offer in compromise to settle their tax bill for less than the amount owed. [IRS FOIA Response #2025-00032, October 2024 and IRS Data Book 2024, Table 27] Taxpayers who require a collection alternative must act timely in order to avoid the adverse consequences of enforced IRS collection activity.

IRS Collection Enforcement Functions

Most IRS collection enforcement originates from IRS computer systems (called the Automated Collection Systems or ACS). More serious IRS collection enforcement is usually assigned to Collection Field function (local IRS collection offices staffed with special collection enforcement personnel called revenue officers). The rules and procedures to obtain each type of collection alternative differ and the rules change frequently. Most of these rules are in the IRS's operational guidelines that are explained in the Internal Revenue Manual. Part 5 of the IRM contains many of these procedures. Other rules can also be found in other IRS guidance including publications and forms instructions. It is important to accurately follow the most current IRS procedures to successfully secure an IRS collection alternative.

Chapter 1.02: Basic IRS Collection Principles

Taxpayers who cannot pay the amounts owed need to be aware of the ten basic principles of IRS collection:

1. *The four IRS alternatives to full payment of taxes*: if a taxpayer cannot pay, the IRS has four collection alternatives to full payment: extension to pay, installment agreement, currently not collectible temporary status, and an offer in compromise. There are different rules for each alternative. Bankruptcy can also be a collection option, but this program operates within the guidelines of the U.S. Bankruptcy Code.
2. *The IRS can enforce payment:* taxpayers who do not pay their balances owed to the IRS or make other collection arrangements can face IRS collection enforcement in the forms of levies, federal tax liens, and possible passport restrictions. [IRC sections 6331, 6321, and 7345]
3. *Agreements require filing and payment compliance*: in order to enter into a collection alternative, taxpayers must file all required returns and have sufficient withholding and/or estimated tax payments in order to avoid owing additional taxes on future return filings. [IRM 5.14.1.4.2 (12-23-2022)]
4. *Only one agreement allowed:* for taxpayers who owe for multiple years, the IRS requires that the taxpayer enter into only one agreement to pay. Additional balance-owed years will cause a default on existing agreements with the IRS. [IRM 5.14.1.4.2 (12-23-2022)]
5. *Penalties and interest continue to accrue:* balances owed to the IRS will continue to accrue a failure to pay penalty (up to 25%) and interest (the rate determined by quarter) on the outstanding balances owed. [IRC sections 6651 and 6601]
6. *Refunds are taken to offset balance owed:* when a taxpayer owes back balances, the IRS will take the taxpayer's refunds and overpayments to offset against the balanced owed until the balance is paid in full. [IRC §6402(c)]

7. *IRS has ten years to collect:* the collection statute of limitations is ten years from the date of assessment. The IRS can collect all balances until the collection statute expiration date. [IRC §6502]

8. *Certain taxes and taxpayers get more serious enforcement:* taxpayers who owe payroll and other trust fund taxes, who owe higher balances and/or for repeated years, or have unfiled tax returns, in addition to balances owed, face more scrutiny from the IRS.

9. *Most IRS collection enforcement is automated:* collection of back taxes can be enforced by IRS automated systems or by local IRS field personnel. Most collection activity is pursued by the automated systems. Most interactions to resolve collection issues can be done by phone to the IRS campuses or "service centers" that send these automated notices and collection enforcement activity.

10. *Importance of agreement to avoid enforcement:* taxpayers who do not make an agreement with the IRS can be subject to enforcement by levy, federal tax lien, and, possibly, passport restrictions. Taxpayers need to execute a collection agreement and complete the terms of their agreement to stay in good standing with the IRS to avoid enforced collection.

Chapter 1.03: Relevant Internal Revenue Manual Sections

The IRS's Internal Revenue Manual (IRM) contains most of the rules related to IRS collection procedures and collection alternatives. Part 5 of the IRM contains most of the IRS collection procedures. The following sections are most often used in assisting taxpayers with IRS collection issues:

IRM Section	Topic
Part 5	IRS collection process
5.19	IRS automated collection procedures
5.15	Financial analysis rules for installment agreements and CNC
5.16	Currently not collectible status and rules
5.14	Installment agreement rules and options
5.1.19	Collection statute of limitation rules
5.12	Federal tax lien rules and options
5.11	Levy rules
5.9	Bankruptcy rules for tax debtors
5.8	Offer in compromise rules

Chapter 1.04: Frequently Used IRS Collection Phone Numbers

IRS Hotline	Phone Number	Hours/Availability (times subject to change)
Individual Accounts	(800) 829-1040	For taxpayers, tax pros use PPS M-F, 7AM-7PM, local time
Business and Specialty Accounts	(800) 829-4933	For taxpayers, tax pros use PPS M-F, 7AM-7PM, local time
Taxpayer Advocate National Hotline (central intake)	(877) 777-4778	M-F, 7AM-7PM, local time Local offices: 8AM-4:30PM
Balance Due Questions: Taxpayer Not in IRS Collection	(800) 829-0922	M-F, 7AM-7PM, local time
Automated Collection: Individuals	(800) 829-7650 (W&I)	M-F, 8AM-8PM, local time
Automated Collection: Self-Employed and Businesses	(800) 829-3903 (SB/SE)	M-F, 8AM-8PM, local time
Centralized Offer in Compromise Unit (on Form 656-PPV)	(844) 398-5025 (Memphis) (844) 805-4980 (Holtsville)	M-F, 8AM-5PM (CST) M-F, 8AM-11PM (EST)
Centralized Lien Unit	(800) 913-6050	M-F, 8AM-5PM, local time
Treasury (Tax) Offset Program (not an IRS number)	(800) 304-3107	M-F, 7:30AM-5:30PM (CST), plus automated options
Practitioner Priority Service	(866) 860-4259 Option #2: Individual accounts Option #3: Business accounts Option #4: Automated Collection System	M-F, 7AM-7PM, local time
Automated Substitute for Return Unit	(866) 681-4271	M-F, 10AM-5PM, local time
IRS Special Compliance Program	(833) 282-7220	M-F, 8AM-8PM, ET

Chapter 1.05: Useful IRS Website Resources and Online Tools

Website	URL	Description
IRS Collection Financial Standards	https://www.irs.gov/businesses/small-businesses-self-employed/collection-financial-standards	Updated IRS collection standards for expenses allowed in ability to pay agreements.
IRS Online Payment Agreement	https://www.irs.gov/payments/online-payment-agreement-application	Request streamlined payment agreement or extension to pay online.
IRS "View your tax account" online tool	https://www.irs.gov/payments/your-online-account	Taxpayer IRS online account that provides transcripts and account information, including balances owed.
IRS Get Transcript service	https://www.irs.gov/individuals/get-transcript	Obtain IRS transcripts for each tax year/form.
IRS e-Services Transcript Delivery System (tax pros only)	https://www.irs.gov/tax-professionals/transcript-delivery-system-tds	Tax pro electronic account with features to access authorized taxpayer transcripts.
IRS OIC Pre-qualifier tool	https://irs.treasury.gov/oic_pre_qualifier/	Tool to use to see if a taxpayer qualifies for an OIC.
IRS Collection Process	https://www.irs.gov/businesses/small-businesses-self-employed/collection-process-for-taxpayers-filing-and-or-paying-late	IRS resources and forms for resolving back taxes.

Chapter 1.06: Key Terms and Definitions

Term	Definition
Ability to Pay (ATP)	The amount a taxpayer can afford to pay based on equity in assets and income and allowable expenses.
Automated Collection System (ACS)	Refers to the IRS automated function of issuing past-due notices and triggering enforced collection actions, including levies and liens.
Collection Appeals Program (CAP)	An informal IRS appeals function generally used to dispute the terms of an installment agreement. A taxpayer uses Form 9423 to request a CAP hearing.

Collection Due Process Hearing (CDP)	A formal IRS appeals hearing that is triggered by a Notice of Federal Tax Lien filing or a Final Notice of Intent to Levy. Taxpayers are given an opportunity to contest the liability, including penalties, or offer a collection alternative. The taxpayer requests this hearing 30 days after the lien filing or intent to levy notice using IRS Form 12153.
Collection Field Function (CFf)	The CFf is a local IRS collection office staffed with revenue officers who collect on the more complicated taxpayers (high wealth, employers, business entities), and more serious delinquent tax obligations (high amount owed, payroll trust fund taxes, corporate taxes, and abusive transactions).
Collection Information Statement (CIS)	Financial disclosure by a taxpayer to the IRS. This includes personal information, assets, liabilities, income, and expenses. The purpose of this statement is for the IRS to determine collectability and collection options for the taxpayer. Individuals: File Form 433-A, 433-F, or 433-H. Businesses: File Form 433-B.
Collection Notice Stream	Series of IRS notices sent by the IRS to collect on back taxes owed.
Collection Statute of Limitations (CSED)	Refers to the amount of time the IRS has to collect on a balance owed. The collection statute expiration date (CSED) is ten years from the date the tax was assessed. It can be extended by several taxpayer or IRS actions.
Conditional Expenses	Actual household expenses that may be allowed as a necessary expense or as another expense in determining monthly disposable income for installment agreements when the taxpayer can pay within six years, or the CSED, whichever is shorter.
Currently Not Collectible (CNC)	A status granted by the IRS to a taxpayer who has no ability to pay the tax owed (based on the ATP calculation).
Equity in Assets and Net Realizable Equity in Assets (NRE)	The calculation of the amount of equity available to pay toward outstanding liabilities.
Extension to Pay Agreement (ETP)	IRS one-time extension to pay for each tax year in which the taxpayer is given 180 days to pay. Only available from the IRS ACS. There can be other ETP that the IRS provides if it is in the best interest of the government and the taxpayer to provide a short-term extension.
Federal Tax Lien	There are two types of liens: a "silent lien" and a public "Notice of Federal Tax Lien" (NFTL). Once a taxpayer owes the IRS, the government has a claim on the taxpayer's assets – called a "silent lien." A filed NFTL is the government's legal claim that alerts creditors of the government's legal right to

	property and rights to property for an amount of unpaid tax liability. An NFTL is an enforcement action taken by the IRS on a taxpayer who is in the IRS Collection compliance unit.
Financial Disclosure	The process of disclosing financial information to the IRS for the purposes of collection.
Full-pay non-streamlined installment agreement (NSIA)	A payment plan that allows a taxpayer who owe between $50,000 and less than $250,000 to make monthly payments before the collection statute expiration date. This agreement is new for 2020 and beyond. This agreement usually requires the IRS to file a Notice of Federal Tax Lien as part of the terms.
Installment Agreement (IA)	An agreement between a taxpayer and the IRS to make payments in monthly installments to pay the balance owed. There are several different types of IAs that have varying payment terms.
IRS Fresh Start Initiative	The 2012-2013 IRS collection program initiatives that eased IRS collection rules on installment agreements, lien filings, and OIC offer amounts. Most of these initiatives have been permanently implemented into IRS collection policy and procedures.
Levy	An enforcement action taken by the IRS on a taxpayer who is in the IRS Collection compliance unit. A levy is a seizure of taxpayer income and assets in order to pay an outstanding tax liability.
Monthly Disposable Income (MDI)	Used to calculate your client's ATP. MDI is the amount of income remaining after necessary expenses have been paid.
Necessary Living Expenses	Household expenses that are allowed in determining monthly disposable income of a taxpayer in an ability to pay analysis. Some expenses are limited by IRS Collection Financial Standards (food/clothing, housing/utilities, transportation).
Not Allowable Expenses	Discretionary expenses that the IRS does not allow in determining the taxpayer's ability to pay on an installment agreement.
Offer in Compromise (OIC)	A settlement of a balance owed for less than the amount owed. There are three types of OICs: Doubt as to Collectability (owe but cannot afford to pay – the most common type of OIC), Doubt as to Liability (do not owe the amount), and Effective Tax Administration (owe and can pay but special circumstances exist requiring the government to accept less than the amount owed).
Passport Restrictions	IRS enforcement provision that allows the IRS to "certify" that a taxpayer has seriously delinquent tax debt to the U.S. State Department for purposes of restricting use or renewal of

	his/her passport. Taxpayers can decertify by getting into good standing with the IRS.
Private Debt Collection (PDC)	IRS outsource of old tax debt accounts to one of the four private debt collectors. The PDCs can contact taxpayers directly to solicit payment or enter into an installment agreement to pay. PDCs cannot enter into complex collection alternatives such as currently not collectible or an OIC.
Reasonable Collection Potential (RCP)	In an IRS OIC, this is the calculated amount of future income and equity in assets that the IRS can reasonably expect to receive if the taxes are settled. This is also referred to as the "offer amount" for an OIC.
Repeater	A taxpayer who has multiple tax years with a balance owed. These taxpayers are likely to see quicker IRS collection enforcement because of the continuous balances owed, which default IRS installment agreements and add to the balances owed.
Revenue Officer (RO)	A local IRS person responsible for securing collection of an unpaid balance and/or delinquent tax returns. Also referred to as the Collection Field function (CFf).
Seriously Delinquent Tax Debt (SDTD)	Taxpayers with tax debt over $64,000 (underlined adjusted annually) and not in good standing with the IRS are certified as having "seriously delinquent tax debt" for purposes of notifying the State Department for passport restrictions.
Simple Installment Agreement (SIA)	The most common IRS collection alternative that taxpayers execute. In 2025, this agreement and its terms replaced the streamlined installment agreement (SLIA). The SIA allows taxpayers who owe less than $50,000 and can pay within the collection statute expiration date. Commonly used to avoid an NFTL.
Taxpayer Delinquent Account (TDA)	IRS term for a taxpayer who owes and is in IRS collection enforcement.
Taxpayer Delinquent Investigation (TDI)	IRS term for a taxpayer who has an unfiled tax return and is in IRS collection enforcement.
Taxpayer Relief Initiative (TRI)	IRS COVID-19 collection relief provisions, which provided taxpayers easier terms for extensions to pay, installment agreements, and accepted offer in compromises.

Chapter 1.07: Overview of IRS Collection Alternatives

The IRS has four basic categories of collection alternatives:

1. *Extension to pay*: these alternatives allow taxpayers to receive an extension to pay an outstanding balance owed. These extensions can be up to 180 days. [IRM 5.14.1.6 (12-23-2022)]

> **Pro Tip:** In response to the COVID-19 pandemic, the IRS announced in its Taxpayer Relief Initiative (TRI) that the IRS will expand extension to pay agreements from 120 days to 180 days. This provision was made permanent in 2022. Taxpayers should stay up to date as the IRS may change these relief provisions in the future. [IRS News Release IR-2020-248, November 2, 2020]

2. *Installment agreement*: these agreements create a monthly payment plan for the taxpayer with the IRS. There are two types of installment agreements:
   a. *Simple installment agreements*: these are the most widely used payment plans as they are easy to obtain and avoid the filing of a Notice of Federal Tax Lien. These plans allow qualifying taxpayers to pay the amount owed over a specific period without the need to provide detailed financial information to the IRS. One simple payment plan, the full-pay non-streamlined installment agreement, does require the IRS to file a Notice of Federal Tax Lien.

   > **Pro Tip:** From 2012-2024, most IRS installment agreements were the Simple installment agreements, including the replaced Streamlined Installment Agreements (SLIA) and the new Simple Installment Agreement (SIA).

   b. *Ability to pay installment agreements*: in these payment plans, the taxpayer cannot qualify and/or afford the terms for the simple installment agreements. These agreements require the taxpayer to provide financial information (called collection information statements) and documentation to prove their ability to pay.

   [IRM 5.19.1.6.4 (1-26-2023)]

3. *Currently not collectible status*: when taxpayers experience a financial hardship and only have enough income to pay for their necessary living expenses they can qualify and receive a temporary payment deferral from the IRS. Like proving the inability to pay installment agreements, the taxpayer must provide financial information and documentation to prove they cannot pay. [IRM 5.16.1.2 (3-3-2025)]
4. *Offer in compromise*: taxpayers who are unable to pay the IRS in full with their assets or future installment agreement payments can settle their taxes for less than the amount owed. Taxpayers who qualify can offer their reasonable collection potential (a calculation) to settle their tax bill. [IRM 5.8.1.2.1 (9-23-2008)]

Bankruptcy can also be a legal alternative to address serious back tax issues and financial hardship. Under certain conditions, bankruptcy can eliminate taxes, penalties, and interest and/or provide more favorable payment terms. Because bankruptcy is a legal alternative, taxpayers should consult legal counsel to determine how bankruptcy can be applied as a collection alternative. [IRM 5.9.1 (2-3-2025)]

Chapter 1.08: Overview of IRS Collection Enforcement

The IRS has two primary compliance units that enforce the payment of back taxes:

- *Automated Collection System* (ACS): the ACS is staffed with IRS collection personnel who interact with delinquent taxpayers by phone and correspondence. They can set up extensions to pay, installment agreements, and currently not collectible status. They can also issue liens and levies.
- *Collection Field function* (CFf): the CFf are local area IRS collection offices staffed with revenue officers (RO). A RO investigates the most egregious tax debtors including those taxpayers subject to employment tax delinquencies, high tax debt owed, with multiple years owed, non-filers with potential high balances owed, and business tax liabilities. ROs have broad authority and can swiftly file a tax lien and issue a levy to collect on balances owed.

Offer in compromise applications can be investigated locally or through the IRS Centralized Offer in Compromise Units that are in the Holtsville, NY or Memphis, TN IRS Service Centers. Both ACS and the CFf are also responsible for enforcing filing of back tax returns — called taxpayer delinquency investigations (TDI). TDI enforcement is a critical component to overall IRS collection enforcement because taxpayers must file all unfiled past-due tax returns in order to secure an IRS collection alternative.

> **Pro Tip:** Most OIC applications are worked by COIC OIC examiners. Field Revenue officers generally can provide input and opinion as to whether they approve on the OIC via Form 657.

IRS Collection Personnel

The IRS has two main personnel who collect taxes: field collection personnel, called Revenue Officers, and IRS Campus collection representatives in the Automated Collection System (ACS) function. IRS collection enforcement staffing has been up and down in the past several years. Through 2022, field collection (revenue officers) has declined. [TIGTA Report 2024-300-011, Trends in Compliance Activities Through Fiscal Year 2022, December 20, 2023]

	FY 2019	FY 2020	FY 2021	FY 2022
Collection				
Revenue Officers (Field Collection)	2,239	2,078	1,937	1,906
Campus Collection (including ACS Staff)	3,969	5,168	4,872	5,472

In 2023 and 2024, IRS revenue officers increased to 4,309 as of 9/30/2024. [IRS Data Book 2024, Table 34] However, 2025 cutbacks saw a initial layoff of 611 revenue officers (18%) in

February 2025. [TIGTA Report 2025-IE-R017, Snapshot Report: IRS Workforce Reductions as of March 2025, May 2, 20205]

These personnel collect on the millions of IRS delinquent accounts. In 2023 and 2024, the IRS had millions of taxpayers in IRS collection [IRS Data Book, 2024, Table 27]:

Table 27. Delinquent Collection Activities, Fiscal Years 2023 and 2024
[Money amounts are in thousands of dollars]

Activity	2023	2024
Returns filed with additional tax due:		
Gross total yield from unpaid assessments [1]	104,146,372	120,236,449
Less: Credit transfers [2]	35,884,592	42,686,156
Equals: Net total amount collected	68,261,781	77,550,293
Taxpayer delinquent accounts:		
Number in beginning inventory	9,379,515	11,375,720
Number of new accounts	7,735,469	9,630,933
Number of accounts closed	5,739,264	6,105,145
Ending inventory:		
Number	11,375,720	14,901,508
Balance of assessed tax, penalties, and interest [3]	158,575,455	208,410,722

Chapter 1.09: IRS Collection Process: The Collection Notice Stream and the IRS Collection Roadmap

IRS collection enforcement generally follows a coordinated series of notices requesting payment of the balances owed. This process is called the IRS Collection Notice Stream. The normal Collection Notice Stream provides the taxpayer a series of five notices prior to IRS enforced collection actions can begin. This process can take 3-8 months, depending on the amount of debt and the taxpayer's compliance history. In 2024, the IRS announced that it would increase the time gap between notices from 5 weeks to 8 weeks to allow taxpayers more time to make arrangements with the IRS on back balances owed.

> **Pro Tip:** For an April 15 filer with no other balance due years, the collection notice stream will end late in the calendar year. The taxpayer can receive notices during that time but is likely to be subject to levies and lien filing after the deadline is past on the final notice in the notice stream.

The following is the normal IRS notice stream for an April 15 filer with a balance due that goes directly to IRS collection enforcement:

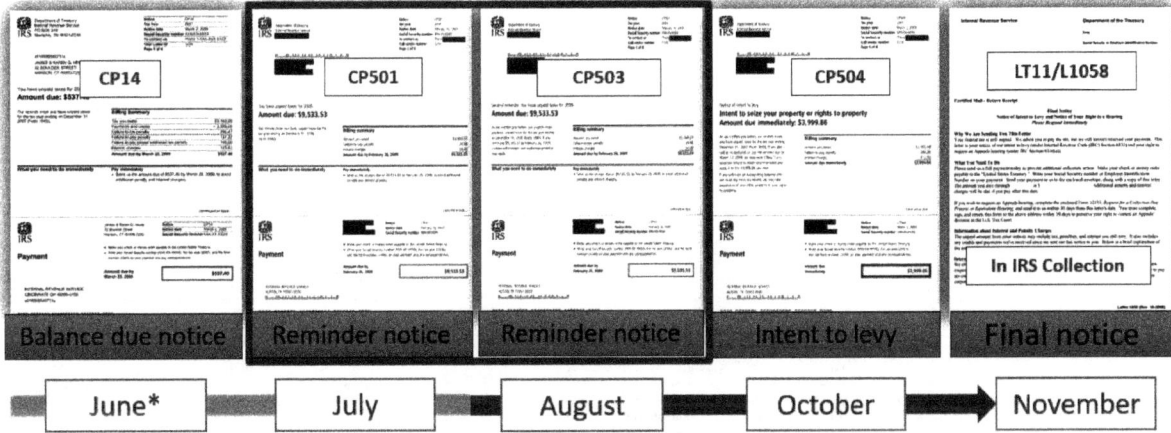

Normal IRS Collection Notice Stream: 4/15 e-filer

Taxpayer files on 4/15 with a balance owed, will receive the following notices before IRS will enforce collection:

CP14	CP501	CP503	CP504	LT11/L1058
Balance due notice	Reminder notice	Reminder notice	Intent to levy	Final notice
June*	July	August	October	November

*4/15 e-filers receive CP14 notices in the first week of June

If the taxpayer has another year with a balance owed, the IRS can skip the CP501 and CP503 – shortening the collection notice duration

The entire collection process can be complicated. The Taxpayer Advocate detailed the "Collection Roadmap" in the 2018 Annual Report to Congress. This chart accurately illustrates the detailed collection process. It is important to understand where the taxpayer is in the process to determine the available alternatives, options, and appeal rights.

[Collection Roadmap: Taxpayer Advocate Service]

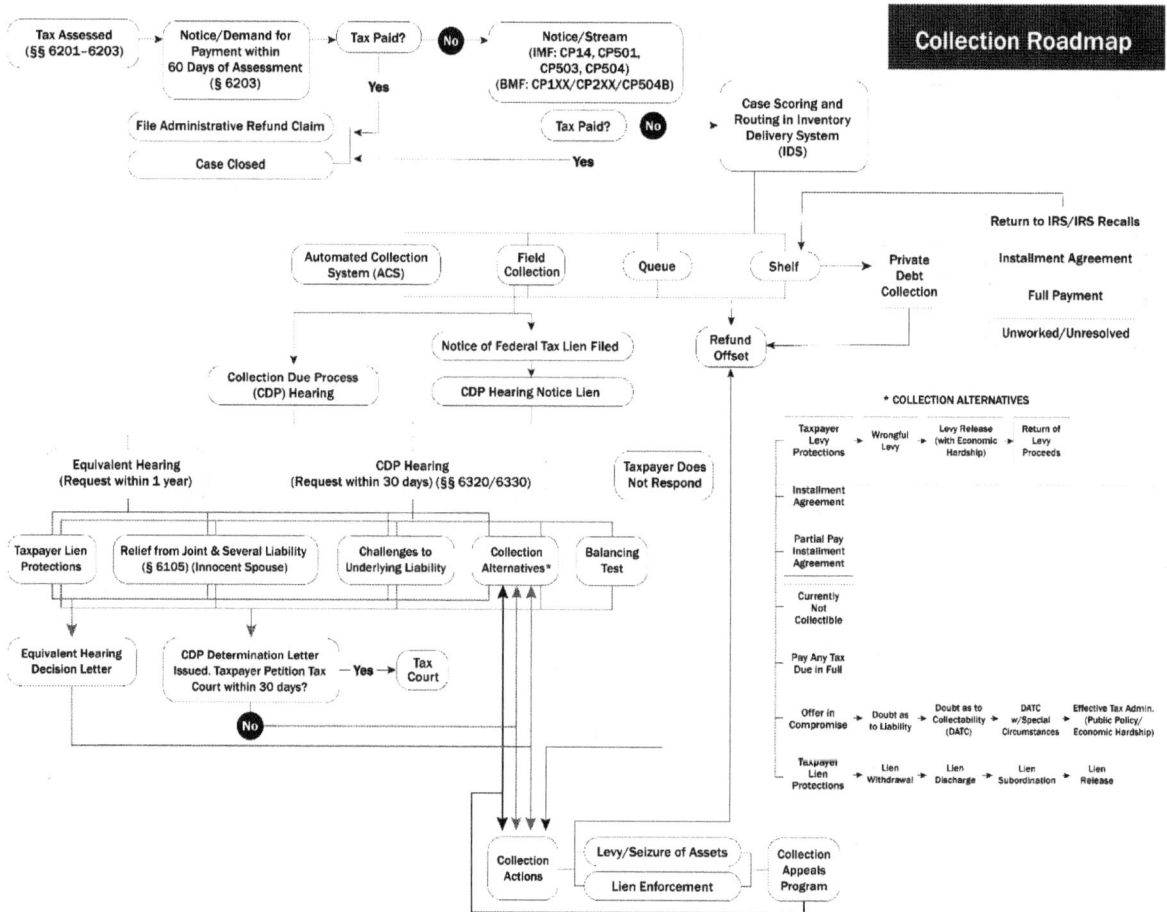

Chapter 1.10: IRS Collection Enforcement: Levies and Liens

The IRS has two primary collection enforcement tools: a levy and the Notice of Federal Tax Lien. A levy is a seizure of the taxpayer's income or assets held by a third party. The most common IRS levies are wage garnishments, financial account (bank) levies, accounts receivable levies, and levies on social security.

IRS Levy Requirements

The requirements for issuance of a levy are:

1. *Tax due notice:* the IRS assessed tax and sent a notice and demand for payment,
2. *Non-payment:* the taxpayer refused or neglected to pay,
3. *Notice of a right to a Collection Due Process (CDP) hearing*: the IRS sent a Final Notice of Intent to Levy ("FNIL") at least 30 days before the levy is issued,

4. *No Collection Due Process (CDP) request is filed*: the taxpayer does not respond to the Final Notice of Intent to Levy and Notice of Your Right to a Hearing (i.e., request a hearing), or a CDP hearing is conducted sustaining the proposed levy, and

5. *Notice of third-party contact*: when a notice of levy is issued to a third party, it is a third-party contact. IRS letters L1058 and LT11 give proper advance notice of third-party notification. Note: when a Notice of Levy is issued to a third-party, it is a Third-Party Contact (TPC). IRC 7602(c)(1) requires that the IRS provide advance written notification of intent to contact third parties for each module that will be referenced in the TPC. The IRS is required to carefully review each module to determine if the taxpayer received advance TPC notification and that the date of TPC notification is less than one year old. If it has been more than one year since the taxpayer last received advance written notification of TPC, on one or more modules, a new notification is required. The calculates the one-year period from the 46th day after the date of the notice, provided the 46th day is the first day of the contact period specified in the letter. IRS employees may not contact a third-party (levy) until the 46th day following the date of the TPC notice. [IRM 5.11.1.3.2 at (2) (4-3-2025)]

[IRM 5.11.1.3.2 (4-3-2025)]

> **Pro Tip:** The IRS does not have to issue the FNIL prior to levying a state income tax refund. The FNIL notice provides the taxpayer a right to a CDP hearing to provide a collection alternative, contest the tax owed, or provide another remedy.

> **Pro Tip:** IRS procedures used to require the IRS to "renotify" the taxpayer of the intent to levy if no action is on the account for 180 days before a new levy can be issued. However, in 2021, the IRS removed the 180-day requirement for revenue officer "manual levies." [IPU SB/SE-05-0221-0290 (2-22-2021)] IRS officials have stated that they intend to renotify taxpayers every 180 days despite the removal of the 180-day requirement from its procedures. In 2024, the IRS used Letter LT38 to notify taxpayers that they owe back taxes, meeting the IRS's renotification procedures. Changes to IRM 5.11.1.3.2 at (2) indicate that the IRS will provide a renotification for ACS notices if the taxpayer has not received a prior notification in 1 year.

IRS Lien Requirements

An IRS Notice of Federal Tax Lien (IRS Form 668(Y)) secures the government's interest in a taxpayer's property when he owes and does not pay his taxes. An NFTL should not be confused with an IRS levy. A lien secures the IRS interest in the property, whereas a levy takes the property from a third-party to pay the tax bill. The requirements to file a Notice of Federal Tax Lien are:

1. *Assessment of a tax liability*: records the tax owed from a filed return or from an assessment like an audit, CP2000 assessment, or a trust fund recovery penalty assessment,
2. *Demand for payment:* the IRS sends a bill for payment, and
3. *Non-payment:* taxpayer neglects or refuses to pay.

[IRC §6321 and IRM 5.12.1.3 (7-11-2018)]

Collection Notices and Enforcement Due Process

The IRS Collection Notice Stream satisfies the legal requirements to enforce collection through levies and liens. In practice, the IRS rarely issues a levy or files an NFTL prior to the completion of the notice stream.

Since 2011, the IRS has reduced the number of levies and liens issued to taxpayers as part of an effort to help struggling taxpayers. In 2019, the IRS started increasing its levy and lien actions to taxpayers. However, during the years 2020-2024, IRS levy and lien enforcement has been at a low volume. IRS campus levy and lien enforcement has been limited, severely lowering the volume of lien and levies issued. [IRS Data Boks 2014-2024, Table 37]

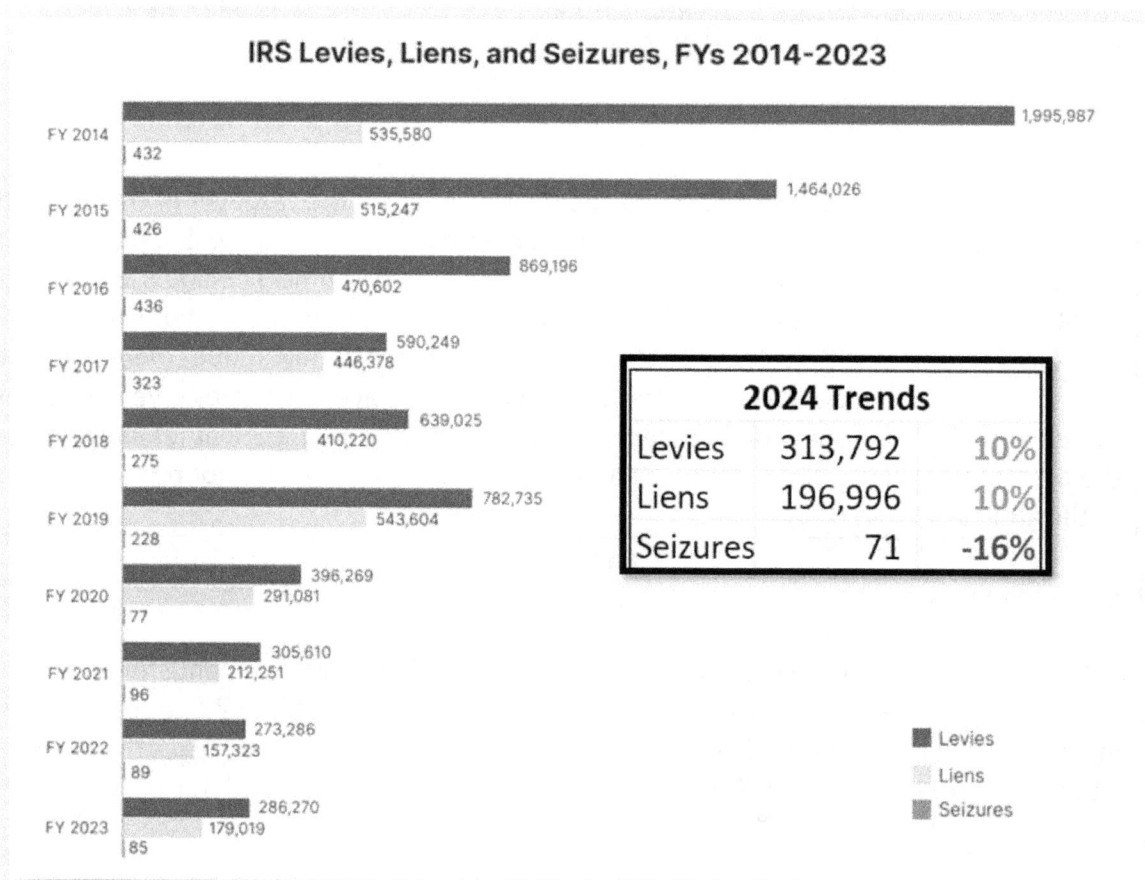

IRS Levies, Liens, and Seizures, FYs 2014-2023

FY	Levies	Liens	Seizures
FY 2014	1,995,987	535,580	432
FY 2015	1,464,026	515,247	426
FY 2016	869,196	470,602	436
FY 2017	590,249	446,378	323
FY 2018	639,025	410,220	275
FY 2019	782,735	543,604	228
FY 2020	396,269	291,081	77
FY 2021	305,610	212,251	96
FY 2022	273,286	157,323	89
FY 2023	286,270	179,019	85

2024 Trends		
Levies	313,792	10%
Liens	196,996	10%
Seizures	71	-16%

■ Levies
　Liens
■ Seizures

Most of the traditional relaxed collection enforcement activities, relaxed payment terms, and increased access to the Offer in Compromise program are referred to as the IRS's "Fresh Start Initiative." [IR-2011-20, February 24, 2011, IRS Announces New Effort to Help Struggling Taxpayers Get a Fresh Start; Major Changes Made to Lien Process]

Most of the IRS Fresh Start changes to IRS collection policy remain in effect. During the COVID-19 pandemic, the IRS ceased many automated liens (unless the lien was required as a result of the taxpayer's requested collection agreement) and levies. However, Field Collection (revenue officers) still issued liens and levies during this time. In 2025, liens from the ACS have resumed.

> **Pro Tip:** If the taxpayer is assigned to the Collection Field function, i.e., a revenue officer, the revenue officer is more likely to issue a levy or lien very quickly if all requirements have been met and the taxpayer has not made arrangements to pay.

Chapter 1.11: IRS Collection Enforcement: Passport Restrictions

In early 2018, the IRS began sending notices to taxpayers with seriously delinquent tax debt. [IRS News Release IR-2018-7, January 16, 2018] Such taxpayers received IRS Notice CP508C indicating that they have been certified as having seriously delinquent tax debt. The State Department also receives this certification and can deny the issuance or renewal of a passport, or fully restrict or limit its use. The State Department notifies the taxpayer separately in writing of any restrictions imposed on an existing passport. Before denying a new or renewed passport application, the State Department will hold the passport application for 90 days to allow the taxpayer to get in good standing with the IRS and request decertification. [IRM 5.19.25.9 (1-24-2024)]

Seriously delinquent tax debt is defined as outstanding tax debt (including penalties and interest) over $64,000 (this amount is indexed annually for inflation) in which the taxpayer has not made an agreement (i.e., a collection alternative) with the IRS on the outstanding balance owed. Certification requires that the IRS has tried to enforce collection through a lien or levy issuance. To remove these restrictions, a taxpayer must decertify themselves from having seriously delinquent tax debt by paying the outstanding balance in full or taking other actions to get in good standing with the IRS. These actions include entering into collection alternatives, such as an installment agreement, currently not collectible status, or an offer in compromise. Appealing a levy with a CDP hearing or applying for innocent spouse relief also decertifies the debt.

To explore this topic in greater depth, see Chapter 17: Passport Restrictions on Seriously Delinquent Tax Debt.

Chapter 1.12: Collection Statute of Limitations

General Rule

The IRS Collection Statute Expiration Date, or "CSED," is the last day the IRS can collect on an assessed tax debt (and associated penalties and interest). [IRC §6502(a) and IRM 5.1.19.1.1 (12-18-2023)] CSEDs are an important factor in deciding which collection option is appropriate. For example, the IRS Simple and Full pay Non-Streamlined Installment Agreement Terms call for the outstanding balances to be paid before the CSED. Offer in compromise qualification also considers the CSED in determining if the taxpayer can fully pay the liability before the statute expires. If the taxpayer can pay before the CSED expires, the taxpayer generally will not qualify for an offer in compromise.

Determining the CSED(s)

The CSED begins ten years from the date of assessment. [IRC §6502(a)(1) and IRM 5.19.1.4.4.3 (11-30-2020)] For example, the CSED for a return filed on a 2018 return with a tax assessment date of June 3, 2019, is June 3, 2029. Each tax year has its own CSED because each tax year results in a separate assessment. A taxpayer can have multiple CSEDs during a year if they have multiple assessments. For example, the taxpayer may file and assess tax on June 3, 2019, and then be audited for the same year. The IRS audit adjustment would be assessed after the June 3, 2019, filing assessment date and create a second CSED associated with the amount of the audit assessment. Additional assessments can be found on IRS account transcripts.

> **Pro Tip:** Most timely filed tax returns mailed on or before the deadline (i.e., April 15) with a balance owed will have an assessment date a few weeks after the return is filed (i.e., usually in the last week of May or the first week of June). The assessment date, not the filing date, triggers the ten-year CSED. Taxpayers can find their assessment date as the corresponding date on the IRS Account Transcript transaction code TC 150. In IRS non-filer investigations, the IRS can file a return for the taxpayer which will trigger the tax assessment date. If the IRS files a return for a taxpayer (called a "substitute for return" or SFR), the IRS will establish a TC 150 for the taxpayer with the SFR that will start the CSED.

Common IRS account transcript transaction codes that carry their own CSEDs appear below. [IRM 5.1.19.2.1 (6-4-2009)]

Transaction Code	Definition
TC 150	Tax Assessed
TC 160	Manually Computed Delinquency Penalty
TC 166	Delinquency Penalty
TC 170	Estimated Tax Penalty
TC 176	Estimated Tax Penalty
TC 180	Deposit Penalty

TC 186	FTD Penalty
TC 234	Daily Delinquency Penalty (if it is the only CSED in the module)
TC 238	Daily Delinquency Penalty
TC 240	Miscellaneous Civil Penalty
TC 246	Form 8752 or Form 1065 Penalty
TC 290	Additional Tax Assessment
TC 294	Tentative Carryback Disallowance with Interest Computation Date
TC 298	Additional Tax Assessment with Interest Computation Date
TC 300	Additional Tax or Deficiency Assessment by Examination or Appeals
TC 304	Tentative Carryback Disallowance by Exam with Interest Computation Date
TC 308	Additional Tax or Deficiency Assessment by Examination or Appeals with Interest Computation Date
TC 320	Fraud Penalty
TC 350	Negligence Penalty

CSED Extension Actions

The CSED can be extended based on taxpayer actions. These actions extend the CSED because the IRS is precluded from collecting if the taxpayer takes these actions. [IRM 5.1.19.3 (2-7-2020)] Some common ways taxpayers can extend the CSED appear in the table below.

Action	CSED extended time
Bankruptcy [IRM 5.1.19.3.1 (5-19-2016)]	Bankruptcy period, plus six months.
Collection Due Process Appeal Request [IRM 5.1.19.3.3 (4-26-2018)]	Appeals request through decision period (not less than 90 days).
Offer in Compromise [IRM 5.1.19.3.4 (12-18-2023)]	Offer review/appeal period, plus 30 days (Offers after 3/9/2002).
Installment agreements [IRM 5.1.19.3.5 (12-18-2023)]	• Time for proposed installment agreement is pending. • 30 days after rejection of an installment agreement. • 30 days after a termination of an installment agreement. • Any appeal of the termination or rejection of an installment agreement.
Innocent Spouse [IRM 5.1.19.3.6 (4-26-2018)]	The collection period is suspended from the filing of the claim until the earlier of the date a waiver is filed, or until the expiration of the 90-day period for petitioning the Tax Court, or if

	a Tax Court petition is filed, when the Tax Court decision becomes final, plus, in each instance, 60 days.
Taxpayer living outside US [IRM 5.1.19.3.7 (4-26-2018)]	Period outside of U.S. (if absence > 6 months). (*Note:* The IRS does not automatically input this CSED extension. It is usually applied when the IRS investigates the taxpayer for collection and discovers the taxpayer was outside the country.) [IRM 5.1.19.3.7 (4-26-2018) and IRM 5.1.19.3.7.1 (5-19-2016)]
Combat zone [IRM 5.1.19.3.8 (4-26-2018)]	Period while in combat zone plus 180 days.
Taxpayer Assistance Order [IRM 5.1.19.3.13 (12-18-2023)]	Period receiving assistance from Taxpayer Advocate Service. (*Note:* The IRS rarely "inputs" this extension.)

The IRS does not readily provide taxpayers with their CSED. For example, IRS transcripts do not contain the CSED(s) for that year. Taxpayers need to ask the IRS for their CSED by contacting the IRS accounts hotline. Alternatively, a simpler approach may be for a taxpayer to authorize a tax professional to contact the Practitioner Priority Service to obtain the CSED(s). The Practitioner Hotline is accustomed to releasing this information; taxpayer hotlines, on the other hand, rarely get CSED requests.

The IRS does not provide a CSED computation document that details how the CSED was computed. Taxpayers can attempt to estimate their CSED date using IRS account transcripts. The transcript will contain these codes that would indicate that the CSED was extended. [IRM 5.1.19.2.2 (5-23-2013)]

Account Transcript Transaction Code	Description
TC 480	Offer in Compromise Pending
TC 488	Installment and/or Manual Billing
TC 500	Military Deferment
TC 520 cc 76-81	Tax Court or IRS Litigation Instituted
TC 520	Bankruptcy
TC 520	Collection Due Process Hearing
TC 550	Waiver Extension of Date Collection Statute Expires (extends the CSED to date input)
TC 550	Innocent Spouse
TC 971	Pending Installment Agreement
TC 971 Action Code 163	Terminated Installment Agreement
TC 971	Taxpayer Living Outside the U.S.

Example: Consider the following:

1. Taxpayer files her 2007 return on April 15, 2008, and owes $45,000.
2. The tax assessment date is June 1, 2008, and establishes the initial CSED as June 1, 2018, ten years from the date of assessment.
3. The taxpayer files for an offer in compromise (OIC) on March 1, 2009 (IRS Account Transcript transaction code 480).
4. The OIC is rejected by the IRS on October 1, 2009 (IRS Account Transcript transaction code 481).

The OIC extends the CSED by 243 days (213 days during the offer investigation pending period from March 1, 2009, to October 1, 2009, plus 30 days) to January 29, 2019.

CSED Errors

Taxpayers who question their CSED dates have good reason to suspect an error. Several Treasury Inspector General for Tax Administration ("TIGTA") and National Taxpayer Advocate reports indicate that there are often serious errors in computing the CSED. A 2022 TIGTA study found that 20% of sampled accounts had incorrect CSED calculations. [TIGTA Report 2022-10-043, Review of the Independent Office of Appeals Collection Due Process Program, August 18, 2022]

A transcript review is a good starting point to evaluate whether the IRS has the CSED correct. The IRS has internal transcripts that can provide more specific actions that can show the CSED. This transcript is called a "TXMODA" (named after the IRS internal transcript name). Taxpayers can request this transcript on the account hotline. Tax professionals can contact the IRS Practitioner Priority Service hotline and request the TXMODA. If the IRS denies the taxpayer this information, taxpayers can submit a Freedom of Information Act request for this information. Taxpayers will need to use IRS Document 6209 to help interpret the codes on the TXMODA transcript.

For more details on this topic, visit www.TaxProblemsHandbook.com and navigate to the **IRS Collection Solutions Handbook** tab to access more on IRS Transcripts.

One common miscalculation by the IRS that will incorrectly extend the CSED, is the pending installment agreement. In practice, the IRS can put a "Pending Installment Agreement" indicator on a taxpayer account but not later record an accepted agreement after the agreement is completed. These "open-ended" pending installment agreements may serve to incorrectly extend the CSED for long periods. If the taxpayer believes the pending installment agreement is in error and the CSED has expired, the taxpayer should analyze the CSED extending events carefully and determine the correct CSED.

> **Pro Tip:** CSED extensions for pending installment agreements require that the taxpayer has met four requirements:
>
> 1. Provided sufficient information to identify the taxpayer (name and TIN are sufficient).
> 2. Identified the tax liability to be covered in the agreement.
> 3. Proposed a monthly installment agreement amount.
> 4. Filed all required returns.
>
> [IRM 5.14.1.3 at (5) (7-2-2024)]

Once the CSED expires, the IRS writes off the debt. Taxpayers are not given notice by the IRS that the CSED has expired. Account transcripts will show a transaction code 608 with the balance amount that was written off because the collection statute has expired.

```
608   Write-off of balance due              02-13-2017      -$32,703.61
```

Chapter 1.13: Additions to Unpaid Taxes: Failure to Pay Penalty and Accrued Interest

Taxpayers who cannot pay face both imposition of the failure to pay penalty and accrual of interest on their outstanding balances owed. [IRC §6651]

Failure to Pay Penalty Rates

The failure to pay penalty is 0.5% per month, up to a maximum of 25%. If the IRS is actively collecting on the taxpayer, the rate rises to 1% per month. If a taxpayer obtains an installment agreement to pay on a timely filed return, the rate drops to 0.25% per month.

Interest on Underpayments

The interest rate charged fluctuates by quarter. [IRC §6601]

The table below provides the underpayments since 1995.

History of IRS Interest Rates, by quarter				
Year	Q1	Q2	Q3	Q4
2025	7%	7%	7%	See IRS Notice 746
2024	8%	8%	8%	8%
2023	7%	7%	7%	8%
2022	3%	4%	5%	6%

2021	3%	3%	3%	3%
2020	5%	5%	3%	3%
2019	6%	6%	5%	5%
2018	4%	5%	5%	5%
2017	4%	4%	4%	4%
2016	3%	4%	4%	4%
2015	3%	3%	3%	3%
2014	3%	3%	3%	3%
2013	3%	3%	3%	3%
2012	3%	3%	3%	3%
2011	3%	4%	4%	3%
2010	4%	4%	4%	4%
2009	5%	4%	4%	4%
2008	7%	6%	5%	6%
2007	8%	8%	8%	8%
2006	7%	7%	8%	8%
2005	5%	6%	6%	7%
2004	4%	5%	4%	5%
2003	5%	5%	5%	4%
2002	6%	6%	6%	6%
2001	9%	8%	7%	7%
2000	8%	9%	9%	9%
1999	7%	8%	8%	8%
1998	8%	7%	7%	7%
1997	8%	8%	8%	8%
1996	8%	7%	8%	8%
1995	8%	9%	8%	8%

IRS Notice 746 provides the most updated IRS interest rates by quarter.

Chapter 1.14: Payment Methods

The IRS offers several options for taxpayers to pay their balances owed. The IRS regularly updates and modifies payment methods. Taxpayers should visit irs.gov/payments for updated payment information.

Option	Location	Days for IRS to post to account	Fees
Check or money order to "United States Treasury" https://www.irs.gov/payment	• Mail	10-14 days	None

s/pay-by-check-or-money-order	• Taxpayer Assistance Center		
Cash https://www.irs.gov/payments/pay-with-cash-at-a-retail-partner	• Retail partners for up to $500 per payment/no limit on number of payments. https://map.payithere.com/	2 business days	$1.50 for ACI Payments and $1.50 for Pay1040.com payments.
Electronic funds withdrawal during e-filing https://www.irs.gov/payments/pay-taxes-by-electronic-funds-withdrawal	• Online, with e-filed return • Phone • With tax software	5-14 days	No IRS fee. Software provider may have a fee.
Electronic Federal Tax Payment System (EFTPS) https://www.irs.gov/payments/eftps-the-electronic-federal-tax-payment-system	• Online	5-7 days	None
Debit card through IRS Direct Pay (ACH) https://www.irs.gov/payments/direct-pay	• Online	5-7 days	None
Debit/credit card through third-party provider *Note:* The IRS is going to offer payment by credit card through the IRS in the future https://www.irs.gov/payments/pay-your-taxes-by-debit-or-credit-card	• Online, through 3 private service providers	5-7 days	Fees apply based service provider selected

Designating Payments

Taxpayers can designate voluntary payments in a manner they choose. For example, a taxpayer can designate a voluntary payment to a tax year and tax form or a specific liability. [IRM 5.1.2.9 (6-20-2013)] Taxpayers can also designate a payment within a tax year. For example, in order to qualify for a simple installment agreement (SIA), a taxpayer can pay the "assessed" balance for a tax year only to allow the taxpayer to bring the assessed balance under $50,000 to qualify for the SIA.

Example- Consider the following facts:

1. John owes $4,000 of mostly remaining interest and penalties for 2016 and $51,000 for 2017 Forms 1040.
   a. $51,000 of the balance is the original assessed tax, penalties, and interest owed. There is $200 in assessed balance for 2016 ($3,800 in accrued penalties and interest). The assessed balance for 2017 is $50,800 (with $200 in accrued penalties and interest).
2. In order to qualify for a simple installment agreement, John only needs to pay the "assessed" amount, reducing it to $50,000.
3. John could designate a payment to the IRS for the 2017 Form 1040 to the "assessed balance only" for $1,000 and be able to enter into the SIA.
4. If John does not so designate, depending on his circumstances and the priority of payments, John may need to pay the total balance ($5,000) under the $50,000 threshold to qualify.

John sends in his payment for $1,000 with the following request to designate payment:

Request to designate payment

PAYMENT FOR 2017 TAX YEAR TO THE ASSESSED BALANCE ONLY

Taxpayers:
John Doe 123-45-6789

Please process the attached payment of $1,000 to the ASSESSED BALANCE ONLY for the tax year 2017 for the Form 1040 for the above taxpayer.

Check # 13192

Amount: $ 1,000

Another common situation where taxpayers designate payments is for back payroll tax issues. Taxpayers who are responsible for collecting or paying employees' withheld income and employment taxes and willfully fail to collect or pay them (called a "responsible person"), can be assessed the taxes personally. [IRC §6672] As a result, the responsible person(s) in the business are assessed the trust fund portion (income tax and FICA/Medicare taxes withheld from their employees) to them personally (called the "trust fund recovery penalty"). The business can reduce the exposure of the responsible persons for the trust fund recovery penalty by designating all voluntary payments the "trust fund portion only." This designation will limit the responsible person(s) liability for the trust fund recovery penalty.

For the template, Request to designate payments, refer to the **Appendix B**—and visit www.TaxProblemsHandbook.com under the IRS Collection Solutions Handbook tab for downloadable resources.

Chapter 1.15: Private Debt Collection

In April 2017, the IRS began using private collection agencies (PCAs) to collect on cases involving inactive tax receivables. In 2024, the IRS had assigned 7.6 million cases to PCAs. [TIGTA Report 2025-300-004, FY2025 Biannual Independent Assessment of the Private Collection Agency Performance, December 20, 2025] An inactive receivable is defined as one which meets any of the following criteria:

1. Removed from active inventory for lack of resources or inability to locate the taxpayer,
2. More than two years have passed since assessment and such receivable has not been assigned for collection to any employee of the IRS, or
3. Assigned for collection, but more than 365 days have passed without interaction with the taxpayer or a third party for purposes of furthering the collection.

[IRC §6306(c)(2)]

Taxpayers who are assigned to a PCA and have new tax years with a balance owed may also have the more current balance due years also assigned to the PCA for collection.

Exclusions from PDC

The 2015 law that enacted PCA collection excluded taxpayers from private debt collection who are:

1. Subject to a pending or active offer-in-compromise or installment agreement,
2. Classified as an innocent spouse case,
3. One of the following: (a) deceased, (b) under the age of 18, (c) in a designated combat zone, or (d) a victim of tax-related identity theft,
4. Currently under examination, litigation, criminal investigation, or levy, or
5. Currently subject to a proper exercise of a right of appeal.

Taxpayers in presidentially declared disaster areas are also excluded. [IRC §6306(d)] The Taxpayer First Act, signed into law on July 1, 2019, also excluded taxpayers whose income substantially consists of Social Security Disability Insurance benefits as well as those with adjusted gross income that does not exceed 200% of the applicable poverty level. It also defined an "inactive receivable" to be an assessment that is more than two years old.

Taxpayers can identify if they are assigned to a PCA on their IRS account transcript. In the transaction section, a TC 971 with the description "Account assigned to PCA" will appear. [IRM 5.19.1.5.21.2.1 (9-14-2021)]

| 971 | Collection referred to a private debt collection agency | 12-03-2018 | $0.00 |

PDC Agencies

There are three private collection agencies (PCAs) assigned to collect IRS inactive tax debtor cases. [IR-2021-191, September 22, 2021]

CBE
P.O. Box 2217
Waterloo, IA 50704
1-800-910-5837

ConServe
P.O. Box 307
Fairport, NY 14450-0307
1-844-853-4875

Coast Professional, Inc.
P.O. Box 425
Geneseo, NY 14454
888-928-0510

IRS Notification of Assignment to a PDC

Taxpayers assigned to a PCA will receive a letter from the IRS (IRS Letter CP40). [IRM 5.19.1.5.21.1 (5-1-2023)] The PCA will also send a letter to the taxpayer and then proceed to contact the taxpayer by phone to collect the tax. Taxpayers can request in writing to have their account sent back to the IRS for collection.

Taxpayers working with a PCA have limited payment options available: fully pay or enter into a PDC payment plan (i.e., not an IRS payment plan) lasting up to seven years (or the collection statute of limitations, whichever is less). The PCA can also take partial payments of the tax owed. Any other resolution requested (longer payment terms or hardship status) is referred back to the IRS for approval. PCAs can only ask the taxpayer to pay directly to the IRS through one of the IRS payment methods. PCAs can secure a preauthorized direct debit payment or series of payments from the taxpayer. [IRS News Release IR-2019-165, October 8, 2019]

PCAs cannot enforce collection. That is, they cannot file an NFTL or issue a levy. However, many taxpayer scams have impersonated private debt collectors in order to defraud taxpayers into making payments. As a best practice and to limit confusion, most taxpayers should deal directly with the IRS when making payments or obtaining a collection alternative.

> **Pro Tip:** Taxpayers who are assigned to a PCA and trying to resolve their account with an IRS agreement should request to have their account sent back to IRS collection. IRS personnel have the ability to approve other collection alternatives and to agree to potentially lower amounts owed through penalty abatement or reconsideration of an additional assessment. PCAs do not have access or the ability to lower the amounts owed or provide guidance on reducing the amounts owed. They also do not offer other collection alternatives that the taxpayer may need based on their financial circumstances. Taxpayers can request that the PDC stop contacting them for collection. To do so, taxpayers can send a letter to the PDC with this request. The IRS Taxpayer Advocate has a sample letter to use at: https://www.taxpayeradvocate.irs.gov/wp-content/uploads/2020/10/R3_Do_Not_Contact_Sample_Letter.pdf.

See IRS Publication 4518, *What You Can Expect When the IRS Assigns Your Account to a Private Collection Agency*, for more information on the private debt collection process and answers to frequently asked questions.

Chapter 1.16: Tax Debtors: Annual Notices of Balances Owed and Activity

Taxpayers who owe the IRS will receive periodic notices from the IRS outlining the balance owed and any activity on the account. [IRM 21.2.1.6.34 (10-2-2023) and IRM 21.3.1.6.39 (10-3-2022)]

The primary notices issued to taxpayers are listed below.

Notice	Taxpayer Status	Information Provided
IRS CP89, Annual Installment Agreement Statement [IRM 21.3.1.6.39 (10-3-2022)]	In an installment agreement with the IRS.	Provides one-year accounting of all payments submitted; shows all years and balances owed.
IRS CP71 and 71A, Reminder Notice (annual) [IRM 21.3.1.6.34 (10-2-2023) and IRM 21.3.1.6.34.1 (10-2-2023)]	Taxpayer is in currently not collectible (CNC) status. CP71 indicates that the taxpayer is in good standing and has a agreed CNC status with the IRS. CP71A is not an agreed CNC status and the taxpayer is NOT in good standing with the IRS	Provides balance owed and accrued penalties and interest.

	and is subject to IRS collection.	
IRS CP71C, 171, Bi-annual Reminder Notices [IRM 21.3.1.6.34.2 (5-23-2018)] and CP 71D Annual Reminder Notice – Balance Due [IRM 21.3.1.6.34.3 (10-2-2023)], Reminder Notice (annual)	Taxpayer is in IRS collection and the account is not in good standing (i.e., collection alternative not reached). 71C: in queue to be assigned to CFf 71D: assigned to CFf (revenue officer)	Separate notice per tax year/form. Provides balance owed with penalties and interest.

Taxpayers in installment agreements in which the payment is being made monthly by mail will receive IRS Notice CP521, *Your Installment Agreement*. This notice is a monthly reminder to pay the monthly payment amount and provides the taxpayer a voucher for the payment. This notice can also be viewed in the taxpayer's online account. Taxpayers may elect to receive the CP521 notifications by email and digitally only; CP521 notices come through the online account (in the "profile" section).

Chapter 2:
IRS COLLECTION ALTERNATIVES

This section will provide an overview of the IRS collection alternatives.

Topic	Covers
Introduction to IRS Collection Alternatives	The four categories of collection alternatives and the options within each category.
Option #1: Extensions to Pay	The 180-day extension to pay and the hardship extension to pay options.
Option #2A: Installment Agreements That Do Not Require an Ability to Pay Determination	The guaranteed installment agreement, the simple installment agreement, and the non-streamlined payment plan options.
Option #2B: Installment Agreements That Require an Ability to Pay Determination	The components of determining the ability to pay. The requirement to use existing assets to pay. The routine ability to pay installment agreement, the conditional installment agreement, and the partial pay installment agreement.
Option #3: Not Collectible Status (Currently Not Collectible or "CNC")	Temporary not collectible status based on the taxpayer's ability to pay determination.
Option #4: Offer in Compromise	The three types of OICs and the rules for the most common OIC: doubt as to collectability.
Comparison of IRS Collection Alternatives and Options	A chart that shows the major distinctions between the collection alternative categories and options.

Key Highlights:

- There are four categories of IRS collection alternatives: extensions to pay, payment plans (installment agreements), not collectible status, and offer in compromise.
- To be able to evaluate which alternative is best, a taxpayer needs a basic understanding about the options and how they work.
- It is important to stay up to date on the latest IRS collection alternatives. The IRS can add/change/remove collection alternatives frequently based on changes in law or administrative enforcement procedures.

Chapter 2.01: Introduction to IRS Collection Alternatives

When a taxpayer cannot immediately pay the IRS in full, they have four categories of collection alternatives. Some categories have more than one alternative:

1. *An extension to pay* (ETP) — a short period to pay the tax bill. There are two types of extensions to pay: [IRM 5.19.1.6.3 (12-20-2022) and IRM 5.1.12.26 (9-20-2012)]

   - 180-day extension to full-pay
   - Hardship extension to pay

   > **Pro Tip:** During the COVID-19 pandemic, the IRS extended the ETP terms from 120 days to 180 days. In 2022, the IRS made the ETP terms of 180 days permanent.

2. *A monthly installment agreement (payment plan)* — there are six types of installment agreements: [IRM 5.19.1.6.4 (1-26-2023)]
   a. "Simplified" installment agreements that are not based on an ability to pay determination:
      i. Guaranteed Installment Agreement (GIA)
      ii. Simple Installment Agreement (SIA)
      iii. Full-pay Non-streamlined installment agreement (NSIA) payment plan for those who owe between $50,000 and $250,000 (*note*: this payment plan will involve the filing of a Notice of Federal Tax Lien)
   b. "Complex" installment agreements that are based on an ability to pay determination:
      i. Routine ability to pay installment agreement (ATP IA)
      ii. Conditional installment agreement
      iii. Partial Pay Installment Agreement (PPIA)
3. *Not collectible status* (called "currently not collectible status" or "CNC"). [IRM 5.16.1 (3-3-2025)]
4. *An offer in compromise* (OIC) [IRM 5.8.2.1.6 (6-14-2024)] — there are two primary OIC collection alternatives:

   - Doubt as to collectibility (OIC-DATC): a tax settlement where the taxpayer cannot pay the amount owed with equity in assets or future income.
   - Effective Tax Administration (ETA OIC): a tax settlement where the taxpayer has the ability to pay but has special circumstances that warrant settling the balance owed for less than the amount owed.

Practical Considerations

The most common option for taxpayers who owe is to obtain an installment agreement. 4.6 million taxpayers were in installment agreements in 2024, far surpassing all other payment alternatives combined. Many taxpayers inquire about a tax settlement, called an Offer in compromise. However, few taxpayers actually receive an Offer in compromise as the program usually applies to taxpayers with a financial hardship. In 2024, there were only 7,199 approved OICs allowing taxpayers to settle their debt. [IRS Data Book, 2024, Table 27]

Taxpayers may use more than one collection alternative. For example, it is common for a taxpayer to use an Extension to Pay to lower the amount owed and then obtain an Installment Agreement. Another example is when a taxpayer obtains an Installment Agreement and then applies for Not Collectible Status or an Offer in Compromise due to a new financial hardship, such as unemployment.

It is important to understand how each of these options work to evaluate which is best.

To explore this topic in greater depth, see Chapter 2.07: Comparison of IRS Collection Alternatives and Options, where we provide help in comparing alternatives and determining which is best

Chapter 2.02: Option #1: Extensions to Pay.

There are two extension to pay agreements: the 180-day extension to pay and the hardship extension to pay.

180-Day Extension to Pay

The simplest and easiest agreement to set up is the 180-day extension to pay (ETP) option. Taxpayers who owe any balance to the IRS can obtain the 180-day extension to pay.

Important Facts and Considerations for ETP Agreements [IRM 5.19.1.6.3 (12-20-2022)]	
Who Qualifies?	This alternative is open to taxpayers who owe any amount and are not assigned to the Collection Field Function for enforcement.
Terms	Pay full balance owed within 180 days.
Fees	None.
Timing	May request any time.
How long does it take?	Can be completed quickly online or by phone.
How to request	• May request online for balances up to $100,000. • May request by phone to the IRS function that the taxpayer is assigned (IRS Accounts Management or IRS Collection).
Effect on Notice of Federal Tax Lien	Important to request prior to the filing of a Notice of Tax Lien. ETP will usually put a hold on the filing of an NFTL. ETP will not remove an NFTL after a lien has been filed.
Effect on Levy	• May use ETP to release a levy or garnishment. • Levies will not be issued during the ETP time period.
Restrictions	• Can only use once for each tax form/year.

	• Collection Field Function is not authorized to accept ETP agreements [IRM 5.14.1.6 at (4) (12-23-2022)] but may allow collection holds while a taxpayer arranges for a collection alternative. • Cannot use ETP to decertify seriously delinquent tax debt in order to release passport restrictions. [IRM 5.19.25.4 (1-24-2024)] • Interest will still accrue and the failure to pay penalty will still apply during the extension period. • A new ETP agreement of up to 180 days may be granted only after all years/periods from any prior payment agreement have been full paid. • Cannot be used for business employment taxes • Collection appeal rights do not extend to ETP agreements
Confirmation notice	Taxpayer will receive Letter 681C, *Proposal to Pay Later Accepted*, confirming ETP with balance to be paid at the end of 180 days.
Useful alternative for:	• A short-term cash flow problem. • Liquidate assets or borrow money to pay outstanding balance. • Avoid premature enforced collection activity (lien, levy, passport restrictions). • Remove levy or garnishment. • To obtain funds to lower the balance to qualify for an SLIA. • Limiting financial disclosure.

During the extended time to pay, the IRS will not enforce collection, i.e., issue liens and levies. The IRS does expect full payment, including accrued penalties and interest, at the completion of the 180-day extension period.

> **Pro Tip:** In practice, the IRS often gives taxpayers the 180-day extension to pay down the amount owed by selling existing assets or by borrowing funds. The IRS calls the agreement a "180-day extension to full pay," but in practice, the IRS routinely provides taxpayers the 180 days to pay down the balance and enter into one of the simple Installment agreements (i.e., simple or full pay non-streamlined installment agreement). [IRM 5.14.5.2 at (12) (10-14-2021)]

Example- Extension to Pay Example. John owes $74,000 for a 2022 tax return filed on October 15, 2023. John cannot pay the amount owed and will need to get a home equity loan in order to pay. John calls the IRS and requests a 180-day extension to pay. The IRS provides John 180 days to pay and a payoff amount at the end of the 180 days. John receives a Letter 681C in three weeks confirming the extension and the amount to be paid at the end of the 180 days.

Hardship Extension to Pay

There is also a less common hardship extension to pay alternative for taxpayers who owe and are unable pay due to hardship. [IRM 20.1.1.3.3.3 (8-5-2014)] The taxpayer must apply for the extension with the filed tax return. If the amount owed is related to an audit or CP2000 adjustment, the request must be sent with the first tax bill. Taxpayers use Form 1127, *Application for Extension of Time for Payment of Tax Due to Undue Hardship*. The IRS may approve an additional six-month extension to pay with a filed return and up to 18 months for an audit or CP2000 adjustment. The taxpayer must have an undue hardship to be granted this extension to pay. During the hardship extension, the taxpayer is not charged the failure to pay penalty. However, they are charged interest on the outstanding balance.

Chapter 2.03: Option #2A: Simplified Installment Agreements That Do Not Require an Ability to Pay Determination

There are three simplified installment agreements that are easy to set up and the terms are fixed:

- Guaranteed Installment Agreement (GIA)
- Simple Installment Agreement (SIA)
- The full-pay non-streamlined installment agreement (NSIA) for those who owe between $50,000 and $250,000 (tax lien filing is required)

[IRM 5.19.1.6.4 (11-18-2021)]

> **Pro Tip**: the "Simple" installment agreement or SIA replaces the "streamlined installment agreement" (SLIA) as of March 5, 2025.

These agreements do not require extensive IRS interaction or detailed financial disclosures while still allowing taxpayers to completely pay the IRS over a certain number of months. Of utmost importance is that a timely executed GIA or SIA avoids the filing of a Notice of Federal Tax Lien. The simple installment agreement is the most common IRS collection alternative, with most taxpayers taking this option.

> **Pro Tip:** The IRS frequently changes terms of their simplified installment agreements. For example, in 2020, the IRS replaced the old "84 month payment plan" with the full pay non-streamlined agreement. In 2025, the IRS replaced the streamlined installment agreement with new terms in the simple installment agreement. Also, the IRS periodically changes terms within these agreements, including requirements on direct payments from financial accounts, ability to obtain online, and user fees to set up these agreements.

Guaranteed Installment Agreement (GIA) and Simple Installment Agreement (SIA) Plans

The GIA and SIA are popular payment plan alternatives because they avoid the filing of a federal tax lien and are very easy to set up. The terms and considerations for each of these agreements are discussed below.

Important Facts and Considerations for GIA and SIA Agreements IRM 5.14.5.3 (10-14-2021) for GIA and IRM 5.14.5.2 (10-14-2021) and IRS.gov for SIA		
	Guaranteed Installment Agreement (GIA)	**Simple Installment Agreement (SIA)**
Qualification	May be used by taxpayers owing $10,000 or less, excluding of penalties and interest. • Cannot have failed to file any income tax returns or to pay any tax shown on such returns during any of the preceding five taxable years. • Must agree to fully pay the tax liability (plus accruals) within three years. • Must agree to file and pay all tax returns during the term of the agreement. • Cannot have entered into an installment agreement during any of the preceding five taxable years.	May be used by taxpayers owing $50,000 or less of original assessed taxes, penalties, and interest. • No requirement on payment method. Payments can be made by check, online, or by direct draft from a financial account. • All required returns must be filed.
Terms	• Must pay total balance owed within 36 months, or the collection statute expiration date, whichever is less. • Must make a payment each month to avoid default.	• Must pay total balance owed before the collection statute expiration date. • Must make a payment each month to avoid default.
Fees	Payment by direct debit or payroll deduction: • Apply online: $22 setup fee. • Apply by phone, mail, or in-person: $107 setup fee. • Low income: Apply online, by phone, mail, or in-person: setup fee waived.	

	Pay by check, money order, or using IRS Direct Pay or debit/credit card: • Apply online: $69 setup fee (low income: only $43 setup fee that may be reimbursed if certain conditions are met). • Apply by phone, mail, or in-person: $178 setup fee (low income: $43 setup fee that may be reimbursed if certain conditions are met).	
Timing to request	• Can request anytime. • Can request at time of filing a balance due return by attaching Form 9465 to filed return (paper or e-filed).	
How long does it take?	• If filed with return, takes two months to set up. • By phone or online, instantaneous. • Add more time if need to send Form 433-D or Form 2159 to establish direct debit or payroll deduction.	• By phone or online, instantaneous. • Add more time if need to send Form 433-D or Form 2159 to establish direct debit or payroll deduction.
How to request	• The IRS' Online Payment Agreement or an IRS Phone Representative can determine the minimum payment amount required under the SIA. • For a GIA, the minimum payment proposed can be the balance divided by 36 months. • Online, using IRS Online Payment Agreement. • Mail, via Form 9465. • Phone, to IRS unit assigned: IRS Accounts management or IRS Collection.	
Effect on filing of Notice of Federal Tax Lien	Important to request prior to the filing of a Notice of Tax Lien. GIA/SIA will not remove an NFTL after the lien has been filed. The IRS may file an NFTL for a GIA or SIA, but rarely does so. Exception: when a taxpayer is assigned to local field collection and the revenue officer believes that the taxpayer will default in the future due to past history, projected new balances owed, and/or assets are available to collect in the future with a lien.	
Effect on Levy	• Can use GIA/SIA to release a levy or garnishment. • Levies will not be issued during the GIA/SIA.	
Restrictions	• Interest and the failure to pay penalty will still accrue. • IRS will take refunds until balance is fully paid. • Taxpayer will default if there is another unpaid assessment (filed return, audit, etc.).	

	• Taxpayer can miss one payment per year and not default on the agreement.
Confirmation notice	Letter 2273C will arrive 2-3 weeks after agreement is processed by IRS. May take 3-6 weeks to receive letter if payments are by direct debit or payroll deduction.
Useful alternative for:	• Fixed payment terms, possibly providing better monthly payment than ability to pay. • Avoid lien filing. • Remove levy/garnishment.

Pro Tip: Taxpayers generally do not need to distinguish between requesting a GIA or an SIA when requesting a simple installment agreement with the IRS. When contacting the IRS by phone or setting up a payment plan online, the IRS often looks for the taxpayer to pay within the SIA terms (i.e., before the CSED). The GIA is most often used when a taxpayer files a return, has a balance owed under $10,000, and wants to pay it off quickly. But, in practice, the IRS does not differentiate between the GIA or SIA — they are all simplified payment plans that pay off the balance within the collection statute and do not require financial disclosure, asset liquidation, or a lien determination.

Guaranteed Installment Agreement Example. Mary files her 2022 tax return with a balance due of $6,800 due to early distributions from her retirement plan in which she did not have enough withheld. Mary has filed all her required returns in the past and has never had a balance owed to the IRS. Mary sends a Form 9465 with her return requesting a payment plan extending over 36 months with a payment of $200 a month. Mary requests the payment to be debited from her checking account on the 28th of each month. The fee to set up Mary's GIA is $107 and will be taken along with the first payment. Mary receives IRS Letter 2273C in three weeks stating that the first payment will start on the 28th of the next month.

Simple Installment Agreement Example. Joe has balances owed from 2019-2021. Joe owes $48,000 ($36,000 in assessed balances plus $12,000 in accrued penalties and interest). The IRS has not yet filed a tax lien for 2019, 2020, or 2021. Joe cannot pay and has corrected his withholding so that he will not owe again in the future. Joe has filed all required past returns. Joe calls the IRS and asks for a simple installment agreement to be paid before the collection statute expiration date for each year. The IRS states the payment plan as low as $550 a month to full pay all three years before the collection statute expiration dates for each year (IRS has an internal tool to compute the minimum payment amount). Joe elects to have the payments directly debited from his checking account on the 15th of each month. On the phone call, Joe faxes a completed Form 433-D to the IRS providing them his bank information and authority to make these withdrawals from his checking account. The fee for Joe to set up the agreement is $107. Joe receives IRS Letter 2273C in three weeks stating that his payment will start on the 15th of the next month.

Full-pay Non-streamlined Payment Plan

If a taxpayer owes an assessed balance between $50,000 and $250,000, he or she may choose to pay the IRS in full in a payment plan. (*Note*: if the taxpayer owes less than $50,000, they will qualify and receive the simple installment agreement that provides the same payment terms as the full pay non-streamlined agreement and does not require the IRS to file a tax lien). This payment plan, called a "full-pay non-streamlined installment agreement" (NSIA), allows the taxpayer to pay the entire amount before the collection statute of limitations expires. [IRM 5.19.13.3 at (1b) (11-4-2024)] The IRS began offering this option in March 2020. The NSIA replaced the IRS's 84-month payment plan option that was in place from 2016-2020.

> **Pro Tip:** Taxpayers who owe above $64,000 and are not in an agreement face possible passport restrictions. The full-pay NSIA is especially helpful in obtaining a quick agreement with the IRS to avoid being certified as having seriously delinquent tax debt and subject to passport restrictions.

> **Pro Tip:** Like the old 84-month agreement, the NSIA is only available if the taxpayer is not assigned to a local Collection Field function (IRS revenue officer) for collection enforcement. Taxpayers who are waiting for an assignment to an RO (called being in the "queue for an RO") can execute an NSIA plan before their case is actually assigned an RO. After assignment to an RO, NSIA is not an available option. However, taxpayers can always request the NSIA plan from the RO if the plan terms facilitate collection of the tax by reducing the default rate on the plan.

The NSIA payment plan has some advantages. Taxpayers can avoid detailed financial disclosure to the IRS, avoid asset liquidation to pay the balance, and may offer better payment terms as compared to an installment agreement based on their ability to pay. However, taxpayers who obtain the NSIA plan face a federal tax lien.

Below are the facts and considerations for the NSIA payment plan.

Important Facts and Considerations for Full-pay NSIAs [IRM 5.19.13.3 (11-4-2024)]	
Qualification	Applicable for total assessed balance between $50,000 and $250,000: • Payment can be made by direct debit or payroll deduction or by check. • All required returns must be filed.

	• Cannot be assigned to the Collection Field function for enforcement.
Terms	• Pay total balance owed before the collection statute expiration date. • Must make a payment each month to avoid default.
Fees	Payment by direct debit or payroll deduction: • Apply by phone or by mail: $107 setup fee. • Low income: setup fee waived. Pay by check, money order, or using IRS Direct Pay or debit/credit card: $178 setup fee (low income: $43 setup fee that may be reimbursed if certain conditions are met).
Timing to request	May request anytime.
How long does it take?	1-2 months. Time is needed for the IRS to process direct debit or financial information and for an IRS manager to approve the agreement.
Method to request	• Unable to request online. • Mail, via Form 9465. • Phone, to IRS unit assigned: IRS Accounts Management or IRS Automated Collection.
Effect on filing of Notice of Federal Tax Lien	An NSIA plan will trigger the filing of an NFTL. *Note*: For 2019 balances only, the IRS will not file an NFTL pursuant to the Taxpayer Relief Initiative COVID-19 relief if the taxpayer obtains the agreement before the taxpayer enters IRS collection. (IRS Notice CP504, LT11, or L1058).
Effect on levy	• May use the NSIA plan to release a levy or garnishment. • Levies will not be issued while on the plan.
Restrictions	• Interest and the failure to pay penalty will still accrue. • IRS will take refunds until balance is fully paid. • Taxpayer will default if with another unpaid assessment (filed return, audit, etc.). • Limited financial disclosure required if the taxpayer has a levy or if the taxpayer has seriously delinquent tax debt (passport restrictions) [IRM 5.19.13.2.2 (1-30-2023)]
Confirmation notice	Letter 2273C will arrive 3-6 weeks after agreement is processed by IRS.

Useful for:	<ul><li>Fixed payment terms.</li><li>Avoiding detailed financial disclosure</li><li>Avoiding asset liquidation.</li><li>Avoiding or removing passport restrictions.</li><li>Removing levy/garnishment.</li></ul>

Full-pay NSIA Payment Plan Example. Jeff owes $84,000 ($74,000 assessed balance plus $10,000 in accrued interest and penalties) for the tax years 2020 and 2021. He has more than 100 months remaining on the collection statute of limitations (for both years) and cannot pay the taxes owed. Jeff has corrected his withholding so that he does not owe again in the future. Jeff has filed all required past returns. Jeff calls the IRS and asks for an NSIA. The IRS representative states that Jeff will need a payment of $1,040 to pay off the entire balance before the collection statutes expire on the debt. To avoid providing financial information related to his assets, liabilities, income, and expenses, Jeff agrees to have the payment directly debited from his checking account on the 15th of each month. On the phone call, Joe faxes a completed Form 433-D to the IRS providing them his bank information and authority to make withdrawals from his checking account. The fee for Joe to set up the agreement is $107. Joe receives IRS Letter 2273C in three weeks stating that his payment will start on the 15th of the next month. The IRS does not file a tax lien as Joe already had a Notice of Federal Tax Lien filed before the agreement was set-up.

Chapter 2.04: Option #2B: Installment Agreements That Require an Ability to Pay Determination

If an ETP or simplified installment agreements are not options, the taxpayer must look to his ability to pay to determine which collection alternative is best. Ability to pay installment agreements (ATP IA), currently not collectible status (CNC), and the offer in compromise (OIC) all require an analysis of the taxpayer's financial status to determine the taxpayer's ability to pay. A taxpayer's ability to pay is the IRS's determination of the collectability of the taxpayer. The determination has two primary ability to pay components:

i.   Ability to pay through the *Net Equity in Assets* (NEA), and
ii. Ability to pay through monthly installment agreements, called *monthly disposable income* ("MDI")

Payment with Net Equity in Assets

If a taxpayer's payment arrangements will not pay the entire balance owed before the collection statute expires (for example, with an ETP or a simplified installment agreement), the IRS may ask the taxpayer to pay with existing assets. [IRM 5.14.2.2 (4-26-2019)]

The IRS will conduct a financial analysis and determine whether the taxpayer should attempt to borrow against or sell property. The taxpayer will be required to make a good faith attempt to utilize the equity before the IRS agrees to approve an ability to pay installment agreement or currently not collectible status. Taxpayers are required to submit copies of all documents that are used in the loan application process.

> **Pro Tip:** Taxpayers with larger balances owed (i.e., over $250,000 and not in a full-pay NSIA) or past noncompliance history (defaulted agreements, non-filing, or under withholding/estimated tax deficiencies) will have more pressure from the IRS to use equity to pay. In all "ability to pay" agreements, the IRS will look for any assets that are not for the production of income or for the health and welfare of the family to be liquidated to pay the balance owed. Excess cash and investments, recreational assets, and equities in other assets likes homes and real estate can be requested by the IRS to pay the outstanding balance before any monthly payment plan is agreed. Taxpayers assigned to the Collection Field function will often be requested to liquidate or borrow against equity in assets.

If the taxpayer does not comply with the requirement of making a good faith attempt to use equity in assets or is not willing to make monthly payments consistent with ability to pay, the taxpayer will be considered a "won't pay" and the IRS may proceed with levy and, in egregious circumstances, seizure of property.

> **Example- Payment with Assets Example.** Karen owes $150,000 for the tax years 2012-2014. Karen can only pay $200 a month in an installment agreement based on her current ability to pay. Karen is 34 years old and is in good health. Karen has a vacation home with $200,000 in net equity. The IRS requests that Karen sell her vacation home to pay her tax bill. Karen elects to refinance her vacation property and use the equity to pay the IRS.

The following factors should be considered when the IRS wants the taxpayer to access existing equity in assets to pay. [IRM 5.14.2.2.2 (6-25-2025)]

When IRS will want taxpayer to use assets to pay	When IRS will NOT request equity in assets
Taxpayer is healthy and has future income potential and does not need the equity for necessary living expenses.	Taxpayer needs to access equity to pay for future necessary living expenses or medical expenses.
Taxpayer has recreational assets.	Taxpayer has minimal (less than 20%) equity in an asset.
Taxpayer has retirement assets that he can borrow against (401k) and will not need these assets for necessary living expenses.	The asset is necessary to generate income and the government will receive more from the future income generated by the asset than from its sale.
Taxpayer has available equity in home.	Taxpayer is on a fixed income and the asset is his home.

| Taxpayer has liquid assets (savings, investments) that can be used to pay and these are not needed for necessary living expenses. | Taxpayer's loan payment would exceed his disposable income. |
| | Taxpayer has unmarketable assets. |

Taxpayers who are requested to access equity by sale or by borrowing against the equity in property will need to show the IRS that they have made a good faith effort to pay. The IRS normally accepts a loan denial letter as a good faith attempt to access equity and as proof that they cannot borrow.

> **Pro Tip:** The taxpayer may find it difficult to borrow against the equity in property if the IRS has filed a Notice of Federal Tax Lien. To avoid complications in being approved for a loan to pay the tax bill, taxpayers should be proactive in requesting loans from third parties before the IRS files an NFTL. Alternatively, taxpayers may need a lien relief option when obtaining the loan.

Payment with Monthly Installment Payments

After consideration of assets, ability to pay agreements consider the taxpayer's ability to pay with monthly payments. If the assets are not sufficient to pay the balance owed, the IRS will want the taxpayer to pay the regular monthly installment agreement payments with monthly disposable income (MDI) (i.e., a payment plan).

> **Pro Tip:** Taxpayers in an IRS installment agreement must make a payment to the IRS each month. Taxpayers who "double-up" payments in a month and skip the following month risk default because the IRS treats the second payment as a voluntary payment — not as a payment for the following month. It is best for taxpayers to set up payments by direct debit from their financial account to avoid defaulting on their agreements.

To determine monthly disposable income, the taxpayer will have to provide the IRS with information to demonstrate average household monthly income and necessary living expenses (Collection Information Statements, Forms 433 series, with substantiation). The living expenses for food/clothing, housing/utilities, and transportation may be limited by IRS collection financial standards. These standards provide national and/or local limits on these expenses and are usually updated annually in March or April.

The MDI, the amount of tax owed, and the collection statute will determine what type of ability to pay agreement is applicable. If a taxpayer owes more than $10,000, the IRS will generally file an NFTL on all ability to pay agreements.

> **Pro Tip:** IRS procedures call for a lien determination if the taxpayer owes more than $10,000 and is not in a qualifying agreement (usually an ETP, GIA, or SIA.) However, in practice, the IRS is not consistent on following these rules. Taxpayers who want to avoid a lien should always consider qualifying options or face the risk that the IRS will file an NFTL.

Ability to pay agreements include not only installment agreements, but currently not collectible status and the offer in compromise alternatives also.

The taxpayer has three types of ability to pay installment agreements:

- *Routine ability to pay installment agreement* (ATP IA): this is an agreement where the taxpayer agrees to fully pay before the collection statute expires. There are four circumstances that call for a routine ATP IA: Collection Field function (revenue officer) assignment, balances owed greater the $250,000 in assessed balances, business agreements, and "tiered" agreements where the taxpayer requests a lower payment in year 1 to allow for household expense adjustments to afford future higher payments. In routine ATP IA cases, the taxpayer cannot utilize any of the simplified installment agreements, including the simple installment agreement (SIA) time period (owe less than $50,000 and can pay within collection statute) or the full-pay non-streamlined installment agreement (NSIA) payment plan terms (if they owe between $50,000 and $250,000 and can full-pay before the CSED expires).

- *Conditional installment agreement* (also referred to as the "six-year" rule): this payment plan applies to taxpayers who do not qualify for any of the simplified installment agreements (i.e., SIA or full pay NSIA) and can fully pay the balance, plus accruals, within six years or before the expiration of the collection statute, whichever is shorter. In cases where the taxpayer can pay within six years, or the collection statute, whichever is shorter, the IRS will allow the taxpayer funds to pay for living expenses even if these exceed IRS standards or are not normally allowed under IRS allowable living expense standards. [IRM 5.14.1.4.1 (3-31-2023)]

  > **Pro Tip:** The release of the 2020 full-pay non-streamlined installment agreement (NSIA) option has diminished much of the need for conditional installment agreements because taxpayers who owe up to $250,000 may have a longer time to pay using the NSIA option. Both the conditional installment agreement and the NSIA require the IRS to file a tax lien. In many cases, the NSIA option may allow for longer payment terms than six years because the NSIA allows the taxpayer to have payment terms until the collection statute expiration date (CSED). For more recent balances, the CSED date may be longer than six years (the CSED date is ten years from the date of assessment), which allows for more time to pay.

- *Partial pay installment agreement* (PPIA): the PPIA is a payment agreement in which the taxpayer is not projected to pay the entire balance owed before the collection statute expires. For PPIAs, the IRS looks closely at the taxpayer's financial situation to first see if the taxpayer can pay with existing equity in assets. [IRM 5.14.2.2 (4-26-2019)] Second, in determining MDI, the IRS only allows necessary living expenses and expenses to produce income. Under IRS procedure, IRS collection is required to review PPIAs every two years to determine if the payment terms should be changed. [IRC §6159(d)] In 2024, the IRS had 32,388 taxpayer accounts with a PPIA [IRS FOIA Response # 2025-07325, February 2025]

The following is a summary of the important facts about the three ability to pay installment agreements:

Ability to pay (ATP) installment agreement	Routine ATP IA	Conditional IA (6-year rule)	Partial Pay IA
Maximum unpaid balance limitation	None.		
Conditions	Taxpayer can fully pay balance before CSED.	Taxpayer owes over $50,000 and can fully pay liability within 72 months.	Taxpayer is unable to pay entire balance before CSED.
Expenses allowed in MDI determination	Only necessary living expenses and expenses to produce income.	Actual expense amounts allowed up to what would allow the taxpayer to pay within 72 months. Can allow the taxpayer a lower first year payment based on actual expenses (called a "tiered IA" or a "lifestyle adjustment" IA) to allow taxpayer to adjust finances to pay a higher monthly payment in years 2-6.	Only necessary living expenses and expenses to produce income.
Maximum term	CSED	6 years.	CSED IRS will review terms every two years and may

			request new ATP determination.
Effect on filing of Notice of Federal Tax Lien	A lien will be filed if amount owed is over $10,000.		
Financial disclosure required	Yes		
Asset liquidation determination	Yes		
Fees	Payment by direct debit or payroll deduction: • Apply by phone, mail, or in-person: $107 setup fee. • Low income: Apply, by phone, mail, or in-person: $31 setup fee waived. Pay by check, money order, or using IRS Direct Pay or debit/credit card: • Apply by phone, mail, or in-person: $225 setup fee (low income: $43 setup fee that may be reimbursed if certain conditions are met).		
Timing to request	May request anytime.		
How long does it take?	• By phone/fax: 1-2 months (if taxpayer has completed Collection Information Statement and supporting documentation faxed to the IRS). • By mail: 2-6 months: depending on whether the IRS has additional requests for information. • Time is needed for IRS to process direct debit or financial information.		
Method to request	• May not request online • Mail, via Form 9465, Form 433, and supporting documents. • Phone, to IRS Collection. Can fax documents or follow up by mail.		
Effect on levy	• Can use to release a levy or garnishment. • Levies will not be issued while in the plan.		
Restrictions	• Interest and the failure to pay penalty will still accrue. • IRS will take refunds until balance is fully paid.		

	• Taxpayer will default with missed payment or if taxpayer has other unpaid assessment (filed return, audit, etc.).		
Confirmation notice	Letter 2273C will arrive 3-6 weeks after agreement is processed by IRS.		
Useful alternative for:	• Cannot use the SLIA or full-pay NSIA option. • Owe > $250,000 • Avoids passport restrictions. • Remove levy/garnishment • Revenue officer assignment. • Business agreements. • For tiered IAs to allow for expense adjustments for future higher payments.	• Lower default rate because allows actual household expenses. • Lower monthly payment than routine ATP agreement. • Avoids passport restrictions. • Remove levy/garnishment • Revenue officer assignment.	• May be better alternative than OIC due to no requirement to offer asset equity. • Poor financial condition and waiting out the CSED to allow IRS to write off remaining balance owed. • Avoids passport restrictions. • Remove levy/ garnishment. • Revenue officer assignment. Business agreements.
Changes	Can renegotiate if financial situation worsens. IRS can request new PPIA terms if financial condition improves.		

Comparison Example of Ability to Pay Installment Agreements

Following are three examples of ability to pay installment agreements.

Routine ATP IA:

Example- George files a 2023 return and owes $120,000. He cannot pay and has no assets that can be used to pay down the liability. George has 115 months remaining on the collection statute of limitations at the time he sets up his agreement. George has filed all his required returns and has sufficient withholding/estimated tax payments to ensure that he will not file and owe in the future.

Situation #1: George has the following average monthly household income and expenses:

Monthly disposable income computations	Amount	Terms
Average monthly gross household income (A)	$7,000	Averaged over period that best reflects average monthly income.
Expenses:		
Total household expenses (B)	$7,100	Necessary and other expenses.
Necessary household expenses only (C)	$5,500	Necessary, limited by IRS Collection Financial Standards.
Monthly Disposable Income:		
MDI: using actual expenses (A) – (B)	($100)	Taxpayer cannot pay based on actual household budget.
MDI: using only necessary expenses (A) – (C)	$1,500	Taxpayer can pay based on expenses allowed by the IRS. Taxpayer will pay off amount owed before CSED expires ($1,500 for 115 months) = $172,500 (greater than balance owed of $120,000).
Installment agreement amount to pay off balance with six-year rule (or CSED whichever is shorter) (D)	$1,667 minimum	Minimum conditional IA payment amount – does not apply here because ATP shows $1,500 a month.

Ignoring the full-pay NSIA terms (*note*: in our example, this is not likely, but assume that the ability to pay is lower than the full-pay NSIA terms), in this case, the IRS will want a routine ability to pay installment agreement of $1,500 a month. A $1,500 monthly payment will not pay the amount owed with six years (see (D) above) and therefore the taxpayer will only be allowed the necessary expenses in determining MDI. The taxpayer is projected to pay off the full balance owed well before the CSED expires in 115 months.

Conditional IA:

Example- *Situation #2*: Tiffany owes $120,000 and has the following average monthly household income and expenses and an IRS CSED of 115 months:

Monthly disposable income computations	Amount	Terms
Average monthly gross household income (A)	$7,000	Averaged over period that best reflects average monthly income.

Expenses:			
	Total household expenses (B)	$5,200	Necessary and other expenses.
	Necessary household expenses only (C)	$4,500	Necessary, limited by IRS Collection Financial Standards.
Monthly Disposable Income:			
	MDI: using actual expenses (A) – (B)	$1,800	Taxpayer can pay within six years based on actual household budget. ($1,800 for 115 months) = $207,000 (greater than the $120,000 owed).
	MDI: using only necessary expenses (A) – (C)	$2,500	Taxpayer can pay based on expenses allowed by IRS. Taxpayer will payoff amount owed before CSED expires ($2,500 for 115 months) = $287,500 (greater than balance owed of $120,000).
	Installment agreement amount to pay off balance with six-year rule (or CSED whichever is shorter) (D)	$1,667 minimum	Minimum conditional IA payment amount to meet six-year rule. Taxpayer's actual expenses can be used to reduce MDI and payment amount to this amount.

In this case, Tiffany qualifies for a conditional installment agreement of $1,800 a month based on her actual expenses. Tiffany's MDI, using actual expenses, will pay the amount owed within six years. (*Note*: Assume that the taxpayer does not take advantage of the full-pay NSIA terms to pay the balance before the CSED.)

PPIA:

Example- *Situation #3*: Vijay owes $120,000 and has the following average monthly household income and expenses and an IRS CSED of 115 months:

Monthly disposable income computations	Amount	Terms
Average monthly gross household income (A)	$7,000	Averaged over period that best reflects average monthly income.
Expenses:		
Total household expenses (B)	$7,100	Necessary and other expenses.
Necessary household expenses only (C)	$6,500	Necessary, limited by IRS Collection Financial Standards.
Monthly Disposable Income:		
MDI: using actual expenses (A) – (B)	($100)	Taxpayer cannot pay based on actual household budget.

| MDI: using only necessary expenses (A) – (C) | $500 | Taxpayer can pay based on expenses allowed by IRS. Taxpayer will NOT pay off amount owed before CSED expires ($500 for 115 months) = $57,500 (less than balance owed of $120,000). |
| Installment agreement amount to pay off balance with six-year rule (or CSED whichever is shorter) (D) | $1,667 minimum | Minimum conditional IA payment amount – does not apply here because ATP shows only $500 a month. |

Vijay qualifies for a PPIA of $500 a month. The IRS will limit his expenses to only the household expenses that are necessary living expenses or expenses necessary to produce income. The IRS will review his agreement every two years. If the IRS does not change the agreement, Vijay will only pay $57,500 of the amount owed before the IRS writes off the remaining balance owed.

Chapter 2.05: Option #3: Not Collectible Status (Currently Not Collectible or "CNC")

If a taxpayer's ability to pay determination concludes that they have $25 or less in MDI, the taxpayer is considered uncollectible. Taxpayers would have to prove that they are uncollectible by providing their financial status to the IRS. Taxpayers would provide a Collection Information Statement (Form 433 series) and supporting documentation to prove their hardship. Some taxpayers may not have to provide a Collection Information Statement (if they owe a low amount that is not published by the IRS) and are terminally or seriously ill, incarcerated, on fixed income, or unemployed with no source of income) to obtain CNC. [IRM 5.16.1.2.9 at (6) (3-3-2025)]

CNC is a temporary status. When the taxpayer's financial situation improves, the IRS can request that the taxpayer provide updated information and make a new ability to pay determination. [IRM 5.16.1.6 (3-3-2025)] The IRS monitors CNC taxpayers for increases in income reported on tax return filings and through Forms W-2 and 1099 filed with the IRS.

If the taxpayer has assets that can be used to pay the tax bill, the IRS may request the taxpayer to access the assets if the taxpayer does not need them for necessary living expenses.

> **Pro Tip:** It is likely that a CNC taxpayer will need to access equity in assets to meet necessary living expenses. Loans against assets are rarely requested because it would put an additional liability on the taxpayer for which they cannot pay. However, the IRS may ask the taxpayer to liquidate non-essential assets such as recreational assets.

Example of CNC. Tom has monthly income of $3,000 and average monthly necessary living expenses of $3,500. Tom lives in an area where the economy is poor, and unemployment is high. Tom has worked as a store clerk and has earned about the same amount of income over the past three years. Tom has had several jobs and has long periods of unemployment in the past. Tom has $5,000 in a savings account from an inheritance from his late relative who died two months ago. Tom would not be required to provide the $5,000, as he will need it for his necessary living expenses over the next year.

Below are the important facts about CNC status.

Currently Not Collectible Status (CNC) [IRM 5.16.1.2 (3-3-2025)]	
Maximum unpaid balance limitation	None.
Conditions	Taxpayer has MDI of $25 or less.
Expenses allowed in determining MDI	Only necessary living expenses and expenses to produce income.
Maximum term	• Temporary status. • IRS will review terms every year based on tax return and information statement (W-2s/1099s) data and may request new ATP determination.
Effect on filing of Notice of Federal Tax Lien	A lien will be filed if amount owed is over $10,000.
Financial disclosure required	Yes (exception if terminally/seriously ill, incarcerated, fixed income and unemployed).
Asset liquidation determination	Yes.
Fees	None.
Timing to request	• Can request anytime. • All required returns do not have to be filed.
How long does it take?	• By phone/fax: 1-4 months (if taxpayer has completed Collection Information Statement and supporting documentation to fax to the IRS). • By mail: 2-9 months: depending on whether the IRS has additional requests for information by the IRS.
Method to request	• May not request online. • Mail, via Form 433, and supporting documents. • Phone, to IRS Collection. Can fax documents or follow up by mail.
Effect on levy	• Can use to release a levy or garnishment. • Levies will not be issued while in CNC.

Restrictions	• Interest and the failure to pay penalty will still accrue. • IRS will take refunds until balance is fully paid. • Taxpayer will default with other unpaid assessment (filed return, audit, etc.).
Confirmation notice	Letter 4223 will arrive 3-6 weeks after agreement is processed by IRS. [IRM 5.16.1.2.9 at (16) (3-3-2025)]
Useful alternative for:	• Temporary hardship. • OIC alternative if the taxpayer cannot afford to pay asset equity in an OIC offer amount. • Avoids passport restrictions. • Remove levy/garnishment. • Business agreements. • Revenue officer assignments.

CNC Example. Tony owes the IRS $19,000 for years 2015-2017. He cannot pay and has no assets that can be used to pay down the liability. Tony has filed all his required returns and has sufficient withholding/estimated tax payments so that he will not file and owe in the future.

Monthly disposable income computations	Amount	Terms
Average monthly gross household income (A):	$7,000	Averaged over period that best reflects average monthly income.
Expenses:		
Total household expenses (B)	$7,500	Necessary and other expenses.
Necessary household expenses only (C)	$7,100	Necessary, limited by IRS Collection Financial Standards.
Monthly Disposable Income:		
MDI: using actual expenses (A) – (B)	($500)	Taxpayer cannot pay based on actual household budget.
MDI: using only necessary expenses (A) – (C)	($100)	Taxpayer cannot pay based on expenses allowed by IRS.

Tony qualifies for CNC status. The IRS will limit the expenses to only the necessary household living expenses and the expenses necessary to produce income. The IRS will not review Tony's CNC status until his income exceeds his annual expenses proven in his CNC approval.

> **Pro Tip:** It is important for the taxpayer to provide all necessary expenses to the IRS when proving CNC. If not, the taxpayer will set a lower threshold for IRS review of the account. For example, if a taxpayer only has $2,000 of income and only provides expenses up to $2,000, but has allowable expenses of $2,500, the IRS will establish $2,000 ($24,000 a year) rather than $2,500 ($30,000 a year) as the threshold to ask for new ability to pay determination. [IRM 5.16.1.2.9 at (13) (3-3-2025)]

In 2024, the IRS had 421,125 taxpayers in CNC status due to financial hardship. [IRS FOIA Response # 2025-07325, February 2025]

Chapter 2.06: Option #4: Offer in Compromise

Taxpayers should consider the offer in compromise (OIC) if they have no means to pay the balance owed before the collection statute of limitations expires. It is common for taxpayers who have little to no assets and qualify for CNC status or a PPIA to consider the OIC.

There are three types of OICs:

i.   *OIC—Doubt as to Collectibility (OIC-DATC):* this is the most common OIC request. A taxpayer qualifies for an OIC-DATC when they have no ability to pay the balances owed with net equity in assets or future installment agreement payments before the CSED. [IRM 5.8.4.3 at (3) (4-25-2025)] Taxpayers who apply for an OIC-DATC would offer an amount to settle the tax bill in full. The amount offered is not arbitrary but is based on future reasonable collection potential (RCP), which is calculated as net equity in assets plus 12 or 24 months of future monthly disposable income, depending on the type of payment method the taxpayer selects.

ii. *OIC—Doubt as to Liability (OIC-DATL):* these OICs are not frequently used. In an OIC-DATL, the taxpayer is questioning the validity of the taxes owed and proposes a correct tax amount. [IRM 4.18.1.2.1 (1-10-2022)] Sometimes, OIC-DATLs are filed when a taxpayer has new information to contest the findings in an audit (in essence, requesting audit reconsideration) or when contesting the assessment determination of the trust fund recovery penalty for unpaid payroll taxes. However, in the IRS FY2024, the IRS only accepted 2 OIC-DATL out of the 1,350 applications received. [IRS FOIA Response # 2025-00032, October 2024]

iii. *OIC—Effective Tax Administration (ETA OIC):* these OICs are also infrequent. Taxpayers who owe balances to the IRS and do not qualify for an OIC-DATC based on their ability to pay may be able to use the ETA OIC if they have extenuating circumstances that warrant settlement. [IRM 5.8.4.2 (4-25-2025)] The most common instance of an ETA OIC is when a taxpayer's liability can be collected in full, but collection would create an economic hardship. The definition of economic hardship as it applies to ETA OICs is derived from Treasury Regulation §301.6343-1. Economic hardship occurs when a taxpayer is unable to pay reasonable basic living expenses. The determination of a reasonable amount for basic living expenses will be made by the IRS and will vary according to the unique circumstances of the individual taxpayer. Unique circumstances, however, do not include the maintenance of an affluent or luxurious standard of living. In the IRS FY2024, the IRS accepted only 293 ETA OICs. [IRS FOIA Response #2025-000321, October 2024]

OICs have historically low acceptance rates by the IRS. From 2007-2017, the IRS accepted a total of 44% of all individual taxpayer OICs. [National Taxpayer Advocate Annual Report to Congress for 2018, TAS RESEARCH AND RELATED STUDIES—A Study of the IRS Offer in Compromise Program for Business Taxpayers] In 2024, the IRS accepted 21% of all OICs. [IRS Data Book 2024, Table 27] The low acceptance rate generally applies to the OIC-DATC, the most common OIC requested. In IRS FY2024, the IRS accepted 6,904 OIC-DATC out of the 31,876 applications received. [IRS FOIA Response #2025-00032, October 2024]

There are four primary reasons that OIC-DATCs are not accepted:

1. Can fully pay before the statute expires: the taxpayer does not qualify because she can pay the balance with asset equity and monthly payments before the CSED.
2. Cannot pay the offer amount: the taxpayer incorrectly computed too low of an offer amount. When the IRS corrects the offer amount, the taxpayer cannot pay the new amount and the offer is rejected or withdrawn.
3. Does not include all asset equity in the OIC offer amount: the taxpayer fails to include all assets in the OIC. A commonly missed asset is the "dissipated asset." [IRM 5.8.5.18 (9-24-2021)] A dissipated asset is an asset that the taxpayer has sold, transferred, encumbered, or otherwise disposed of in an attempt to avoid the payment of the tax liability or the taxpayer used the assets or proceeds (other than wages, salary, or other income) for other than the payment of items necessary for the production of income or the health and welfare of the taxpayer or her family, after the tax has been assessed or during a period of up to six months prior to or after the tax assessment. Generally, a three-year time frame is used to determine if it is appropriate to include a dissipated asset in an OIC. Common dissipated assets include withdrawal of funds from an IRA or pension plan.
4. The taxpayer cannot stay compliant: the taxpayer does not file all required returns or make required estimated tax payments while the OIC is being considered.

Below are the important facts and requirements for an OIC-DATC.

OIC-DATC [IRM 5.8.1 (5-25-2023)]	
Maximum unpaid balance limitation	None
Conditions	Taxpayer must: • File all required returns before the OIC is submitted. • Qualify by not being able to pay the entire amount from equity in assets or monthly payments before the CSED expires.

	• Pay the calculated offer amount, according to the OIC payment method selected. • Remain in filing and payment compliance for the next five years.
Expenses allowed in determining MDI	• Only necessary living expenses and expenses to produce income. • OIC financial analysis has special rules regarding valuation of assets and inclusion of expenses.
Term	OIC-DATC is a complete settlement of all open balances, including any shared responsibility payments owed.
Effect on filing of Notice of Federal Tax Lien	The OIC examiner can request that a lien be filed if the IRS has not already filed the lien. IRS procedures require a lien to be filed if the taxpayer owes more than $10,000 and is not in a qualified payment plan.
Financial disclosure required	Yes. <u>Form 656</u> with a <u>Form 433-A(OIC) and/or Form 433-B(OIC)</u> with supporting documentation is required.
Asset liquidation determination	Net realizable equity in assets is included in the OIC amount to be offered to settle the amount owed.
Fees	A $205 application fee (subject to change) plus payments of the offer amount (payment amounts depend on the payment type selected). Low-income taxpayers do not have to pay the application fee or make OIC payments (either the down payment of the payments during offer consideration).
Timing to request	• Can request any time. • All required returns must be filed prior to the application.
How long does it take?	• 6-12 months. • Taxpayers who owe less than $50,000 come under the "streamlined OIC" procedures which will lower processing and approval times. • ~11% of OICs are appealed — this will add 4-10 months to the process. • IRS must approve or reject the OIC within 24 months after receipt of the OIC application or the OIC is deemed to be accepted.
Method to request	By mail, using <u>Form 656</u>, OIC application.
Effect on levy	• Can use to release a levy or garnishment

	• Levies will not be issued during OIC investigation process.
Restrictions	• Interest and the failure to pay penalty will still accrue. • Taxpayer will default with other unpaid assessment or unfiled return in the next five years after approval.
Confirmation notice	Letter 673 will arrive 3-6 weeks after agreement is processed by IRS.
Useful alternative for:	• Financial hardship situation in which it is clear that the taxpayer can never pay the balance owed and can afford to pay the offer amount. • Avoids passport restrictions. • Remove levy/garnishment.

Pro Tip: On November 1, 2021, the IRS removed the OIC requirement to keep any refund for tax periods extending through the calendar year in which the IRS accepts the OIC. The Form 656 (OIC Application) has this agreement provision, and the provision was removed in the April 2022 Form 656 update.

OIC-DATC Example. Kathy owes $150,000 for the tax year 2018. When submitting the OIC, Kathy has 72 months remaining on the collection statute of limitations. Kathy has filed all of her required returns and has sufficient withholding/estimated tax payments so that she will not file and owe in the future.

Kathy's financial situation is as follows:

Net realizable equity in assets	$5,000	Computed using IRS OIC rules. Includes any dissipated assets.
Monthly disposable Income	$500	Expenses allowed only for necessary living expenses and expenses for the production of income, limited by IRS Collection Financial Standards.

OIC Qualification. Based on the information provided, Kathy qualifies for an OIC-DATC because she cannot pay the balance owed before the CSED expires. Her net equity in assets plus future income to be collected before the collection statute expires ($41,000) is less than the tax balance owed ($150,000).

OIC-DATC Qualification	Calculation
(1) Net realizable equity in assets, plus	$5,000
(2) Future Income (A) × (B)	
(A) MDI	$500
(B) CSED – months remaining to collect	72 months
(A) × (B)	$36,000
(3) Ability to pay (ATP) before CSED expires ((1) + (2))	$41,000
(4) Tax balance owed	$150,000
Qualification (Is (4) > (3)?)	Yes (ATP < tax owed)

Although Kathy has the ability to pay $41,000 on her debt before the collection statute expires, Kathy will only have to offer her "reasonable collection potential" ("RCP") based on OIC rules.

Taxpayers who qualify for CNC or a PPIA and have little/no assets will want to see if they qualify and can pay an IRS OIC-DATC. An OIC may be an option if the taxpayer has little to no asset equity to offer the IRS.

OIC Offer Amount to Settle Balance Owed. If Kathy selects the "lump-sum" OIC payment method, she will only have to offer 12 months of MDI in her offer amount. As a result, she will offer the IRS $11,000 to settle her debt using the OIC-DATC. (This example assumes the net equity in assets and the MDI are the same for the qualification and offer amount computations- this is rarely the case and the offer amount calculation has additional asset exclusions and MDI allowances.)

	Qualification	Offer Amount (Lump-Sum OIC)
(1) Net equity in assets	$5,000	$5,000
(A) MDI	$500	$500
CSED (expires in six years)	72 months	N/A
(B) Future Income Multiplier	N/A	12 months
(2) Future income (A) × (B)	$36,000	$6,000
Reasonable Collection Potential for offer ((1) + (2))	$41,000	$11,000
Tax balance owed	$150,000	$150,000
Qualification	Yes (ATP < tax owed)	
Offer amount		$11,000

Kathy applies for the OIC-DATC. Kathy selects the lump-sum OIC payment method. She does not meet the qualification for low income and so must pay the $205 application fee plus 20% of the offer amount ($2,200) with the <u>Form 656</u> application that is required with the lump-sum OIC payment method. Kathy provides all necessary documentation to prove her assets, liabilities, income, and expenses to the OIC examiner and is approved for the OIC. Kathy makes the remaining offer payments over the next five months after approval and her tax liability is settled. For the next five years, Kathy files and pays all taxes due on time to complete the conditions of her OIC.

If Kathy chose the PPIA alternative, she likely would have a payment nearing the OIC MDI amount and the IRS would have asked about accessing her equity in assets. If Kathy could not access the equity, she still would have to pay the $500 a month for 72 months – or $36,000 of the total tax bill. The OIC offer amount of $11,000 was obviously a better option for Kathy assuming she could afford to pay the OIC offer amount.

> **Pro Tip:** MDI calculations for the OIC-DATC and installment agreements differ. It is possible that the MDI amounts would be different if the taxpayer has certain expenses that allowed for the OIC as opposed to an installment agreement. For example, the taxpayer is allowed an additional transportation operating expense of $200 for an older vehicle for an OIC offer amount. This expense is not allowed in determining MDI for a PPIA.

To explore these topics in greater depth:

- See **Chapter 9: Determining Ability to Pay for IRS Collection Options**, where we break down how to compute the ability to pay for the OIC-DATC.

- See **Chapter 12: Qualify and Obtain an Offer in Compromise for Doubt as to Collectibility (OIC-DATC)**, where we break down how to file for an OIC-DATC.

Chapter 2.07: Comparison of IRS Collection Alternatives and Options

See the Collection Alternatives Evaluation Chart below for a comparison of the major terms and qualifications for each type of collection alternative.

IRS Collection Alternatives Evaluation Chart

| | Installment Agreements (IA) | | | | | | Hardship relief | |
| | Simplified Installment Agreements | | Full-pay non-streamlined IA (owe <$250K) | Complex Ability-to-pay installment agreements | | | Based on Ability-to-pay | |
	Guaranteed installment agreement (GIA)	Simple installment agreement (SIA)		Conditional IA	Ability to Pay IA	Partial Pay IA	Currently not collectible	Offer in Compromise
Maximum unpaid balance	$10,000 total balance owed	$50,000 assessed balance; total balance can be higher	Assessed balance between $50K-250K	No limit	No limit	No limit	No limit	No limit
Maximum payment terms	36-months	Until CSED	Until CSED	6 years or by CSED, whichever is shorter	Before CSED	Paid through end of CSED, then IRS writes off remaining amount owed	N/A	5-24 months
Other collection actions	Refunds used to offset balances owed					Refunds used to offset balances; IRS reviews every 2 years	Increase in income may exit CNC status; refunds taken	Taxpayer must file and pay timely for next 5 years
Advantages	Simple to setup. Avoids tax lien filing and financial disclosure. IRS must accept.	Simple to set up. Avoids tax lien filing and financial disclosure. Favorable payment terms.	Avoids financial disclosure. May lead to favorable payment terms.	Provides payment terms based on actual expenses which lowers default rate.	Limits payment based on income and allowable expenses. Required for field collection.	Does not pay full balance owed before CSED. May not have to pay assets like an OIC.	No payment required based on financial status.	Settle taxes based on calculation of future reasonable collection potential.
Lien filing if balance over $10,000	No	No	Yes	Yes	Yes	Yes	Yes	Yes, if payment plan term is greater than 5 months

IRS Collection Alternatives Evaluation Chart

| | Installment Agreements (IA) | | | | | | Hardship relief | |
| | Simplified Installment Agreements | | | Complex Ability-to-pay installment agreements | | | Based on Ability-to-pay | |
	Guaranteed installment agreement (GIA)	Simple installment agreement (SIA)	Full-pay non-streamlined IA (owe <$250K)	Conditional IA	Ability to Pay IA	Partial Pay IA	Currently not collectible	Offer in Compromise
Financial disclosure required	No	No.	No, unless taxpayer has passport restrictions or prior defaulted IA	Yes	Yes	Yes	Yes	Yes
Expense limitations	N/A	N/A	N/A	Reasonable actual expenses allowed	Limited to expenses for production of income and allowable, necessary living expenses (limits set in IRS Collection Financial Standards)			
Asset liquidation required	No	No	No	No	Considered based on financial information, collection history, and balances owed	Yes	Yes for assets not essential for health and welfare of family or to produce income.	Yes, net equity in assets have to be offered as payment in an OIC
Fees	Set-up by phone/mail: fees range from $107-$225 Set-up online (only available for GIA and SLIA): $31-$149 Setup fee for low-income: $0-43 Penalties and interest accrue until balance is paid						No fee. Penalties and interest continue to accrue	Fee: $205, plus offer amount payments; Low-income waiver available.

- CSED (Collection Statute Expiration Date) – The last date the IRS can legally collect the tax (typically 10 years from the date the taxes were assessed)
- Collection financial standards – Published IRS standards that provides limits on amounts spent for necessary living expenses
- Ability to Pay – based on the taxpayer's equity in assets and/or monthly disposable income that can be used to pay balances owed
- *Note: the IRS also has an Extension to Pay agreement (ETP or referred to by IRS as "short-term payment agreement) that allows individual taxpayers a one-time, up to 180 days, to pay the balance (in full or partially). ETP agreements do not apply if the taxpayer is in default status on a prior agreement, owe greater than $1M (assigned to Collection Field Function), or is assigned to the Collection Field Function (revenue officer).

Chapter 3:
STEPS TO RESOLVE AN IRS COLLECTION ISSUE

This section explains the eight steps to successfully resolve a taxpayer's collection issue. It is especially helpful when a taxpayer does not know where to start to resolve the situation.

Topic	Covers
Goals and Approach of the Collection Taxpayer	The three goals in resolving collection issues and the best approach to meet the goals.
Overview of the Eight Steps to Resolving a Collection Issue	The steps to get the best outcome in the least amount of time for a collection issue taxpayer. With reference sections for how to complete each step.
Example of the Eight-Step Process	Practical example to illustrate how the eight-step process works.
Collection Issue Resolution Checklist	Eight-step checklist to use to solve collection taxpayer issues.

Key Highlights:

- There are eight steps a taxpayer should follow when he has a collection issue. The taxpayer will pay the least amount, get the best alternative, and avoid future IRS enforcement if he follows all eight steps.
- It is necessary to evaluate the taxpayer's tax, financial, and personal information when trying to obtain a collection agreement. With this information, the taxpayer can evaluate options and understand the actions required in order to effectively resolve all outstanding issues and successfully be given a collection alternative.
- It is in the best interest for the taxpayer to resolve all outstanding issues when he has a collection issue. Any additional balances owed will default any agreement set up with the IRS. Some issues will prevent the taxpayer from obtaining a collection alternative, such as filing noncompliance.

Chapter 3.01: Goals and Approach of the Collection Taxpayer

There are three goals when a taxpayer has a balance due to the IRS:

- *Pay the minimum amount*: ensure that the taxes, penalties, and interest paid are minimized.

- *Keep the IRS away*: avoid IRS collection enforcement actions (liens, levies, and passport restrictions).
- *Secure the most appropriate terms for the taxpayer's situation*: obtain the most appropriate collection alternative to get into good standing with the IRS.

Taxpayers facing a balance owed may need to resolve other issues before they can obtain a successful collection agreement with the IRS. Their balance owed may result from other noncompliant behavior such as an audit adjustment, lack of sufficient withholding, or a penalty for filing late. To optimize their outcome, taxpayers need to review their entire tax situation and approach collection resolution by addressing both the causes for the balance owed and the collection alternative solution.

Chapter 3.02: Overview of the Eight Steps to Resolving a Collection Issue

A systematic approach to resolving a collection issue will produce the best outcome with the least amount of effort. The process is similar to how a doctor approaches a medical issue. The first step for the doctor is to understand the relevant facts. Obtaining relevant facts may require some diagnostic tests, like a blood test or an x-ray. Next, with the facts known, the doctor can evaluate options to remedy the patient's ailment(s). The doctor and the patient will develop a treatment plan and execute each step of the plan until the situation is resolved. There may be follow up check-ins to make sure that the patient is in good health.

Resolving any IRS issue mirrors how a doctor and a patient resolve a health issue. The process starts with a diagnosis of the facts that are relevant in determining resolution options. This step may require contacting the IRS to collect the relevant facts. It will always involve understanding the taxpayer's situation to be able to evaluate options. With the relevant facts, the taxpayer can evaluate options, develop a plan of action, and execute the steps required to resolve the issue(s). The taxpayer may have to take follow-up steps to make sure that he stays in compliance and the issue(s) does not return.

> **Pro Tip:** It is best to conduct a "compliance check" with the IRS and obtain a tax history and transcripts for at least the past six years and any years in which taxes or penalties are owed/paid. This can be done by phone, and transcripts can be obtained by mail or online. Taxpayers may find unfiled tax returns, opportunities for penalty abatement, return errors and adjustments, and even identify theft when reviewing the information. The taxpayer will need to assess any errors and consider any actions needed to clear up any past or current issues.

A taxpayer should follow these eight steps below to resolve the tax debt situation to attain the best outcome in the least amount of time:

Step 1: *Obtain the relevant account information.*

- *IRS account and compliance information*: includes information from the IRS on balances owed, years owed, CSEDs, filing and payment compliance, enforcement status (lien filed, levies issued, passport restrictions), and deadlines for next action(s). Obtain tax history documents (transcripts) to review tax history and transactions in detail for possible errors and opportunities.

> **Pro Tip:** For more guidance on obtaining taxpayer information to evaluate collection alternatives, see **Chapter 4: Obtaining IRS and Taxpayer Information for Collection Issues.**

- *Taxpayer information*: includes information from the taxpayer such as copies of notices received, copies of past tax returns with balances owed, initial information on the ability to pay, reasons for past non-compliance, and information to evaluate whether the taxpayer will file and owe in the future.

Step 2: *Request additional time, if needed, to resolve matters to avoid enforced collection actions.*

- *Collection hold*: if the taxpayer is facing pending IRS enforcement, request an extension of time to obtain a collection agreement.
- *Enforcement relief*: If the IRS has already issued a levy, evaluate levy release criteria and request levy release.

> **Pro Tip:** For more information on obtaining an extension to pay or collect hold, see **Chapter 6: IRS Collection Alternatives: Extensions to Pay.**
>
> For more information on avoiding or relief from a garnishment/levy, see **Chapter 15: Avoid/Release an IRS Wage Garnishment and Levy.**

Step 3: *Resolve compliance issues, if needed.*

- *Filing compliance*: file required past-due tax returns.
- *Payment compliance*: adjust withholding and/or make estimated tax payments to avoid owing on future tax filings.

> **Pro Tip:** For more details on this topic, visit www.TaxProblemsHandbook.com and navigate to the **IRS Collection Solutions Handbook** tab to access more information on filing compliance (filing back tax returns).

Step 4: *Evaluate options to reduce taxes, penalties, and associated interest.*

- *Lower tax owed*: consider filing amended returns and/or audit/CP2000 reconsideration, if applicable.
- *Lower penalties owed*: consider penalty abatement options.

> **Pro Tip:** For more details on this topic, visit www.TaxProblemsHandbook.com and navigate to the **IRS Collection Solutions Handbook** tab to access more information on CP2000/audit reconsideration and more information on penalty abatement.

Step 5: *Evaluate collection alternative options in this order:*

- *Simple agreements*: evaluate extensions to pay and simplified installment agreements first.
- *Complex agreements*: If extensions or simple agreements are not feasible, conduct an ability to pay financial analysis to evaluate all options.
- *Settlement option*: evaluate whether the client should consider an OIC as an option.
- *Important considerations*: consider the implications of lien filing and the collection alternative selected.

> **Pro Tip:** For more information on IRS Collection Alternatives, see **Chapter 2: IRS Collection Alternatives**.
>
> For more information on evaluating which collection alternative is best, see **Chapter 5: Evaluating Collection Alternatives**.
>
> For more information on determining ATP, see **Chapter 9: Determining Ability to Pay for IRS Collection Options**.

Step 6: *Complete agreement option with the IRS.*

- *Required format*: complete required forms and documentation.
- *Apply*: request option from IRS (phone, mail, in-person, or online).
- *Follow-through*: complete any follow-up items and secure agreement.
- *Good standing*: confirm taxpayer future collection enforcement (i.e., lien filed) and if applicable, request remaining collection enforcement relief (relief from levy, lien, passport restrictions).

Step 7: *Confirm agreement is accepted by the IRS.*

- *Agreement terms accepted*: validate with IRS notice or contact the IRS 3-4 weeks after completing agreement with IRS. Confirm all years affected obtain the desired agreement by analyzing account transcripts for each year.

- *Enforcement relief granted*: if applicable, confirm enforcement relief was provided (levy relief, lien relief, and decertification of seriously delinquent tax debt for passport restrictions).

Step 8: *Maintain compliance and monitor ongoing notices.*

- *Future compliance*: complete terms of agreement.
- *Avoid future issues*: avoid default by filing and paying on-time in the future.
- *Mark calendar and take action*: take action on any follow-up issues, such as future first-time penalty abatement for the accrued failure to pay penalty.

Pro Tip: For more information on extensions to pay, see **Chapter 6: IRS Collection Alternatives: Extensions to Pay.**

For more information on simplified installment agreements, see **Chapter 7: IRS Collection Alternatives: Simple Installment Agreements.**

For more information on full-pay non-streamlined installment agreement plans, see **Chapter 8: Full-pay Non-Streamlined Installment Agreement Plan (Owe between $50,000 and $250,000.)**

For more information on CNC, see **Chapter 11: Obtain Currently Not Collectible Status (CNC.)**

For more information on OIC, reference see **Chapter 12: Qualify and Obtain an Offer in Compromise for Doubt as to Collectibility (OIC-DATC).**

For more information on levy relief, see **Chapter 15: Avoid/Release an IRS Wage Garnishment and Levy.**

For more information on lien relief, see **Chapter 16: Avoid/Obtain Relief from a Federal Tax Lien.**

For more information on passport restrictions, see **Chapter 17: Passport Restrictions on Seriously Delinquent Tax Debt.**

It is very common for taxpayers with collection issues to have additional future problems (defaulted agreements, questionable notices, etc.). Tax pros should consider monitoring their client's account through IRS account transcripts analysis periodically. Tax pros can use Form 8821, *Tax Information Authorization*, to get copied on future notices and routinely request account transcripts for analysis and action on important items. Taxpayers can monitor their account online using the Taxpayer Individual Online Account at: https://www.irs.gov/payments/online-account-for-individuals

To explore this topic in greater depth, see **Chapter 3.04: Collection Issue Resolution Checklist**.

For the IRS Collection Templates, refer to **Appendix B**—and visit www.TaxProblemsHandbook.com under the **IRS Collection Solutions Handbook** tab for downloadable resources.

Chapter 3.03: Example of the Eight-Step Process

Example: Alan receives a notice that he owes $24,212 for two prior years and the IRS is threatening collection activity.

Step 1: Gather the relevant account information. After reviewing the notice, Alan contacts the IRS and learns that the amount owed was because of an additional assessment from a matching notice (CP2000). Alan also learns that he never responded to the notice and the IRS proceeded with assessing him the proposed additional interest and penalties. The assessment originated from stock sales that were not reported on the return. Alan requested the IRS to send him a copy of the CP2000 notice that he never received because he had moved. Alan also learns that he owes a small amount from another year and his refunds have been used to offset the balance for the past two years. He also discovers that he has not filed a required return from three years ago. Alarmingly, Alan discovers that he is 30 days from a levy and a lien.

With this information, Alan can assess any discrepancies that he has with the IRS and the actions he needs to take to potentially lower taxes, penalties, and interest. He also learns that he needs to file an overdue tax return. Ultimately, because Alan has a collection issue, he will need to work urgently toward a collection option, knowing that he will need to file his returns first to be able to request a collection alternative.

Step 2: Request additional time, if needed, to resolve to avoid enforced collection actions. With these facts, Alan requests a collection hold on the account to allow him to correct the amounts owed and to file back tax returns. The IRS grants him 60 days to correct the prior CP2000 assessment, request penalty abatement, and to file his late return.

Step 3: Resolve compliance issues, if needed. Alan knows he needs to get into compliance before he can request a collection agreement. He will file his overdue return using the wage and income transcripts for that year (received from the IRS) that shows all W-2s and 1099s received. He will owe $1,200 in tax, plus penalties and interest on the late return. He will track the mailing of the return to ensure that the IRS received the return. He keeps a copy of his return to use in the event that he needs to obtain an agreement before the IRS will give him an extension to pay. The return posts to the IRS system in six weeks and Alan can confirm the return was accepted by reviewing his IRS transcript.

Alan's withholding is adequate so that when he files his current year return, he will not owe money to the IRS.

Step 4: Evaluate options to reduce taxes, penalties, and associated interest. Alan develops a plan to lower the liability owed by requesting CP2000 reconsideration (he has basis in the stock sold that he can use to lower the amount owed) and request penalty abatement for the other balance owed year. Over the next two months, Alan reduces the amount that he owes through a successful CP2000 reconsideration and receives first time penalty abatement for the other balance due year. In the end, Alan owes the IRS a final balance of $2,121. He believes he will qualify for a simplified installment agreement and can pay the balance owed before the collection statute expires with a small payment plan amount.

Step 5: Evaluate collection alternative options. Alan has enough income to pay his liability. Alan makes over $120,000 a year and only supports himself. Alan will execute a simplified payment plan to pay back the amount owed.

Step 6: Complete agreement option with the IRS. After he successfully lowers his liability to $2,121, Alan sets up a payment plan with payments of $100 a month (guaranteed installment agreement) by contacting the IRS by phone and arranging for the payment to be made by direct debit. Alan will have his payments drafted on the 28th starting the following month and for each month thereafter until the amount is paid in full. Alan completes the Form 433-D to set up the payment by direct debit.

Step 7: Confirm agreement is accepted by the IRS. Alan reviews his transcripts and confirms that the CP2000 assessment has been correctly changed and that he has received penalty abatement for the other year for which he had a balance owed. Alan receives a Letter 2273C that confirms the terms of the agreement.

Step 8: Maintain compliance and monitor ongoing notices. Several months later, Alan files his current year return and is entitled to a $4,234 refund. The IRS takes $1,344 to pay the remaining balance and sends Alan the remaining refund. Alan receives IRS letter CP89 later in the year confirming the amount paid and that there is no balance owed.

Chapter 3.04: Collection Issue Resolution Checklist

Use the eight-step Collection Issue Resolution Checklist to address a taxpayer collection issue.

Collection Issue Resolution Checklist

☐ Step #1: Obtain taxpayer information

    o IRS information

- Account information and tax history
- Compliance enforcement status, assignment, and history
- Filing and payment compliance status
- IRS documents (transcripts for years in question, payoff calculator)
- Deadlines for next actions and enforcement

    o Taxpayer information

- Years in question
- Reasons for noncompliance
- Notices and interactions with IRS
- Prior and current IRS enforcement actions
- Current filing and payment compliance
- Ability to pay

☐ Step #2: Request additional time, if needed

    o Request collection hold if needed to understand facts and resolve issues and to avoid future collection enforcement
    o Request levy relief, if needed

☐ Step #3: Resolve pre-requisite compliance issues, if needed

    o File all required back tax returns and confirm acceptance by IRS
    o Correct withholding and/or make estimated tax payments so that the taxpayer will not owe for the next filed tax return (tax payments can also be used as an expense to lower monthly payment plan amount in any ATP agreement)

☐ Step #4: Evaluate options to reduce taxes, penalties, and interest

    o Correct tax on recent three years and any year in which tax owed/paid within past two years with an amended return o Review IRS account transcripts for opportunities for penalty abatement and request abatement of penalties

☐ Step #5: Evaluate which collection alternative option is best

o Identify if simplified agreement is best
o If simplified agreements are not used, calculate ability to pay and which alternative is best
o Obtain all information and documentation needed to obtain the selected agreement

☐ Step #6: Complete agreement with IRS

o Complete all required forms and required substantiation
o For urgent situations, apply by phone or online and fax all required information to IRS collection personnel. Request levy relief when applying by phone, if needed. Otherwise, can apply by mail.
o Monitor IRS letters for requests for additional information. Reply by the deadline.

☐ Step #7: Confirm agreement is accepted

o Review IRS notices and/or contact the IRS to confirm that the terms of the agreement are in place.
o Confirm all years/periods are included by reviewing IRS account transcripts.
o Validate that enforcement relief has been granted. If needed

☐ Step #8: Maintain terms of agreement and compliance

o Confirm estimated tax payments and withholding actions are complete to not owe in future
o Monitor future IRS notices for any issues
o If taxpayer needs to miss payment, contact IRS to avoid default of agreement
o File and pay all future tax returns and balances

For the Collection Issue Resolution Checklist, refer to **Appendix B**—and visit www.TaxProblemsHandbook.com under the **IRS Collection Solutions Handbook** tab for downloadable resources.

Chapter 4:
OBTAINING IRS AND TAXPAYER INFORMATION FOR COLLECTION ISSUES

This section covers the information needed from the taxpayer and the IRS to evaluate and execute IRS collection alternatives and agreements.

Topic	Covers
Due Diligence: Gathering Taxpayer and IRS Information to Evaluate and Execute Collection Alternatives	The two sources of information needed to evaluate collection alternatives: from the taxpayer and the IRS.
Taxpayer Information Needed in Collection Issues	Taxpayer information needed to evaluate collection alternatives.
Taxpayer Information Task List — IRS Collection Issue	Task list of information to be gathered from the taxpayer in collection issues.
IRS Information Needed in Collection Issues	IRS information to be requested in order to evaluate collection alternatives.
IRS Account Research Worksheet — Collection Issue (Contact by Phone/in Person)	Worksheet used to request IRS information for the taxpayer to evaluate collection alternatives.
IRS Transcripts and Payoff Calculator	Important collection information contained in IRS transcripts and the payoff calculator.

Key Highlights:

- The first step in resolving an IRS collection issue is to obtain all the relevant information needed to evaluate alternatives and identify other issues that need to be addressed.
- To effectively evaluate IRS collection alternatives, a taxpayer will collect all pertinent information about her personal and financial situation.
- IRS account and enforcement information are needed to understand options and specific actions required to resolve a tax debt problem and to avoid collection enforcement actions.
- IRS information is also needed to determine additional issues that may need to be resolved to obtain a collection agreement, such as filing compliance issues.

Chapter 4.01: Due Diligence: Gathering Taxpayer and IRS Information to Evaluate and Execute Collection Alternatives

Conducting effective due diligence is necessary to effectively resolve a collection issue. The first step is to gather all the relevant facts to effectively address the issue(s).

The first source of information is the taxpayer's personal and financial circumstances. Many taxpayers will wish to avoid IRS scrutiny as quickly as possible and want to avoid the negative effects of a federal tax lien. These taxpayers may just need limited information, such as a payoff amount, to fully pay their liability and may not have to interact with the IRS in the future. However, if the taxpayer needs a collection alternative or wants to investigate solutions to lower the liability, more information is needed from the taxpayer and from the IRS.

The second source of information is the IRS account and enforcement information. Often IRS collection issues cannot be solved in isolation. For example, to enter into most IRS collection alternatives such as an installment agreement or an offer in compromise, taxpayers will need to have filed all required returns (be filing compliant) and be up to date on withholding or estimated tax payments so that they will not owe on their next filed return (be payment compliant). To obtain all the relevant information, the taxpayer can contact the IRS directly – either the accounts management function for account information or the IRS collection function for enforcement information. The IRS can provide to the taxpayer transcripts that can be used to analyze and resolve the tax issue(s).

IRS notices and letters can also be useful to understand the status and account information. However, transcripts are often limited to a specific tax period/form, and may not provide the entire picture and all of the information needed to resolve a collection matter effectively.

Chapter 4.02: Taxpayer Information Needed in Collection Issues

If a taxpayer requires a collection alternative from the IRS, she will need to evaluate her circumstances to determine which alternative is best and how to obtain the alternative with the IRS.

Generally, the taxpayer will only need to assess and provide in-depth personal and financial information if she is obtaining an ability to pay collection alternative (ATP installment agreement, CNC, or an OIC). A taxpayer who qualifies and can meet the terms of an extension to pay or a simplified installment agreement may only need to provide limited information. For example, if a taxpayer wants to pay with a simple installment agreement, she will only need to assess if she can pay within the collection statute. Taxpayers will always need to demonstrate filing compliance and payment compliance. Taxpayers need to evaluate their current year tax situation to determine if their payments and withholdings are sufficient so that they will not owe again in the future. Even if the IRS allows the taxpayer an agreement without payment compliance, the taxpayer may default on the agreement if she owes an additional balance that she cannot pay.

It also may be necessary to assess the taxpayer's willingness to pay the IRS in full to avoid future interaction. Taxpayers who face a federal tax lien may also want to consider the impact of a tax lien and obtain a collection alternative that does not require a tax lien determination by the IRS.

However, if the taxpayer's situation is more complex, more information will be needed to assess available collection options.

In these cases, the taxpayer's information will be needed to specifically address:

- *Net equity in assets*: what assets does the taxpayer own and what is the equity in each of these assets that could be used to pay the IRS based on the various collection alternatives available to the taxpayer.
- *Liquidity in assets*: determine immediate assets that may be accessed to pay the IRS.
- *Average household monthly income (from all sources):* used to determine monthly disposable income, i.e., the amount that the IRS will want in a payment plan.
- *Average household monthly expenses*: also used in determining monthly disposable income (MDI), i.e., the monthly amount that the IRS will want in a payment plan.
- *Future earning capability*: this is used in evaluating alternatives such as extension to pay or an offer in compromise.
- *Future wealth and income to be acquired*: used in evaluating an offer in compromise.
- *Personal circumstances*: this includes factors used to determine the ability to make future payments and the need for assets to pay for necessary future living expenses.
- *Future tax liability*: whether the taxpayer will file and owe in future years based on their tax situation.

IRS Collection Information Statements provide the minimum information needed for an application for an ability to pay collection alternative. Taxpayers should complete the following forms as part of the information gathering process: [IRM 5.15.1.2 at (2) and (3) (11-22-2021)]

- *Form 433-A*: *Collection Information Statement for Wage Earners and Self-Employed Individuals* (for more complex individual taxpayers and those who are assigned to the Collection Field function (CFf or revenue officer assignment))
- *Form 433-B*: *Collection Information Statement for Businesses* (businesses that are not sole proprietorships)
- *Form 433-F*: *Collection Information Statement* (for wage earners and self-employed persons assigned to the Automated Collection System). *Note*: The Collection Field Function can use Form 433-F for trust fund recovery cases where the potential penalty is less than $100,000 and for self-employed and individual wage earners who owe less than $250,000.
- *Form 433-H*: *Installment Agreement Request and Collection Information Statement* (wage earner requesting an installment agreement, and the liability is either greater than $50,000). Does not apply to taxpayers who owe up to $250,000 and are requesting a full-pay non-streamlined installment agreement plan (NSIA).

> **Pro Tip:** Technically, a revenue officer can accept a Form 433-F for any taxpayer who owes less than $250,000 (or trust fund taxes up to $100,000). However, in practice, many ROs prefer the more extensive Form 433-A document.

The table below contains the personal and financial information needed from the taxpayer.

	IRS Collection Issue: Information Needed from the Taxpayer	
	Taxpayer Information	**Why It Is Needed**
1	Tax return filings and payments • Obtain copies of last three years returns and any years with a balance owed. • Confirm current and past six years have been filed. • Obtain payment history on balances owed.	• Review returns for accuracy and ability to file amended returns to lower amount owed. • Confirm filing compliance. • Review payment(s) made on balances owed.
2	IRS notices • All notices received from the IRS, even if the taxpayer does not believe they are relevant. • All state tax notices received to find related state tax issues. • Notice of Federal Tax Liens.	• Determine status with the IRS and where taxpayer is at in the collection process, including any pending enforcement and deadlines. • Determine prior agreements with IRS. • Identify nature of any additions to tax, such as from an audit or CP2000 adjustment.
3	Collection Information Statement information • Form 433-A, B, F, or H required information. • Employer/customer/bank contact information for levy issues.	• Help in determining ability to pay and which collection alternatives are available. • Address questions required for an ability to pay agreement. • Information for immediate garnishment or levy release.
4	Ability to pay information: assets and liability	• Determine ability to pay with current assets.

	<ul><li>List of all household assets with associated liabilities.</li><li>All financial account balances.</li><li>All retirement account balances.</li><li>All recreational assets and associated liabilities.</li><li>Cash on hand.</li><li>Student loans or state/local tax debt owed.</li><li>Any assets disposed of in the past three years.</li><li>Any other assets and liabilities.</li></ul>	<ul><li>Determine net equity in assets in determining ability to pay.</li></ul>
5	Ability to pay information: income and expenses <ul><li>Gross household income for the past three months.</li><li>Gross household income for the past 12 months.</li><li>Any bonuses or other income that is due to be received.</li><li>Reconciliation of past three months bank deposits to source of income with explanation of non-taxable sources/sources not reported on Form 433.</li><li>Non-liable spouse income and household expenses, including how they are paid (commingled with liable spouse, not commingled).</li></ul>	<ul><li>Determine ability to pay with household monthly income.</li><li>Determine monthly disposable income for collection alternative evaluation.</li></ul>
6	Ability to pay: documents needed <ul><li>Form 433 (A, B, F, or H as required).</li><li>Last three months paystubs for all members of the family.</li><li>Last three months financial account statements (all accounts and all pages).</li><li>Bills, receipts, and payments for last three months of household living expenses and any other allowable expenses.</li><li>Bills, receipts, and payments for any household living expenses and other</li></ul>	<ul><li>Must be provided to IRS for an ability to pay agreement.</li><li>Source documents to reconcile the ability to pay with financial information provided to the IRS.</li></ul>

	allowable expenses paid on an annual basis. • Self-employed: profit and loss statement for the past 12 months.		
7	Personal information • Household family member information (age, health, income, assets). • Employment information. • Past employment history. • Bankruptcy history. • Residences in the past ten years. • Beneficiary of trust, estate or life insurance policy. • Safety deposit box contents, if any. • Business information, if applicable. • Level of education. • Past unemployment or underemployment history. • Effects of a federal tax lien. • Retirement timeline, if applicable.		• Determine factors for computing ability to pay. • Determine future need to use assets. • Determine factors that may hinder future MDI. • Determine income history for proper income averaging and computation of future income. • Determine if there are dissipated assets. • Determine effect of NFTL.

Chapter 4.03: Taxpayer Information Task List — IRS Collection Issue

Use the Taxpayer Information Task List below to select and track the taxpayer information needed to evaluate collection alternatives and to execute a collection agreement with the IRS.

Taxpayer Information Task List – IRS Collection Issue

Information Category	Taxpayer Task List Deadline to provide: _____

(1) IRS collection documents	☐ Complete Collection Information Statement:
	    ☐ Form 433-A
	    ☐ Form 433-B
	    ☐ Form 433-F
	    ☐ Form 433-H
	☐ Provide current employer/customer/banking information who has received garnishment or levy:
	    ☐ Employer/customer/bank name: _____
	    ☐ Employer/customer/bank contact person: _____
	    ☐ Contact person phone and fax number: _____
	☐ Provide all copies of IRS notices, State/local tax notices

(2) Tax returns and payments information	☐ Tax returns for past three years: _____
	☐ Tax returns for any years with issues: _____
	☐ Did you file last year's returns and the past six years returns? (Y/N) _____
	    a. If no, why?
	    _____
	    _____
	☐ Do you expect to owe again for your next return that you file?
	    (Y/N)_____ Explain:
	    _____
	    _

(3) Financial information: Assets and liabilities (for most items are listed on the Form 433)	☐ List of household assets and liabilities (real property, vehicles, personal assets, etc.) ☐ All financial account balances (checking, savings, investment, ☐ Other investments and their values (businesses, stocks, land, rental property, intellectual property, etc.) ☐ All retirement account balances (pension, 401K, IRS, etc.) ☐ List of all life insurance policies and their cash value, if any ☐ All recreational assets and associated liabilities (vacation homes, recreational vehicles, etc.) ☐ Cash on hand (in possession) ☐ Student loans or state/local tax debt owed ☐ Any assets disposed of in the past three years ☐ Any other assets and liabilities ☐ Credit lines, with balances and available credit ☐ Assets transferred or sold in past three years (real property, investments, retirement, businesses, etc.)

(4) Financial information: Household income and expenses **(for most items are listed on the Form 433)**	☐ Wage earners: Gross household income for the past three months ☐ Self-employed: Profit and loss for the past 12 months ☐ Any bonuses or income that is due to be received ☐ Other income (taxable and non-taxable): rental, child support, alimony, retirement, Social Security, investment, etc.) for the past 12 months ☐ Reconciliation of past three months bank deposits to source of income with explanation of non-taxable sources/sources not reported on Form 433 ☐ Other than family members, are there any other members of the household? For each person, provide their name, relationship, age, their monthly income, and expenses that the pay for the household.
(5) Source documents: Provide these supporting documents	☐ Last three months paystubs for all members of the family ☐ Last three months financial account statements (all accounts and all pages) ☐ Bills, receipts, and payments for last three months of household living expenses and any other allowable expenses ☐ Bills, receipts, and payments for any household living expenses and other allowable expenses paid on an annual basis ☐ Self-employed: profit and loss statement for the past 12 months ☐ Estimated tax payment made for the past year ☐ State and local income taxes paid for the last year, including any installment agreement payments for back taxes owed ☐ Court ordered payments: court order and payments made for past year ☐ Student loan payments made in the past year ☐ Payments to other debts in the past year: include loan document and payments ☐ Professional fees for the past year: include invoice, description of services performed, and payments made ☐ Other: _____ ☐ Other: _____ ☐ Other: _____
(6) Personal Information to evaluate collection alternatives	☐ Household family member(s) information (age, health, income, assets) ☐ Employment information ☐ Past employment history ☐ Bankruptcy history ☐ Residences in the past 10 years ☐ Beneficiary of trust, estate or life insurance policy ☐ Safety deposit box contents, if any ☐ Business information, if applicable ☐ Level of education ☐ Past unemployment or underemployment history ☐ Effects of a federal tax lien ☐ Retirement timeline, if applicable ☐ Other: _____ ☐ Other: _____ ☐ Other: _____

For the IRS Collection Templates, refer to **Appendix B**—and visit www.TaxProblemsHandbook.com under the **IRS Collection Solutions Handbook** tab for downloadable resources.

Chapter 4.04: IRS Information Needed in Collection Issues

It is especially important to understand the taxpayer's status and his relevant information from the IRS's perspective. It is necessary to obtain IRS account and enforcement information to understand what options are available and the actions that are needed to resolve the collection issues and avoid enforcement. IRS information will also reveal any opportunities to lower the amount owed through filing amended returns, reconsideration requests, and penalty abatement.

There are three sources of IRS information available:

1. IRS tax history and account information.
2. IRS collection enforcement information.
3. IRS transcripts and payoff information.

If a taxpayer is assigned to the Collection Field function (CFf or revenue officer assignment), the revenue officer can provide both account and enforcement information.

> **Pro Tip:** If a taxpayer is assigned to IRS collection, only IRS collection can provide payoff amounts.

However, taxpayers and tax pros can obtain this information from the sources in the table below.

IRS Account Information Phone Contacts for Collection Issues		
Taxpayer account and enforcement information	**Tax professional**	**Taxpayer**
In IRS Automated Collection: wage earner	(M-F, 8AM-8PM, local time) (866) 860-4259, option 4 (through IRS PPS)	(M-F, 8AM-8PM, local time) (800) 829-7650
In IRS Automated Collection: small business or self-employed		(M-F, 8AM-8PM, local time) (800) 829-3903
Not in IRS Collection or assigned to IRS Collection Field Function (CFf, i.e., a revenue officer)	(M-F, 8AM-8PM, local time) (866) 860-4259, option 2 (PPS line, can also be used to get account information at any time from the IRS)	(M-F, 7AM-7PM, local time) (800) 829-0922 or (800) 829-8374
In IRS Special Compliance Program	(M-F, 8AM-8PM, ET) (833) 282-7220	

Specifically, the information that is needed from the IRS, including what transcripts should be requested, is detailed below.

	IRS Collection Issue: Information Needed from the IRS	
	IRS Account Information	**Why It Is Needed**
1	Tax Return Filing Compliance • Confirm that the current and past six years returns have been filed.	Unable to complete most collection alternatives, including installment agreement or OIC, without demonstrated filing compliance.
2	Balances Owed – total and detail by tax year Total balances: • Total balance owed. • Assessed balance owed. For each year: • Additional tax assessments made after return was filed. • Assessed failure to file penalty. • Accrued failure to pay penalty. • Other penalties on the account. • Collection Statute Expiration Date(s) (CSED).	Balances: to determine payoff amount, which installment agreements are available, and for OIC qualification. Each year detail: assessments and penalties are opportunities to lower balances by filing amended returns, audit/CP2000 reconsideration, and/or penalty abatement. CSED: used to determine limitations on length of simplified installment agreements and for OIC qualification.
3	Enforcement Status • In IRS Collection? • Lien issued? Years? • Levy issued? Years? Employer/bank/customer levied? • If owe > $59,000, passport restrictions started?	To determine if pending IRS enforcement is imminent. Determine if relief will need to be requested for liens, levies, and passport restrictions.
4	Deadline for Action: • Date/next action required. • Ramifications for missing next deadline.	To determine timing of next actions and to avoid enforced collection actions.
5	IRS documents:	To more closely examine taxes owed, penalties assessed, other assessments, and actions on the

	<ul><li>Obtain IRS account transcripts for past seven years and balance due years.</li><li>Obtain wage and income transcripts for most recent year and unfiled years (if MFJ, request both spouses).</li><li>Payoff calculator showing amounts owed.</li></ul>	account that may need to be addressed. To obtain wage and income information to evaluate accuracy of current income reported and for preparation of unfiled tax returns.

Chapter 4.05: IRS Account Research Worksheet — Collection Issue (Contact by Phone/in Person)

When interviewing the IRS, the taxpayer can use the IRS Account Research Worksheet to guide the information gathering process.

IRS Account Research Worksheet– Collection Issue (contact by phone/in person)

Information	Notes
Document who gave you the information at the IRS	IRS Phone Number called: _____ IRS Function: _____ IRS representative's name: _____ Badge/ID #: _____
(1) Tax return filing compliance	Current year filed: (Y/N/on extension) _____ Past 6 years filed: (Y/N) _____ Years needed to be filed: _____ *Note: request Wage and Income and Account Transcripts for any unfiled years to help with tax preparation*
(2) Balance(s) owed information	<u>Totals:</u> Total balance owed: _____ Total assessed balance owed:_____ Years owed: _____ <u>Breakdown by year:</u> <table><tr><td>Year</td><td>Total balance owed</td><td>Assessed balance</td><td>Collection statute expiration date</td><td>Additional assessments/penalties assessed (list)</td></tr><tr><td></td><td></td><td></td><td></td><td></td></tr><tr><td></td><td></td><td></td><td></td><td></td></tr><tr><td></td><td></td><td></td><td></td><td></td></tr><tr><td></td><td></td><td></td><td></td><td></td></tr><tr><td></td><td></td><td></td><td></td><td></td></tr></table>
(3) Enforcement status	<u>IRS Collection Status:</u> Assigned to IRS Collection? (Y/N) _____ IRS Collection assigned (ACS/CFf) _____ <u>Lien filing:</u> Lien filed: (Y/N/in process) _____ Years lien filed: _____ <u>Garnishments/levies:</u> Garnishment/levy issued? (Y/N) _____ If yes: levy source: _____ Passport certification notice sent? (Y/N or N/A) ___ Date of CP508: _____

(4) Deadline for action	**Deadlines:**
	IRS follow up date:_____
	Actions required to be completed by that date:
	☐ File back returns: (years/due date)_____
	☐ Change withholding: (due date) _____
	☐ Make estimated tax payments: (due date) _____
	☐ Provide collection information statement or enter into simplified installment agreement to avoid enforced collection: (date/action) _____
	☐ Other: (action/due date)_____
	☐ Other: (action/due date)_____
	☐ Other: (action/due date)_____
	☐ Other: (action/due date)_____
(5) Request transcripts	**Account transcripts:** (request all balance due years and any other years with issues)
	Years ordered: _____
	Wage and Income transcripts (W-2s, 1099s, etc.): *request all unfiled return years and any years with possible need for amended return)*
	Years ordered (Primary): _____
	Years ordered (spouse, if applicable): _____
	Return transcripts: *request last three years if amended returns will be considered or filed*
	Years ordered: _____
	Delivery of transcripts: *IRS will not fax transcripts Can be hand delivered at local IRS office*
	Delivery method: (taxpayer by mail/tax pro through e-services account) _____
	Date to be delivered to taxpayer: _____

For the IRS Collection Templates, refer to **Appendix B**—and visit
www.TaxProblemsHandbook.com under the **IRS Collection Solutions Handbook** tab for
downloadable resources.

For more information on accessing and using IRS transcripts, visit
www.TaxProblemsHandbook.com and navigate to the **IRS Collection Solutions Handbook** tab
to access more information on IRS Transcripts.

Chapter 4.06: IRS Transcripts and Payoff Calculator

IRS documents can provide an in-depth analysis of collection information. IRS documents include the three types of transcripts (tax account, tax return, and wage and income) and the IRS payoff calculator.

Account Transcripts

Account transcripts can be used to identify important information for collection issues, including:

- *Filing compliance*: whether required returns were filed.
- *Account Information*: includes payments and adjustments to the account, including audit adjustments, CP2000 notices and adjustments, and penalties assessed.
- *Enforcement data*: includes important notices that trigger appeals, such as the issuance of a Final Notice of Intent to Levy which provides the taxpayer with an opportunity to request a Collection Due Process hearing. An issuance of a Notice of Federal Tax Lien is also indicated on an account transcript.
- *Agreement status*: includes installment agreements, currently not collectible, and OICs.
- *Some notices*: not all collection notice stream notices are listed. The CP14 initial balance owed, Letter LT11 (Final Notice of Intent to Levy) and the CP523 (Defaulted Installment Agreement Notice) are examples of collection notices that are listed on the account transcript.
- *Collection statute of limitations insights*: provides processing date that triggers the start of the CSED and other transactions that extend the CSED.

To explore this topic in greater depth, see **Chapter 1.12: Collection Statute of Limitations**, for CSED and account transcript codes that extend the CSED.

The following is a list of important account transcript codes (called "TCs" or "transaction codes") that contain important collection information. [IRS Document 6209 (Section 8A)]

Analysis	Code	Transcript Description	What Happened
Payments	610	Remittance with return	Payment received when return was filed.
	670	Payment	Payment received on the balance owed.
	706	Credit transferred	A refund or overpayment from another year has been applied to the tax year with a balance owed.
Installment agreement	971	Miscellaneous transaction – installment agreement	An installment agreement was established and is in effect.

Currently not collectible	530	Balance due account – currently not collectible	The taxpayer has negotiated and is in currently not collectible status with the IRS for the tax period.
Lien	971	Issued notice of lien filing and right to Collection Due Process hearing	Notice of lien filed and right to challenge within 30 days with a CDP hearing.
	582	Lien indicator	IRS has filed a tax lien on taxpayer's account.
	583	Reverse lien indicator	IRS manually released a lien from account.
Levy	670	Payment levy	Payment received from a levy source posted to the account.
	971	Collection due process Notice of Intent to Levy issued	IRS will send a letter via certified mail indicating its intent to levy within 30 days notifying the taxpayer of the right to file for a CDP hearing within 30 days. *Note:* Another 971 will indicate whether the taxpayer received the notice.
Offer in compromise	480	Offer in compromise pending	OIC request under consideration; has not been rejected, returned, withdrawn, or terminated.
	481	Offer in compromise rejected	IRS rejected the OIC request.
	482	Offer in compromise withdrawn/terminated	Taxpayer withdrew or terminated the OIC request.
	780	Offer in compromise accepted	IRS accepted the OIC request.
Passport restrictions	971	Passport certified seriously delinquent tax debt	IRS provided taxpayer Letter CP508C stating that they face potential passport restrictions if tax debt issue is not resolved.
Private debt collection	971	Collection referred to a private debt collection agency	Debt sent to a PDC for collection action.

> **Pro Tip:** Taxpayers need to be aware that account transcripts have limitations. Account transcripts do not contain many notices issued, causes for notices and adjustments to the account, pending transactions, status indicators, statute dates – including the CSED, and deadlines. Taxpayers should interview the IRS to obtain this information. The account transcript should never be used to obtain a payoff amount. The current balance on the account transcript may not be accurate because it is possible that accrued penalties and interest have not yet posted to the account transcript. Contacting the IRS directly for a payoff amount or having the taxpayer access the IRS account on irs.gov ("View my account" feature) is the only way to obtain the exact payoff amount.

For more information on accessing and using IRS transcripts, visit www.TaxProblemsHandbook.com and navigate to the **IRS Collection Solutions Handbook** tab to access more information on IRS Transcripts.

Return Transcripts

Return transcripts can be obtained for the current year return and any returns filed within the past three years. [IRM 21.2.3.2.1 (8-15-2024) and IRM 21.2.3.3.1 (5-22-2024)] These are the returns that the IRS originally processed and do not include any adjustments made to the return from amended returns, audits, and CP2000 notices. Taxpayer who do not have copies of their prior year returns can access the return transcripts. Return transcripts are helpful in discovering opportunities to lower the tax liability as originally reported on the return. Taxpayers can compare their return transcripts against the wage and income transcripts to see if they missed any deductions. For example, the taxpayer may identify that they missed an education credit from a reported Form 1098-T, *Tuition Statement*.

> **Pro Tip:** Return transcripts can also be used to provide a historical comparison with current income. Taxpayers who request an ability to pay collection alternative with the IRS may have to explain year-to-year reductions in income.

For more information on accessing and using IRS transcripts, visit www.TaxProblemsHandbook.com and navigate to the **IRS Collection Solutions Handbook** tab to access more information on IRS Transcripts.

Wage and Income Transcripts

Taxpayers should always request wage and income transcripts for any required unfiled tax year. The IRS keeps wage and income information (W-2s, 1099s, etc.) for the current and past nine years under the taxpayer's identification number (i.e., SSN). [IRM 21.2.3.2.4 (5-30-2023)] Wage and income transcripts can greatly reduce the amount of time needed to prepare a late-filed return. Reporting all income listed on the wage and income transcript is also necessary for the IRS to initially accept the return as filed.

The last three year's wage and income transcripts also can be used to conduct due diligence before filing for an OIC. Taxpayers should review prior wage and income information and be prepared to explain any assets that were dissipated (that is, assets that were transferred or sold and were not used to pay the outstanding balance owed or for necessary living expenses). For example, Form 1099-R or Form 5498 may indicate prior IRA balances or distributions. The taxpayer will need to explain how these assets were used for necessary living expenses or be prepared to include them in the OIC offer amount.

It is always a good practice for taxpayers to review their last year's wage and income information when considering all ability to pay agreements. The IRS will review this document closely and ask the taxpayer to explain any accounts, income, or assets on the wage and income transcript that do not appear on the Collection Information Statement. Taxpayers should be prepared to address these issues.

For more information on wage and income transcripts, visit www.TaxProblemsHandbook.com and navigate to the **IRS Collection Solutions Handbook** tab to access more information on IRS Transcripts.

IRS Payoff Calculator

The IRS payoff calculator provides important information about the taxpayer's balances.

For each tax year and form filed by the taxpayer, the payoff calculator provides the following:

- *Assessed tax/penalty:* the amount of tax, penalties, and interest at the time the return or assessment is made. This amount is important as it is the amount used to determine the taxpayer's qualification for both the simple installment agreement (assessed balance under $50,000) or for the non-streamlined installment agreement (for assessed amounts owed between $50,000 to $250,000).

- *Accrued Interest and Penalties*: the total accrued amounts for the failure to pay penalty and interest at two target dates. Taxpayers can get a specific payoff amount based on a date they provide the IRS.

- *Total amount owed:* if multiple years and/or forms are present, the payoff calculator will total the assessed balances and accruals and provide a total payoff amount.

Below is an example of a payoff calculator.

PAYOFF CALCULATOR

Name: JOHN Q. TAXPAYER   SSN: 000-00-0000

Calculation Result Based on INTST

MFT	Tax Period	Assessed Tax/Penalty	01/22/2019 (Target Date)			02/21/2019 (Target Date + 30 Days)			IDRS Hold Conditions
			Total FTP	Total Interest	Balance	Total FTP	Total Interest	Balance	
30	201112	-133.80	0.00	1,407.93	1,274.13	0.00	1,418.87	1,285.07	COMPUTATION HOLD ON FTP UNREVERSED TC 270 OR TC 271 START DATE MISSING/FTP FROZEN BY MF; REPLACED TARGET DATE 01/22/2019 WITH NOTICE DATE 12/31/2018 *
30	201412	1,173.15	547.47	557.19	2,277.81	547.47	568.45	2,289.07	
30	201512	9,978.08	3,656.96	2,490.44	16,125.48	3,656.96	2,562.56	16,197.60	
30	201612	49,223.38	7,829.01	4,108.32	61,160.71	8,269.54	4,381.06	61,893.98	
30	201712	0.00	726.76	579.97	1,306.73	726.76	588.16	1,314.92	REPLACED TARGET DATE 01/22/2019 WITH NOTICE DATE 01/14/2019 *
	Total	60,240.81	12,760.20	9,143.85	82,144.86	13,220.73	9,519.10	82,980.64	

Installment Agreement present.   Determine whether to include the User Fee in the above total.

* Recalculated using NOTICE DATE because (Target Date) or (Target Date + 30 Days) was WITHIN GRACE OF A NOTICE.

Note: The IRS will now only mail taxpayers and tax professionals a payoff calculator upon request. If the taxpayer has a tax lien, the taxpayer can also call the IRS Centralized Lien Unit and they will fax a payoff calculator letter for the total amounts owed (IRS Letter 3640-B). However, the IRS PPS hotline will provide the tax professional this information verbally.

Taxpayers can view their online account for total and assessed balances. Also, tax pros can see the authorized taxpayer's balances in their Tax Pro Account online.

The MFT code ("Master File Transaction Code") refers to the type of return filed, or assessment made when the taxpayer has a balance owed. Below are common MFT codes and their returns/assessments for individuals:

MFT Code	Form/Assessment
30	Form 1040
31 or 65	Form 1040 – separate assessment (split spousal assessments)
35	Individual shared responsibility penalty assessment
55	Trust fund recovery penalty assessment

> **Pro Tip:** Often, the IRS is unwilling to fax the payoff calculator to the taxpayer when the taxpayer calls the IRS to obtain this written confirmation of the amount owed. The taxpayer can request that the document be mailed to the taxpayer directly. To help with immediate needs for payoff details, the taxpayer or tax pro can ask the IRS phone representative to verbally provide this information or call the IRS Centralized Lien Unit (CLU) for a formal letter to be sent that has the payoff amounts owed by year. The CLU will also fax this information to the taxpayer or their representative.

For more information on the IRS payoff calculator and the information available on the different types of tax modules, visit www.TaxProblemsHandbook.com and navigate to the **IRS Collection Solutions Handbook** tab to access more information on IRS Transcripts.

IRS.gov Online Tools

Taxpayers can also access their online account through "View Your Tax Account" or through the "Online Payment Agreement" application on IRS.gov to obtain their payoff amounts.

For more details on this topic, visit www.TaxProblemsHandbook.com and navigate to the **IRS Collection Solutions Handbook** tab to links to viewing your tax account and the online payment agreement.

The online account provides current payoff information:

Your Balance Due

According to our records, this is the full balance due including penalties and interest computed on **09/20/2018**.

Tax Period	Tax Form	Assessed Balance	Accrued Penalties and Interest	Balance Due
2014	1040	$18,414.35	$4,937.94	$23,352.29
2015	1040	$21,191.65	$3,283.90	$24,475.55
2016	1040	$14,313.08	$2,363.48	$16,676.56
Total Amount Owed:				**$64,504.40**

Note: Only tax periods with a current <u>balance due</u> are displayed. Your balance due may not reflect <u>recent activity</u> that occurred within the last 3-10 weeks.

For a detailed overview of the information available on the "<u>View my tax account</u>" application at IRS.gov, visit www.TaxProblemsHandbook.com and navigate to the **IRS Collection Solutions Handbook** tab to access more information on IRS Transcripts.

Chapter 5:
EVALUATING COLLECTION ALTERNATIVES

This section explains how to evaluate which alternative is best.

Topic	Covers
Approach to Evaluating Alternatives	Overview of how to approach collection alternatives.
Categories of Collection Alternatives	Overview of the four IRS collection alternatives.
Comparison of Collection Alternatives	Chart to compare the terms and applicability of each of the IRS collection alternatives.
Factors to Determine Which Alternative Is Best	Factors to consider when evaluating collection options.
Get the Facts from the IRS	IRS facts needed to evaluate options available to the taxpayer.
Get the Taxpayer's Facts	Taxpayer facts that should be obtained to help determine which alternative is best.
Evaluation Steps to Determine the Best Collection Alternative	Order to review collection alternatives.
Evaluation Steps Based on Amount Owed	Steps to follow if a taxpayer owes: • Under $50,000 • $50,000 to $250,000 • More than $250,000
Timetable to Complete Collection Alternatives	Estimate of time to obtain each type of IRS collection alternative.
Example Collection Alternative Evaluation	A practical example of a typical taxpayer situation and the steps to take when evaluating which alternative is best.

Key Highlights:

- Most taxpayers can pay the IRS. Most collection agreements are extensions to pay and simple installment agreements.
- There are four types of collection alternatives. The best approach is to start with the simplest alternatives. If the taxpayer cannot utilize the simple alternatives, the taxpayer will have to evaluate the ability to pay alternatives.

- Taxpayers must review their personal financial situation and circumstances and their IRS information to effectively evaluate which collection alternative is best for them.
- Many taxpayers believe that they can settle their taxes. However, few taxpayers will be able to settle because their financial situation will allow them to fully pay their tax liability before the IRS collection statute of limitations expires.

Chapter 5.01: Approach to Evaluating Alternatives

Once a taxpayer is satisfied that she owes the balance in question, she should then turn to evaluating the collection options. Taxpayers should evaluate collection alternatives by understanding each alternative, and then applying their ability to pay to their personal circumstances to find the right alternative.

It may be obvious which alternative is best. For example, many taxpayers who owe small amounts and make substantial income may only need an extension to pay to access the funds needed to pay. Many taxpayers just need payment terms and can execute a simple installment agreement (SIA).

If a taxpayer is under financial duress, the taxpayer will have to evaluate all of the ability to pay options and even consider settling their taxes with an offer in compromise.

Chapter 5.02: Categories of Collection Alternatives

The IRS has four basic categories of collection alternatives:

1. *Extensions to pay:* taxpayers can get an extension of up to 180 days to pay an outstanding balance owed. [IRM 5.19.1.6.3 (12-20-2022)]
2. *Installment agreements:* taxpayers can enter into a monthly payment plan with the IRS. [IRM 5.19.1.6.4 (1-26-2023)] There are two categories of installment agreements:
   a. *Simple installment agreements*: these plans allow qualifying taxpayers who to pay the amount owed over a specific period of time without the need to provide detailed financial information to the IRS. These are the most widely used payment plans as they are easy to obtain and avoid the filing of a Notice of Federal Tax Lien. However, one simple installment agreement, the full-pay non-streamlined installment agreement, does require the IRS to file a Notice of Federal Tax Lien.

> **Pro Tip:** From 2012-2024, most IRS collection agreements were simple streamlined installment agreements.

   b. *Ability to pay installment agreements*: in these payment plans, the taxpayer cannot qualify and/or afford the terms for the simple installment agreements. These agreements require the taxpayer to provide financial information (called collection information statements) and documentation to prove their ability to pay.

3. *Currently not collectible status:* taxpayers who experience a financial hardship and only have enough income to pay for their necessary living expenses can qualify and receive a temporary payment deferral from the IRS. [IRM 5.16.1.2 (3-5-2025)] Like ability to pay installment agreements, the taxpayer must provide financial information and documentation to prove that they cannot pay.

4. *Offer in compromise:* taxpayers who cannot pay the IRS with their assets or by making future installment agreement payments can settle their taxes for less than the amount owed. [IRM 5.8.1.2.1 (9-23-2008)] Taxpayers who qualify can offer their reasonable collection potential (a calculation) to settle their tax bill.

When evaluating payment alternatives, most taxpayers choose and obtain a simple installment agreement. This simple option allows taxpayers to avoid a tax lien and make payments for a period of up to collection statute expiration date (10 years from the date of assessment). Most taxpayers do not opt for other ability to pay payment options (ability to pay installment agreements, currently not collectible or offers in compromise) that require providing the IRS with detailed financial information and an analysis of the taxpayer's ability to pay.

Bankruptcy can also be a legal alternative to address serious back tax issues and financial hardship. [IRM 5.9.1.2 (8-11-2014)] Under certain conditions, bankruptcy can eliminate taxes, penalties, and interest and/or provide more favorable payment terms. Because bankruptcy is a legal alternative, taxpayers should consult legal counsel as to how bankruptcy can be applied as a collection alternative.

Chapter 5.03: Comparison of Collection Alternatives

The IRS Collection Alternatives Evaluation Chart is useful in understanding the difference between the IRS collection options.

IRS Collection Alternatives Evaluation Chart

| | Installment Agreements (IA) | | | | | | Hardship relief Based on Ability-to-pay | |
| | Simplified Installment Agreements | | | Complex Ability-to-pay installment agreements | | | | |
	Guaranteed installment agreement (GIA)	Simple installment agreement (SIA)	Full-pay non-streamlined IA (owe <$250K)	Conditional IA	Ability to Pay IA	Partial Pay IA	Currently not collectible	Offer in Compromise
Maximum unpaid balance	$10,000 total balance owed	$50,000 assessed balance; total balance can be higher	Assessed balance between $50K-250K	No limit	No limit	No limit	No limit	No limit
Maximum payment terms	36-months	Until CSED	Until CSED	6 years or by CSED, whichever is shorter	Before CSED	Paid through end of CSED, then IRS writes off remaining amount owed	N/A	5-24 months
Other collection actions	Refunds used to offset balances owed					Refunds used to offset balances; IRS reviews every 2 years	Increase in income may exit CNC status; refunds taken	Taxpayer must file and pay timely for next 5 years
Advantages	Simple to setup. Avoids tax lien filing and financial disclosure. IRS must accept.	Simple to set up. Avoids tax lien filing and financial disclosure. Favorable payment terms.	Avoids financial disclosure. May lead to favorable payment terms.	Provides payment terms based on actual expenses which lowers default rate.	Limits payment based on income and allowable expenses. Required for field collection.	Does not pay full balance owed before CSED. May not have to pay assets like an OIC.	No payment required based on financial status.	Settle taxes based on calculation of future reasonable collection potential.
Lien filing if balance over $10,000	No	No	Yes	Yes	Yes	Yes	Yes	Yes, if payment plan term is greater than 5 months

IRS Collection Alternatives Evaluation Chart

| | Installment Agreements (IA) | | | | | | Hardship relief | |
| | Simplified Installment Agreements | | | Complex Ability-to-pay installment agreements | | | Based on Ability-to-pay | |
	Guaranteed installment agreement (GIA)	Simple installment agreement (SIA)	Full-pay non-streamlined IA (owe <$250K)	Conditional IA	Ability to Pay IA	Partial Pay IA	Currently not collectible	Offer in Compromise
Financial disclosure required	No	No.	No, unless taxpayer has passport restrictions or prior defaulted IA	Yes	Yes	Yes	Yes	Yes
Expense limitations	N/A	N/A	N/A	Reasonable actual expenses allowed	Limited to expenses for production of income and allowable, necessary living expenses (limits set in IRS Collection Financial Standards)			
Asset liquidation required	No	No	No	No	Considered based on financial information, collection history, and balances owed	Yes	Yes for assets not essential for health and welfare of family or to produce income.	Yes, net equity in assets have to be offered as payment in an OIC
Fees	Set-up by phone/mail: fees range from $107-$225. Set-up online (only available for GIA and SLIA): $31-$149. Setup fee for low-income: $0-43. Penalties and interest accrue until balance is paid						No fee. Penalties and interest continue to accrue	Fee: $205, plus offer amount payments; Low-income waiver available.

CSED (Collection Statute Expiration Date) – The last date the IRS can legally collect the tax (typically 10 years from the date the taxes were assessed)
Collection financial standards – Published IRS standards that provides limits on amounts spent for necessary living expenses
Ability to Pay – based on the taxpayer's equity in assets and/or monthly disposable income that can be used to pay balances owed
*Note: the IRS also has an Extension to Pay agreement (ETP or referred to by IRS as "short-term payment agreement") that allows individual taxpayers a one-time, up to 180 days, to pay the balance (in full or partially). ETP agreements do not apply if the taxpayer is in default status on a prior agreement, owe greater than $1M (assigned to Collection Field Function), or is assigned to the Collection Field Function (revenue officer).

• • •

For more information on each of these alternatives, refer to the sections indicated below.

Collection Alternative	Chapter
IRS Collection Alternatives: Extensions to Pay	Chapter 6
IRS Collection Alternatives: Simple Installment Agreements	Chapter 7
Full-pay Non-streamlined Installment Agreement (Owe between $50,000 and $250,000)	Chapter 8
Determining Ability to Pay for IRS Collection Options	Chapter 9
Obtain an Installment Agreement Based on Ability to Pay Analysis	Chapter 10
Obtain Currently Not Collectible Status (CNC)	Chapter 11
Qualify and Obtain an Offer in Compromise for Doubt as to Collectibility (OIC-DATC)	Chapter 12

Chapter 5.04: Factors to Determine Which Alternative Is Best

If a taxpayer is unable to pay with an extension to pay, taxpayers must consider which alternative is best. There are several factors to consider. These factors will affect which options are available to and best for the particular taxpayer:

1. *The amount of taxes owed*: taxpayers who owe larger balances, especially over $50,000, should consider all collection alternatives. Taxpayers owing under $50,000 and who can pay, should consider the simple installment agreement.
2. *The taxpayer's personal circumstances*: the taxpayer's personal circumstances, such as a disability or unemployment, may warrant the taxpayer to look more closely at ability to pay solutions, including an offer in compromise. If a taxpayer is in a payment plan and subsequently becomes unemployed, he or she should consider requesting currently not collectible status from the IRS until the situation improves.
3. *Future income and ability to pay with monthly payments*: determine what the taxpayer can afford to pay the IRS in monthly installment agreement payments. Taxpayers who think they do not have the ability to pay may be surprised that the IRS limits their expenses allowed and determines that they can pay a much higher amount than they initially thought.
4. *Using assets to pay*: the IRS may look for the taxpayer to liquidate assets or borrow against/sell assets to pay the tax liability. Taxpayers with little or no assets and income may want to consider an offer in compromise.
5. *Impact of a tax lien*: certain options will result in a lien filing. Taxpayers should consider the impact of a federal tax lien on the taxpayer's ability to produce income and access credit.
6. *Ability to stay in compliance*: the ability to stay in compliance with filing and to pay on future tax returns. For example, the inability to stay in compliance is fatal for taxpayers considering an offer in compromise which requires five years of timely filing and payment by the taxpayer.

7. *The collection statute of limitations*: the collection statute of limitations may affect the time period to repay under an installment agreement. The CSED is also used in determining whether a taxpayer qualifies for an OIC.

Chapter 5.05: Get the Facts from the IRS

If taxpayers are unable to fully pay via an extension to pay or an installment agreement, they should research their account information at the IRS to determine their ability to pay:

- *Balance owed*: this shows how much is owed for each year, including the assessed balance — necessary to evaluate the simplified installment agreement options.
- *Collection statute expiration dates*: determine how long the IRS can collect and how this will impact installment agreements and the offer in compromise.
- *Compliance status*: confirms whether the taxpayer has filed all required tax returns and, if needed, made required estimated tax payments in order to not owe for future tax year filings.
- *Enforcement status*: determine whether the taxpayer is already assigned to collection which may reduce the options available.

The taxpayer can get the above information from the IRS through the following two sources:

- *Interviewing the IRS*: IRS accounts management personnel can provide balances owed, assessed balances, collection statute dates, unfiled tax return(s) issues, and enforcement status.
- *IRS account transcripts and payoff calculators*: these documents can provide amounts owed by year with assessed totals by year. Account transcripts will also provide other information related to multiple CSEDs and estimated taxes paid for the current year.

Chapter 5.06: Get the Taxpayer's Facts

The taxpayer will provide important information needed to evaluate collection alternatives. If a taxpayer needs to evaluate an ability to pay agreement, the following facts are needed:

- *Current equity in assets*: necessary to determine assets available to pay the IRS, including any assets that were disposed of in the past three years.
- *Liquidity in assets*: to determine immediate assets that may be accessed to pay the IRS.
- *Average household monthly income from all sources*: to be used in determining monthly disposable income, i.e., the amount that the IRS will want in a payment plan.
- *Average household monthly expenses*: to be used in determining monthly disposable income, i.e., the amount that the IRS will want in a payment plan.
- *Future earning capability*: to be used in evaluating alternatives such as extension to pay or an offer in compromise.
- *Future wealth and income to be acquired*: to be used in evaluating an offer in compromise.

- *Personal circumstances*: including factors determining the ability to acquire future income and the need to retain assets to pay for necessary future living expenses.
- *Future tax liability*: whether the taxpayer will file and owe tax in future years based on the current tax situation.
- *The impact of a tax lien*: certain collection alternatives warrant the filing of a Notice of Federal Tax Lien by the IRS. Taxpayers will want to consider the impact of this on their ability to earn income and to access credit when evaluating options.

Most of the taxpayer facts will be used in negotiating collection alternatives and on making financial disclosures to the IRS (IRS Forms 433-A, B, F, and H).

For taxpayer questionnaires and financial analysis templates, refer to the **Appendix B**—and visit www.TaxProblemsHandbook.com under the **IRS Collection Solutions Handbook** tab for downloadable resources.

Chapter 5.07: Evaluation Steps to Determine the Best Collection Alternative

Before evaluating which collection alternative is best, the taxpayer should confirm that the amount owed is correct.

First Issue to Address: Determine If the Amount Owed Is Correct

The first step in evaluating collection alternatives is to determine if the amount claimed to be owed by the taxpayer is correct. If the taxes or penalties can be reduced, the taxpayer should consider requesting the appropriate reduction using the proper IRS procedure. Options include:

1. *Filing an amended return to lower the taxes owed*: taxpayers can file an amended return to lower the amount owed on the past three years, any year with an open balance, and any year in which payment has been made within the last two years.
2. *Requesting penalty abatement*: if the taxpayer has a balance due, the taxpayer can request abatement of penalties for any year – not just the years with balances. The penalty abatement will be applied against the tax years with a balance due and reduce the amount owed

> **Pro Tip:** Taxpayers can request quick abatement as far back as 2001 by reviewing IRS transcripts for first time penalty abatement qualification. The IRS will abate any penalties paid if the taxpayer does not have a balance owed or has paid the penalty in the past two years.
>
> For more details on this topic, visit www.TaxProblemsHandbook.com and navigate to the **IRS Collection Solutions Handbook** tab to access more information on how to use penalty abatement.

3. *CP2000 or audit reconsideration*: the taxpayer may consider contesting incorrect assessments, additional taxes and penalties from a CP2000 or audit. The taxpayer can request CP2000 or audit reconsideration to adjust the amount owed.

Evaluation Steps: Start with Evaluating the Simplest and Most Common Alternatives

Taxpayers should always begin the approach to collection alternatives starting with the simplest and most common options (extensions to pay and simplified installment agreements) before moving to the more complicated and less frequently used options (ability to pay agreements, currently not collectible, or the offer in compromise).

> **Pro Tip:** Actions taken to reduce taxes and penalties may take considerable time to complete. In order to avoid enforced collection through liens and levies, taxpayers should request a "collection hold" while the IRS processes any request for tax reduction through amended returns or audit/CP2000 reconsideration and/or penalty abatement.

In general, all taxpayers should review the collection options in this order:

1. Extension to pay (ETP)
2. Simplified installment agreements (SIA or full-pay NSIA)
3. Ability to pay installment agreement (ATP) or currently not collectible (CNC) status
4. Offer in compromise (OIC)

Taxpayers who are able to pay will likely obtain the ETP or SIA agreements. In fact, historically, approximately nine out of ten taxpayers chose the ETP or SIA as their collection alternative. If the taxpayer is unable pay with an ETP or qualify or pay with an SIA, then the taxpayer will need to evaluate more complex collection alternatives that involve the taxpayer having to prove his ability to pay the IRS.

Chapter 5.08: Evaluation Steps Based on Amount Owed

Below are the steps the taxpayer should follow to evaluate the best options based on the amount owed:

Taxpayers Who Owe $50,000 or Less

Taxpayers who owe $50,000 or less (assessed balance) have the option of a simple installment agreement. For these taxpayers, the steps and order to follow to evaluate which alternative is best are laid out below.

Steps		What to do
1	Evaluate whether the taxpayer can afford to pay with a short-term extension to pay.	Evaluate whether the taxpayer has available liquid assets or future income stream that can be used to pay the taxes owed. In this case, the

		taxpayer's best option may be to limit penalties and interest, pay the balance owed and look for possible penalty abatement. This agreement will avoid a federal tax lien and the taxpayer can look to penalty abatement at the end of the payment plan to reduce penalties paid.
2	Evaluate the guaranteed installment agreement. This option can be used if the taxpayer owes less than $10,000 (total balance), is able to pay over 36 months, and meets the conditions of a guaranteed installment agreement.	Evaluate the taxpayer's finances to see if he can pay the total balance owed in 36 months. If so, he should execute a guaranteed installment agreement. This agreement will avoid imposition of a federal tax lien and the taxpayer can look to penalty abatement at the end of the payment plan to reduce penalties paid.
3	Evaluate whether the taxpayer is able to pay before the collection statute(s) and whether he meets the conditions necessary to qualify for a simple installment agreement.	Evaluate the taxpayer's finances to see if he can pay the balance owed before the collection statute expiration date(s) (CSED). If so, he should execute a simple installment agreement. Execution of this timely agreement will avoid a federal tax lien and the taxpayer can look to penalty abatement at the end of the payment plan to reduce penalties paid.
4	If the taxpayer is unable to pay with a simple installment agreement, compute the ability to pay and select the most appropriate ability to pay agreement (CNC, routine ability to pay IA, conditional IA, PPIA, or an offer in compromise).	Taxpayer will need to determine net equity in assets and monthly disposable income. Using these two calculations, the taxpayer can determine which ability to pay option should be obtained. These agreements are likely to result in a federal tax lien filing if the taxpayer owes more than $10,000.

Taxpayers Who Owe Between $50,000 – $250,000 and can pay in full before the collection statute expires

Taxpayers with assessed balances between $50,000 and $250,000 may still avoid detailed financial disclosure to the IRS if they are able to execute a simplified plan by utilizing the full-pay non-streamlined installment agreement (NSIA). However, when a taxpayer owes more than $50,000, he is likely to have a federal tax lien filed against him. If a taxpayer has an assessed balance owed between $50,000 and $250,000, the following are the steps and order to evaluate which collection alternative is best.

Steps		What to do
1	Evaluate whether the taxpayer can afford to pay with a short-term extension to pay.	Evaluate whether the taxpayer has available liquid assets that can be used to pay the taxes owed. In this case, the taxpayer's best option may be to limit penalties and interest, pay the balance owed and look for possible penalty abatement. This agreement will avoid a federal tax lien and the taxpayer can look to penalty abatement at the end of the payment plan to reduce penalties paid.
2	Evaluate whether the taxpayer is able to pay down the debt to bring it under $50,000 (assessed balance) by designating payments to the assessed balance owed and thus qualify for a simple installment agreement. Taxpayer will want to consider the SIA to avoid a federal tax lien filing.	Evaluate the taxpayer's finances to see if they able to pay the assessed balance with available assets to bring it under $50,000 and pay the remaining balance owed within the CSED. The taxpayer may want to obtain a 180-day extension to pay to allow him time to bring the debt under $50,000 and to avoid a federal tax lien. If so, he should execute a timely simple installment agreement. This timely agreement will avoid imposition of a federal tax lien and the taxpayer can look to penalty abatement at the end of the payment plan to reduce penalties paid.
3	If the taxpayer is unable to pay down the debt and obtain an SIA, evaluate whether the taxpayer can pay the balance owed within the CSED, using the full-pay non-streamlined installment agreement (NSIA) option.	Obtain the collection statute of limitation information from the IRS and ask the IRS representative for the amount to qualify for the NSIA. Evaluate the taxpayer's finances to see if he is able to pay the balance within the NSIA terms. If so, execute an NSIA using Form 433-D.
4	If the taxpayer is unable to pay within the NSIA-required time period (i.e., before the CSED), compute his ability to pay and select the most appropriate ability to pay agreement (CNC, routine IA, conditional IA, PPIA, or an offer in compromise).	Taxpayer will need to determine his net equity in assets and monthly disposable income. Using these two calculations, the taxpayer can determine which ability to pay option should be sought. These agreements are likely to result in a federal tax lien filing.

Taxpayers Who Owe More Than $250,000

If a taxpayer owes more than $250,000 (assessed balance amounts), the filing of a federal tax lien and providing financial information is much more probable unless the taxpayer can pay down the amount owed and obtain a simplified agreement.

Pro Tip: Taxpayers who have an assessed balance of $1,000,000 or more and are not in an agreement with the IRS will be assigned to the Collection Field function for local collection enforcement and/or agreement. Simplified agreements are not available when assigned to field collection and the revenue officer assigned will look for full payment from assets first, then monthly disposable income.

Below are the steps and order to follow to evaluate which collection alternative is best when a taxpayer has an assessed balance greater than $250,000.

	Steps	What to do
1	Evaluate whether the taxpayer is able to afford to pay with a short-term extension to pay.	Evaluate whether the taxpayer has available liquid assets that may be used to pay the taxes owed. In this case, the taxpayer's best option may be to limit penalties and interest and pay the balance owed and look for penalty abatement. This agreement will avoid a federal tax lien and the taxpayer can use penalty abatement at the end of the payment plan to reduce penalties paid. Note: the ETP agreement is not available if the taxpayer owes more than $1M. Taxpayer who owe over $1M are assigned to Field Collection who do not allow ETP agreements.
2	Evaluate whether the taxpayer has the ability to pay down the debt bringing it under $50,000 (assessed balance) by designating payments to the assessed balance owed and thus qualify for a simple installment agreement. Taxpayers will want to consider the SIA to avoid a federal tax lien filing.	Evaluate the taxpayer's finances to see if they are able to pay the assessed balance to bring it under $50,000 with available assets and then pay the remaining balance owed within the CSED(s). The taxpayer may want to obtain a 180-day extension to pay to allow him time to bring the debt under $50,000 and to avoid a federal tax lien. If so, he should execute an ETP, pay down the assessed balance under $50,000, and obtain a simple installment agreement. This agreement will avoid a federal tax lien and the taxpayer can look to penalty abatement at the end of the payment plan to reduce penalties paid.
3	Evaluate whether the taxpayer is able to pay down the debt to bring it under $250,000 (assessed balance) by designating payments to the assessed balance owed and thus qualify for a full-pay non-streamlined installment	Evaluate the taxpayer's finances to see if he has the ability to pay the assessed balance to bring it under $250,000 with available assets and then to pay the remaining balance before the collection statute expiration date (CSED). The taxpayer may want to obtain a 180-day extension to pay to allow enough time to bring the debt under $250,000. This may allow the taxpayer to obtain

	agreement (NSIA). The taxpayer will want to consider the NSIA plan to avoid having to complete detailed financial information for the IRS and/or to obtain more favorable payment terms.	better payment terms and avoid providing detailed financial information to the IRS.
4	If the taxpayer is able to pay within the simple or full pay NSIA terms, compute the ability to pay and select the most appropriate ability to pay agreement (CNC, routine IA, conditional IA, PPIA, or an offer in compromise).	Taxpayer will need to determine his net equity in assets and monthly disposable income. Using these two calculations, the taxpayer can determine which ability to pay option should be obtained. These agreements are likely to result in a federal tax lien filing.

Chapter 5.09: Timetable to Complete Collection Alternatives

Taxpayers can quickly set up simplified payment plans, such as extensions to pay and simple installment agreements online or by phone. For more complicated agreements (such as the full pay NSIA, ability to pay installment agreements, currently not collectible, and the offer in compromise), the taxpayer will need to apply and submit detailed financial information to the IRS for approval. This process takes much longer.

Below is an estimate of what the taxpayer can expect with each option.

Payment option	Time to complete	Factors that add time
Extension to pay of up to 180 days for any amount.	Online: 15 minutes using the IRS's online payment agreement tool (online can only serve if you owe $100,000 or less). Phone: Usually one hour.	If the taxpayer has prior extensions or collection agreements that were broken.
Simplified installment agreements for assessed balances up to $50,000 (guaranteed or simple installment agreements).	Online: less than one hour using the IRS's online payment agreement tool. Phone: Usually one hour.	If the taxpayer had a prior installment agreement and defaulted, the taxpayer may need to set up the agreement by phone and/or give the IRS limited financial information. If the taxpayer is paying by direct debit or payroll deduction, the process can add 4-6 weeks to the set-up time if the direct

		debit form (433-D or 9465) is sent by mail.
Full-pay non-streamlined installment agreements for assessed balances between $50,000 and $250,000.	By phone/pay by check: about 1 hour. Direct debit/payroll deduction: about 1 hour for the initial agreement by phone, plus 4-6 weeks to finalize the direct debit setup (if 433-D or 9465 to set up the direct debit is done by mail).	If the taxpayer has prior noncompliance issues and the IRS demands the payment by direct debit or payroll deduction, add 1-2 months for a review of the financial information. If the IRS requires financial information, it will take additional time to complete the agreement and get manager approval.
Ability to pay installment agreements, currently not collectible status, and all agreements.	By phone: Can take 1-4 months to complete by phone if the taxpayer is prepared with detailed financial information to be provided over the phone/fax. By mail: The IRS will take 2-6 months to review the request. More requests for information will add time if the initial submitted documentation is not sufficient. The taxpayer can shorten this process by initiating the agreement by phone with IRS collection.	Additional requests for information and incomplete responses will add more time to this process. Requests to liquidate or borrow against assets will add more time to allow the taxpayer to access equity, or to prove that the taxpayer cannot obtain a loan against assets to pay down the amount owed. Appeals can add 1-4 months to this process.
Offer in compromise (OIC) to settle tax debt for less than the full amount owed.	Tax bills of less than $50,000: 5-7 months. Tax bills of more than $50,000: 7-12 months. *Note:* OICs must be finalized within two years of the time that the IRS receives the OIC application.	Applications to the Memphis OIC unit take longer due to volume. Appeals can add 4-10 months to this process.

Chapter 5.10: Example Collection Alternative Evaluation

Example This is an example of a collection taxpayer who owes between $50,000 and $250,000. The taxpayer has gathered all her personal and financial information and retrieved her IRS information. The taxpayer has also computed her ability to pay, and determined her net equity in assets and her monthly disposable income.

The facts appear below.

Factor	Facts				
Total amount owed	$69,212				
Requested agreement date	5/1/2025				
Years detail	*Year*	*Total Balance*	*Assessed Balance*	*CSED*	*Months remaining on CSED*
	2022	$13,000	$9,400	6/5/2027	97
	2023	$56,212	$51,100	6/3/2028	109
	Totals	$69,212	$60,500		
Net equity in assets	$55,000				
Assets that can be used to pay down the amount owed	$15,000 (shares of stock owned that can be sold)				
Monthly disposable income (using actual expenses)	$500 (has a high mortgage which is $1,300 over the allowable living expense for the area as allowed by IRS Collection Financial Standards)				
Monthly disposable income (limited by IRS Collection financial standards)	$1,800				
Filing compliance	Yes – past six years returns are filed				
Payment compliance	Yes – will not owe when she files the next year's return				

Penalty history	Has failure to pay penalties for every year since 2012. Does not qualify for first-time abatement due to prior FTA abatement. Does not have reasonable cause for abatement.
Cause of tax owed	Liquidated IRAs in each year to build a vacation home.
IRS enforcement status and agreement history	Received 4th notice – CP504 14 days ago. Will be in IRS collection in three weeks. Had installment agreement for $1,000 a month that she defaulted on four months ago. The IRS has not yet filed a Notice of Federal Tax lien.
Taxpayer personal information	Taxpayer wants to avoid a tax lien because she wants to refinance her house and believes the tax lien will disqualify any refinance. Taxpayer is in good health, has worked in sales and has consistent income over last several years, and is age 43. Taxpayer's family of 4 is also in good health and has normal living expenses.

Using the steps for a taxpayer who owes between $50,000 – $250,000, the collection evaluation appears below.

Steps		What to Do/Analysis
1	Evaluate whether the taxpayer can afford to pay with a short-term extension to pay.	Evaluate whether the taxpayer has available liquid assets that can be used to pay the taxes owed. In this case, the taxpayer's best option may be to limit penalties and interest and pay the balance owed and look for possible penalty abatement. This agreement will avoid a federal tax lien and the taxpayer can look to penalty abatement at the end of the payment plan to reduce penalties paid. *The taxpayer can look to borrow and use existing funds to pay the entire IRS liability. To avoid a federal tax lien, the taxpayer would request an extension to pay in order to access or borrow the funds to pay the IRS.* *Taxpayer has exhausted all penalty abatement opportunities. The taxpayer should look for any opportunity to review the 2022 and 2023 tax years to reduce the amount owed by filing an amended return.*
2	Evaluate whether the taxpayer has the ability to pay down the debt and bring it under $50,000 (assessed balance) by	Evaluate the taxpayer's finances to see if she is able to pay down the assessed balance to bring it under $50,000 with available assets and pay the remaining balance owed within the collection

		designating payments to the assessed balance owed and thereby qualify for a simple installment agreement. Taxpayers will want to consider the SIA to avoid a federal tax lien filing.	statute expiration dates. Taxpayer may want to get a 180-day extension to pay to allow time to pay down the debt to bring it under $50,000 and to avoid a federal tax lien. If so, the taxpayer should execute a timely simple installment agreement. This timely agreement will avoid imposition of a federal tax lien and the taxpayer can look to penalty abatement at the end of the payment plan to reduce penalties paid. *Taxpayer has the option to pay currently with assets and negotiate a streamlined installment agreement. To avoid a premature lien filing, the taxpayer can obtain an extension to pay, apply a payment to the 2023 assessed balance to reduce the total assessed amount to bring it under $50,000, and then enter into a simple installment agreement. The taxpayer would have to make a designated payment to the 2023 tax year to the "assessed balance only" of $10,500. This will reduce the assessed amount to $50,000 and qualify the taxpayer for a payment plan over the remaining months before the collection statute expiration dates. The minimum payment when contacting the IRS by phone would be: $680 (IRS provides using their minimum payment agreement tool that accounts for future penalties and interest before the collection statute expiration dates). This payment would be lower (and less likely for default) than the prior $1,000 a monthly payment that was defaulted on by the taxpayer, and much lower than the calculated $1,800 ability to pay according to IRS rules.*
3		If the taxpayer is unable to pay down the debt and obtain an SIA, evaluate whether the taxpayer can pay the balance owed within the time period before the CSED, using the non-streamlined installment agreement payment plan option (NSIA).	Obtain the collection statute expiration dates and amount needed to execute an NSIA. Evaluate the taxpayer's finances to see if she is able to pay the balance before the CSED. If so, execute an NSIA payment plan using Form 433-D. *If the taxpayer does not what to use her funds to pay under the $50,000 assessed balance to avoid a lien, the taxpayer can qualify for the NSIA. However, this option will require the IRS to file a Notice of Federal Tax Lien unless the taxpayer can show that the lien impairs the ability to earn*

		income. The minimum NSIA payment, according to the IRS, would be $801 a month.
4	If the taxpayer is unable to pay within the full-pay NSIA terms, compute the ability to pay and select the most appropriate ability to pay agreement (CNC, routine IA, conditional IA, PPIA, or an offer in compromise).	Taxpayer will need to determine her net equity in assets and her monthly disposable income. Using these two calculations, the taxpayer can determine which ability to pay option should be obtained. These agreements are likely to result in a federal tax lien filing. *Per the example, the taxpayer's finances were analyzed, and the taxpayer has significant equity in assets ($55,000) and has MDI of $1,800 (limited by IRS standards). The taxpayer has more expenses than allowed which will not be allowed unless it can be shown that the taxpayer can pay within six years.* *Ability to pay IA options: The taxpayer's ability to pay is $1,800 a month when limited by IRS collection standards. Her MDI based on her actual expenses is $500 a month. The IRS will limit the taxpayer to expenses that will allow her to pay within 72 months (a conditional IA). The IRS will not allow the $500 as it would be a PPIA and the IRS would project to write off a remaining balance at the end of the CSED. The taxpayer could request that the IRS give her a 12-month lifestyle adjustment by allowing a $500 monthly payment and increase the payment to a minimum of $909 ($60,500 – $6,000 first year payments/remaining 60 months) a month for the remaining 60 months.* *OIC option: The taxpayer does not qualify for an OIC because her ability to pay is greater than the tax owed. The net equity in assets ($55,000) plus the remaining payments before the statute expires ($1,800 × 109 = $196,200), or $251,200, far exceeds the amount of tax owed.* *The best option: The taxpayer will likely choose to pay down the debt so that it is under the $50,000 assessed balance to obtain a direct debit SLIA. That will avoid an NFTL and provide a reasonable monthly payment of $680 a month. Future refunds will also be used to offset and lower the amount owed.*

Chapter 6:
IRS COLLECTION ALTERNATIVES: EXTENSIONS TO PAY

The section covers the three extension to pay agreements and how to obtain each of these alternatives.

Topic	Covers
Extension to Pay Options	The three extension to pay options that provide additional time to pay without collection enforcement.
ETP Option #1: IRS "Collection Holds"	Informal requests and reasons for short-term extensions to pay.
ETP Option #2: 180-Day Extension to Pay Qualifications and Rules	The terms and conditions for a 180-day extension to pay agreement.
ETP Option #3: Hardship Extension to Pay Agreements	The terms, conditions, and how to apply for a hardship extension to pay agreement.
Steps to Obtain a 180-Day Extension to Pay	How to request a 180-day extension to pay agreement.

Key Highlights:

- The 180-day extension to pay (ETP) is the easiest and least expensive IRS collection alternative.
- ETP agreements provide additional time to pay the IRS or pay down the balance owed to qualify for a more favorable, simplified IRS installment agreement option.
- Timely ETP agreements are qualifying agreements to avoid a premature Notice of Federal Tax Lien and to release a wage garnishment or levy. However, an ETP agreement cannot be used to remove passport restrictions.
- The IRS also has other formal and informal extensions to pay that taxpayers can request from the IRS to avoid collection enforcement.

Chapter 6.01: Extension to Pay Options

There are three types of extensions to pay:

- The informal "Collection Hold."

- A formal agreement to pay called the "180-day extension to full pay." [IRM 5.19.1.6.3 (12-20-2022)]
- The hardship extension to pay application via Form 1127 that applies to balance due returns and audit adjustments and provides relief from the failure to pay penalty. [IRC §6161 and IRM 20.1.1.3.3.3 (8-5-2014)]

Interest will continue to accrue on all three extension types. Only the hardship extension to pay provides relief from the failure to pay penalty.

Note: The IRS expanded the 120-day extension to pay to 180 days as part of the Taxpayer Relief Initiative due to the COVID-19 pandemic on November 19. 2020. The 180-day terms were made permanent in 2022.

Chapter 6.02: ETP Option #1: IRS "Collection Holds"

The IRS can provide collection taxpayers a "collection hold" (also referred to as a "stay on collection" or a "STAUP" by the IRS collection agents) on their account which delays any enforcement action such as the imposition of liens or levies. Some actions get an automatic collection hold such as for taxpayers who have filed for an installment agreement, an offer in compromise, or for innocent spouse relief. Taxpayers who have requested collection appeals hearings will also have a collection hold on their account. If a taxpayer has a hardship and needs assistance from the Taxpayer Advocate, it is common for the TAS to put a collection hold on the account while the problem is being resolved.

Taxpayers can request a short-term collection hold on their account. Taxpayers commonly get a collection hold if the IRS or the taxpayer has an unforeseen delay which will result in premature IRS collection activity. The IRS commonly provides collection holds for the following issues:

- *To allow for the posting of a refund or a pending adjustment that will reduce or eliminate the balance owed:* examples include newly filed returns with refunds, amended returns, requests for audit or CP2000 reconsideration, or penalty abatement pending adjustments.
- *To accommodate for delays in processing returns that are needed for filing compliance and installment agreement*: for example, the taxpayer may have filed a past-due return and the IRS has not yet posted the return to the taxpayer's account. Another common example is when a taxpayer files an original return to replace an IRS-filed return (called a substitute for return or "SFR"). The IRS takes several months to replace SFRs with original returns and it is common for the taxpayer to obtain a collection hold when the new return shows little or no tax due.
- *To accommodate for delays in posting payments:* for example, the taxpayer may have made a payment to reduce the amount owed to qualify for an SIA. If the IRS has not processed the payment to reduce the balance owed, the IRS will provide a collection hold to allow time for the payment to post.

- *To accommodate for delays in reviewing taxpayer correspondence:* if the IRS has not been able to review taxpayer correspondence, such as installment agreement follow-up information, the taxpayer should get an automatic collection hold. However, the IRS may not associate the correspondence with the pending collection issue and therefore not provide the hold on the account. Taxpayers should follow up and request the collection hold to avoid unexpected collection enforcement activity.

Informal collection holds are usually for a short period of time. If the taxpayer makes multiple collection hold requests, the IRS may interpret the requests as an attempt to delay enforced collection and deny the hold request.

> **Pro Tip:** Taxpayers should always be aware of their enforcement timing with the IRS to avoid unnecessary collection hold requests. If a taxpayer is not yet assigned to IRS Collection, they may not be in enforced collection for several months. A request for a collection hold is likely not needed in such a case. If a lengthy period of time is needed, the taxpayer can request the more formal 180-day extension to pay.

Chapter 6.03: ETP Option #2: 180-Day Extension to Pay Qualification and Rules

A common collection alternative is a 180-day extension to pay agreement (also referred by the IRS as the "short-term payment plan"). [IRM 5.19.1.6.3 (12-20-2022)] The ETP agreement is an informal arrangement with the IRS to pay within a prescribed time frame without IRS enforcement action. The IRS will allow up to 180 days for the taxpayer to "full pay the outstanding balance(s) owed." If the taxpayer is unable to fully pay the balance owed, she can use other remaining collection alternatives.

> **Pro Tip:** The IRS encourages taxpayers to use ETP agreements to pay down their balances and reduce the amounts owed under a payment plan.

Below are the relevant terms and conditions for the 180-day ETP agreement.

Terms and conditions	180-day extension to pay agreement [IRM 5.19.1.6.3 (12-20-2022)]
Agreement terms	• Pay the balance in full, including interest and penalties, within 180 days. • Does not extend the time the IRS has to collection (CSED). • Interest will still accrue and the failure to pay penalty will still apply during the extension period.
Fees	No fees apply.
Eligible taxpayers	• Individuals, businesses that are out of business or owe income taxes only.

	• Not for taxpayers assigned to the Collection Field function or for employment taxes. (Includes individual taxpayers who owe >$1M)
Amounts owed	Available for up to $1M owed for individuals.
IRS function to contact	• IRS Accounts Management, IRS Practitioner Priority Service, or IRS Collection. • If taxpayer is in IRS Collection, only IRS Collection can set up the agreement.
Limitations	• IRS CFf (revenue officers) cannot grant 180-day extension to pay. • Cannot use ETP to decertify seriously delinquent tax debt in order to release passport restrictions. [IRM 5.19.25.4 (1-24-2024)] • Can only use once for each tax form/year. • A new ETP agreement of up to 180 days may be granted only after all years/periods from any prior payment agreement have been full paid. • Collection appeal rights do not extend to ETP agreements
Method	• Phone or online payment arrangement (ETP through OPA is only available for individuals who owe less than $100,000).
Tax return filings	All required tax returns do not have to be filed in order to qualify for an ETP. However, the IRS will give the taxpayer a deadline to fully file all back returns within the 180-day extension period. [IRM 5.19.1.6.3 at (11) (12-20-2022)]
Request	• Can request fewer than 180 days. • Multiple extension requests cannot total more than 180 days for the tax period. [IRM 5.19.1.6.3 at (7) (12-20-2022)] • Requests can be made at any time, including immediately after the tax return is filed. [IRM 5.19.1.6.3 at (2) (12-20-2022)]
IRS Notice	• IRS Letter 681C, *Proposal to Pay Later Accepted*, should be sent 2-3 weeks after securing ETP confirming deadline and amount due at the deadline. [IRM 5.19.1.6.3 at (16) (12-20-2022)]
Best for:	• A short-term cash flow problem. • Providing time to liquidate assets or borrow money to pay outstanding balance. • Avoiding premature enforced collection activity (lien and levy). • Obtaining funds to lower the balance to qualify for a more favorable payment plan. • Limiting financial disclosure and documents to be filed with the IRS.

	• To allow for a refund offset for an amended return or a refund return to pay the balance owed.

ETP agreements are simple to obtain and the IRS provides clear instructions of the amount owed at the end of the 180-day period.

> **Example-** John files his tax return on March 15, 2025, with a balance owed of $15,312. He cannot pay the balance owed with the return. He needs to get a home equity line of credit to pay his tax bill, but it will take three months to apply, be approved, and have access to the funds to pay. On June 22, 2025, John contacts the IRS and requests a 180-day extension to pay. The IRS sends John a notice (Letter 681C) providing him the final date (180 days from June 22, 2025 or December 19, 2025) and the exact amount to pay, which includes interest and failure to pay penalties through December 19, 2025.

> **Pro Tip:** Taxpayers may want to wait until they are farther down the IRS collection notice stream to maximize the amount of time needed to obtain funds to pay their liability without IRS enforcement. Note that 180-day agreements start from the date that the agreement is made, not the date that the tax return is filed, or additional tax is assessed.

> **Example-** John files his return on April 15, 2025, and owes $29,222. He receives a big bonus in November that will pay his taxes in full, including any accrued interest and penalties. John receives two notices from the IRS to pay (CP14 dated June 7, 2025 and CP501 dated July 31, 2025). After the second notice, John is safely within his 180 days to receive his bonus. John contacts the IRS on July 31, 2025, and obtains a 180-day extension to pay. He has until January 28, 2026 (180 days from the agreement date) to pay his tax bill and avoid IRS enforcement.

For taxpayers who owe more than $50,000, an advantage of a timely ETP agreement is to provide the taxpayer time to either pay the tax in full or lower the balance to get into an agreement that avoids the filing of an NFTL. However, if the IRS has already filed an NFTL, an ETP agreement does not remove the lien. Taxpayers need to be timely in requesting the ETP agreement before the lien is filed.

> **Example-** Mary files her 2023 tax return on April 15, 2024, with a $92,000 balance due. Mary cannot pay the amount owed but believes she can refinance and borrow additional funds to pay a significant amount of the balance owed. Mary also wants to avoid filing of an NFTL because it would blemish her reputation in her community and impede her ability to borrow additional funds to run her business. Mary contacts the IRS on June 10, 2024, and obtains an extension to pay agreement. The 180-day deadline is December 6, 2024. Mary borrows enough funds to reduce her balance to $48,000 (below $50,000) and qualify for an IRS simple installment agreement (SIA) payment plan. On December 6, 2024, Mary contacts the IRS and sets up an SIA on the remaining $48,000 to be paid before the

collection statute expiration date. Mary sets up the agreement and avoids the filing of an NFTL.

Chapter 6.04: ETP Option #3: Hardship Extension to Pay Agreements

Taxpayers who experience an undue hardship may request a hardship extension of time to pay for up to six months by filing Form 1127, *Application for Extension of Time for Payment of Tax Due to Undue Hardship*, and attaching hardship substantiation. [IRM 20.1.1.3.3.3 (8-5-2014)] Form 1127 allows the taxpayer to avoid the failure to pay penalty during the extension period. If the amount owed is due to a deficiency (for example, the amount owed from an audit or CP2000 notice), the taxpayer can receive an extension up to 18 months to pay. In the past, taxpayers who had been assessed an accuracy or fraud penalty in the audit or CP2000 assessment did not qualify for the undue hardship relief. However, this requirement is no longer in the Internal Revenue Manual.

An undue hardship means that the taxpayer would experience a substantial financial loss (such as selling property at a sacrifice price), if forced to pay the IRS by the due date. The taxpayer must provide substantiation to prove the undue hardship. The mere inability to pay does not ordinarily provide the basis for granting relief. [Treasury Regulation §301.6651-1(c)] Taxpayers must show that they exercised ordinary business care and prudence in planning for the payment of the tax liability owed. The taxpayer may have had an unanticipated event that caused him to use the available funds and therefore could not pay his taxes. The taxpayer must show that if the taxes were paid, the taxpayer would have suffered an undue hardship. To support the request, the taxpayer must send an explanation of the hardship, a statement of assets and liabilities at the end of the most recent month (showing book and market value of assets and whether securities are listed or unlisted), and an itemized list of income and expenses for the past three months (prior to the due date of the tax). If the taxpayer meets the hardship criteria, the IRS may grant additional time to pay. The taxpayer will be responsible for paying the balance due (including interest) before the extension period expires.

If the request is for an extension of time to pay the tax due on an upcoming return, the IRS must receive Form 1127 on or before the due date of that return, not including extensions. For deficiencies, the IRS must receive Form 1127 on or before the payment due date indicated in the tax bill. [Form 1127]

Form 1127 is filed with the local IRS Advisory Group (see Publication 4235 for the address), for the area where the taxpayer maintains his legal residence.

> **Pro Tip:** Taxpayers rarely file Form 1127 to request relief. In 2012, 33,000 taxpayers filed for relief with only 10,175 taxpayers actually granted relief. Taxpayers who need additional time may request an extension to pay their tax bill. However, extensions to pay do not relieve the taxpayer of the failure to pay penalty. Only undue hardship requests via Form 1127 enable the taxpayer to avoid the failure to pay penalty. As an alternative, taxpayers who have a financial hardship and cannot pay can look for penalty abatement due to reasonable cause or first-time abatement.

Example- John prepares his 2024 return and owes $28,000. Just before he files his return, he has a heart attack and incurs $30,000 in medical expenses. John files his return with a Form 1127 explaining his circumstances and provides financial information and bank statements to support his undue hardship. John receives a six-month extension to pay, without penalty. Alternatively, if John failed to file Form 1127, he could request abatement of the failure to pay penalty due to reasonable cause (unforeseen illness) or use the first-time penalty abatement if he qualifies.

Chapter 6.05: Steps to Obtain a 180-Day Extension to Pay

An Extension to Pay (ETP) can only be granted by the IRS ACS and Accounts Management personnel. ETP cannot be granted by the CFf (revenue officers). Note that taxpayers cannot request an extension to pay until the return has been processed by the IRS. The CP14 indicates that the IRS has processed the return. Generally, the CP14 letter arrives 4-7 weeks after filing. If a taxpayer needs the maximum amount of time, she can request her ETP later in the collection process (i.e., after the IRS issues its Final Notice of Intent to Levy (Letter LT11)).

> **Pro Tip:** It is best to at least wait until the IRS issues its first balance due notice — the CP14 notice — before requesting an ETP.

There is also no IRS form to obtain an ETP agreement. A taxpayer requests a post-filing ETP by phone or by using the IRS Online Payment Agreement application at irs.gov.

Below are the steps to take to obtain an ETP agreement.

Steps	Action	What to do
1	Contact the IRS and confirm that the taxpayer qualifies: no prior ETP agreement has been granted.	Confirm that the taxpayer has not had a 180-day ETP agreement in the past (if they have received less than 180 days in the past, the IRS will only allow the additional days, not to exceed 180 days in total). *Pro Tip:* IRS transcripts do not clearly indicate if an ETP agreement has been received in the past. If a taxpayer does not know if they have had an extension in the past, he can ask the IRS when the ETP is requested.

| 2 | Contact the appropriate IRS function and request an ETP. | By phone:

1. *Request when the taxpayer is not in IRS Collection:*

   a. Taxpayers: contact IRS Accounts Management at (800) 829-0922.
   b. Tax professionals with Form 2848: contact Practitioner Priority Service Line at (866) 860-4259, option 2.

2. *All requests when taxpayer is in IRS Collection: after the IRS issues a Final Notice of Intent to Levy (Letter 1058, LT11, or the equivalent), contact IRS collection directly:*
   a. Wage earner taxpayers: 800-829-7650.
   b. Self-employed taxpayers (file Schedule C, E, F, or Form 2106): 800-829-3903.
   c. Tax pros: contact ACS through the Practitioner Priority Service hotline at 866-860-4259, option 4.

By IRS Online Payment Agreement: (OPA ETP only available for balances less than $100,000)

1. Go to https://www.irs.gov/payments/online-payment-agreement-application
2. Taxpayer: follow the IRS workflow screens.
3. Tax professionals (must have Form 2848 on file with the IRS and know the signature date of the Form 2848): follow the IRS workflow screens.

Pro Tip: The IRS OPA is typically unavailable from 10PM on Saturdays through 6PM on Sundays, daily between 12:30AM and 6AM, and periodically for maintenance. [See system availability at http://irs.gov/payments/online-payment-agreement-application] Although the IRS has made improvements to the OPA tool, some taxpayers are directed to call the IRS for various reasons. Taxpayers should not be alarmed if they cannot complete the agreement using the OPA as the IRS continues to enhance and improve the OPA tool so that more |

		taxpayers can complete their agreements online. See <u>IRM 21.2.1.57</u> at (8) (5-29-2024) for specific circumstances in which the OPA cannot be used. Tax Pros with a <u>Form 2848</u> with the "Intermediate Service Provider" checkbox selected cannot use the IRS' OPA.
3	Confirm the ETP agreement was granted.	• Successful phone or online OPA requests will provide the ETP terms and conditions and payoff amount. • Taxpayers will receive Letter 681C that will confirm the years, forms, and deadline date along with the payoff amount and instructions to pay. • If the taxpayer does not receive this notice, he should contact the IRS immediately by phone and confirm that it has been granted or re-request as needed.

Taxpayers will need to pay the balance owed before the extension to pay date or otherwise seek another available collection alternative. No additional ETP (i.e., Option #1 – the "collection hold") will be provided without special circumstances (i.e., additional time needed by the IRS to process amended return, etc.).

Chapter 7:
IRS COLLECTION ALTERNATIVES: SIMPLE INSTALLMENT AGREEMENTS

This section covers the guaranteed installment agreement and the simple installment agreement collection alternatives. The simple installment agreement is the most commonly used IRS collection alternative.

Topic	Covers
Overview of Simple Installment Agreements	The two simplest installment agreements to set up with the IRS.
Guaranteed Installment Agreements	How to set qualify and set up a GIA.
Simple Installment Agreements	How to qualify and set up an SIA.
Installment Agreement User Fees	The setup fees that apply to all installment agreements and how to minimize the cost of setting up an installment agreement with the IRS.
Where to Mail Form 9465	Specific addresses to send Form 9465 when setting up an installment agreement.
Important Pro Tips for Simple Payment Plans	Seven tips to consider when setting up a simple installment agreement.

Key Highlights:

- The easiest and most common IRS monthly payment plan arrangements are the simple payment plans which allow payment terms over a fixed time period.
- Taxpayers who can execute a simple installment agreement (i.e., owe $50,000 or less, can pay before the collection statute expiration date) will avoid a federal tax lien and not have to provide the IRS detailed financial information.
- The IRS replaced the streamlined installment agreement in March 2025 with the new "simple installment agreement" (SIA). The new SIA allows for longer payment terms v. the retired streamlined agreement and does not require direct debit payment when the balance owed is between $25,000 and $50,000 to avoid a lien filing.
- Installment agreements have set-up fees ranging from $0 to $178. Low-income taxpayers, online setup, and automatic payment agreements have the lowest fees.

Chapter 7.01: Overview of Simple Installment Agreements

The IRS has two payment plans that are simple to obtain and, if obtained timely, can avoid imposition of a Notice of Federal Tax Lien. These payment plans may also offer the taxpayer the best payment options, depending on the circumstances.

There are two types of simple installment agreements offered that help the taxpayer avoid a Notice of Federal Tax Lien:

- *Guaranteed Installment Agreement* (GIA): up to 36-month payment terms for amounts owed that are less than $10,000. If the taxpayer meets all the qualification rules for the GIA, they are guaranteed a payment plan with the IRS. [IRM 5.14.5.3 (10-14-2021)]
- *Simple Installment Agreement* (SIA): a payment plan for individuals who owe up to $50,000 in assessed balance and can pay before the collection statute expiration date(s) (CSED). [IRM 5.14.5.2 (10-14-2021)] Note: The IRS retired the streamlined installment agreement on March 5, 2025, and replaced it with the new Simple installment agreement (SIA). However, most IRS guidance and its Internal Revenue Manual have not been updated with its new terms. The new SIA terms are found mostly on IRS.gov.

SIAs are the most common collection alternative. In 2014, 95% of all payment plans were SIAs and in 2016, 85% of all plans were SIAs. [Taxpayer Advocate Research Study, The Importance of Financial Analysis in Installment Agreements in Minimizing Defaults and Preventing Noncompliance, 2016 Annual Report to Congress] SIAs are the only installment agreements that can all be established online using the IRS's Online Payment Agreement. In 2024, 2/3rds of all installment agreements were completed online, indicating that SIAs are still the vast majority of all payment plans.

As with all IRS installment agreements, the taxpayer must be in compliance for filing and payment in order to obtain the agreement. That is, the taxpayer must have filed all required back returns and have adequate withholding and/or estimated tax payments, so they are not projected to owe in future filed returns. [IRM 5.19.1.4.4.1 (7-9-2024)]

> **Pro Tip:** IRS policy generally requires that only the past six years need to be filed in order to be considered "filing compliant." [IRS Policy Statement 5-133 (8-4-2006)] IRS collection personnel are less stringent on requiring payment compliance (i.e., current withholding and/or estimated tax payments are sufficient to ensure that the taxpayer will not owe on future returns) for simple installment agreements unless the taxpayer has defaulted on past payment plans. Prior defaults in the past five years also disqualify taxpayers from the GIA.

In all installment agreements, the IRS will make every attempt to make sure that the tax bill is paid before the time to collect expires. The collection statute of limitations is ten years from the date of assessment. [IRC §6502(a)(1)] The GIA payment terms may be shorter if the taxpayer has old tax debts where the collection statute expiration date (CSED) is less than the GIA (36-months).

The SIA payment terms are always before the CSED. [IRM 5.14.5.2 at (2c) (10-14-2021) and IRS.gov] The IRS will always want full payment of the balance owed and will request a payment amount to be paid before the CSED expires.

Example- John owes $24,000 ($8,000 each year) to the IRS for 2013, 2014, and 2015 on June 1, 2024. The CSEDs for each year are as follows:

Tax year	CSED	Months remaining until CSED	Amount owed
2013	6/1/2025	12	$8,000
2014	6/1/2026	24	$8,000
2015	6/1/2027	36	$8,000

If the taxpayer were to obtain an SIA, the SIA payment period would be the remaining months on the CSEDs that would full pay the amount owed (plus accrued penalties and interest). John would have to offer at least $667 a month ($8,000/12), plus accrued interest (in our example, it is likely that the maximum failure to pay penalty would have already be included in the balance), as a payment plan to fully pay the liability for each year before the expiration of the CSED.

Chapter 7.02: Guaranteed Installment Agreements

Guaranteed installment agreements (GIA) are the easiest of all payment plans to setup with the IRS. The maximum number of payments for a GIA is 36 months. If a taxpayer owes $10,000 (not including any assessed or accrued penalties and interest), has filed all required returns, and has not entered into an installment agreement in the past five years, the IRS must and will automatically allow the GIA. [IRM 5.14.5.3 at (1) (10-14-2021)]

> **Pro Tip:** Taxpayers qualifying for a guaranteed installment agreement would generally also qualify for a simple installment agreement. If the taxpayer does not automatically qualify for a GIA, the taxpayer should seek an SIA. In fact, if the taxpayer wants a lower payment than the GIA allows, it is common for the IRS to just put the taxpayer in an SIA with the desired payment amount. Most importantly, both a timely executed GIA and SIA avoid a federal tax lien.

Taxpayers can setup the agreement online, by phone, or by using Form 9465. As with all installment agreements, taxpayers who agree to the GIA must make a payment each month until the balance is paid in full or face default on their agreement.

> **Pro Tip:** In situations where there are CSED limitation issues, the taxpayer does not have to compute the minimum payment amount. The IRS has a tool that computes the minimum payment amount that considers CSED limitations. To find out the minimum payment amount, contact the IRS or use the Online Payment Agreement tool.

Like all installment agreements, future refunds are taken to pay the outstanding balance owed. Taxpayers are not required to liquidate or borrow against assets to pay the balance. Taxpayers are also allowed to miss one payment each year and not default on their payment plan.

> **Pro Tip:** Taxpayers must make a payment each month to avoid default. Taxpayers cannot "double-up" payments in a month to avoid this requirement. Any payment in advance of the month is treated as a voluntary payment outside of the payment plan.

Taxpayers have the option to make the monthly installment payment by any accepted means. Taxpayers are encouraged to set up their payment as direct debit to avoid defaulting on the agreement for missed payments. However, for a GIA, direct payments are not required to avoid a federal tax lien.

Computing the GIA Payment Amount

GIA payment terms are simple to compute. The taxpayer can simply take the tax owed and divide by 36 to determine the payment amount. [IRM 5.14.5.3 at (1) (10-14-2021)] If refund offsets do not significantly lower the balance owed, the taxpayer may have to make additional payments past the 36 months due to accrued penalties and interest.

> **Pro Tip:** Taxpayers should set up the GIA online and pay by automatic debits from their bank account to reduce setup fees to $22 (setting up by phone or form with check payment carries a $178 setup fee.) Automatic payment will also lower the chances for missing payments and subsequent payment plan default.

Example- Jeremy files his 2018 return with tax owed of $7,200. Jeremy cannot pay and wants an installment agreement. This is the first time Jeremy has owed the IRS and he has filed all required prior year returns. Jeremy submits Form 9465 to request a guaranteed installment agreement payment for $200 a month starting on the 28th of the next month and continuing for each month thereafter. Jeremy also wants to pay by direct debit and provides his banking information on Form 9465.

Form 9465
(Rev. September 2020)
Department of the Treasury
Internal Revenue Service

Installment Agreement Request

▶ Go to *www.irs.gov/Form9465* for instructions and the latest information.
▶ If you are filing this form with your tax return, attach it to the front of the return.
▶ See separate instructions.

OMB No. 1545-0074

Tip: If you owe $50,000 or less, you may be able to avoid filing Form 9465 and establish an installment agreement online, even if you haven't yet received a tax bill. Go to *www.irs.gov/OPA* to apply for an Online Payment Agreement. If you establish your installment agreement using the Online Payment Agreement application, the user fee that you pay will be lower than it would be with Form 9465.

Part I	Installment Agreement Request

This request is for Form(s) (for example, Form 1040 or Form 941) ▶   1040

Enter tax year(s) or period(s) involved (for example, 2018 and 2019, or January 1, 2019, to June 30, 2019) ▶   2018

1a	Your first name and initial	Last name	Your social security number
	Jeremy	Taxpayer	123456789
	If a joint return, spouse's first name and initial	Last name	Spouse's social security number

Current address (number and street). If you have a P.O. box and no home delivery, enter your box number.	Apt. number
123 Cantpay St.	

City, town or post office, state, and ZIP code. If a foreign address, also complete the spaces below (see instructions).
Broke, NC 27777

Foreign country name	Foreign province/state/county	Foreign postal code

1b If this address is new since you filed your last tax return, check here . . . . ▶ ☐

2 Name of your business (must no longer be operating) | Employer identification number (EIN)

3	335-555-1212	8-5PM	4			
	Your home phone number	Best time for us to call		Your work phone number	Ext.	Best time for us to call

5	Enter the total amount you owe as shown on your tax return(s) (or notice(s))	5	7200
6	If you have any additional balances due that aren't reported on line 5, enter the amount here (even if the amounts are included in an existing installment agreement)	6	0
7	Add lines 5 and 6 and enter the result	7	7200
8	Enter the amount of any payment you're making with this request. See instructions	8	0
9	Amount owed. Subtract line 8 from line 7 and enter the result	9	7200
10	Divide the amount on line 9 by 72.0 and enter the result	10	100

11a Enter the amount you can pay each month. Make your payment as large as possible to limit interest and penalty charges, **as these charges will continue to accrue until you pay in full.** If you have an existing installment agreement, this amount should represent your total proposed monthly payment amount for all your liabilities. **If no payment amount is listed on line 11a, a payment will be determined for you by dividing the balance due on line 9 by 72 months** . . . . . . | **11a** $ | 200

b If the amount on line 11a is less than the amount on line 10 and you're able to increase your payment to an amount that is equal to or greater than the amount on line 10, enter your *revised* monthly payment | **11b** $ |

• If you can't increase your payment on line 11b to more than or equal to the amount shown on line 10, check the box. Also, complete and attach Form 433-F, Collection Information Statement . . . . ☐

• If the amount on line 11a (or 11b, if applicable) is more than or equal to the amount on line 10 and the amount you owe is over $25,000 but not more than $50,000, then you don't have to complete Form 433-F. However, if you don't complete Form 433-F, then you must complete either line 13 or 14.

• If the amount on line 9 is greater than $50,000, complete and attach Form 433-F.

12 Enter the date you want to make your payment each month. **Don't** enter a date later than the 28th | **12** | 28th

13 If you want to make your payments by direct debit from your checking account, see the instructions and fill in lines 13a and 13b. This is the most convenient way to make your payments and it will ensure that they are made on time.

▶ **a** Routing number [1 1 1 1 1 1 1 1 1]   ▶ **b** Account number [1 1 1 1 1 1 1 1 1 1 1 1 1 1 1 1 1 1]

I authorize the U.S. Treasury and its designated Financial Agent to initiate a monthly ACH debit (electronic withdrawal) entry to the financial institution account indicated for payments of my federal taxes owed, and the financial institution to debit the entry to this account. This authorization is to remain in full force and effect until I notify the U.S. Treasury Financial Agent to terminate the authorization. To revoke payment, I must contact the U.S. Treasury Financial Agent at **1-800-829-1040** no later than 14 business days prior to the payment (settlement) date. I also authorize the financial institutions involved in the processing of the electronic payments of taxes to receive confidential information necessary to answer inquiries and resolve issues related to the payments.

c **Low-income taxpayers only.** If you're unable to make electronic payments through a debit instrument by providing your banking information on lines 13a and 13b, check this box and your user fee will be reimbursed upon completion of your installment agreement. See instructions . . . . ☐

14 If you want to make payments by payroll deduction, check this box and attach a completed Form 2159 . . . . ☐

By signing and submitting this form, I authorize the IRS to contact third parties and to disclose my tax information to third parties in order to process this request and administer the agreement over its duration. I also agree to the terms of this agreement, as provided in the instructions, if it's approved by the IRS.

Your signature	Date	Spouse's signature. If a joint return, **both** must sign.	Date

For Privacy Act and Paperwork Reduction Act Notice, see instructions.   Cat. No. 14842Y   Form **9465** (Rev. 9-2020)

The table below summarizes the steps necessary to obtain a GIA.

Steps	Action	How to Do
1	Confirm that the taxpayer meets the conditions for a GIA.	Meets these conditions: 1. Total tax owed is $10,000 or less (does not include any assessed or accrued penalties and interest). 2. All required returns have been filed (i.e., last six years). 3. No installment agreements in the past five years.
2	Compute monthly payment amount.	Compute minimum monthly payment. (Balance due/36 months) The payment should be *at least* this amount.
3	Contact the appropriate IRS function and secure GIA.	By mail: 1. Complete IRS <u>Form 9465</u>, *Installment Agreement Request*. (*Note:* The taxpayer can also use the Form 433-D, *Installment Agreement*.) 2. Form 9465, line 11a should reflect the minimum or greater payment amount. 3. Form 9465 should include the direct debit payment information in Box 13 (not required if paying by check). 4. Attach to return or mail to IRS. By phone: 1. Request when the taxpayer is not in IRS Collection: a. Taxpayers: contact IRS Accounts Management at (800) 829-0922. b. Tax professionals with <u>Form 2848</u>: contact Practitioner Priority Service Line at (866) 860-4259, option 2. c. Request GIA from IRS representative. Give the representative payment amount, day of each month for the payment, and method of payment (check/other v. direct debit). d. If by direct debit, provide the <u>Form 9465</u> by fax to the IRS representative on the call. 2. All requests when taxpayer is in IRS Collection: after the IRS issues a Final Notice of Intent to Levy (Letter 1058, LT11, or the equivalent), contact IRS Collection directly: a. Wage earner taxpayers: 800-829-7650.

		b. Self-employed taxpayers (file Schedule C, E, F, or Form 2106): 800-829-3903. c. Tax pros: contact ACS through the Practitioner Priority Service hotline at 866-860-4259, option 4. d. Request GIA from IRS representative. Give the representative payment amount, day of each month for the payment, and method of payment (check/other v. direct debit). e. If by direct debit, provide the Form 9465 by fax to the IRS representative on the call. By IRS Online Payment Agreement: 1. Go to https://www.irs.gov/payments/online-payment-agreement-application 2. Taxpayer: follow the IRS workflow screens. 3. Tax professionals (must have <u>Form 2848</u> on file with the IRS and know the signature date of the Form 2848, and not select the "Intermediate Service Provider" checkbox in section 5a): follow the IRS workflow screens. **Pro Tip:** The IRS OPA is typically unavailable from 10PM on Saturdays through 6PM ET on Sundays, daily between 12:30AM and 6AM ET, and periodically for maintenance. [See system availability at http://irs.gov/payments/online-payment-agreement-application] Although the IRS has made improvements to the OPA tool, some taxpayers are directed to call the IRS for various reasons. Taxpayers should not be alarmed if they cannot complete the agreement using the OPA as the IRS continues to enhance and improve the OPA tool so that more taxpayers can complete their agreements online. See <u>IRM 21.2.1.57</u> at (8) (5-29-2024) for specific circumstances in which the OPA cannot be used.
4	Confirm the agreement is setup	Receipt of IRS Letter 2273C, *Installment Agreement Accepted*, or its equivalent

		• If the taxpayer does not receive this notice, they should contact the IRS immediately by phone and confirm that it has been granted or re-request as needed.

Chapter 7.03: Simple Installment Agreements

Taxpayers who owe less than $50,000 in assessed balances can use the simple installment agreement (SIA) to pay up to the collection statute expiration date(s). An SIA can be used to pay individual taxes owed, including income taxes, individual shared responsibility assessments, and trust fund recovery penalty assessments. Out-of-business sole proprietors can also use an SIA to pay any back income taxes, penalties, and interest owed. Small businesses may also use an SIA to for income taxes and late-filing penalties (i.e., Form 1120-S/1065) but they must only owe $25,000 or less. [IRM 5.14.5.2 at (3) (10-14-2021)]

> **Pro Tip:** The SIA is new as of March 5, 2025, and replaces the streamlined installment agreement which limited the number of payments to 72 months or the CSED, whichever is shorter. Taxpayers cannot accurately determine the exact minimum payment amount of the SIA. Taxpayers must call the IRS or use the Online Payment Agreement tool to obtain the minimum payment amount, which would include a projected amount of interest and penalties included in the minimum payment amount.

The SIA payment plan is the most common payment plan with the IRS. A SIA can usually be set up quickly and will likely provide taxpayers better payment terms. Taxpayers who are unable pay according to the SIA terms face tax liens if the amount they owe is over $10,000. Taxpayers also need to timely request the SIA before a tax lien is filed. After the lien is filed, taxpayers must pay the balance owed for a lien release or lower the amount to $25,000 to start lien withdrawal proceedings.

To obtain an SIA, individuals must meet the following conditions:

- The total "assessed" balance (not including accruals of penalties and interest after assessment) is $50,000 or less. [IRM 5.14.5.2 at (2) and (3) (10-14-2021)]
- Must pay within the CSED.
- All required tax returns have been filed. [IRM 5.14.5.2 at (10) (10-14-2021)]
- Payment by direct debit from a financial institution or by payroll deduction is NOT required.

> **Pro Tip:** For an SIA, taxpayers can owe more than $50,000 and get into an SIA because the SIA threshold is based on the "assessed balance" — not the total amount owed. The unpaid balance of assessments includes tax, assessed penalty and interest, and all other assessments for each tax year. It does not include accrued penalty and interest after the original assessment. A taxpayer can have an original assessment under $50,000 for an older tax year and accrue additional penalties and interest that put the total balance owed over the $50,000 threshold but still qualify for an SIA. Taxpayer can designate payments to reduce the "assessed balance only" and qualify themselves for an SIA.

Taxpayers who have defaulted on an installment agreement during the past 12 months due to missed payments may have to provide financial information to the IRS to prove their ability to pay. [IRM 5.14.5.2 at (10) (10-14-2021)] Taxpayers can provide this financial disclosure on Form 9465, Part II. [Instructions to Form 9465]

Form 9465 (Rev. 9-2020)   Page **2**

Part II	**Additional Information**

Complete this Part only if all three conditions below apply:

    1. You defaulted on an installment agreement in the past 12 months;

    2. You owe more than $25,000 but not more than $50,000; and

    3. The amount on line 11a (or 11b, if applicable) is less than line 10.

Note: If you owe more than $50,000, also complete and attach Form 433-F.

15   In which county is your primary residence? _____

16a   Marital status:

    ☐ Single. Skip question 16b and go to question 17.

    ☐ Married. Go to question 16b.

  b   Do you share household expenses with your spouse?

    ☐ Yes.

    ☐ No.

17   How many dependents will you be able to claim on this year's tax return? . . . .   **17** |

18   How many people in your household are 65 or older? . . . .   **18** |

19   How often are you paid?

    ☐ Once a week.

    ☐ Once every 2 weeks.

    ☐ Once a month.

    ☐ Twice a month.

20   What is your net income per pay period (take home pay)? . . . .   **20** |$

Note: Complete lines 21 and 22 only if you have a spouse and meet certain conditions (see instructions). If you don't have a spouse, go to line 23.

21   How often is your spouse paid?

    ☐ Once a week.

    ☐ Once every 2 weeks.

    ☐ Once a month.

    ☐ Twice a month.

22   What is your spouse's net income per pay period (take home pay)? . . . .   **22** |$

23   How many vehicles do you own? . . . .   **23** |

24   How many car payments do you have each month? . . . .   **24** |

25a   Do you have health insurance?

    ☐ Yes. Go to question 25b.   ☐ No. Skip question 25b and go to question 26a.

  b   Are your health insurance premiums deducted from your paycheck?

    ☐ Yes. Skip question 25c and go to question 26a.   ☐ No. Go to question 25c.

  c   How much are your monthly health insurance premiums? . . . .   **25c** |$

26a   Do you make court-ordered payments?

    ☐ Yes. Go to question 26b.   ☐ No. Go to question 27.

  b   Are your court-ordered payments deducted from your paycheck?

    ☐ Yes. Go to question 27.   ☐ No. Go to question 26c.

  c   How much are your court-ordered payments each month? . . . .   **26c** |$

27   Not including any court-ordered payments for child and dependent support, how much do you pay for child or dependent care each month? . . . .   **27** |$

Form **9465** (Rev. 9-2020)

Computing the SIA Payment Amount

The minimum SIA payment can only be computed by the IRS. The taxpayer can contact the IRS by phone, or use the IRS' <u>Online Payment Agreement</u> tool to see the minimum payment amount. The total balance, including penalty and interest accruals, must be paid before the CSED expires. The IRS has an internal tool that will compute the minimum payment that considers future accrued penalties and interest.

Taxpayers can set up an SIA online using the <u>Online Payment Agreement</u> tool at irs.gov, file <u>Form 9465</u>, *Installment Agreement Request*, with the IRS, or contact the IRS by phone. (*Note:* Taxpayers can also use <u>Form 433-D</u>, *Installment Agreement*, instead of Form 9465.)

The table below lists the steps to be taken to obtain an SIA.

Steps	Action	How to Do
1	Confirm that the taxpayer meets the conditions for an SIA.	Meets these conditions: • Total assessed balance is $50,000 or less. • All required returns have been filed (i.e., last six years).
2	Contact IRS for the minimum monthly payment amount.	Use the IRS <u>Online Payment Agreement</u> tool or contact IRS Collection for the minimum payment amount. The taxpayer can pay more than the minimum.
3	Complete any required financial disclosure	Taxpayers who have defaulted on an installment agreement due to a missed payment in the past 12 months may be required to complete Part II of <u>Form 9465</u> to include limited taxpayer collection information. You can provide this information to the IRS by phone when setting up the SIA.

4	Contact the appropriate IRS function and secure SLIA.	By mail:
		
		1. Complete IRS <u>Form 9465</u> or <u>433-D</u>, *Installment Agreement* (with direct debit or payroll deduction information).
		2. <u>Form 9465</u>, line 11a should reflect the minimum or greater payment amount.
		3. Complete Part II of <u>Form 9465</u> if have defaulted on a prior payment agreement in the past 12 months.
		4. Mail to IRS.
		
		By phone:
		
		1. Request when the taxpayer is not in IRS Collection:
		    a. Taxpayers: contact IRS Accounts Management at (800) 829-0922.
		    b. Tax professionals with Form 2848: contact Practitioner Priority Service Line at (866) 860-4259, option 2.

		c. Request SIA from IRS representative. Give the representative payment amount, day of each month for the payment, and method of payment (check/other v. direct debit). Provide any financial information from Part II of <u>Form 9465</u> if there is a prior defaulted agreement in the past 12 months.
		d. If by direct debit, provide the <u>Form 9465</u> by fax to the IRS representative on the call.
		2. All requests when the taxpayer is in IRS Collection: after the IRS issues a Final Notice of Intent to Levy (Letter 1058, LT11, or the equivalent), contact IRS collection directly:
		    a. Wage earner taxpayers: 800-829-7650.
		    b. Self-employed taxpayers (file Schedule C, E, F, or Form 2106): 800-829-3903.
		    c. Tax pros: contact ACS through the Practitioner Priority Service hotline at 866-860-4259, option 4.
		    d. Request SIA from IRS representative. Give the representative payment amount, day of each month for the payment, and method of payment (check/other v. direct debit).
		    e. If by direct debit, provide the <u>Form 9465</u> by fax to the IRS representative on the call. If Form 9465, Part II information is required, the information can be provided to the IRS representative on the phone.
		
		By IRS Online Payment Agreement:
		
		1. Go to <u>https://www.irs.gov/payments/online-payment-agreement-application</u>
		2. Taxpayer: follow the IRS workflow screens.
		3. Tax professionals (must have <u>Form 2848</u> on file with the IRS and know the signature date of the Form 2848, and without the "Intermediate Service Provider" checkbox selected in section 5a of Form 2848): follow the IRS workflow screens.

5	Confirm the agreement is setup.	Receipt of IRS Letter 2273C, *Installment Agreement Accepted*, or its equivalent

		• If the taxpayer does not receive this notice, they should contact the IRS immediately by phone and confirm that it has been granted or re-request as needed.

Example- Greg owes $4,891 to the IRS for 2024. His assessed balance is the same as the accrued balance. He has 119 months remaining on the CSED for 2024. The IRS likely will not file a Notice of Federal Tax Lien as the amount owed is under $10,000. Greg can pay the minimum payment amount of $147.20 per month. Greg uses the IRS's Online Payment Agreement (OPA) and provides his payment amount, banking information, and sets up the agreement. His fee to set up the agreement is $22.

Greg sees the amount owed in OPA: (*Note:* All OPA screens are not shown)

Account Home / Payment Options

Payment Options

All fields marked with an asterisk (*) are required.

Make a Payment

Pay towards any amount you owe to minimize penalties and interest.

Balance Payment: Pay your balance due as shown on your account or as much as possible.

Other Payment: Make another type of payment such as:

- Amended Return ?
- Estimated Tax ?
- Proposed Tax Assessment ?
- Offer in Compromise ?

[Make a payment]

Short-Term Plan

✓ No setup fee

$ Lower penalties and interest ?

Select one term *:

○ **$4,891.00**
within 90 days

◉ **$5,038.20**
within 180 days

[Apply for short-term plan]

Long-Term Plan

$ Setup fee applies ?

$ Higher penalties and interest ?

Pay Monthly
View personalized plan terms and monthly amounts after you select a payment method option.

Select one option *:
◉ Pay by Direct Debit
$22 setup fee
Pay by automatic withdrawal

○ Pay by Other Method
$69 setup fee
Pay manually each month via credit card or Make a Payment

[Apply for long-term plan]

Account Home / Payment Options / Create Short-Term Plan

Create Short-Term Plan

```
  1 ──────── 2 ──────── 3
 Plan      Terms &    Plan Approval
Summary   Conditions
```

Plan Summary Details

Plan Type	Short-Term Payment Plan
Payoff Amount	$5,038.20* (includes accrued penalties & interest)
Accrued Penalties & Interest ?	$147.20
Setup Fee	$0
Pay Within	180 days
Due Date	December 13, 2025

*Important notice:

- This information is only an estimate of the cost of the payment plan and accruals.

- It does not constitute a quote, offer, or contract by the IRS, and it is not a guarantee of the final cost of the payment plan and accruals.

- The cost is subject to change without notice.

- The IRS makes no representation or warranties about the accuracy of the estimate and accepts no liability arising out of your use of this estimate.

Please note that all correspondence will be sent to the address from when you last filed your taxes, which can be found in your Profile. You can still set up a payment plan with the address we have on file and then, if necessary, update your address immediately after establishing your plan.

[Back] [Next]

Greg agrees to the terms, conditions and payment amount:

Account Home / Payment Options / Create Short-Term Plan

Create Short-Term Plan

Plan Summary — Terms & Conditions (2) — Plan Approval (3)

All fields with an asterisk (*) are required.

Terms and Conditions

If your account is not fully paid by the date promised, we may begin enforced collection actions. We could:

- Collect the entire amount you owe by levying your wages, other income, bank accounts, other assets, or by seizing property.
- Terminate this payment plan at any time if we find that collection of the tax is in jeopardy.
- File a Notice of Federal Tax Lien ⬀ if one has not been filed previously.

All federal taxes that become due must be filed and paid on time. We will apply any federal tax refund to the amount you owe until your balance is paid in full.

Note: The Internal Revenue Service may have already initiated enforcement actions on your account. If you have received a "Notice of Intent to Levy and Notice of Your Right to a Hearing", it is important that you contact the IRS representative listed on that notice to prevent further enforcement actions.

Accept Terms and Conditions

☑ I have read the above Terms and Conditions and authorize the creation of a short-term payment plan.*

[Back] [Submit]

Chapter 7.04: Installment Agreement User Fees

All IRS installment agreements require a setup fee. The fees range from $178 for installment agreements set up by phone and paid by check, to $22 for agreements set up online and paid by automatic direct debit. [IRM 5.14.1.2 (3-31-2023)]

Installment Agreement User Fees as (*Note:* Subject to Change)	
Manual setup method (by phone or by mailed form):	*Fee*
Low-income non-direct debit installment agreement (DDIA) payment	$43 (may be reimbursed)
Low-income DDIA payment	$0
DDIA payment	$107
Pay by check	$178
Setup using IRS.gov _Online Payment Agreement_ (OPA):	*Fee*

OPA Low-Income Non DDIA	$43 (may be reimbursed)
OPA Low-Income DDIA payment	$0
OPA pay by check	$69
OPA DDIA payment	$22
Reinstatement/Restructuring:	*Fee*
Low-income Non DDIA reinstatement/restructuring	$43 (reimbursed the $43 after the agreement is completed)
Low-income DDIA reinstatement/restructuring	$0
Revise online	$10 (low-income reimbursed after agreement is completed)
Revise by phone, mail, or in-person	$89

Note: All payments made by payroll deduction carry a $178 user fee. Low-income taxpayers can have this fee reduced to $43. [Form 2159]

Taxpayers who meet low-income thresholds can have the fee reduced to $43. For taxpayers paying by direct debit, the $43 user fee will be reimbursed when the taxpayer completes the installment agreement. Low-income criteria can be found on Form 13844, *Application for Reduced User Fee for Installment Agreements.* It is based on the taxpayer's prior year adjusted gross income, family size, and place of residence. [Form 13844, *Application for Reduced User Fee for Installment Agreements* (2-2025)]

Low-Income Taxpayer Adjusted Gross Income Guidance			
Size of Family Unit	48 Contiguous States and D.C., and U.S. Territories	Alaska	Hawaii
1	$39,125	$48,875	$44,975
2	$52,875	$66,075	$60,800
3	$66,625	$83,275	$76,625
4	$80,375	$100,475	$92,450
5	$94,125	$117,675	$108,275
6	$107,875	$134,875	$124,100
7	$121,625	$152,075	$139,925
8	$135,375	$169,275	$155,750
For each additional person, add	$13,750	$17,200	$15,825

Source: Based on 2025 US Department of Health & Human Services Poverty Guidelines, January 17, 2025.

The IRS will automatically apply the low-income waiver if the most recent filed tax return meets the low-income criteria (adjusted gross income is at or below 250% of the federal poverty guidelines). If the taxpayer qualifies based on her current financial situation, she should use Form 13844, *Application for Reduced User Fee for Installment Agreements.* The IRS must receive this form within 30 days of the date on the installment agreement acceptance letter (Letter 2273C or its equivalent). [IRM 5.14.1.2 at (11) (7-2-2024)]

> **Pro Tip:** In most circumstances, when setting up the payment plan by phone, IRS employees will review the taxpayer's prior year AGI and determine if the taxpayer meets low-income criteria and will reduce the fee without the need for filing the Form 13844.

Chapter 7.05: Where to Mail Form 9465

Form 9465, *Installment Agreement Request*, is used to set up an IRS installment agreement. It is not necessary to provide this form to set up the agreement online or by phone. Online payment arrangements do not require the taxpayer to submit any follow-up information to the IRS. However, if a taxpayer sets up a direct debit payment method by phone, he must send Form 9465 or 433-D to the IRS by mail (or fax when on the phone call with the IRS). Taxpayers setting up a payroll deduction payment method must send Form 2159 to their employer for completion. The IRS will provide instructions on where to mail both Forms 433-D and Form 2159.

> **Pro Tip:** Taxpayers who set up a direct debit installment agreement can either fax the Form 433-D/9465 directly to the IRS collection agent while on the phone or ask for a fax number to send the form within 48 hours after the call. However, for SIAs, it is always best to set them up online using the IRS Online Payment Agreement.

With regard to Form 9465 installment agreement requests, taxpayers can attach the form to the return (paper filed or e-file with most tax preparation software) or mail to the address listed in the Form 9465 instructions.

For all taxpayers except those filing Form 1040 or 1040-SR with Schedule(s) C, E, or F for any tax year for which this installment agreement is being requested	
IF you live in…	**THEN use this address…**
Alaska, Arizona, Colorado, Connecticut, Delaware, District of Columbia, Hawaii, Idaho, Illinois, Maine, Maryland, Massachusetts, Montana, Nevada, New Hampshire, New Jersey, New Mexico, North Dakota, Oregon, Rhode Island, South Dakota, Tennessee, Utah, Vermont, Washington, Wisconsin, Wyoming	Department of the Treasury Internal Revenue Service 310 Lowell St. Stop 830 Andover, MA 01810
Alabama, Florida, Georgia, Kentucky, Louisiana, Mississippi, North Carolina, South Carolina, Texas, Virginia	Department of the Treasury Internal Revenue Service P.O. Box 47421 Stop 74

	Doraville, GA 30362
Arkansas, California, Indiana, Iowa, Kansas, Michigan, Minnesota, Missouri, Nebraska, New York, Ohio, Oklahoma, Pennsylvania, West Virginia	Department of the Treasury Internal Revenue Service Stop P-4 5000 Kansas City, MO 64999-0250

For taxpayers filing Form 1040 or 1040-SR with Schedule(s) C, E, or F for any tax year for which this installment agreement is being requested...

IF you live in...	THEN use this address...
Connecticut, Maine, Massachusetts, New Hampshire, New York, Rhode Island, Vermont	Department of the Treasury Internal Revenue Service P.O. Box 480 Stop 660 Holtsville, NY 11742-0480
Alabama, Arkansas, Georgia, Illinois, Indiana, Iowa, Kansas, Kentucky, Louisiana, Michigan, Minnesota, Mississippi, Missouri, Nebraska, New Jersey, North Dakota, Ohio, Oklahoma, Pennsylvania, South Dakota, Tennessee, Texas, West Virginia, Wisconsin	Department of the Treasury Internal Revenue Service P.O. Box 69 Stop 811 Memphis, TN 38101-0069
Alaska, Arizona, California, Colorado, Hawaii, Idaho, Montana, Nevada, New Mexico, Oregon, Utah, Washington, Wyoming	Department of the Treasury Internal Revenue Service P.O. Box 9941 Stop 5500 Ogden, UT 84409
District of Columbia, Delaware, Florida, Maryland, North Carolina, South Carolina, Virginia	Department of the Treasury Internal Revenue Service Stop 4-N31.142

	Philadelphia, PA 19255-0030
For all taxpayers living outside the 50 states, for any tax year for which the installment agreement is being requested...	
IF you live in...	**THEN use this address...**
A foreign country, US territory*. or use an APO or FPO address, or file Form 2555 or 4563, or are a dual-status alien	Department of the Treasury Internal Revenue Service 3651 South I-H 35 5501USC Austin, TX 78741
*For all taxpayers who are bona fide residents of American Samoa, Puerto Rico, Guam, the U.S. Virgin Islands, or the Northern Mariana Islands, see Pub. 570, Tax Guide for Individuals with Income from U.S. Territories.	

Chapter 7.06: Important Pro Tips for Simple Payment Plans

1. *Avoid a tax lien — pay down and get into an SIA*: many taxpayers who owe more than $50,000 and are able to access funds to lower the amount receive an extension to pay within 180 days, so that they can pay the balance down under $50,000 and obtain an SIA. The timely extension to pay, payment, and execution of the SIA will avoid the filing of a tax lien.

2. *Reduce fees — apply online and pay by direct debit*: the IRS increases the setup fees for paper requests and payment by check. Reduce the setup fee by setting up the agreement online using the Online Payment Agreement tool and agree to direct debit automatic payments. Automatic payments will also avoid a monthly reminder letter from the IRS of the payment due.

3. *Reduce default — pay by direct debit or payroll deduction*: IRS installment agreements have a high default rate. To avoid a default, a taxpayer must make payments monthly. The best way to avoid missing a payment is to have the payment automatically deducted from the taxpayer's financial account.

4. *Avoid unpaid taxes in the future*: future tax filings with unpaid balances owed is a common reason for default of a payment arrangement. Taxpayers need to change withholding and/or make estimated tax payments to avoid future balances owed that they cannot pay. Taxpayers in an installment agreement who file a return in a future year with an unpaid balance can often fold the new balance into a new agreement if they still qualify for an SIA.

5. *Potential to miss one payment a year without default:* most IRS GIA and SIA payment plans allow the taxpayer to miss one payment per year and not be in default. It is best for the taxpayer to notify the IRS in advance if they cannot make a payment.

6. *If financial situation worsens, apply for an ability to pay plan*: payment plans can always be renegotiated if the taxpayer's financial circumstances change. For example, if a

taxpayer becomes unemployed, he may not have the means to pay the IRS. In these cases, the taxpayer can contact the IRS and provide them with documentation confirming his ability to pay. This may mean they can negotiate a lower payment or even payment deferral (currently not collectible status). Be careful here: if the taxpayer owes more than $10,000 and cannot pay with an ETP or SIA, the IRS will likely file a tax lien.

7. *Remember to ask for penalty abatement at the end of the plan*: one important end of payment plan action is to request abatement of the failure to pay penalty. Taxpayers should consider using first-time abatement or reasonable cause abatement if they qualify.

Chapter 8:

FULL-PAY NON-STREAMLINED INSTALLMENT AGREEMENT PLAN (OWE BETWEEN $50,000 AND $250,000)

The section covers the full-pay non-streamlined payment plan for taxpayers who owe between $50,000 and $250,000. However, taxpayers who owe less than $50,000 should consider the terms of the simple installment agreement to avoid a tax lien filing.

Topic	Covers
Overview of the Full-pay Non-streamlined Installment Agreement	Explanation of the non-streamlined installment agreement.
Full-pay Non-streamlined Installment Agreement Payment Plan Terms, Conditions, and Minimum Payment Amount	Terms to qualify and how to determine the minimum payment amount for the full-pay non-streamlined installment agreement plan.
Steps to Obtain a Full-pay Non-Streamlined Installment Agreement	How to obtain a full-pay non-streamlined installment agreement with a practice example.

Key Highlights:

- The full-pay non-streamlined Installment Agreement (NSIA) payment plan collection alternative is an IRS payment plan that began in 2020. Many taxpayers and tax pros are still unaware of the full-pay NSIA alternative. It replaced the 84-month payment plan for taxpayers who owed between $50,000-$100,000 in 2020. The NSIA changed the payment period from 84 months to the collection statute expiration date (CSED). The NSIA also expanded the amount owed from $50,000-$100,000 under the old 84-month agreement to amounts between $50,000 and $250,000 under the new NSIA terms.

- Recent changes to the streamlined installment agreement (SLIA) to the simple installment agreement (SIA) altered the full pay NSIA. The full-pay NSIA previously could be used if the taxpayer owes less than $50,000, but does not meet/want the old SLIA terms. However, on March 5, 2025, the SLIA was replaced by the new SIA. The new SIA has the same payment terms (pay before the CSED). However, unlike the full pay NSIA which applies to amounts over $50,000, the SIA does avoid a filing of a tax lien.

- Only the IRS Automated Collection System function can enter into the NSIA plan. The NSIA plan is not available to taxpayers assigned to the Collection Field function. Also, taxpayers cannot use the IRS' Online Payment Agreement to obtain a full pay NSIA.

Chapter 8.01: Overview of the Full-pay Non-streamlined Installment Agreement

On October 1, 2016, the IRS initiated a pilot program where taxpayers who owe between $50,000 and $100,000 can quickly set up a payment plan over 84 months. This pilot was referred to as the "Streamlined Processing for Balances Owed Between $50,000-$100,000, 84-month" payment plan or "expanded IA payment plan." [IRM 5.19.1.2.6.4.3 at (3) (2-2-2021)] The 84-month installment agreement was discontinued in March 2020 by the IRS. [IRM Procedural Update SBSE 05-0320-0413 (3-11-2020)]

The IRS replaced the 84-month agreement by expanding the terms and making the non-streamlined installment agreement (NSIA) more accessible to taxpayers. Compared to the old 84-month agreement, the NSIA expanded the ceiling on the assessed amount owed from $100,000 to $250,000. The NSIA also changed the time to pay from 84 months to the number of months remaining before the collection statute expiration date (CSED). Taxpayers who can full-pay their liability before the CSED can more easily set up a payment plan without having to provide a detailed financial disclosure and proof of their ability to pay. They also do not have to liquidate assets for the full pay NSIA.

The NSIA payment plan is simple to set up. However, the NSIA plan differs from the other IRS simple payment plans (the GIA and SIA). Taxpayers who obtain this installment agreement will have a Notice of Federal Tax Lien filed. [IRM 5.19.1.6.4 at (11) (1-26-2023)]Procedural Update SBSE 05-0320-0413 (3-11-2020)]

> **Pro Tip:** A taxpayer who will be harmed by a tax lien should consider paying the assessed amount to bring it under $50,000 and obtaining the SIA, which avoids the tax lien filing. Taxpayers who want to avoid a lien will need to act before the IRS makes a lien determination. Taxpayers can get an extension to pay in order to pay the assessed amount to bring the assessed balance under $50,000 and enter into an SIA.

The NSIA payment terms depend on the time period for the IRS to collect (i.e., the CSED). This is especially true for older tax debt, where the CSED is imminent. In an NSIA, the taxpayer must full-pay the balance before the CSED expires.

> **Pro Tip:** If a taxpayer has an older year with an imminent CSED, he should consider paying off that year to get the more favorable payment terms over the maximum period. Taxpayers can pay off a year by designating a voluntary lump-sum payment for a year.

Chapter 8.02: Full-pay Non-streamlined Installment Agreement Payment Plan Terms, Conditions, and Minimum Payment Amount

Individual taxpayers can use the full-pay non-streamlined installment agreement (NSIA) plan if the assessed balance owed is between $50,000 and $250,000. Taxpayers who owe less than $50,000 will use the SIA to avoid a tax lien. The SIA has the same payment terms as the NSIA (pay until CSED). Taxpayers may pay by direct debit or payroll agreement. If the taxpayer is unable to pay with automatic payments, they are still eligible for the NSIA payment terms. All NSIAs are made through IRS Automated Collection System campus locations (not allowed in local IRS collection offices).

> **Pro Tip:** To provide COVID-19 relief to taxpayers, the IRS's Taxpayer Relief Initiative allowed individual taxpayers who only owe for the 2019 tax year and owe less than $250,000 to qualify to set up a full-pay NSIA without a Notice of Federal Tax Lien filed by the IRS. The taxpayer must enter into the agreement before a CP504 notice is issued to the taxpayer in order to qualify.

Taxpayers requesting a full-pay NSIA will receive a preliminary approval by the IRS ACS agent. The full-pay NSIA must be approved by an IRS manager. [IRM 5.19.1.6.4.1 at (11) (1-26-2023)] The IRS will send a letter in 14 days informing the taxpayer of the approval/disapproval. [IRM 5.19.1.6.4.8 at (6) (7-9-2024)] Letter 2273C will be issued to explain any rejection of the request with the items needed to correct the request.

On January 30, 2023, the IRS changed the terms for the full-pay NSIA for those who have a levy or have passport restrictions. In these cases, the IRS required a Collection Financial Statement in order to enter into the full-pay NSIA. [IRM 5.19.1.6.4.1 at (11) (1-26-2023)]

> **Pro Tip:** In many cases, taxpayers will have a passport restriction (CP508C notice) if they owe more than $64,000 and have been in IRS collection for enforcement. It is important for the taxpayers to quickly get into a full-pay NSIA if they want to avoid providing detailed financial information to obtain this favorable agreement.

Computing the NSIA Payment Amount

The NSIA payment terms require that the taxpayer pay the entire balance owed, including any accrued penalties and interest, before the CSED. In order to obtain the NSIA payment amount, the taxpayer should contact IRS Collection to obtain the IRS-calculated payment amount. [IRM 5.19.1.6.4 at (11) (1-26-2023)] The IRS can calculate the payment required to satisfy the total balance, including penalty and interest accruals, before the CSED. The IRS will continue to use the taxpayer's future refunds to offset the balances owed.

> **Pro Tip:** The NSIA procedures for taxpayers who will pay in full before the CSED are unknown to some IRS Collection employees. The IRS has some challenges, including many taxpayers experiencing questionable monthly payment amount calculations from IRS systems. Taxpayers should be prepared to go through the calculation of the required monthly payment amount with IRS collection representatives before agreeing to a payment amount. If necessary, involve the IRS collection representative's manager if the payment amount appears to be incorrectly excessive.

There is not a set formula to compute the NSIA-required monthly payment amount. The taxpayer must anticipate that the monthly payment amount will include the projected total balance owed before the CSED, including accrued penalties and interest.

> **Example-** Tony owes the IRS $75,000. He has 75 months remaining on this debt before the CSED. If Tony only paid $1,000 a month (his current balance over 75 months), he would fail to pay any penalty and interest. When contacting the IRS, he learns that his payment will be $1,250 to account for projected future penalties and interest on the unpaid balance.

Chapter 8.03: Steps to Obtain a Full-pay Non-streamlined Installment Agreement

After the taxpayer confirms that she qualifies for the NSIA, she must contact the IRS Automated Collection System unit to secure the NSIA. The Collection Field function (revenue officers) is unable to enroll taxpayers in the NSIA payment option. [IRM 5.19.1.6.4 at (11) (1-26-2023)] IRS ACS employees may take the Collection Information Statement information by phone when setting up the NSIA plan.

The steps to obtain an NSIA appear below.

Steps	Action	How to Do
1	Confirm that the taxpayer meets the conditions for the NSIA.	Meets these conditions: • Total assessed balance is between $50,000 and $250,000. • Taxpayer is not assigned to the Collection Field function (i.e., local IRS collection office and assigned to a revenue officer). • All required returns have been filed (i.e., last six years). • Taxpayer will not owe for future years (has adequate current withholding and/or estimated tax payments). • If the taxpayer has a levy or passport restrictions, obtain a collection information statement (Form

		433A or F) prior to the call.
2	Compute payment amount.	Contact IRS collection to obtain minimum payment (i.e., projected total balance/months remaining before CSED). The payment should be at least this amount. *Note:* Review the IRS-calculated payment amount for reasonableness. If the amount appears unreasonable, consider requesting intervention from the IRS employee's manager.
3	Complete direct debit or payroll deduction information or submit the appropriate Collection Information Statement.	To avoid potential default, complete direct debit information (Form 433-D) or payroll deduction information (Form 2159). If the taxpayer has prior compliance issues and/or a levy or passport restrictions, they may have to provide a Collection Information Statement to the IRS. Complete the appropriate Collection Information Statement (Form 433 (A or F)). Be advised that the taxpayer will receive a Notice of Federal Tax Lien. The taxpayer can provide the Form 433 information directly to the IRS collection person if securing the NSIA by phone.

4	Contact IRS automated collection and request the NSIA.	By mail:
		
		1. Complete IRS Form 433-D, *Installment Agreement*. Add the direct debit information to the Form 433-D or include Form 2159 (if the taxpayer is making automatic payments via a payroll deduction information).
		2. Form 433-D should reflect the minimum or greater payment amount.
		3. Mail to IRS.
		
		By phone:
		
		1. All requests must be to IRS Automated Collection System:
		    a. Wage earner taxpayers: call 800-829-7650.
		    b. Self-employed taxpayers (file Schedule C, E, F, or Form 2106): call 800-829-3903.

		2. Send the <u>Form 433-D</u> by fax to the IRS collection representative for the direct debit agreement (Form 2159 for a payroll deduction).
5	Confirm the agreement is setup.	Receipt of IRS Letter 2273C, *Installment Agreement Accepted*, or its equivalent. • If the taxpayer does not receive this notice, she should contact the IRS immediately by phone and confirm if the agreement has been granted or re-request as needed.

Example- Cort owes $201,000 for 2021 as of August 1, 2023. The assessed balance is $184,000. The collection statute expiration date (CSED) is 106 months. The taxes owed on investment income in those two years is related to gain on the sale of stock. Cort will not owe for future years. Cort would like to pay by direct debit to avoid potentially missing payments and defaulting the agreement. Cort contacts the IRS and requests the minimum monthly payment to pay the total balance in full before the CSED. The IRS provides Cort with a payment of $2,375 a month as a minimum payment. Cort prepares and sends the <u>Form 433-D</u>, which includes his direct debit information, and faxes it to the IRS while setting up the agreement on the phone. Three weeks later, Cort receives a Letter 2273C from the IRS confirming the payment arrangement of $2,375 a month, starting on the 28th of the following month and continuing each month thereafter, until the balance is paid in full.

Form **433-D** (August 2022)	Department of the Treasury - Internal Revenue Service # Installment Agreement *(See Instructions on the back of this page)*

Name and address of taxpayer(s)	Social Security or Employer Identification Number (SSN/EIN)
Cort Taxpayer 123 Iwoe St Debttown, NC 27777	*(Taxpayer)* 000-00-0000 *(Spouse)*
	Your telephone numbers *(including area code)* *(Home)* *(Work, cell or business)* 336-555-1212
	For assistance, call: **1-800-829-3903 (Individual - Self-Employed/Business Owners, Businesses), or** **1-800-829-7650 (Individuals - Wage Earners)**

☐ Submit a new Form W-4 to your employer to increase your withholding.	Or write _____ *(City, State, and ZIP Code)*

Kinds of taxes *(form numbers)*	Tax periods	Amount owed as of 8/1/2023
1040	2021	$ 201,000

I / We agree to pay the federal taxes shown above, PLUS PENALTIES AND INTEREST PROVIDED BY LAW, as follows

$ 2375 _____ on 9/28/2023 _____ and $ 2375 _____ on the 28th _____ of each month thereafter

I / We also agree to increase or decrease the above installment payments as follows:

Date of increase *(or decrease)*	Amount of increase *(or decrease)*	New installment payment amount

The terms of this agreement are provided on the back of this page. Please review them thoroughly.

CT	By initialing here and my signature below, I agree to the terms of this agreement, as provided in this form, if it is approved by the Internal Revenue Service.

Additional Conditions / Terms *(To be completed by IRS)*	By signing and submitting this form, I authorize the IRS to contact third parties and to disclose my tax information to third parties in order to process and administer this agreement over its duration.

DIRECT DEBIT — Attach a voided check or complete this part only if you choose to make payments by direct debit. Read the instructions on the back of this page.

a. Routing number | 1 | 1 | 1 | 1 | 1 | 1 | 1 | 1 | 1 |

b. Account number | 1 | 1 | 1 | 1 | 1 | 1 | 1 | 1 | 1 | 1 | 1 | 1 | 1 | 1 | 1 | 1 | 1 | 1 |

I authorize the U.S. Treasury and its designated Financial Agent to initiate a monthly ACH debit (electronic withdrawal) entry to the financial institution account indicated for payments of my federal taxes owed, and the financial institution to debit the entry to this account. This authorization is to remain in full force and effect until I notify the Internal Revenue Service to terminate the authorization. If I wish to stop payment under my direct debit installment agreement, I may do so by contacting my financial institution either orally or in writing at least three (3) business days before the next scheduled electronic funds transfer. Alternatively, if there are at least fourteen (14) business days before the next scheduled electronic funds transfer, I may contact the Internal Revenue Service at the applicable toll-free number listed above. I also authorize the financial institutions involved in the processing of the electronic payments of taxes to receive confidential information necessary to answer inquiries and resolve issues related to the payments.

Debit Payments Self-Identifier

If you are unable to make electronic payments through a debit instrument (debit payments) by providing your banking information in a. and b. above, please check the box below:

☐ I am unable to make debit payments

Note: Not checking this box indicates that you are able but choosing not to make debit payments. See Instructions to Taxpayer below for more details.

Your signature	Date	Title *(if Corporate Officer or Partner)*	Spouse's signature *(if a joint liability)*	Date

FOR IRS USE ONLY

AGREEMENT LOCATOR NUMBER: __ __ __ __

Check the appropriate boxes:

☐ RSI "1" no further review	☐ AI "0" Not a PPIA
☐ RSI "5" PPIA IMF 2 year review	☐ AI "1" Field Asset PPIA
☐ RSI "6" PPIA BMF 2 year review	☐ AI "2" All other PPIAs

Agreement Review Cycle __ __ __ __ __ __ Earliest CSED _____

☐ Check box if pre-assessed modules included

Originator's ID number _____ Originator Code _____

Name _____ Title _____

A NOTICE OF FEDERAL TAX LIEN *(Check one box below)*

☐ **HAS ALREADY BEEN FILED**

☐ **WILL BE FILED IMMEDIATELY**

☐ **WILL BE FILED WHEN TAX IS ASSESSED**

☐ **MAY BE FILED IF THIS AGREEMENT DEFAULTS**

NOTE: A NOTICE OF FEDERAL TAX LIEN WILL NOT BE FILED ON ANY PORTION OF YOUR LIABILITY WHICH REPRESENTS AN INDIVIDUAL SHARED RESPONSIBILITY PAYMENT UNDER THE AFFORDABLE CARE ACT.

Agreement examined or approved by *(Signature, title, function)*	Date

Catalog Number 16644M www.irs.gov Form **433-D** (Rev. 8-2022)

Part 1 — IRS Copy

Chapter 9:
DETERMINING ABILITY TO PAY FOR IRS COLLECTION OPTIONS

This section explains the ability to pay agreements and how to determine a taxpayer's ability to pay using equity in assets and monthly income.

Topic	Covers
IRS Ability to Pay Agreements	Types of IRS ability to pay agreements and the two components of a taxpayer's ability to pay.
Key Terms for ATP	IRS terms used in determining a taxpayer's ability to pay.
ATP Analysis Determines Available Collection Options	How the ATP analysis determines which collection option(s) are available to resolve the balance owed.
ATP Components and IRS Collection Options	How equity, assets and monthly income are computed to determine each ATP collection option.
ATP Financial Disclosure to the IRS	Required forms and documentation by the IRS for ATP determinations.
Ability to Pay Component #1: Equity in Assets	Guidance to determine ATP using equity in assets, including: • Assets included in ATP agreements. • Jointly held assets with non-liable persons. • Income-producing assets for ATP IA and CNC. • Income-producing assets for an OIC. • Valuing a business as a going concern for an OIC. • Equity in assets for ability to pay installment agreement/currently not collectible status. • Equity in assets: offer in compromise. • Dissipated assets. • Worksheets for determining equity in assets for ATP agreements.
Ability to Pay Component #2: Monthly Disposable Income	Guidance to determine ATP through monthly income, including: • Components of MDI. • Determining average household income. • Determining average living expenses. • Shared expenses with non-liable persons. • MDI Analysis Worksheet (for determining ability to

	pay for installment agreements, CNC, and OIC-DATC). • Forms 433-A and 433-A (OIC) MDI Computation Worksheet. • Self-employed and rental income taxpayers. • Forms 433-A and 433-A(OIC): Net Business Income Analysis for Ability to Pay Calculation Worksheet. • Applying IRS Collection Financial Standards. • Applying CSED to ATP determinations: CNC and installment agreements. • Applying CSED for OIC-DATC. • Worksheets for determining MDI for ATP agreements.
Determining Total Ability to Pay: CNC and the ATP IA, and the OIC-DATC	Completing the computation of total ability to pay from both components: equity in assets and MDI for: • CNC and ATP IAs. • OIC-DATC ability to pay (qualification) and reasonable collection potential (offer amount). • OIC-DATC Worksheets.
ATP Examples	References to links to view examples of an ATP calculation for an ATP IA, CNC, and the OIC-DATC.

Key Highlights:

- If a taxpayer is unable to pay with an extension to pay or a simple IRS payment plan, their collection option will be determined by their ability to pay.
- The goal of an ability to pay determination is to understand how much the taxpayer can pay the IRS with current assets and future income.
- The ability to pay calculation determines the amount that can be paid using equity in assets and monthly disposable income. The IRS has specific rules that are used in determining ability to pay.
- The ability to pay calculation for an Offer in Compromise–Doubt as to Collectibility is more complicated than the computation for currently not collectible and ability to pay installment agreements. The IRS has special rules for determining ability to pay for an OIC-DATC, including additional computations of the reasonable collection potential (offer amount) for an OIC.
- If a higher debt taxpayer can full-pay the amount owed, plus accrued penalties and interest, before the collection statute expiration date(s), the taxpayer should consider the full-pay non-streamlined installment agreement, which avoids the ability to pay calculation and asset liquidation.

Chapter 9.01: IRS Ability to Pay Agreements

When taxpayers are unable to qualify or utilize the extensions to pay or the simple installment agreements as a collection alternative, they will determine their best option by analyzing their ability to pay. A taxpayer's ability to pay is calculated by applying the IRS's collection financial analysis rules to a taxpayer's financial situation. [IRM 5.15.1 (financial analysis rules for ability to pay agreements) and IRM 5.8.5 (specific financial analysis rules for an offer in compromise)] Once a taxpayer knows his ability to pay, according to the IRS rules, he can determine which collection option is best.

Taxpayers may conclude that it is in their best interest to use their existing assets to pay down the balance owed and enter into a simple or non-streamlined installment agreement. Both the simple installment agreement and full-pay non-streamlined installment agreement, which pays the total balance before the collection statute expiration date, can avoid the detailed financial disclosure required for all other ability to pay agreements. [IRM 5.19.1.2.6.4.2 (2-2-2021) and IRM 5.19.1.2.6.4.3 (2-2-2021)] The ability to pay analysis may also conclude that the taxpayer should utilize another option including one of the following ability to pay alternatives:

- Routine ATP, conditional, or a partial pay installment agreement.
- Currently not collectible status.
- Offer in compromise, doubt as to collectibility.

There are two components of the taxpayer's ability to pay:

1. *Equity in assets*: the taxpayer's assets less liabilities. For ATP agreements other than the OIC, the IRS will want the taxpayer to use assets to pay the liability. For an OIC, the taxpayer will compute the net realizable equity in assets to determine if he qualifies for an OIC and whether this can be included in any offer amount. [IRM 5.14.1.4 at (5) (7-2-2024)]
2. *Monthly disposable income*: the amount the taxpayer can pay in monthly payments to the IRS after allowing for necessary living expenses. [IRM 5.14.1.4 at (4a) (7-2-2024)]

The IRS rules for determining ability to pay are found in the Internal Revenue Manual and IRS.gov. These resources include:

Ability to pay help with:	Found at:	Updated:
Ability to pay financial analysis	IRM 5.15.1 (Collection Field function)	November 22, 2021
	IRM 5.19.13 (ACS)	March 21, 2025
Financial analysis: special rules for OICs	IRM 5.8.5	April 8, 2024

Financial analysis for CNC	IRM 5.16.1	March 3, 2025
IRS Collection Financial Standards (provides limits and allowances for certain living expenses)	IRS.gov at: https://www.irs.gov/businesses/small-businesses-self-employed/collection-financial-standards	Updated annually, usually in late March or April
Property exempt from levy (for help in determining ability to pay from equity in assets) and exemption for tools of trade	Updated annually—2025 amounts found at Revenue Procedure 2024-40, section 3.50	Updated annually in November

Chapter 9.02: Key Terms for ATP

The following terms are commonly used in ATP calculations and agreements.

Term	Definition
Ability to pay (ATP)	The taxpayer's equity in assets and future monthly payments that can be used to pay a tax balance owed.
Ability to pay installment agreement (ATP IA)	An IRS payment plan in which the taxpayer must provide a financial disclosure and proof of ability to pay. Required when the taxpayer cannot pay according to the terms for a guaranteed, streamlined, or non-streamlined installment agreement (in which the taxpayer can pay in full before the collection statute expires) payment plan.
Average monthly household income	Used in determining MDI. The average gross income received from in the household from all sources.
Average monthly household living expenses	Used in determining MDI. The average of the total actual household expenses. Expenses are separated into two categories: necessary living expenses or expenses necessary to produce income, and other expenses that are not considered necessary.
Collection Information Statement	IRS form (Form 433 series) used to disclose the taxpayer's financial information to determine ability to pay.
Collection statute expiration date (CSED)	The last day in which the IRS can collect on a tax balance owed. CSED is an important component in determining which collection option is appropriate in an ability to pay determination.
Currently not collectible (CNC)	A temporary status where the taxpayer does not have to pay the IRS in monthly installment payments because he does not have the ability to pay. CNC requires that the taxpayer provide proof (financial disclosure) of the inability to pay.

Dissipated asset	Used in an OIC financial analysis. An asset sold, transferred, encumbered, or otherwise disposed of in an attempt to avoid the payment of the tax liability. Also includes assets or proceeds used (other than wages, salary, or other income) for other than the payment of items necessary for the production of income or the health and welfare of the taxpayer or his family, after the tax has been assessed or during a period of up to six months prior to or after the tax assessment.
Equity in assets	The taxpayer's assets less liabilities that can be used to pay the IRS in a lump sum payment or in an offer in compromise. Generally, the IRS looks at each asset individually to determine the amount that can be used to pay the balance owed.
Fair market value (FMV)	The value of an asset as determined by what a willing buyer will pay to a willing seller.
Financial disclosure	Financial information, including IRS Form 433 series and financial documents, provided to the IRS to determine the taxpayer's ability to pay.
Income averaging	Used in determining monthly disposable income. Methods to determine the taxpayer's average monthly household income. The proper income averaging method is based on what method best reflects the taxpayer's future income.
Income-producing asset	A taxpayer's asset that is used to generate income. These assets are generally exempt from collection and ATP determinations.
IRS Collection Financial Standards (CFS)	Used in determining the expenses allowed in computing monthly disposable income in ATP agreements. Also called allowable living expense (ALE) standards. The IRS limits placed on certain necessary living expenses. The limitations are based on the taxpayer's location and/or family size.
Monthly disposable income (MDI) for an installment agreement	The amount of disposable income each month (gross income less all allowable expenses) that is available to pay monthly toward the balance owed in the form of an installment agreement.
Monthly disposable income (MDI) for an OIC	The amount of disposable income each month (gross income less all allowable expenses) that is reflective of the taxpayer's future income for an OIC qualification and offer amount calculations. The MDI calculation for the OIC offer amount (reasonable collection potential) has a few differences (additional allowable expenses) compared to other MDI calculations for ATP agreements and OIC qualification computations.
Necessary living expenses	Expenses that are necessary to provide for a taxpayer's and his or her family's health and welfare and/or production of income.
Net realizable equity in assets (NRE)	In an OIC, assets are valued at net realizable equity (NRE). Net realizable equity is defined as the quick sale value (QSV) less

	amounts owed to secured lien holders with priority over the federal tax lien, if applicable, and applicable exemption amounts. NRE differs in an OIC for the qualification and offer amount computations as the IRS allows additional asset exclusions in computing the offer amount.
Offer in Compromise–Doubt as to Collectibility (OIC-DATC)	A settlement of a taxpayer's tax bill for less than the amount owed. Requires that the taxpayer prove that he cannot pay with net equity in assets and future income. There are specific ability to pay calculations for determining qualification for an OIC-DATC and the amount of an acceptable offer to settle the balance owed.
Other household expenses	Actual household expenses that may be allowed in determining MDI depending on the taxpayer's circumstances and collection options selected.
Quick sale value (QSV)	Used in an OIC financial analysis to value assets to determine net realizable equity in assets. QSV is defined as an estimate of the price a seller could get for the asset in a situation where financial pressures motivate the owner to sell in a short period of time, usually 90 calendar days or less.
Reasonable collection potential (RCP)	Also referred to as the offer amount in an OIC. The calculation of the taxpayer's net realizable equity in assets and future income that the IRS can reasonably collect in an offer in compromise. RCP becomes the amount that the taxpayer offers in an OIC to settle the tax bill. The IRS provides the rules for determining RCP.
Shared expenses	A factor used in computing monthly disposable income. Situations in which the liable taxpayer shares household living expenses with a non-liable person (spouse, partner, roommate). The non-liable person's income and expenses are considered in determining the liable person's ability to pay.

Chapter 9.03: ATP Analysis Determines Available Collection Options

The taxpayer's ATP determines which collection options are available to them to resolve their balance owed. Extension to pay (ETP), simple IAs (guaranteed and simple installment agreements), and the full-pay non-streamlined IA (when the taxpayer can pay in full before the CSED expires) do not require ATP determinations. The only calculation involves determining the payment over the term of the agreement, or within the CSED, whichever is lower.

However, when a taxpayer cannot utilize the ETP, simple IAs, or the full-pay non-streamlined IA payment plan, they must execute an "ATP agreement." Because these agreements are not simple or "streamlined" to set up, the ATP agreements are often referred to as "non-streamlined installment agreements" or "NSIA." The specific ATP agreements and their criteria are as follows:

ATP Agreement type	ATP conclusion	Taxpayer result
Routine ATP IA	Taxpayer can fully pay before the CSED expires with assets and MDI.	A payment plan that only allows the taxpayer necessary living expenses.
Conditional IA	Taxpayer can fully pay with assets and MDI in six years and before the CSED expires. *Note:* The routine and conditional IAs will be used less because the full-pay non-streamlined installment agreement rules allow payment until the CSED.	A payment plan where the taxpayer can use actual household expenses up to the amount that allows payment in six years. Can be used in a "tiered" or "lifestyle adjustment" IA to lower the first-year payments to allow the taxpayer a lower payment in year 1 in order to adjust their expenses for future higher payments in years 2-6.
Partial-pay installment agreement (PPIA)	Taxpayer has MDI and can make monthly payments, but the amount of the payment will not fully pay the liability before the CSED expires.	Monthly payment plan that allows only necessary living expenses. The IRS will re-evaluate the arrangement every two years.
Currently not collectible status (CNC)	Taxpayer cannot currently pay with monthly installment payments. MDI is $25 or less.	Temporary non-payment status.
Offer in Compromise– Doubt as to Collectibility (OIC-DATC)	Taxpayer cannot full-pay the liability with net realizable equity in assets and future payments (MDI) before the CSED expires.	Taxpayer will settle based on their "reasonable collection potential" calculated offer amount.

Taxpayers who are unable to pay for the tax liability before the CSED expires (i.e., who qualify for CNC or a PPIA) may also qualify for an OIC-DATC - especially if they have little or no assets. If the ATP calculation concludes PPIA or CNC is appropriate, the taxpayer should always evaluate the OIC as a collection alternative.

Example- Bryan owes the IRS back taxes. His financial situation is as follows:

- Total tax liability: $50,000
- Net realizable equity in assets: $5,000 (none can be accessed or used to pay in an installment agreement)

- MDI: $200 (necessary expenses only — assume MDI is the same for IA and OIC calculations)
- Months remaining on collection statute: 72 months

Bryan has two collection options.

Option #1: PPIA of $200 a month for 72 months, subject to re-evaluation every two years:

ATP Example: ATP concludes PPIA – taxpayer will pay $200 a month for 72 months			
ATP Calculation	**ATP – Installment Agreement (PPIA)**	**Amount paid before CSED (72 months)**	**Assumptions**
Net realizable equity in assets	$5,000	0	Assume taxpayer cannot access equity.
MDI	$200	$14,400	Taxpayer's financial situation does not change.

Based on the above facts, Bryan's payment plan will be a PPIA of $200 a month, projected for 72 months. Assuming Bryan's financial situation will not change, the IRS is projected not to collect the full amount of the tax owed ($50,000) before the expiration of the CSED (payment is $200 a month for 72 months or $14,400). Note: the IRS can review Bryan's ability to pay every 2 years and ask for a different payment amount from assets and MDI.

In total, Bryan's ability to pay is $19,400 ($5,000 net realizable equity in assets plus the remaining installment payments of $14,400). Note: the example assumes that net realizable equity in assets and MDI are the same for qualification and the offer amount, which is not likely. We assume the same amount in this example for simplicity of analysis.

ATP Example: ATP concludes qualification for an OIC – amount to settle is $7,400	
OIC Qualification: Bryan qualifies for an OIC because he currently is not projected to have the ATP his total balance owed before the expiration of the CSED	
OIC Qualification	**Qualification Calculation**
Net realizable equity in assets (1)	$5,000
MDI	$200
Collection statute (expires in 72 months)	72 months
Future income = MDI × months remaining on collection statute (2)	$14,400
Ability to pay before CSED (1) + (2)	$19,400
IRS balance owed	$50,000
Qualification	YES (ATP < tax owed)

OIC Offer Amount: Bryan can offer $7,400 to settle his balances owed (assumes taxpayer selected OIC lump-sum payment method which only requires the taxpayer to pay 12 months of MDI)	
OIC Offer Amount Calculation	**Lump Sum Offer Amount**
Net realizable equity in assets (1)	$5,000
MDI	$200
Future income multiplier for IRS RCP offer amount	12 months
RCP Future income (2)	$2,400
Offer amount to settle (RCP) (1) + (2)	$7,400

Because Bryan's total current ATP is not projected to pay off the amount owed before the expiration of the CSED, he qualifies for an OIC. His reasonable collection potential (offer amount to settle his tax bill) would be $7,400 for a lump-sum method OIC ($5,000 net realizable equity in assets plus the MDI of $200 for 12 months using the OIC lump-sum payment method future income multiplier to determine RCP).

To explore this topic in greater depth, see **Chapter 12: Qualify and Obtain an Offer in Compromise for Doubt as to Collectibility (OIC-DATC).**

Bryan has two options: he can choose to enter into a PPIA for $200 a month or request an OIC that would settle his liability for $7,400.

Chapter 9.04: ATP Components and IRS Collection Options

ETP, simple IAs, and full-pay non-streamlined IAs do not require ATP determinations. However, the other collection alternatives are all based on the taxpayer's ATP including assets and monthly disposable income (MDI). ATP determinations are different for each collection option:

Collection Options: Asset Equity Considerations and ATP Computation Components			
Collection Option	**Amount Owed**	**ATP: Equity in Assets**	**ATP: MDI Computation**
Extension to pay	Any amount	Not applicable. Taxpayer does not have to use assets to pay balances owed.	None
Simple IAs – GIA and SIA	$50,000 or less in assessed balances owed	Not applicable. Taxpayers are not required to use assets to pay the balance owed.	None — taxpayer opts out of ATP and pays over GIA (36 months) or SLIA (pay until CSED) term.
Full-pay non-streamlined installment	$50,000 to $250,000 in	Generally, not applicable. Taxpayers are not required to	None — taxpayer opts out of ATP and pays total amount before CSED.

agreement (NSIA) payment plan	assessed balance owed	use assets to pay the balance owed. May have asset review if levy or passport restriction is in place.	
Routine ATP IA	Any amount owed	Yes, IRS may want the taxpayer to use assets to pay if taxpayer's IA requires payment over more than six years.	MDI will determine amount to be paid in an installment agreement to the IRS. Routine IA MDI payments will pay the IRS before the CSED expires. Only taxpayer's necessary living expenses are allowed and are limited by the IRS Collection Financial Standards.
Conditional IA	Any amount owed	Taxpayer may have to access equity. IRS will press for taxpayer to pay with available assets for higher amounts owed and for taxpayers who have defaulted on prior agreements.	MDI will determine amount to be paid in an installment agreement to the IRS. Conditional IA MDI payments will pay the IRS within six years, or the term of the CSED, whichever is earlier. Taxpayer's reasonable actual living expenses are allowed to the extent that he can pay within six years.
PPIA	Any amount owed	Yes, IRS will request taxpayer to access available equity if the equity is not needed for necessary living expenses or does not put taxpayer in economic harm.	MDI will determine amount to be paid in an installment agreement to the IRS. MDI payments will NOT pay the IRS before the CSED expires. Only taxpayer's necessary living expenses are allowed and are limited by IRS Collection Financial Standards.
CNC	Any amount owed	Not likely. The IRS may request the taxpayer to pay with available equity in	MDI will determine if the taxpayer qualifies for CNC. MDI must be $25 or less to qualify for CNC.

		assets if the assets are not needed for future necessary living expenses.	Only taxpayer's necessary living expenses are allowed and are limited by IRS Collection Financial Standards.
OIC-DATC	Any amount owed	The taxpayers net realizable equity in assets (NRE) is a component to determine if taxpayer qualifies and must be offered as part of settlement (offer) amount if not needed for future necessary living expenses. There are special rules to determine NRE for an OIC.	MDI is a component in determining whether the taxpayer qualifies for an OIC. If a taxpayer qualifies, a future number of monthly payments, determined by MDI, must be offered as a settlement amount depending on the type of OIC payment method selected. For OIC calculations, only taxpayer's necessary living expenses are allowed and are limited by IRS Collection Financial Standards. There are special rules to determine MDI for an OIC.

Chapter 9.05: ATP Financial Disclosure to the IRS

In ATP agreements, taxpayers will disclose their assets, liabilities, income, and expenses to the IRS on a Collection Information Statement (CIS) and supporting documentation. Taxpayers use the CIS Form 433-A, B, F, or H for ATP IAs and CNC. When requesting an OIC-DATC, taxpayers use Form 656, *Offer in Compromise*, and its specific CIS Form(s) 433-A(OIC) (individual financial disclosure) and/or 433-B(OIC) (business financial disclosure). Depending on the amount owed and the ATP agreement requested the IRS may also require supporting documentation, including, but not limited to, bank statements to support all income amounts.

> **Pro Tip:** Most wage earner taxpayers with individual income tax liabilities will use Form 433-F for ATP IAs and CNC requests. The IRS's Automated Collection System employees will take information directly from the 433-F to determine a taxpayer's ability to pay. Taxpayers calling the IRS can provide the 433-F information orally to speed up the establishment of agreements. IRS Collection Field function revenue officers generally prefer a Form 433-A when collecting from individual taxpayers. If the taxpayer has an interest in an outside business entity, revenue officers usually request a Form 433-B unless the taxpayer is agreeing to a streamlined installment agreement.

The proper Form 433 is determined by the taxpayer's source of income and ATP option requested.

Form	Used for:	Collection Option
433-A	Long form for individual and Schedule C taxpayers. Generally required if taxpayer owes higher balances, is responsible for payroll tax trust fund recovery penalty, or is assigned to a revenue officer.	ATP IA or CNC
433-B	Business entity taxpayers. Individual taxpayer may have to file Form 433-B in addition to Form 433-A to provide the IRS disclosure of closely-held business interests.	ATP IA or CNC
433-F	Short form for individual and small Schedule C taxpayers.	ATP IA or CNC
433-H	Installment Agreement Request and Collection Information Statement. Used for wage earners who owe more than $50,000 and cannot pay within the full-pay NSIA payment terms.	ATP IA (earn wages, requesting an installment agreement, and liability is greater than $50,000 and cannot pay using full- pay NSIA terms). Note: not used often and likely will be obsoleted given the new simple IA option.
433-A(OIC)	Individuals filing for an OIC. Individuals can use if they are an individual wage earner, operate or operated as a sole proprietor, a disregarded single member LLC taxed as a sole proprietor prior to 2009, or are submitting an offer on behalf of a deceased individual.	OIC-DATC or Effective Tax Administration OIC (ETA OIC)
433-B(OIC)	Businesses filing for an OIC. Use if the business is a Corporation, Partnership, LLC classified as a corporation, single member LLC taxed as a corporation, or other multi-owner/multi-member LLC.	OIC-DATC or ETA OIC

Supporting Documentation

The IRS does not have an exhaustive listing of documents needed when requesting an ATP agreement.

Taxpayers with more complex financial circumstances, higher liabilities owed, and/or are assigned to the Collection Field function receive more extensive requests for documentation to support their ability to pay.

In general, the IRS requests substantiation of assets, liabilities, income sources, and expenses if a taxpayer meets any of the following three conditions:

1. A taxpayer is requesting an ATP agreement that is projected not to be fully paid before the collection statute expires (i.e., a PPIA or CNC),
2. A taxpayer cannot pay within six years (i.e., routine IA), or
3. A taxpayer wants to settle the balance owed for less than the amount owed (OIC).

> **Pro Tip**: there are common scenarios in which financial disclosure and supporting documentation are always required, including Collection Field function (revenue officer assignment), business and payroll tax liabilities, individuals owing more than $250,000 in assessment balances, and tiered installment agreement where the payments are changing during the duration of the plan based on actual expenses.

In these cases, the IRS requests can include, but not be limited to, the following financial information and supporting documentation to substantiate each element of the taxpayer's ability to pay:

	Supporting documentation
Household assets and liabilities (real property, vehicles, personal assets, etc.).	• Third-party valuations (appraisals, online valuation tools like NADA and Kelley Blue Book for vehicles). • Loan statements with balances owed and amounts paid. • Property records, such as tax valuations. • Taxpayer listings of assets.
Cash on hand and in financial institutions. Investments. Sources of income. Payment of expenses.	• Last three months financial account statements (all accounts and all pages). • Documents to prove income received.

	• Cancelled checks/payment verification for certain expenses to prove payment.
Other investments and their values (businesses, stocks, land, rental property, intellectual property, virtual currency, etc.).	• Last three months financial account statements (all accounts and all pages).
All retirement account balances (pension, 401K, IRS, etc.).	• Last three months financial account statements (all accounts and all pages). • Social Security statements. • Retirement statements. • Cryptocurrency account statements.
List of all life insurance policies and their cash value, if any.	• Insurance policy. • Statements indicating cash value.
All recreational assets and associated liabilities (vacation homes, recreational vehicles, etc.).	• Tax records. • Appraisals and other third-party valuations.
Credit lines, with balances and available credit.	• Last three months financial account statements (all accounts and all pages).
Assets transferred or sold in past three years (real property, investments, retirement, businesses, etc.).	• Listing of asset and associated liability. • Sales/transfer documents. • Reason for transfer. • Use of proceeds.
Wage earners: Gross household income for the past three months.	• Last three months paystubs for all members of the family.
Self-employed: Profit and Loss for the past 6-12 months.	• Detailed Profit and Loss statement for the past 6-12 months. • Supporting documentation for selected expenses. • Bank statements for the past 6-12 months.

Any bonuses or income that are due to be received.	• Employment contract. • Historical and current projection of bonus to be received.
Other income (taxable and non-taxable): rental, child support, alimony, etc.	• Rental: Profit and Loss for past 6-12 months. • Court ordered payments received: court order and payment receipt.
Non-liable person(s) information.	• Paystubs with total income. • Listing of other income received. • Tax returns. • Profit/Loss statements. • Listing of expenses paid for household expenses. • Financial account statements – past three months.
Household living expenses. (housing, utilities, transportation, medical, insurance, etc.)	• Bills, receipts, and payments for last three months of household living expenses and any other allowable expenses. • Bills, receipts, and payments for any household living expenses and other allowable expenses paid on an annual basis.
Withholding and estimated tax payment made for the past year.	• Last three months paystubs. • Proof of payment for recent estimated tax payments.
State and local income taxes paid for the last year, including any installment agreement payments for back taxes owed.	• Statement of amount owed (notice). • Agreement for monthly payment amount. • Proof of payment.
Court ordered payments.	• Court order. • Proof of payment for past three months.
Student loan payments.	• Student loan statement for past three months.

	• Proof of payment.
Payments to other debts.	• Loan document. • Proof of payment. • Loan statements – last three months.
Other expenses paid (professional fees, childcare, professional fees, etc.) for the past year: include invoice, description of services performed, and payments made.	• Invoices. • Outstanding balances owed. • Description of services performed. • Proof of payments.

Pro Tip: The IRS has the discretion to request supporting documentation to determine the taxpayer's ATP. In many cases, the IRS will only request documentation for necessary living expenses that are questionable or unusual. However, in almost all ATP agreements, the IRS will ask the individual taxpayer for the last three month's statements from all financial accounts. For wage earners, the IRS will also ask for a paystub(s) that can show monthly and year-to-date earnings. The IRS will use prior tax return information and the Forms W-2/1099 on file to validate the taxpayer's income claims and to question additional sources of income. Taxpayers should always obtain their IRS wage and income transcript to review sources of income and be ready to respond to IRS inquiries regarding prior sources of income.

Supporting Documentation for OICs

When submitting an OIC, the taxpayer must submit supporting documentation with the application Form 656, *Offer in Compromise*. The minimum information to provide is listed on the Form 433-A(OIC):

- Copies of the most recent pay stub, earnings statement, etc., from each employer.
- Copies of the most recent statement for each investment and retirement account.
- Copies of the most recent statement, etc., from all other sources of income such as pensions, Social Security, rental income, interest and dividends (including any received from a related partnership, corporation, LLC, LLP, etc.), court order for child support, alimony, and rent subsidies.
- Copies of individual bank statements for the three most recent months.
- For business taxpayers, copies of the six most recent statements for each business bank account.
- Copies of the most recent statement from lender(s) on loans such as mortgages, second mortgages, vehicles, etc., showing monthly payments, loan payoffs, and balances.
- List of accounts and notes receivable, if applicable.

- Verification of delinquent state/local tax liability and amount of monthly payments, if applicable.
- Copies of Trust documents, if applicable.
- Documentation to support any special circumstances described in the "Explanation of Circumstances" on Form 656, if applicable.

For OICs, the taxpayer may consider submitting additional documentation to provide the OIC examiner a full picture of the ability to pay and reasonable collection potential. Taxpayers can also speed up the process by attaching applicable tax returns, credit reports, and third-party documentation that support their case and provides the OIC examiner evidence of their ability to pay.

For a listing of information that should be provided in an OIC application, see **Chapter 12: Qualify and Obtain an Offer in Compromise for Doubt as to Collectibility (OIC-DATC).**

During an OIC investigation, the OIC examiner may request additional documentation on assets, liabilities, income, and expenses in order to determine a taxpayer's ability to pay and future reasonable collection potential. The taxpayer should always respond promptly to avoid IRS rejection of the OIC due to non-response by the taxpayer.

During IRS collection investigations of a taxpayer's ATP (including OICs), the taxpayer may need to provide new ATP supporting information when the financial information is older than 12 months and it appears that significant changes have occurred in the taxpayer's financial status. [IRM 5.15.1.2 at (5) (11-22-2021) for ATP agreements and IRM 5.8.5.3 at (2) (9-24-2021) for OICs]

Chapter 9.06: Ability to Pay Component #1: Equity in Assets

In IRS ATP collection options, the taxpayer's assets are an important component of collectibility. For IA and CNC status, the IRS will request that the taxpayer pay with available asset equity first only when the taxpayer does not need the assets for necessary living expenses or to produce income. For an OIC, the taxpayer's net realizable equity in assets (less specific allowed exclusions) must be offered as part of the settlement unless that taxpayer is requesting an OIC for Doubt as to Collectibility for Special Circumstances of an OIC for Effective Tax Administration.

The OIC collection alternative calculation of ATP differs slightly from that involved where taxpayers are seeking an installment agreement or currently not collectible status. For an IA or CNC, the process of reviewing equity in assets is to determine if a taxpayer can access those assets to pay off or lower the amount owed without creating economic harm to the taxpayer. For an OIC, the taxpayer and the IRS need to know the taxpayer's net realizable equity in assets for purposes of determining whether the taxpayer qualifies for an OIC and, if so, the amount to be offered as a settlement. In an OIC, the IRS will apply special rules to determine which assets are to be included and what expenses are allowed in determining whether a taxpayer qualifies for the OIC. These special allowances are also reflected in the amount that the taxpayer has to offer to settle the tax liability.

> **Pro Tip:** In OICs, the IRS seeks to understand the taxpayer's ability to pay for two reasons: to determine if she qualifies for the OIC and to determine the settlement (offer) amount. Taxpayers who project not to pay the IRS in full before the CSED expires should always do separate ATP calculations for qualification for an OIC and computation of the amount that would be needed to settle their debt. The OIC calculation differs from the IA and CNC calculation and is likely to show less equity in assets and MDI because the IRS allows certain exemptions in the asset and MDI calculations that are not allowed in the IA and CNC ATP calculations. For example, the taxpayer is allowed an equity exclusion of $3,450 for each motor vehicle in determining the OIC offer amount. This amount is not allowed in the OIC qualification calculation. [IRM 5.8.5.12 at (3) (9-24-2021)]

Assets Included in ATP Agreements

In all ATP agreements, the taxpayer must disclose her assets to the IRS on a Collection Information Statement (Form 433-A, B, F, or H). All taxpayer assets, with their related liabilities, must be disclosed, including assets that are owned or effectively owned but are outside of the reach of the government.

These assets include, but are not limited to, the following: [IRS Form 433-A and F]

Asset (domestic and foreign):	Includes:
Cash	All cash on hand and in financial accounts; this includes cryptocurrency accounts.
Cash equivalents	Amounts held on payment cards or in other merchant accounts, such as PayPal.
Investments	Stocks and bonds, business interests in non-publicly traded companies, and other investments.
Retirement accounts	Qualified and nonqualified pensions, IRAs, annuities, and other retirement assets.
Life insurance	Cash value.
Real estate	Home, vacation property, other property held.
Vehicles and recreational assets	Cars, trucks, motorcycles, and boats.
Valuable items	Artwork, jewelry, collectibles, items kept in a safety deposit box, etc.
Personal items	Furniture and other personal effects (personal assets up to $11,390 (for 2024, adjusted annually) in value are not included in asset equity for OIC offer amount purposes).
Business assets	Cash and cash equivalents, office equipment, property, vehicles, machinery, inventory, accounts/notes receivable, and other assets.

Potential future assets	Beneficiary to a trust, estate, or life insurance policy. Party to a lawsuit.
Dissipated assets/assets outside the reach of the government	Assets disposed of in last three years. Assets transferred in last ten years for less than FMV. Assets held by third parties. Assets in foreign countries.

Jointly Held Assets with Non-Liable Persons

Taxpayers with assets held jointly with non-liable persons must include their own ratable ownership in each asset. If the asset is not owned equally, the taxpayer should allocate based on her ownership percentage. Generally, the IRS will look to each owner's contribution to the value of each asset in determining ownership percentage.

For property held as tenancies by the entirety, the taxpayer's portion is usually 50% of the property's equity. It may be necessary to review applicable state law, including the effect community property and registered domestic partnership laws have on property ownership rights in order to determine the taxpayer's interest in such assets.

> **Pro Tip:** It is common in IRS collection investigations to review the assets of all persons in the household as well as transfers of large assets to others to determine the taxpayer's collectability though equity in assets. In cases where the taxpayer has transferred assets to avoid IRS collection, the IRS may seek to collect a taxpayer's unpaid balances by asserting transferee liability when the taxpayer has transferred property to another person or entity without considering payment of the outstanding balance owed.

Income-Producing Assets for ATP IA and CNC

The IRS rules for inclusion of income-producing assets in the taxpayer's ATP depends on the asset. Generally, income-producing assets are excluded as they enable the taxpayer to generate income to make monthly payments.

Income-producing assets: assets that are used to produce income for the taxpayer are generally excluded in all ATP installment agreements and CNC if the asset is necessary to generate income. [IRM 5.15.1.23 (10-2-2012)] As a general rule, the IRS rarely requests taxpayers to liquidate a business asset(s) unless the asset is not needed to generate income. [IRM 5.14.2.2.2 at (2e) (6-5-2025)] The IRS may request that a taxpayer borrow against equity in assets in situations where the taxpayer is able to afford to make additional loan payments.

Receivables: the IRS may request accounts and notes receivable unless it determines that they should be treated as part of the income stream required to produce income. When it is determined that liquidation of a receivable would be detrimental to the continued operation of an otherwise profitable business, it may be treated as future income. [IRM 5.15.1.33 (11-17-2014)]

Tools in a trade or business: individual taxpayer's tools used in a trade or business can be treated differently from other income-producing assets. There is a statutory exemption from a levy that applies to an individual taxpayer's tools used in a trade or business; these will be allowed, in addition to income-producing assets such as inventory, machinery, and equipment. [IRC §6334(a)(3)] The levy exemption amount is updated on an annual basis. [See Revenue Procedure 2024-40, section 3.50 (11-2024) for the 2024 adjusted amount] In practice, unless the taxpayer has unused tools, the IRS rarely requests the taxpayer to liquidate them to pay the balance as they are considered income-producing assets. [IRM 5.15.1.23 at (2) (10-2-2012)]

Exceptions: however, if the taxpayer owns real property that is used in business or rental activity, the value of that property should be included as equity in assets. The IRS will commonly request the taxpayer to borrow against any equity in business or rental real property for PPIAs. If the taxpayer borrows against the asset(s), the resulting loan payment should be considered in reducing the taxpayer's monthly disposable income. If the loan will put the taxpayer in economic harm (i.e., cause her to have negative MDI), the IRS will not request the taxpayer to borrow against the asset(s).

> **Example-** Tony owns rental property that produces $500 in net rental income per month and has total MDI of $1000. Tony has equity in the property of $50,000. The IRS will require Tony to access this equity to pay his tax bill. Tony can get an equity loan on the property for $25,000 which he uses to lower his overall tax bill. His monthly payment on the equity loan is $400. For purposes of determining Tony's MDI, Tony should be allowed his $400 monthly payment on the equity loan to reduce his net rental income to $100. This will reduce Tony's MDI to $600, which will result in a lower ATP installment agreement to the IRS.

> **Pro Tip:** Taxpayers should take a practical approach to using equity in assets to pay the balance owed to the IRS. The IRS will normally not ask the taxpayer to access business asset equity, because it may reduce the taxpayer's ability to generate income. The IRS will focus on accessing equity in obvious discretionary assets such as luxury cars, vacation homes, and substantial amounts of accounts receivable.

Income-Producing Assets for an OIC

The analysis of which income-producing assets to include for an OIC is similar to the ATP determination for IAs and CNC. In an OIC, income-producing assets are generally not included in computing net realizable equity in assets used to determine if a taxpayer qualifies for an OIC (an ATP calculation) and to determine the offer amount (the reasonable collection potential (RCP) calculation).

> **Pro Tip:** As a general rule, equity in income-producing assets will not be added to the RCP of a viable, ongoing business unless it is determined that the assets are not critical to business operations. In practice, IRS inclusion of business assets when they are used to produce income is rare in an OIC. IRM 5.8.5.15 (9-24-2021) has specific examples that the taxpayer can review in deciding whether to include an income-producing asset.

Valuing a Business as a Going Concern for an OIC

For purposes of calculating net realizable equity in assets (NRE) for an OIC, generally, the value of a business as a going concern would not be included in equity in assets for a viable, ongoing business, unless the value is substantially greater than the income produced by the business. For this reason, a business taxpayer may have to prove the value of the business as a going concern in an OIC application. Businesses are sometimes worth more than the sum of their assets because of the value of the business' intangible assets which include, but are not limited to: [IRM 5.8.5.17 at (2) (3-23-2018)]

- Ability or reputation of a professional.
- Established customer base.
- Prominent location.
- Well-known trade name, trademark, or telephone number.
- Possession of government licenses, copyrights, or patents.

> **Example:** The taxpayer operates a business which has been in existence for several years and has a good reputation with current customers. The assets of the business are valued at $100,000. The business also has loans on the assets of $90,000. There is no NRE in the assets ($100,000 FMV @ 80% quick sale value (QSV) = $80,000 less loans of $90,000). An appraisal determines that the business could be sold as a going concern for $150,000. NRE should be recomputed based on the value of the business as going concern. The value, using 80% QSV, is $30,000 ($150,000 @ 80% QSV = $120,000 less loans of $90,000).

> **Pro Tip:** Taxpayers with a viable, open business have very low OIC acceptance rates. Taxpayers with a business should do their due diligence in determining the value of the business as a going concern. Taxpayers can get an appraisal or an independent valuation from a business broker to provide evidence of the value of the business as a going concern.

Equity in Assets for Ability to Pay Installment Agreement/Currently Not Collectible Status

The IRS's review of a taxpayer's assets in an IA or CNC scenario is to determine the ability of the taxpayer to use available equity in assets to pay or lower the balance owed. As such, the first consideration in determining a taxpayer's ability to pay is to review his assets for available and accessible equity. [IRM 5.15.1.2 at (20a) (11-22-2021)] For the simple installment agreements and the full-pay non-streamlined installment agreement, the IRS does not require the taxpayer to consider equity in assets. However, in ability to pay installment agreements (routine ATP IA, conditional IA, or a partial pay IA), the IRS will consider the taxpayer's available equity in assets.

> **Pro Tip:** Taxpayers who enter into a full-pay non-streamlined installment agreement (NSIA) may have to liquidate assets first in order to qualify for an NSIA. Although this scenario is

not likely, it can occur if the taxpayer has prior defaulted IRS agreements due to missed payments or additional unpaid tax balances owed.

When making a determination of whether an asset has equity, the IRS normally looks at the quick sale value (QSV) to determine the amount of equity in an asset. [IRM 5.15.1.21 (10-2-2012)] The Quick Sale Value (QSV) of an asset is an estimate of the price a seller could get for the asset in a situation where financial pressures motivate the seller to sell in a short period of time, usually 90 days or less. Generally, the QSV is calculated at 80% of the fair market value. A higher or lower percentage may be appropriate depending on the type of asset and current market conditions. [IRM 5.15.1.21 at (4) (10-2-2012)] If the taxpayer does not have equity at QSV, the IRS is less likely to pursue the asset's equity in an ATP IA or CNC.

> **Pro Tip:** The IRS is more likely to look closer at the taxpayer's ability to sell non-essential assets or borrow against assets with equity (i.e., take a home equity loan) if the taxpayer has a Collection Field function assignment or cannot pay before the CSED expires. There is higher demand by the IRS for the taxpayer to access equity in assets in situations where the taxpayer has higher amounts owed or is a repeat offender (repeated defaulted agreements or new balances owed).

The IRS request to access equity in assets starts with the taxpayer's financial disclosure on a Collection Information Statement (Form 433-A, B, or F). Taxpayers must disclose the balance of financial accounts, retirement plans, and investments. Taxpayers also must provide asset and related liability information related to real property, vehicles, and other assets. If a taxpayer owns a business, he must disclose asset values, including accounts receivable, and liabilities against the assets.

In an IA or CNC, the IRS is not trying to determine the taxpayer's net worth. The goal is to identify equity in any specific assets and determine if the taxpayer can access this equity. For example, a taxpayer may have a negative net worth (total liabilities exceed total assets). However, when evaluating each asset individually, the taxpayer may have a retirement plan that the taxpayer can borrow against or liquidate to pay the liability owed.

> **Pro Tip:** If the IRS requests that the taxpayer borrow against assets to pay a tax bill, the taxpayer must try to access the equity. Taxpayers who cannot borrow against equity in assets can provide the IRS evidence of their unsuccessful attempt by providing a loan denial letter. Similarly, if the taxpayer has a pension plan, the taxpayer may provide plan documents that show that he cannot borrow or liquidate the assets in the plan.

Equity in Assets: Offer in Compromise

The equity in assets determination for an OIC differs from that for an IA or CNC, and it also differs in the qualification and offer amount computations.

In an OIC, the IRS wants the taxpayer's net realizable equity in assets (or "NRE") to be part of the amount paid to settle the tax liability. For an offer in compromise, the taxpayer must properly value assets and determine the NRE. NRE must be offered in an OIC to the IRS unless special circumstances exist that require the assets to be used for future necessary living expenses.

Taxpayers who are considering an OIC-DATC must do two equity in asset computations:

1. OIC qualification NRE: Compute net equity in assets to determine if the taxpayer qualifies for an OIC. Taxpayers qualify for an OIC if they cannot pay with net equity in assets and monthly installment payments before the collection statute expires. The assets are valued at their quick sale value.
2. OIC offer amount NRE: in addition to the taxpayer's assets being valued at the quick sale value, the taxpayer adds additional exclusions to determine net realizable equity in assets to determine the OIC offer amount. In this computation, the IRS applies these asset exclusions in determining NRE in assets for the offer amount:
   a. Cash exclusion: $1,000 plus one month of living expenses. [IRM 5.8.5.7 at (1) and (3) (4-8-2024)]

> **Pro Tip:** For the OIC offer amount, the IRS actually allows the taxpayer to also exclude one month's living expenses in the cash to be excluded. This exception is not on the IRS Form 656/433-A(OIC) OIC application forms.

   b. Car exemption: $3,450 per vehicle, up to two vehicles (married taxpayers). [IRM 5.8.5.12 at (3) (9-24-2021)]

For each calculation, equity in assets is determined by valuing each of the taxpayer's assets at the quick sale value (QSV). [IRM 5.8.5.4.1 at (1) (4-8-2024)] QSV is an estimate of the price a seller could get for the asset in a situation where financial pressures motivate the owner to sell in a short period of time, usually 90 calendar days or less. [IRM 5.8.5.4.1 at (2) (4-8-2024)] For OIC calculations, most assets are valued at 80% of their FMV, allowing for a 20% reduction due to the QSV allowance. The IRS uses 80% as a general rule in determining QSV. However, taxpayers can adjust QSV if they believe it does not properly estimate the price if the asset were sold within 90 days. [IRM 5.8.5.4.1 at (3) (4-8-2024)]

> **Pro Tip:** Often other factors come into play in determining the QSV estimate. For example, if a taxpayer values the QSV of an IRA, the QSV estimate would reflect the cost of liquidating the IRA, not the reduction of the price for selling within 90 days. Assets in an IRA can be sold immediately, but the tax effect of selling (income tax and early distribution penalty) may cost the taxpayer far in excess of the normal 20% QSV reduction. Taxpayers would take their income tax rate, for federal and state taxes, plus the early withdrawal penalty, to arrive at the QSV. Taxpayers must document any deviations from the standard IRS QSVs.

Guidance on QSV standards is found in the IRS Internal Revenue Manual. [IRM 5.8.5.4.1 (4-8-2024), IRM 5.8.5.8 (4-8-2024), IRM 5.8.5.12 (9-24-2021), IRM 5.8.5.13 (4-8-2024), IRM 5.8.5.14 (3-23-2018)] The standard QSV for the most common individual assets appears below:

Asset type	Standard QSV
Cash	100%
Vehicles, boats, planes	80%
Real estate	80%
IRAs and profit-sharing plans	65%–70% (accounts for withdrawal penalties and tax rate)
Furniture, fixtures, personal effects	80% (exempt assets excluded)
Income-producing assets	80% (if includable)

After applying the QSV, the taxpayer may be allowed an exemption/exclusion of assets. OICs value assets differently than other ATP agreements and allow for certain assets to be exempt in the ATP calculation.

Asset	OIC rule: asset amount excluded from OIC ATP calculation	Other ATP agreements (IA, CNC)
Cash	Qualification: no exclusion. [IRM 5.8.5.7 at (1) (4-8-2024)] Offer amount: $1,000, plus 1 month of living expenses are excluded. [IRM 5.8.5.7 at (1) (4-8-2024)]	No exemptions – IRS looks for cash to pay toward liability.
Household assets (jewelry, antiques, etc.)	Qualification and offer amount: Exemption of $11,710. [Revenue Procedure 2024-40, section 3.50 (11-2024) for 2025 adjusted amount]	No exemption — however, other than recreational assets, IRS rarely pursues to pay liability.
Vehicles	Qualification: No exemption allowed. [IRM 5.8.5.12 at (3) (9-24-2021)] Offer amount: Allows asset exemption of $3,450 for up to two vehicles (married taxpayers). [IRM 5.8.5.12 at (3) (9-24-2021)]	No exemption, but IRS does not look for first two cars (joint liability) to be used toward liability.
Income-producing assets	Generally excluded if they are producing income stream. [IRM 5.8.5.15 at (3) (9-24-2021)]	Generally excluded if they are producing income stream. [IRM 5.15.1.23 at (1) (10-2-2012)]

Tools for trade/profession for self-employed individuals	Qualification and offer amount: $5,860 is exempt. [Revenue Procedure 2024-40, section 3.50 (11-2024) for 2025 adjusted amount]	No exemption, but IRS does not look for taxpayer to liquidate income-producing assets in an IA or CNC agreement.
Dissipated assets	IRS looks at assets liquidated where proceeds not used for necessary living expenses within the last three years or six months before a new assessment (i.e., audit, CP2000, or late-filed return).	Generally, not pursued unless taxpayer transfers out assets to avoid payment of tax. In these cases, IRS may pursue these assets for transferee liability.

> **Pro Tip:** OIC applicants complete IRS Form 433-A(OIC) which provides for the asset exemptions to determine NRE for an OIC. However, in computing the offer amount, the Form 433-A(OIC) does not provide for the taxpayer to exclude one month's living expenses form the cash balance (only provides for $1,000 to be excluded) as allowed by IRM 5.8.5.7 at (1). Taxpayers should reduce the cash valuation by their average monthly living expenses when determining NRE for the offer amount.

To determine Net Equity in Assets for OIC qualification, the taxpayer must complete the following steps:

1. *Value the asset:* determine the FMV of each asset.
2. *Convert value to the quick sale value*: reduce the asset by the applicable QSV percentage.
3. *Determine equity:* reduce by any loan balance on the asset. Exclude all assets with negative equity.
4. *Compute net equity*: apply any exemptions for personal effects, tools of the trade, and income-producing assets to reduce or exclude the equity in the asset to arrive at net equity.

To compute NRE for an OIC to determine the offer amount, the taxpayer will complete the following four steps for each asset:

1. *Value the asset:* determine the FMV of each asset.
2. *Convert value to current value*: reduce the asset by the applicable QSV.
3. *Determine equity:* reduce by any loan balance on the asset.
4. *Compute NRE with additional exclusions allowed*:

   - Cash exclusion: $1,000 and one month of living expenses.
   - Car exemption: $3,450 per vehicle (limited to two for married taxpayers).

> **Pro Tip:** Taxpayers should be cautious in using the IRS website's OIC pre-qualifier tool. This tool incorrectly allows the taxpayer the $1,000 cash exclusion and $3,450 car exemption in determining whether the taxpayer qualifies for an OIC.

Example- Greg is considering submitting an OIC. Greg determines that he has NRE of $33,550.

Asset	FMV	QSV (QSV%)	Reduce by loan and/or exemption = NRE
Cash • Monthly living expenses are $3,000	$10,000	$10,000 (100%)	Qualification: $10,000 Offer amount: $6,000 ($10,000 - $3,000 - $1,000)
Home • Loan: $180,000	$250,000	$200,000 (80%)	$20,000
IRA • Fed/State tax rate = 20% • Early W/D penalty of 10%	$10,000	$7,000 (70%)	$7,000
Car • No loan	$5,000	$4,000 (80%)	Qualification: $4,000 Offer amount: $550 ($4,000 - $3,450)
Totals	$275,000	$221,000	Equity in assets (qualification) = $41,000 NRE (offer amount) = $33,550

Dissipated Assets

Dissipated assets may be included in the taxpayer's ability to pay in an OIC determination depending upon the facts and circumstances.

A dissipated asset is an asset that was sold, transferred, encumbered or otherwise disposed of in an attempt to avoid the payment of the tax liability. It also includes assets or proceeds (other than wages, salary, or other income) used to pay other items that are not necessary for the production of income or the health and welfare of the taxpayer or their family, after the tax has been assessed or during a period of up to six months prior to or after the tax assessment. [IRM 5.8.5.18 at (1) (9-24-2021)]

Dissipated assets are problematic for taxpayers. If a taxpayer knowingly transfers an asset at less than FMV to a third-party to hinder IRS collection, the IRS can pursue collection of the asset (called transferee liability). The IRS can also pursue criminal prosecution for more serious intentional asset transfers to avoid payment of taxes. Taxpayers in these situations should consult legal counsel for advice.

For an OIC determination, dissipated assets must be included in the calculation of the NRE and offered to the IRS as part of the tax settlement amount. There are four rules to follow in determining whether a taxpayer has dissipated assets for an OIC determination:

- *Three-year rule*: any assets disposed of in the past three years (first year is the submission year) that are not used to pay necessary living expenses or to produce income. For example, if the offer was submitted in 2024, only assets in 2022-2024 will be reviewed for asset dissipation. [IRM 5.8.5.18 at (2) (9-24-2021)]
- *Tax assessment rule*: any assets disposed of six months before and six months after a tax assessment. For example, if a taxpayer files a 2012 return two years after its due date (April 26, 2015), the dissipated asset lookback would be six months before and after April 26, 2015, in addition to the past three years. [IRM 5.8.5.18 at (2) (9-24-2021)]
- *Tax examination rule*: any assets disposed of after notification of an examination where such assets are not used for necessary living expenses or to produce income. For example, a taxpayer receives a notice of examination for 2012 on November 15, 2013. The lookback period for dissipated assets should start on November 15, 2013. [IRM 5.8.5.18 at (6) (9-24-2021)]
- *Deliberate payment avoidance:* situations where it can be shown that the taxpayer has sold, transferred, encumbered, or otherwise disposed of assets in an attempt to avoid the payment of the tax liability, or used the assets or proceeds (other than wages, salary, or other income) for other than the payment of items necessary for the production of income or the health and welfare of the taxpayer or their family. For example, after the taxpayer learns that he owes the IRS $105,000 for 2011, the taxpayer deliberately transfers $100,000 to a friend to hold to avoid payment to the IRS. [IRM 5.8.5.6 (3-23-2018)]

If the tax liability did not exist prior to the transfer or the transfer occurred prior to the taxable event giving rise to the tax liability, generally, a taxpayer cannot be said to have dissipated the assets in disregard of the outstanding tax liability. Other situations where dissipated assets should not be considered or only partially considered as part of NRE for an OIC are as follows:

- Taxpayer used the funds for necessary living expenses.
- Taxpayer dissolved a retirement account or withdrew substantial amounts from savings during unemployment or underemployment, if the taxpayer's income was insufficient to meet necessary living expenses. The amount needed to meet necessary living expenses should be excluded from NRE.
- Taxpayer disposes of an asset and uses the funds to purchase another asset that is included in the NRE evaluation. In these cases, a taxpayer should not include the value of the asset disposed of as a dissipated asset.

   [IRM 5.8.5.18 at (7) (9-24-2021)]

Taxpayers who believe that they have a potential dissipated asset should review the guidance and examples in IRM 5.8.5.18 when questioning whether an asset should be included in NRE for an OIC computation.

The taxpayer can review the following documents to investigate potential dissipated assets:

- *IRS account transcripts* for look-back periods. Review account transcripts for assessment dates and audit activity to determine whether to expand the dissipated assets review past the last three years.
- *IRS wage and income transcripts* for assets that could be considered dissipated. Wage and income transcripts include information on IRA balances, investments, bank accounts, property sales, and other potential dissipated asset issues.
- *Prior year returns* for property bought and sold, indicators of loan activity, investments sold, business assets, and other potential assets.
- *Credit reports* for loans that would encumber assets and other funds available to the taxpayer that were used elsewhere.
- *Public records* for property sales, loan activity, and transfers of property.

> **Pro Tip:** Dissipated assets are one of the biggest reasons for rejected OICs. Taxpayers submitting an OIC should always review their situation for potential dissipated assets. If the taxpayer had a dissipated asset(s), he should be prepared to show how the dissipated asset(s) was used for necessary living expenses or be prepared to include the amount in the OIC.

Worksheets for Determining Equity in Assets for ATP Agreements

Use the following worksheets to help determine ATP with equity in assets.

Worksheet	Helps with:
#1: Form 433-A: Equity in Asset Summary (for CNC and Installment Agreements)	Worksheet to determine ability to pay with net equity in assets for CNC status or an ATP IA. Maps to Form 433-A.

#2: OIC: Equity in Asset Summary for OIC Qualification Determination	Worksheet to value net equity in assets for purposes of determining if the taxpayer qualifies for an OIC-DATC.
#3: Form 433-A(OIC): Equity in Asset Summary for Offer Amount Determination	Worksheet to compute net realizable equity in assets (for OIC-DATC offer amounts determination). Maps to Form 433-A(OIC).

#1: Form 433-A: Equity in Asset Summary (for CNC and Installment Agreements):

Use this worksheet to calculate personal and business asset equity (fair market value less encumbrances) for CNC and ATP IAs.

#2: OIC Equity in Asset Summary for OIC Qualification Determination:

Use the MDI worksheet to compute the net realizable equity in asset component for qualifying for an OIC-DATC. To determine qualification, the taxpayer must add the second component: the amount that the taxpayer can pay in monthly installments (MDI) before the CSED expires.

For more information on Monthly Disposable Income, see **Chapter 9.07: Ability to Pay Component #2: Monthly Disposable Income.** For more information on OIC-DATC Qualification Computations, see **Chapter 9.08: Determining Total Ability to Pay: CNC and the ATP IA, and the OIC-DATC.**

#3: Form 433-A(OIC): Equity in Asset Summary for OIC Offer Amount Determination:

Use this two-page worksheet to compute the net realizable equity in asset component of the offer amount for an OIC-DATC. To determine the offer amount, the taxpayer must add the second component: the amount that the taxpayer can pay in monthly installments (MDI) allowed by the terms of the OIC.

Chapter 9.07: Ability to Pay Component #2: Monthly Disposable Income

The second component of a taxpayer's ability to pay is the amount that the taxpayer can pay in monthly payments to the IRS. In ATP agreements, these monthly payments are referred to as monthly disposable income or "MDI." [IRM 5.15.1.3 (8-29-2018)]

MDI is the average income remaining each month after the taxpayer pays necessary living expenses. [IRM 5.15.1.8 (7-24-2019)] In ATP agreements, the IRS will require this amount as an installment agreement payment or a multiplier of this amount as part of the amount to settle the tax liability in an OIC.

The goal in properly determining MDI is to represent the future average cash flow for the taxpayer. Averaging should be done over the applicable time period that best reflects the average income and expenses for the taxpayer. [IRM 5.15.1.12 (8-29-2018) and IRM 5.15.1.3 at (3) (8-29-2018)]

> **Pro Tip:** The IRS sets guidelines for determining the time period to use in averaging income and expenses. Wage earners can average income and expenses over three months and self-employed persons over 12 months. However, the taxpayer should choose the time period that best reflects the average per month. When trying to average household income and household expenses, consider income (i.e., annual bonuses, commission payments, seasonal income) and expenses (i.e., insurance, homeowners dues, real estate taxes not paid through monthly mortgage payments) that do not occur monthly. Taxpayers should select and be able to document the proper income and expense averaging period that best reflects future MDI.

Components of MDI

There are two components in determining MDI for individuals:

- *Total average household monthly income*: the average amount of funds received each month for all members of the household. These funds can come from taxable and non-taxable sources. [IRM 5.15.1.12 (8-29-2018)]
- *Less: Average household monthly living expenses*: the average amount of living expenses each month. Expenses are separated into three categories:

  1. Necessary living expenses that are subject to IRS collection financial standards.
  2. Necessary expenses not subject to IRS collection standards.
  3. Other actual expenses that may or may not be allowed in calculating MDI, depending on the taxpayer's circumstances (conditional expenses).

  [IRM 5.15.1.8 at (1) (7-24-2019)]

MDI can be negative if the taxpayer's monthly expenses exceed income. Negative MDI indicates that the taxpayer does not have an ability to pay with monthly installment agreements. In these cases, CNC status or evaluating the taxpayer for an OIC is appropriate.

> **Pro Tip:** In rare cases, the taxpayer may have negative MDI because the MDI calculation allows for the use of IRS standard amounts for food/clothing/other, transportation operating costs, and out-of-pocket healthcare without proof of actual expenses to the IRS. In cases where the taxpayer has substantial negative MDI, the taxpayer should be prepared to explain to the IRS how they are supporting their household (i.e., gifts, loans, etc.).

Determining Average Household Income

The first step in calculating MDI is to determine the average gross monthly income for all members of the household. Both taxable and non-taxable sources should be included. [IRM 5.15.1.12 at (1) (8-29-2018)]

> **Pro Tip:** A necessary due diligence step when requesting an ATP agreement is to review all deposits in all financial accounts. Each deposit should be verified and documented as to its source. Unexplained deposits will be considered additional sources of income by the IRS. In instances where the taxpayer is going to pay in more than six years or is requesting CNC, the IRS will also verify that the allowable expenses were actually paid by reviewing bank statements, cancelled checks, and other receipts.

These include, but are not limited to, the following: [IRM 5.15.1.12 (8-29-2018)]

Income source	Documentation to support	Averaging period
Wages and commissions	Paystubs for past three months showing gross income (pay period and YTD), taxes, and any payroll deductions that are allowable as expenses (i.e., health insurance).	Past 3 months. Longer if commissions, seasonality, and bonuses are involved.
Self-employment net income	Profit and loss statement, removing non-cash expenses.	6-12 months. Likely 12 months to account for any seasonality.
Net rental income	Profit and loss statement.	Past 12 months.
Distributions from S corporations/partnerships	Prior year K-1s and current year distribution statements.	3-12 months, depending on frequency of payments
Retirement income	Pension and annuity statements.	3 months.
IRA distributions	IRA statements.	12 months.
Social security income	Social security statement or bank statement showing deposit; 1099-SSA from prior year.	Last month.
Investment income	Broker statements and other investment documents.	Likely over past 12 months.
Child support	Child support order and proof of payment received.	Last 3 months unless payments received are not

		regularly received each month.
Alimony	Alimony agreement and proof of payments received.	Last 3 months unless payments received are not regularly received each month.
Subsidies (rent, food, etc.)	Grant documents and proof of payments or subsidies.	Last 3 months.
Unemployment	Unemployment statement and bank account statement.	Last 3 months.
Gambling income	Gambling receipts from casino, etc.	Last 3 months.
Other income received by members of the family and non-liable person(s)	All source documents (paystubs, etc.) and bank statements.	Last 3 months.

> **Pro Tip:** The IRS does not allow negative average monthly income from the taxpayer's business or rental property. If the business or rental income is a loss, the taxpayer should enter zero as the net income.

Determining Average Living Expenses

In determining an individual taxpayer's ability to pay, the IRS allows taxpayers to reduce their income by necessary expenses to provide for a taxpayer and her family's health and welfare, or the production of income. [IRM 5.15.1.8 (7-24-2019) and IRM 5.19.13.3.2 (8-14-2023)]

Expenses are separated in three categories:

- *Category #1 – necessary living expenses subject to IRS limits:* necessary living expenses subject to IRS collection financial standards. Allowable necessary expenses that may be limited or allowed based on annual IRS Collection Financial Standards. Examples include housing and utilities.
- *Category #2 – other necessary expenses not subject to standards:* other expenses specifically allowed for the health and welfare of the family, or to produce income, that are not subject to IRS Collection Financial Standards. An example is medical insurance.
- *Category #3 – other expenses:* expenses that may be necessary or are conditional. Conditional expenses are expenses that are not necessary but may be allowed if the taxpayer is obtaining a conditional installment agreement (payment plan within six years). An example is private school tuition.

    [IRM 5.15.1.8 at (1) (7-24-2019)]

Specific expenses are categorized and allowable as follows:

Category #1: Necessary living expenses: subject to IRS Collection Financial Standard limitations		
Expense	**Amount allowable**	**Reference**
Food, clothing, and other items • Apparel and services • Food • Housekeeping supplies • Personal care products/Services • Misc. (credit card payments, occupational expenses, bank fees, school supplies, etc.)	A standard amount is allowed based on family size (generally, number of dependents on a tax return) without questioning the amount actually spent.	IRM 5.15.1.9 (08-29-2018) and IRM 5.15.1.10 and subsections (11-22-2021)
Housing and utilities • Mortgage/rent • Taxes • Insurance • Electric • Gas/heating oil • Home phone • Cell phone • Water/trash • Repairs/maintenance • Internet/cable • Other	Taxpayers are allowed the standard amount for housing and utilities or the amount actually claimed and verified by the taxpayer, whichever is less. If the amount claimed is more than the total allowed by housing and utilities standards, the taxpayer must provide documentation to substantiate that those expenses are necessary.	
Transportation (up to 2 vehicles) • Ownership costs • Operating costs (flat amount allowed) • Public Transportation	*Ownership*: taxpayer is allowed the full ownership standard amount, or the amount actually claimed and verified by the taxpayer, whichever is less. *Operating*: taxpayer is allowed the full operating standard amount, or the amount actually claimed by the taxpayer, whichever is less.	

	Substantiation for the operating allowance is not required unless the amount claimed exceeds the standard. *Note*: A single taxpayer is normally allowed ownership and operating costs for one vehicle. If a husband and wife own two vehicles, they are allowed the amount claimed for each vehicle up to the maximum allowances for ownership and operating expenses. The taxpayer is allowed the standard for ownership and operating costs, or the amounts actually spent, whichever is less. *Public transportation*: A taxpayer with no vehicle is allowed the standard, per household, without questioning the amount actually spent. The taxpayer is not required to provide documentation unless the amount claimed exceeds the standard. If a taxpayer owns a vehicle and uses public transportation, expenses may be allowed for both, provided they are needed for the health and welfare of the individual or family, or to produce income. However, the expenses allowed would be actual expenses incurred. Documentation would not be required unless the amount claimed exceeds the standards.	

| Out-of-pocket medical expenses

 • Medical services
 • Prescriptions
 • Medical supplies | A standard is allowed based on age without questioning the amount actually spent. Taxpayers will be allowed a greater amount if they can document more expenses were paid.
 Not allowable: elective cosmetic and dental procedures. | |

A taxpayer who claims more than the total allowed by the national standards must provide documentation to substantiate and justify as necessary those expenses that exceed the total national standard amounts. Deviations from the standard amount are not allowed for miscellaneous expenses.

Category #2: Necessary living expenses and expenses to produce income: not subject to standards		
Expense	**Amount allowable**	**Reference**
Health Insurance, plus individual shared responsibility payment made	Amount paid.	IRM 5.15.1.9 (08-29-2018) IRM 5.15.1.11 (11-22-2021) IRM 5.15.1.27 (11-22-2021)
Term life insurance	Only term life insurance is allowed. Not allowed: investment portions of life insurance payments (i.e., whole life) in excess of the term insurance amount.	
Taxes paid • Federal • State • Local	All income taxes paid to federal, state, and local tax authorities. FICA and Medicare taxes. Not allowed: property taxes paid that would be included in housing or transportation operating costs.	
Mandatory retirement	Employer required retirement contributions.	

Category #3: Other expenses: necessary expenses or conditional expenses

Other Necessary Expenses — These expenses must meet the necessary expense test and normally are allowed. The amount allowed must be reasonable considering the taxpayer's individual facts and circumstances.

Other Conditional Expenses — These expenses may not meet the necessary expense test but may be allowable based on the circumstances of an individual case. Other conditional expenses may also be allowable if the taxpayer qualifies for the six-year rule and one-year rule (tiered IA).

Taxpayer should review IRM 5.15.1.11 (11-22-2021) for assistance in determining if a particular expense is allowable.	
Expense	**Necessary if:**
Accounting and legal fees	<ul><li>Tax preparation.</li><li>The fees are for representation before the Service (i.e., to resolve current balances due, delinquent returns, examinations, etc.).</li><li>The fees meet the necessary expense test.</li><li>The amount should not be excessive and must be reasonable given the complexity of the case. *Note:* Fees for small business accounting should be expenses against net business income.</li></ul>
Charitable contributions	If it is a condition of employment or meets the necessary expense test. *Example:* A minister is required to tithe according to his employment contract.
Child/dependent care (baby-sitting, day care, nursery, pre-school)	If paid so that the taxpayer can work (produce income) or for the care of the elderly, invalid, or handicapped if there is no alternative to the taxpayer other than paying the expense. Not allowed: primary school tuition.
Court-order payments <ul><li>Child support</li><li>Alimony</li><li>Other</li></ul>	If alimony and child support payments are court ordered and being paid, they are allowable. If payments are not being made, the expense is not allowed unless the non-payment was due to temporary job loss or illness. Restitution payments made to other victims pursuant to a court order are allowable expenses. Not allowed: court-ordered payments for items that would not be an allowable necessary expense (i.e., payment of a child's college tuition)
Education	If it is required for a physically challenged or special needs child and no public education providing similar services is available. Education expenses are also allowed for the taxpayer if required as a condition of employment (such as continuing professional education). Not allowed: college tuition.
Secured or legally perfected debt payments	Allowed if paid and if for necessary living expenses or the production of income.
Unsecured debts	If the taxpayer substantiates and justifies the expense, the minimum payment may be allowed. The necessary expense test of health and welfare and/or production of income must be met. Except for payments required to produce income, payments on unsecured debts will not be allowed if the tax liability, including projected accruals, can be paid in full within 90 days.

Credit card debt payments	Included in food, clothing, and other expenses category. Generally, minimum payments on credit cards are allowed as a conditional expense under the six-year rule.
Work deductions: union dues, uniforms, etc.	Allowed if it is a requirement of the job.
Student loan payments	If it is guaranteed by the federal government and only for the taxpayer's post-high school education. • Taxpayers must substantiate that the payments are being made. • Taxpayers who have student loan debt but are unable to make payments on the debt because they are suffering an economic hardship or have medical problems, should be advised to request a deferment or forbearance of the student loan payments. • Taxpayers must be advised that if they later decide to pay the student loan, they can request the installment agreement be revised.
Repayment of loans made to pay federal taxes owed	If the IRS has received the proceeds of the loan and the taxpayer can document the loan, the payment amount should be allowed.
Delinquent state and local tax payments (*Note:* In practice, state/local IA payments are generally allowed when the taxpayer state/local debt is assessed BEFORE the IRS agreement.)	Payments for delinquent state and local (county or municipal) tax liabilities may be allowed in certain circumstances: • When a taxpayer does not have the ability to full-pay the tax liability. • When a taxpayer provides complete financial information. • When taxpayer provides verification of the state or local tax liability, and agreement if applicable *Note:* The IRS can allow a payment up to a percentage of IRS and state liabilities to the total liability. However, if the state payment results in the taxpayer being reported as CNC, the IRS will only allow the payment if the taxpayer's state agreement was established before the earliest IRS unpaid assessment.
Veterinary expenses	Not a necessary expense but allowed as a conditional expense if the taxpayer pays within six years.
Voluntary retirement contributions	Not a necessary expense but allowed as a conditional expense if the taxpayer pays within six years.

Shared Expenses with Non-Liable Persons

Determining ATP requires that the taxpayer account for total household income and expenses. In situations where the taxpayer is living with a non-liable person (spouse, domestic partner, roommate) and bills are paid from commingled funds or joint accounts, it will be necessary to review other household income and any expenses shared with the non-liable person in order to determine the taxpayer's allowable portion of the shared household income and expenses. [IRM 5.15.1.5 (11-22-2021) and IRM 5.8.5.24 (9-24-2021)]

A taxpayer must review the entire household information to determine the taxpayer's proportional share of the total household income and expenses. This includes obtaining income and expense information from the non-liable person(s). The liable taxpayer's allowable shared expenses will be determined based on the percentage of the total household income to which the taxpayer contributes. Expenses attributable only to the liable taxpayer can be allowed up to the standard. For example, if the liable taxpayer owns a car (not held jointly), she will be allowed the actual expense paid, subject to the limits imposed by the IRS Collection Financial Standards, for the car that she owns.

> **Pro Tip:** In situations where the taxpayer's income and expenses are not commingled (roommates with shared housing) and responsibility for household expenses is divided equitably between the co-inhabitants, it is not necessary to review the income and expense information for the non-liable person. In these cases, the IRS will limit the living expenses allowed up to the allowable standards per the IRS Collection Financial Standards. [IRM 5.15.1.5 at (5) (11-22-2021)]

To determine the taxpayer's allowable shared expenses when they are commingled with other non-liable persons in the household:

1. *Determine the total actual household income and expenses:* for all persons in the household, including both liable and non-liable persons.
2. *Determine what percentage of the total household income the taxpayer contributes*: the liable spouse's total income divided by total household income.
3. *Determine allowable expenses for the household*: necessary living expenses limited by IRS Collection Financial Standards.
4. *Separate which expenses are shared and which expenses are the sole responsibility of the taxpayer*: expenses that are not shared and are necessary will be allowed (i.e., car payments, child support, allowable educational loan, or state delinquent tax payments).
5. *Apply the taxpayer's percentage* of income to the shared expenses.
6. *Verify that the taxpayer actually contributes at least this amount to the total household expense*: validate that the taxpayer actually pays for necessary living expenses.
7. *Do not allow the taxpayer any amount paid toward a non-liable person's discretionary expenses.*

The following is an IRS example of how to apply the shared expense allocation: [IRM 5.15.1.5 (11-22-2021)]

Facts: Family of 4 One spouse not liable	Household Actual Amount Claimed	Maximum Allowable Amount for Family of 4	Maximum Allowable Amount for one Taxpayer	Taxpayer's Percentage of Total Income and Expenses	Taxpayer Expenses Allowed for Computation
Gross Monthly Income (determines allocation % for shared expenses)	$6667 non-liable person $1667 liable taxpayer $8333 total income			20% ($1667/$8333) Use 20% as proportion of liable person's shared expenses	
National Standard for Food, Clothing and Miscellaneous (shared expense)	$1370	$1370	$565	$274 ($1370 × .20)	$565 the greater amount
Housing and Utilities (shared expense)	$2256	$2465	$1635	$451 ($2256 × .20)	$451 the lesser amount
Ownership Costs – Car 1 (shared expense)	$525 owned jointly	$517	$517	$105 ($525 × .20)	$105 the lesser amount
Ownership Costs – Car 2 (shared expense)	$480 owned jointly	$517	0	$96 ($480 × .20)	$96 the lesser amount
Operating Costs – Both cars (shared expense)	$500	$488	$244	$100 ($500 × .20)	$100 the lesser amount
Out-of-pocket Health Care (shared expense)	$200	$240	$60	$40 ($200 × .20)	$60 the greater amount

Health Insurance (shared expense)	$400 for family paid by non-liable person			$80 ($400 × .20)	$80
Taxes (NOT a shared expense)	$1800 non-liable person $400 liable taxpayer				$400
Child Support Payments (NOT a shared expense)	$300 liable taxpayer				$300
Court Ordered Payments (NOT a shared expense)	$100 non-liable person				$0

Taxpayers who live in community property states (Arizona, California, Idaho, Louisiana, Nevada, New Mexico, Texas, Washington, and Wisconsin) have special rules regarding shared household income and expenses. Taxpayers must follow the community property laws in these states to determine what assets and income of the non-liable spouse are subject to collection of the tax. [IRM 25.18.4.2 (6-5-2017) and IRM 25.18.4.17 (6-5-2017)]

MDI Analysis Worksheet (for Determining Ability to Pay for Installment Agreements, CNC, and OIC-DATC)

Taxpayers can determine their monthly disposable income by averaging their actual income received and expenses paid for a specific time period.

Taxpayers can quantify their actual income and expenses over the past 3 months and past 12 months using the MDI Analysis Worksheet.

This worksheet will provide the taxpayer's MDI using actual expenses. If the taxpayer cannot pay within six years, or before the expiration of the CSED, whichever is shorter, or wishes to determine if she qualifies for an OIC-DATC the taxpayer may have to limit expenses for food/clothing/other, housing/utilities, and transportation expenses to IRS standards.

For the MDI Analysis Worksheet, refer to the **Appendix B**—and visit
www.TaxProblemsHandbook.com under the **IRS Collection Solutions Handbook** tab for
downloadable resources.

Forms 433-A and 433-A(OIC) MDI Computation Worksheet

After determining the taxpayer's average monthly income and expenses, the taxpayer will want
to apply the IRS Collection Financial Standards and disclose them on the appropriate IRS
Collection Information Statement (Form 433 series).

For the MDI Analysis Worksheet for CNC, an ATP IA, or for an OIC-DATC, refer to the **Appendix
B**—and visit www.TaxProblemsHandbook.com under the **IRS Collection Solutions Handbook**
tab for downloadable resources.

Self-Employed and Rental Income Taxpayers

Taxpayers who are self-employed or have rental property may need to provide a profit and loss
statement to provide their income and expenses. The profit and loss statement should reflect
the average monthly cash flow of the business or property. Non-cash expenses, such as
depreciation, are not allowed in determining MDI. [IRM 5.15.1.12 at (2c) (8-29-2018)] In addition,
business expenses should not be duplicated as personal expenses; for example, car ownership
that could appear as both a business expense and a personal living expense.

Many businesses and rental properties have seasonal fluctuation in income and expenses.
Taxpayers should review their past 12 months to determine an accurate net income. The IRS does
not allow business and rental income to be negative in computing MDI. [IRM 5.15.1.12 at (2c) (8-
29-2018)]

> **Pro Tip:** Self-employed and rental property taxpayers should average income and expenses
> over the time period that best reflects future income and expenses. For IAs and CNC, it is
> normal for the IRS to allow averaging over the past 12 months. However, when it comes to
> an OIC, the IRS may want to consider income average for up to the last three years. In the
> OIC investigation, the IRS will review prior year tax returns and ask for clarification if the
> taxpayer is reporting significantly less net income than what is reported in prior returns.
> The IRS looks to past tax returns as a litmus test for average business and rental income.
> The taxpayer should be prepared to explain variances in current year income as compared
> to prior year tax returns if the income reported on prior returns is significantly higher than
> the income reported on the Collection Information Statement.

Forms 433-A and 433-A(OIC): Net Business Income Analysis for Ability to Pay Calculation Worksheet

Business taxpayers can analyze their past 12 months income and expenses to determine average
monthly income by completing the Ability to Pay Worksheet: Forms 433A/433A-OIC: Net

Business Income Analysis (for ability to pay determinations for installment agreements, CNC, and OICs), and add/delete/edit any income and expenses that properly reflect future income.

For the Ability to Pay Worksheet, refer to the **Appendix B**—and visit www.TaxProblemsHandbook.com under the **IRS Collection Solutions Handbook** tab for downloadable resources.

The income and expense items should be verifiable through banks statements and other documentation. The IRS may request more information on any item reported as well as verification of the income reported as deposits in bank accounts.

Taxpayers should be prepared to support the following business expenses as necessary to produce income:

- Travel and entertainment.
- Wages paid to officers, shareholders, and related parties.
- Bonuses paid to officers, shareholders, and related parties.
- Interest paid on loans to officers or owners of the company.
- Pension plan contributions and employee benefits paid to officers, shareholders, and related parties.

Some expenses are never allowed. These include non-cash expenses such as depreciation, depletion, and bad debt accruals. Additionally, taxpayers' net operating losses are not allowed in determining ATP. [IRM 5.15.1.18 (8-29-2018)]

Applying IRS Collection Financial Standards

If the taxpayer is unable to pay within the terms of the full-pay non-streamlined installment agreement or six-year ATP conditional IA, the taxpayer's ability to pay is likely to be reduced by the IRS Collection Financial Standards. These standards provide limits or allowances for the following expenses for individual taxpayers:

Expense category	Limitations/allowances
Food, Clothing, and Miscellaneous • Food • Housekeeping supplies • Apparel and services • Personal care products and services • Miscellaneous (includes minimum credit card payments)	National allowance based on number in household. Limits amount claimed unless additional amounts are needed to provide for the health and welfare of the family.

Housing and utilities • Mortgage/rent • Homeowner association dues • Taxes • Insurance • Electric • Gas/heating oil • Home phone • Cell phone • Water/trash • Repairs/maintenance • Internet/cable	Local standard based on county/state and number in household. Limits amount claimed unless additional amounts are needed to provide for the health and welfare of the family.
Transportation expenses • Car ownership (up to two cars for joint filers) • Operating costs (up to two cars for joint filers) • Public transportation	Regional/local standards. Up to two car ownership/operating expenses allowed based on joint returns. Limits amount claimed unless additional amounts are needed to provide for the health and welfare of the family, or production of income. OICs allow additional operating costs for older/higher mileage vehicles.
Out of pocket medical expenses • Medical services, including doctors • Prescriptions • Medical supplies	Standard amount allowed based on age of family members. The taxpayer is allowed the greater of amount actual paid or the standard allowance.

Example- The Morris family is a family of four, all under age 65. They owe the IRS $60,000 and cannot pay with a simple installment agreement. They have 95 months before their earliest collection statute expiration date. They also have $100,000 in net realizable equity in their home that they cannot access because they do not qualify for a new loan (this will disqualify them from an OIC). They need to understand their payment options with the IRS and likely need an ATP agreement (CNC, routine IA, conditional IA, or partial pay IA, depending on their circumstances). The Morris family lives in Tampa, Florida (Hillsborough County). The primary and the spouse both work and support their two ten-year-old twins. They own their home and have two car payments. Their financial information is as follows:

Actual income/expenses	Average amount (past 3 months)	Notes
Income:		
Primary – gross wages/month	$4,800	Per paychecks (paid bi-monthly)
Spouse – gross wages/month	$4,224	Per paychecks (paid bi-monthly)
No other income	$0	
Total average monthly gross income	$9,024	
Expenses: (actual paid)		
Food, clothing, misc. (all)	$2,300	No special dietary conditions in the family
Housing/utilities (all)	$3,811	No special needs in the family
Car 1 payment (primary)	$290	Primary
Car 2 payment (spouse)	$465	Spouse
Transportation operating costs	$680	All car expenses for both vehicles
Public transportation	$0	None
Out-of-pocket medical expenses	$120	Average paid
Federal taxes paid	$500	Per paychecks
FICA/Medicare taxes paid	$505	Per paychecks
Health insurance premiums	$375	Withheld from Kathy's paycheck
Term life insurance premiums	$120	Premiums paid monthly
Childcare payments	$400	Paid for after school care so parents can work
Total average monthly expenses	$9,566	
Monthly disposable income – ACTUAL EXPENSES	($1,766)	Based on actual expenses, taxpayer does not have an ability to pay

Based on the taxpayers' current average household income and expenses each month, they do not have the ability to pay — their expenses exceed their income by $1,766. In fact, each month, the Morris family has increased their credit card balances to support their household expenses.

However, the IRS Collection Financial Standards for the Morris family limit these expenses. *Note:* This example uses the IRS expense standards for April 2025–March 2026. For the most up-to-date expense standards, see the following: https://www.irs.gov/businesses/small-businesses-self-employed/collection-financial-standards.

Expense	Actual amount paid	IRS Standard allowed	Monthly expense applying IRS Collection Financial Standards
Food, clothing, miscellaneous	$2,300	Amount allowed: $2,129 (National Standard -family of 4)	$2,129
Housing/utilities	$3,811	Up to $2,696 (Hillsborough County, FL, family of 4)	$2,696
Transportation – car payment 1	$290	Up to $662 (National standard per car)	$290
Transportation – car payment 2	$465	Up to $662 (National standard per car)	$465
Transportation operating costs – 2 cars	$680	Amount allowed: $670 (Standard for South Region- Tampa location)	$670
Out-of-pocket medical expenses	$120	Amount allowed: actual expenses paid or $84 per family member (under age 65) or $336	$336

When applying the IRS Collection Financial Standards, the expenses for food/clothing/other, housing/utilities, and transportation operating costs are reduced to the maximum amount allowed (assumes that the taxpayer does not have special conditions warranting an increase to the standard).

The taxpayers' ability to pay the IRS after applying the Standards is as follows:

MDI analysis	Average ACTUAL MDI (past 3 months)	Average MDI applying IRS Collection Financial Standards (past 3 months)
Income:		
Primary – gross wages/month	$4,800	$4,800
Spouse – gross wages/month	$4,224	$4,224
No other income	$0	$0
Total average monthly gross income	$9,024	$9,024
Expenses: (actual paid)		
Food, clothing, miscellaneous (all)	$2,300	$2,129

Housing/utilities (all)	$3,811	$2,696
Car 1 payment (primary)	$290	$290
Car 2 payment (spouse)	$465	$465
Transportation operating costs	$680	$670
Public transportation	$0	$0
Out-of-pocket medical expenses	$120	$336
Federal taxes paid	$500	$500
FICA/Medicare taxes paid	$505	$505
Health insurance premiums	$375	$375
Term life insurance premiums	$120	$120
Childcare payments	$400	$400
Total average monthly expenses	$9,566	$8,486
Monthly disposable income – ACTUAL EXPENSES v. ALLOWABLE EXPENSES (applying IRS CFS)	($542)	$538

The Morris family has an ability to pay off $538 a month and projects to make payments of $51,110 (95 months of $538 per month) toward the current balance of $60,000 plus any accrued penalties and interest before the CSED (95 months before first CSED). Because the Morris family is not projected to pay the full amount of the tax owed (projected payments are $538 a month, or $51,110, and the Morris family owe $60,000), the ability to pay agreement is a "partial pay installment agreement." The Morris family should execute an ATP installment agreement of $538 a month with the IRS. If their financial situation changes, they can request the IRS to change the payment amount based on their current/changed financial condition.

Applying CSED to ATP Determinations: CNC and Installment Agreements

Obviously, for the simple (owe $50,000 or less and can pay in full before CSED) and full-pay non-streamlined installment agreements (owe between $50,000 and $250,000 and can pay in full before CSED), the CSED is important to determine how long a taxpayer can pay the IRS. The full-pay NSIA will allow the IRS and taxpayers to avoid the determination on whether the taxpayer can use the actual or allowable expenses in determining their installment agreement terms if the taxpayer has the ability to pay before the CSED.

The CSED is also an important factor in all ATP agreements. For an ATP IA or CNC status, the CSED will determine what expenses are allowable in determining the taxpayer's agreement. If the taxpayer can pay within six years or the time frame of the CSED, whichever is shorter, some or all the other actual living expenses may be allowed in determining the installment agreement payment. [IRM 5.14.1.4.1 (3-31-2023)] However, if the taxpayer is not projected to pay the balance due before the CSED expires, the IRS will only allow necessary living expenses and expenses to produce income, subject to the IRS Collection Financial Standards.

Example: A taxpayer owes $96,000 for one year and has 120 months remaining on the CSED. The taxpayer has $6,000 in average monthly income. In each scenario, the CSED will determine whether the taxpayer is limited to only the necessary expenses (i.e., not conditional expenses). Below are different scenarios of actual v. allowable expenses (necessary and subject to IRS Collection Financial Standards) and their final ATP determination:

In each scenario, the taxpayer's actual expenses are greater than what the IRS allows under their Collection Financial Standards.
Scenario 1: Taxpayer is limited to necessary expenses only, which will full pay the amount owed before the CSED expires.
Scenario 2: Taxpayer can use actual expenses because they can pay within 6 years or less.
Scenario 3: Taxpayer's cannot pay with actual expenses - but will be limited to expenses allowed by Standards.
Scenario 4: Taxpayer has no MDI under actual or allowable expenses. Qualifies for CNC status.

Taxpayer situation
Amount owed: $96,000
CSED (months): 120

Financials	Scenario 1 Routine ATP IA	Scenario 2 Condtional IA	Scenario 3 Partial pay IA	Scenario 4 CNC
Average Monthly Income	**$6,000**	**$6,000**	**$6,000**	**$6,000**
Expenses: ACTUAL	$5,900	**$4,000**	$6,200	$6,500
Expenses: Necessary Only	**$5,000**	$3,800	**$5,700**	**$6,100**
MDI: ACTUAL	$100	**$2,000**	($200)	($500)
MDI: Necessary	**$1,000**	$2,200	**$300**	**($100)**
IA Payment	**$1,000**	**$2,000**	**$300**	**$0 - CNC status**
Actual expenses allowed?	No- cannot pay within 6 years	Yes- can pay within 6 years	No	No
Expenses limited by standards?	Yes	No	Yes	Yes
# of payments	96 months (plus time to pay accrued P&I)	48 months (plus time to pay accrued P&I)	120 months	No payment
Full payment of liability?	Yes	Yes	IRS projected not to receive full payment before CSED	IRS projected not to receive full payment before CSED
IRS re-determination of payment terms?	No	No	Yes- IRS reviews every 2 years	income may remove CNC status
Should taxpayer consider full pay NSIA terms?	Yes, payment amount could be lower than routine ATP IA (need to contact IRS)	Yes, payment amount will be lower if taxpayer pays currently balance, plus accruals, over CSED period.	Not an option as taxpayer cannot pay before CSED	

Note: in the routine or conditional IA cases, the taxpayer is likely to accept a "full pay NSIA" option to pay the entire balance owed before the CSED. This will result in less disclosure, no asset liquidation, and a less payment amount ($96,000 plus accrued penalties and interest to be paid before the 120 month CSED).

Applying CSED for OIC-DATC

The collection statute of limitations impacts the OIC qualification and offer amount computations. When determining OIC qualification, the ability to pay calculation projects future income to be paid over the life of the CSED. In determining the offer amount, the reasonable collection potential computation allows the taxpayer to compute the offer amount over 12 or 24 months, or the life of the CSED if it is less.

For more on the impact of CSEDs on the OIC qualification and offer amount computations, see **Chapter 12: Qualify and Obtain an Offer in Compromise for Doubt as to Collectibility (OIC-DATC.)**

Worksheets for Determining MDI for ATP Agreements

For the following worksheets to help determine ATP with equity in assets and detailed instructions, refer to the **Appendix B**—and visit www.TaxProblemsHandbook.com under the **IRS Collection Solutions Handbook** tab for downloadable resources.

Worksheet	Helps with:
Forms 433-A and 433-A(OIC): Net Business Income Analysis for Ability to Pay Calculation	For self-employed taxpayers: Worksheet to determine the average net business income for ability to pay determinations for CNC, ATP IAs, and OIC-DATC Maps to Forms 433-A and 433-A(OIC).
MDI Analysis Worksheet (for determining ability to pay for installment agreements, CNC, and OIC-DATC)	Worksheet to analyze the average monthly disposable income for ability to pay determinations for CNC, ATP IAs, and OIC-DATC.
Forms 433-A and 433-A(OIC) MDI Computation	Worksheet to determine final MDI for ability to pay determinations for CNC, ATP IAs, and OIC-DATC. Maps to Forms 433-A and 433-A(OIC).

Chapter 9.08: Determining Total Ability to Pay: CNC and the ATP IA, and the OIC-DATC

The taxpayer's ability to pay is determined by two components:

1. Net equity in assets, plus
2. Amount that can be paid in monthly payments (monthly disposable income).

CNC/ATP IA computations determine the current payment arrangements with the IRS. The OIC computations differ from the CNC/IA ATP calculations and are used to determine if the taxpayer qualifies for an OIC-DATC and the offer amount necessary to settle the liability in full.

CNC and ATP IAs

For CNC and ability to pay IAs, the taxpayer may have to access equity in assets first to pay down the liability. If the equity does not pay down the liability, the taxpayer will then determine how much can be paid with monthly payments (MDI).

The taxpayer will proceed to negotiate payment by accessing equity and negotiating future installment agreements with the IRS.

OIC-DATC Ability to Pay (Qualification) and Reasonable Collection Potential (Offer Amount)

The taxpayer will need do separate computations to determine qualification and the offer amount when considering an OIC-DATC.

Step #1: Determine if the taxpayer qualifies for an OIC.

To determine if a taxpayer qualifies for an OIC-DATC, the taxpayer will compute the total amount that could be paid with net equity in assets plus future installment payments. If that amount exceeds the tax balance owed, the taxpayer qualifies.

Step #2: If the taxpayer qualifies, determine the offer amount.

If the taxpayer qualifies for an OIC-DATC, the next step is to determine their reasonable collection potential (RCP) or the "offer amount." The taxpayer will add the net realizable equity in assets and MDI amount (based on which type of OIC payment method is selected) to arrive at the offer amount. The offer amount computation will differ from the qualification computation. The offer amount will allow additional exclusions from the net equity in assets and monthly disposable income.

The Form 433-A(OIC): OIC Qualification and Offer Amount Computations Worksheet can be used to make the final OIC qualification and offer amount calculation:

OIC-DATC Worksheets

To fully compute the taxpayer's equity in assets and monthly disposable income, as well as to determine OIC qualification and offer amount, refer to the **Appendix B**—and visit www.TaxProblemsHandbook.com under the **IRS Collection Solutions Handbook** tab.

Worksheet	Helps with:
OIC: Equity in Asset Summary for OIC Qualification Determination	NRE calculation: Worksheet to value net equity in assets for purposes of determining if the taxpayer qualifies for an OIC-DATC.
Form 433-A(OIC): Equity in Asset Summary for Offer Amount Determination	NRE calculation: Worksheet to compute net realizable equity in assets (for OIC-DATC offer amounts determination). Maps to Form 433-A(OIC).
Forms 433-A and 433-A(OIC): Net Business Income Analysis for Ability to Pay Calculation	MDI calculation: (self-employed taxpayers) Worksheet to determine the average net business income for ability to pay determinations for CNC, ATP IAs, and OIC-DATC. Maps to Forms 433-A and 433-A(OIC).
MDI Analysis Worksheet (for determining ability to pay for installment agreements, CNC, and OIC-DATC)	MDI calculation: Worksheet to analyze the average monthly disposable income for ability to pay determinations for CNC, ATP IAs, and OIC-DATC.
Forms 433-A and 433-A(OIC) MDI Computation	MDI calculation: Worksheet to determine final MDI for ability to pay determinations for CNC, ATP IAs, and OIC-DATC. Maps to Forms 433-A and 433-A(OIC).
Form 433-A(OIC): OIC Qualification and Offer Amount Computations	Offer qualification and offer amount calculations: Worksheet to determine if the taxpayer qualifies for an OIC-DATC and to compute the offer amount. Maps to parts of Form 433-A(OIC) and Form 656.

Chapter 9.09: ATP Examples

View examples of these ATP agreements at www.TaxProblemsHandbook.com and navigate to the **IRS Collection Solutions Handbook** tab to access the referenced item.

Collection option examples
Ability to pay installment agreement
Currently not collectible
Offer in compromise, Doubt as to collectibility

Chapter 10:
OBTAIN AN INSTALLMENT AGREEMENT BASED ON ABILITY TO PAY ANALYSIS

This section covers the IRS's ability to pay installment agreement options and how to obtain this option with the IRS.

Topic	Covers
Ability to Pay Installment Agreements (ATP IA)	The types of ATP IAs and how they are computed. The terms of each ATP IA.
Steps to Request ATP IA	How to request an ATP installment agreement with the IRS.
Appealing Rejected ATP IA Requests	Appeals options and how to appeal a rejected ATP installment agreement with the IRS.
Comprehensive Example	Link to a practical example of how to analyze and request an ATP installment agreement.

Key Highlights:

- There are three situations where taxpayers must consider an ATP installment agreement (ATP IA): taxpayers who have an assessed balance owed greater than $250,000 and have the ability to pay with monthly payments, taxpayers who owe less than $250,000 and have an ATP with monthly payments but cannot pay based on the simple installment agreement (SIA) or the full-pay non-streamlined installment agreement (NSIA) payment plan terms, and taxpayers assigned to Field Collection (i.e., CFf, revenue officer).

- There are three types of ATP IAs: the routine ATP IA (ATP IA), conditional IA, and the partial pay IA (PPIA). The appropriate ATP IA is determined by an analysis of a taxpayer's current finances (ATP calculation).

- Taxpayers enter into a "partial pay installment agreement" (PPIA) with the IRS when their monthly payment plan will not full-pay the amount owed before the collection statute expires.

- ATP IAs have increased IRS scrutiny and take more time and effort to set up. They require that the taxpayer file a Collection Information Statement with the IRS, with supporting documentation, to prove the ability to pay. Many taxpayers will also find better terms and an easier set-up process using the full-pay NSIA if they can pay the balance in full before the Collection Statute Expiration Date (CSED).

- The new simple IA and the full-pay NSIA terms will remove the need for many ability to pay agreements. The full-pay NSIA allows the taxpayer to pay the amount owed before the CSED without regard to their ability to pay calculation.

- ATP IAs usually result in the filing of a Notice of Federal Tax Lien if the taxpayer owes more than $10,000. The full- pay NSIA also requires a tax lien to be filed.

Chapter 10.01: Ability to Pay Installment Agreements (ATP IA)

Most IRS installment agreements executed each year do not require the taxpayer to prove the ability to pay. At the end of the IRS FY2024, the taxpayers were in 4.6 million installment agreements, most of which were simple installment agreements. [IRS Data Book, 2024, Table 27] Simple Installment Agreements (SIA) and full-pay Non-streamlined Installment Agreement (NSIA) payment agreements (for those who owe assessed balances up to $250,000 and can pay before the CSED) do not require the taxpayer to provide the IRS with financial information and make payment arrangements based on the ability to pay. However, the Treasury Inspector General for Tax Administration also reported that 9% of all payment agreements defaulted in 2020. [TIGTA Report 2022-30-012, Oversight of the Low-Income Housing Tax Credit Program Can Be Improved, January 26, 2022] The high default rate was likely due to the fact that taxpayers did not have an ability to pay the installment agreement amount and should be looking for a different collection alternative.

If a taxpayer does not qualify or cannot meet the terms (i.e., payment amount) for a simple agreement or a full-pay non-streamlined agreement payment plan, and can pay with monthly payments (i.e., has positive monthly disposable income or "MDI" greater than $25 a month), they will need an ATP IA.

There are three types of ATP IAs:

- *Routine IA*: a payment plan based on average monthly income and necessary living expenses that will fully pay the balance owed before the collection statute expiration date (CSED). Usually, these payment plans are longer than six years, or the duration of the CSED, whichever is shorter. [IRM 5.14.1.4 at (4) (7-2-2024)] The full-pay NSIA will remove the need for many routine IA computations because the taxpayer will be allowed to pay the balance owed before the CSED, which may remove the need to compute the taxpayer's ATP
- *Conditional IA*: a payment plan in which the taxpayer will fully pay the liability owed within six years, or the term of the CSED, whichever is shorter. This plan allows the taxpayer to use actual expenses in determining the monthly payment arrangement. Conditional IAs, also known as the "six-year rule" IA, are attractive to both the taxpayer and the IRS because they are less likely to default. Taxpayers pay based on their current expenses which reduces their chances for default. [IRM 5.14.1.4.1 (3-31-2023)] However, the full-pay NSIA will likely remove the need for many taxpayers to use the conditional IA because the full-pay NSIA will allow the taxpayer to pay before the CSED, which may be longer than the six-year conditional IA period.
- *Partial Pay Installment Agreement (PPIA):* a payment plan in which the taxpayer is projected, based on current ability, to be unable to pay the balance owed before the

expiration of the CSED. If the payment arrangement is not changed, the IRS will "write-off" the remaining tax, penalties, and interest owed on the CSED. [IRM 5.14.2.2.1 (10-18-2023)]

IRS Collection Financial Standards (Allowable Living Expenses)

In ATP IAs, the taxpayer is only allowed necessary household living expenses and expenses for the production of income. [IRM 5.15.1.8 at (1) (7-24-2019)] The taxpayers' allowable living expenses (ALEs) may be limited by the IRS's Collection Financial Standards (CFS). The CFS places limits or provides standard amounts allowed on the amount of ALEs for the following types of household living expenses:

- Food, clothing, and other items.
- Out-of-pocket medical expenses.
- Housing and utilities.
- Transportation ownership and operating costs.

[IRM 5.15.1.8 (7-24-2019)]

The standard amounts are guidelines. In some cases, it is appropriate for the IRS to deviate from the standard amount for living expenses when the standard causes the taxpayer economic hardship. [IRM 5.15.1.2 at (13) (11-22-2021)] Unique circumstances do not include the maintenance of an affluent or luxurious standard of living. [IRM 5.15.1.2 at (16) (11-22-2021)]

> **Pro Tip:** IRS collection representatives are very reluctant to allow the taxpayer to exceed their ALEs. Taxpayers must document and prove that the expenses in excess of the standard are needed for the health and welfare of the family. Taxpayers are allowed expenses in excess of the standards if they can pay within six years (or the time limit of the CSED, whichever is lower) under the conditional installment agreement rules. Taxpayers who can full-pay should consider the full-pay NSIA option to avoid disputes on allowable versus non-allowable expenses.

For each ATP IA, the payment plan amount and duration are determined as follows:

ATP IA Type	Payment determination	Payment plan duration
Routine ATP IA	Average monthly household income less average monthly necessary living expenses, subject to limitations imposed by IRS Collection Financial Standards.	Until the amount is paid but before the expiration of the CSED.
Conditional IA	Average monthly household income less average actual monthly necessary living expenses. Actual expenses are only allowed to the extent that the taxpayer	72 months, or the period of the CSED, whichever is shorter. *Note:* The full-pay NSIA terms are likely to

	can pay within 72 months or the CSED, whichever is shorter.	produce a lower monthly payment if the CSED is longer than six years.
Partial pay installment agreement (PPIA)	Average monthly household income less average monthly necessary living expenses, subject to limitations imposed by IRS Collection Financial Standards.	Until the expiration of the CSED. Reviewed by the IRS every 2 years.

ATP IA — Payment with Equity in Assets

The routine ATP IA and the PPIA receive additional scrutiny by the IRS because the taxpayer is requesting payment terms that put the total collection of the balances owed in jeopardy. If the payment plan will last more than six years, is a PPIA, or there is a high dollar amount owed, the IRS will more closely look to see if the taxpayer can liquidate non-essential assets or access equity in assets. [IRM 5.14.2.2 at (2) (4-26-2019)] If the taxpayer borrows against equity in assets, any additional loans would be allowed as a necessary living expense and reduce MDI. In practice, the IRS does not require the taxpayer to borrow against assets in a PPIA if the additional loan payment would put the taxpayer at risk of meeting their monthly living expenses (i.e., reduce the MDI to under $25). [IRM 5.14.2.2.2 at (2e) (6-5-2025)] A common example is when the taxpayer is asked to access home equity via a home equity loan. If the additional loan payment would exceed monthly disposable income and put the taxpayer in financial hardship, the IRS will not look for the taxpayer to access equity in the home. [IRM 5.14.2.2.2 at (2f) (6-5-2025)]

One-Year Rule to Reduce Living Expenses

In an ATP IA, the IRS may allow a taxpayer one year to lower his living expenses. This allowance is called the "one-year rule," "tiered installment agreement," or the "one-year lifestyle adjustment." [IRM 5.14.1.4.1 at (2) (3-31-2023)] Although it is not an IRS requirement, the one-year rule is usually allowed when the taxpayer can pay within six years. Using the one-year rule, it is possible for a taxpayer to enter into an agreement with the IRS in which the first-year payments are based on actual expenses and the remaining payments are higher based on the taxpayer's agreement to reduce excessive necessary living expenses.

> **Example** Ben owes the IRS $60,000 and has 80 months remaining before the expiration of the CSED. He has the following financial information:

Monthly disposable income	Amount
Based on Actual Expenses	$500
Living expenses in excess of the IRS Collection Financial Standard limitations: Excess housing expenses due to a high mortgage payment	$1,000
Based on Allowable Living Expenses, subject to limits imposed by IRS Collection Financial Standards	$1,500

In this case, Ben can petition the IRS for a $500 per month payment for the first year using the one-year rule, and payments of $1,500 a month thereafter until the tax is paid. The IRS will accept this agreement because the full amount will be paid within six years ($6,000 in year one and $18,000 in the three years following (for a total of $54,000) which will pay the amount off in four years). *Note:* Ben may have a few remaining payments after four years to account for accrued interest and penalties. Ben could also use the full-pay NSIA terms, but may not elect to do so because it would result in higher first-year payments.

PPIA Additional Terms

On rare occasions when the taxpayer has a potential future ability to pay, PPIA-requesting taxpayers may be asked to extend the CSED. [IRM 5.14.2.2.3 (1-1-2016)] It is the IRS's policy to request an extension of the CSED only in PPIAs with certain circumstances. [IRM 5.14.1.2 at (14) (7-2-2024)] The IRS can request the taxpayer to extend the CSED up to five years, plus an additional year for any administrative actions needed. The IRS can only request a CSED extension where there is an asset that will come into the possession of a taxpayer after the CSED and liquidation of that asset offers the best-case resolution (in lieu of liquidating existing assets to partially pay the liability). [IRM 5.14.2.2.3 (1-1-2016)]

The IRS uses Form 900, *Tax Collection Waiver*, to extend the CSED. [IRM 5.14.2.2.3 at (4) (1-1-2016)]

Approved PPIAs are tracked by the IRS and the law requires the IRS to review the agreements every two years and redetermine if the taxpayer's ATP should be reviewed and new payment terms requested. [IRC §6159(d)] The IRS procedures trigger a manual review of the PPIA if the taxpayer's total income increases by 6% as compared to the year in which the PPIA was requested (the IRS does this by comparing tax total income on tax returns). [TIGTA Report 2013-30-040, Controls Over Partial Payment Installment Agreements Can Be Improved, May 6, 2013] The IRS may contact taxpayers falling into this category with a request for updated financial information. Taxpayers not responding to the inquiry face termination of their IA and enforced collection by levy.

Taxpayers who obtain a PPIA will receive a Notice of Federal Tax Lien if the amount that they owe is greater than $10,000. [IRM 5.14.2.2.1 at (10) (10-18-2023)]

There is a user fee to set up ATP installment agreements. ATP IAs cannot be completed using the IRS online payment agreement application (OPA) and have a higher fee if set up by mail or phone. Taxpayers can reduce their set-up fee by signing up for a direct debit or payroll deduction payment method. If the taxpayer has defaulted on a PPIA in the past 24 months, a direct debit payment method is required to reinstate the agreement. [IRM 5.14.2.2.1 at (9) (10-18-2023)]

For a list of appropriate fees, see **Chapter 7.04: Installment Agreement User Fees.**

Comparison Example of ATP IAs

To illustrate the differences among the three ATP IAs, see the following three scenarios for a taxpayer who owes $96,000 (total balance), has 120 months until the expiration of the CSED. Assume, the taxpayer cannot pay down their debt to qualify for the simple or full-pay non-streamlined installment agreements.

For each scenario, assume the taxpayer has $6,000 in average monthly revenue, the following actual and allowable expenses, and resulting MDI:

Income	Scenario 1	Scenario 2	Scenario 3
Monthly average	$6,000	$6,000	$6,000
Average Monthly Expenses	**Scenario 1**	**Scenario 2**	**Scenario 3**
Actual	$5,900	$4,000	$6,200
Necessary only, limited by IRS Collection Financial Standards	$5,000	$3,800	$5,700
Monthly Disposable Income (MDI) (Income less expenses)	**Scenario 1**	**Scenario 2**	**Scenario 3**
MDI – actual	$100	$2,000	($200)
MDI – necessary only, limited by IRS Collection Financial Standards	$1,000	$2,200	$300

In scenario 1, the taxpayer only can pay $100 using actual expenses. The IRS will not accept a $100 agreement because the actual expenses exceed the necessary business expenses allowed for the taxpayer according to limits set by IRS Collection Financial Standards (i.e., some actual expenses are not considered necessary and/or necessary expenses exceed the limits imposed by the Standards). In scenario 1, the IRS will only allow $5,000 in necessary expenses. The result is a routine IA where the taxpayer will have a $1,000 a month payment for 96+ months that is projected to fully pay the liability before the expiration of the CSED. In this scenario, the taxpayer should explore the full-pay NSIA as a possible alternative.

In scenario 2, the taxpayer's finances will allow him to use his actual expenses because the taxpayer will be able to pay within six years, or within the CSED (120 months in our example), whichever is shorter. In this case, the taxpayer can use all $4,000 in actual expenses. The result is a conditional IA with a payment of $2,000 a month for 48+ months — within the six years required by a conditional IA. *Note:* In this case, the taxpayer would qualify for a full-pay "non-streamlined" installment agreement. This payment will be the total projected amount owed (the current balance plus the projected accrued penalties and interest) divided by the number of months remaining on the collection statute of limitations. For example, if the taxpayer is projected to owe $120,000 before the CSED (i.e., the current $96,000 plus accrued penalties and interest for the next 120 months before the CSED), the taxpayer could enter into a $1,091 a month payment plan under the full-pay NSIA rules. In this scenario, if the taxpayer wants a lower monthly payment, they should explore the full-pay NSIA as an alternative as the $96,000 current balance, plus accrued interest and penalties, would likely render a smaller monthly payment amount over the 120 months remaining until the CSED.

In scenario 3, the taxpayer will not be able to pay based on actual or necessary living expenses. If actual expenses were allowed, the taxpayer would be currently not collectible. However, when applying the necessary expense rules and IRS Collection Financial Standard limitations, the taxpayer has $500 less in expenses allowed. The result is a PPIA where the taxpayer will have a payment of $300 per month projected to last for the entire 120 months left on the collection statute. The IRS will review the agreement every two years to determine if a new agreement is warranted.

To summarize the three scenarios:

Taxpayer situation
Amount owed: $96,000
CSED (months): 120

	Financials	*Scenario 1* **Routine ATP IA**	*Scenario 2* **Condtional IA**	*Scenario 3* **Partial pay IA**
Income and Expenses	*Average Monthly Income*	$6,000	$6,000	$6,000
	Expenses: ACTUAL	$5,900	$4,000	$6,200
	Expenses: Necessary Only	$5,000	$3,800	$5,700
ATP: MDI	*MDI: ACTUAL*	$100	$2,000	($200)
	MDI: Necessary	$1,000	$2,200	$300
	IA Payment	$1,000	$2,000	$300
ATP Determination	*Actual expenses allowed?*	No- cannot pay within 6 years	Yes- can pay within 6 years	No
	Expenses limited by standards?	Yes	No	Yes
	# of payments	96 months (plus time to pay accrued P&I)	48 months (plus time to pay accrued P&I)	120 months
	Full payment of liability?	Yes	Yes	IRS projected not to receive full payment before CSED
	IRS re-determination of payment terms?	No	No	Yes- IRS reviews every 2 years
Full pay NSIA option	*Should taxpayer consider full pay NSIA terms?*	Yes, payment amount could be lower than routine ATP IA (need to contact IRS)	Yes, payment amount will be lower if taxpayer pays currently balance, plus accruals, over CSED period.	Not an option as taxpayer cannot pay before CSED

Change in Financial Circumstances

Taxpayers who have changes in their financial situation can request a different agreement with the IRS based on their current and future ability to pay. Taxpayers often request a change due to unforeseen circumstances like loss of a job or increased allowable expenses, such as bill related to a medical condition.

> **Pro Tip:** It is common for taxpayers will few assets to obtain a PPIA and subsequently file for an OIC. Though this may or may not be related to a change in financial circumstances, it illustrates that collection agreements can be changed based on taxpayer action.

Chapter 10.02: Steps to Request ATP IA

ATP IAs are always secured with the IRS Collection function. If the taxpayer is assigned to IRS collection, the taxpayer will secure the agreement with the assigned collection function: either the Automated Collection System (i.e., IRS Campus Collection or "Service Center" collection) or local collection (the Collection Field function assignment to a revenue officer). If the taxpayer is in the IRS field collection "queue" awaiting assignment to an IRS revenue officer, the taxpayer may secure the agreement with the revenue officer. IRS ACS can take information on the case, but it is likely that ACS will defer to a revenue officer's collection decision. [IRM 5.19.1.4.1 at (4) (7-9-2024)]

ATP IA requires a financial disclosure. Taxpayers will be required to complete the appropriate Collection Information Statement(s) (Form 433-A, 433-F, 433-H, and/or 433-B) to provide detailed information on their assets, liabilities, income, and expenses to the IRS. [IRM 5.19.1.6.4.1 at (2) (7-9-2024)] Depending on the circumstances, the IRS may request supporting information and documents to determine the taxpayer's ATP with equity in assets and MDI. Taxpayers may propose a collection alternative, including a specific payment amount, or have the IRS compute the acceptable payment.

> **Pro Tip:** It is essential that the taxpayer conduct their due diligence in determining the ability to pay according to IRS procedures. With the ATP calculation, taxpayers can request specific terms (type of ATP IA, payment amount, etc.) in an ATP agreement with the IRS. With the analysis in hand, any disagreements with the IRS can be isolated and immediately addressed. Taxpayers should also keep a full copy of all documents and representations made to the IRS in securing any IRS collection agreement.

Steps to Obtain an ATP IA		
#	Steps	Resources
1	Compute ability to pay with equity in assets (voluntary lump sum payment) and MDI.	IRS Collection Templates (Worksheets, Checklists, etc.)- See **Appendix B**

2	Complete required Collection Information Statement (Form 433-A or F).	IRS Forms Used for Collection Agreements and Issues- See **Appendix C**
3	Gather and attach supporting documentation.	ATP Financial Disclosure to the IRS- See **Chapter 9.05**
4	Complete proposal of collection alternative and required installment agreement forms (Form 433-D or 9465).	IRS Forms Used for Collection Agreements and Issues- See **Appendix C**
5	Submit to IRS Collection (by phone or by mail).	Frequently Used IRS Collection Phone Numbers- See **Chapter 1.04**
6	Resolve disputed issues and finalize agreement.	Appealing Rejected ATP IA Requests- See **Chapter 10.03**
7	Make monthly payments as required.	Payment Methods- See **Chapter 1.14**

If the taxpayer is not assigned to a local revenue officer, the taxpayer can call IRS collection and provide the Collection Information Statement by phone to expedite the ATP IA request. The IRS will take the information on the Collection Information Statement and request the taxpayer to fax the supporting documents while on the call. Alternatively, the IRS will provide an ACS Support address to send in supporting documents in order to complete the agreement.

Chapter 10.03: Appealing Rejected ATP IA Requests

If a taxpayer's ATP IA request is rejected by the IRS, the taxpayer has two informal appeals options:

1. *Manager Review*: the taxpayer may request the IRS collection employee's manager to reconsider the proposed IA. In most cases, the IRS manager has likely already reviewed the rejected IA independently. The taxpayer will have the opportunity to present her position to the manager and this may contradict the facts considered by the manager. [IRM 5.19.8.4.16.4 (5-3-2023)] IRS procedures state that the manager will contact the taxpayer within 24 hours to informally discuss the case. [IRM 5.19.8.4.16.4 at (2) (5-3-2023)] However, in dealing with the IRS ACS, it is common for the taxpayer to not be contacted within 24 hours.

2. *Collection Appeals Program (CAP)*: taxpayers may ask an independent IRS appeals officer to review the case. Taxpayers must use Form 9423, *Collection Appeal Request*, to state her position and disagreement with the IRS IA determination. Taxpayers must request a CAP hearing within 30 days of the rejected IA. [IRM 5.14.9.8 at (1) (12-18-2017)] Taxpayers usually are contacted by the IRS and receive an appeal hearing several weeks after filing the Form 9423. The conclusion of the appeals hearing is final and not subject to further review.

The taxpayer may also utilize the more formal Collection Due Process appeal if she has also received a lien or levy notice within the last 30 days. Rejected IA proposals do not automatically qualify the taxpayer for a CDP appeal. However, if a taxpayer has a lien or levy notice that qualifies her for a CDP, the CDP hearing can be used to both propose a new ATP IA as well as to argue a rejected IA.

> **Pro Tip:** It is common for the IRS and the taxpayer to disagree on ATP IA proposals, especially as they relate to the calculation of monthly income and necessary living expenses. Taxpayers should be prepared to appeal and provide substantiation and explanations to support how their calculation of monthly income and expenses best represents that taxpayer's future ability to pay.

Chapter 10.04: Comprehensive Example

Example Geoff and Tiffany Jones owe the IRS $160,000 for the tax years 2020 and 2021. Their assessed balance is $140,000 and the earliest CSED expiration is 98 months. They are unable to pay according to the full-pay non-streamlined installment agreement payment terms and need an ATP IA. Their date to request the IA is April 30, 2024. *Note:* For this example, Geoff and Tiffany do not qualify for an OIC-DATC as their equity in assets ($167,009) plus future installment payments (98 months @ $1,154 a month) far exceed their taxes owed. *Note:* This example uses the IRS expense standards for April 2024–March 2025. For the most up-to-date expense standards, see the following: https://www.irs.gov/businesses/small-businesses-self-employed/collection-financial-standards.

To view more of this comprehensive example, see www.TaxProblemsHandbook.com and navigate to the **IRS Collection Solutions Handbook** tab to access the referenced item.

Chapter 11:
OBTAIN CURRENTLY NOT COLLECTIBLE STATUS (CNC)

This section covers the IRS's currently not collectible status, its terms, and how to obtain CNC with the IRS.

Topic	Covers
Currently Not Collectible Status (CNC)	CNC status terms and common situations that warrant CNC status.
CNC Ability to Pay Analysis	How to determine and compute if a taxpayer qualifies for CNC status.
Steps to Request CNC	How to request CNC with the IRS.
Appealing Rejected CNC Requests	Appeals options and how to appeal a rejected CNC request.
Comprehensive Example	Link to a practical example of how to analyze and request CNC.

Key Highlights:

- Currently not collectible status (CNC) is a temporary hardship status that allows taxpayers to defer payment on their balances owed to the IRS. To obtain CNC, a taxpayer must prove hardship to the IRS.
- CNC status remains in effect until the taxpayer has an increase in income and/or assets that results in an ability to pay the IRS.
- IRS procedures require a filing of a Notice of Federal Tax Lien on taxpayers who obtain CNC status and owe more than $10,000.

Chapter 11.01: Currently Not Collectible Status (CNC)

Overview

CNC is a hardship status that allows the taxpayer to temporarily defer payment on a tax debt. If a taxpayer owes back taxes and does not have enough income to pay necessary living expenses, he may qualify for CNC status.

IRS Policy Statement 5-71 states that the IRS can stop collection on taxpayers when it has been determined that a taxpayer account is not collectible. [IRM 1.2.1.6.14 (11-19-1980)] As of 9/30/2024, there were 421,125 taxpayers in a hardship CNC status. [IRS FOIA Response #2025-

07325, February 2025)] To determine non-collectibility, the IRS must examine the taxpayer's assets, income, and expenses to determine if payment of the liability would cause a hardship to the taxpayer. The taxpayer qualifies for CNC if their income does not allow them to meet necessary living expenses. Once a taxpayer is in CNC status, the account is removed from IRS collection until she has an ability to pay in the future.

Taxpayers may request CNC status from the IRS for any amount owed. The IRS can put taxpayers in CNC status if the taxpayer can prove that she has an inability to pay. [IRM 5.16.1.2.9 (3-3-2025)]

The IRS may also put taxpayers in CNC status if the IRS has decided not to pursue collection on the taxpayer for internal reasons, such as lack of collection resources. In these cases, a taxpayer can be temporarily removed from "active collection" enforcement. The IRS can also put a taxpayer in CNC status if they are unable to enforce payment. For example, a common reason accounts may be removed from active collection occurs when the IRS cannot locate the taxpayer to enforce payment. In these cases, the taxpayer is likely not working with the IRS to obtain CNC status. The taxpayer receives "CNC–unable to locate" status. [IRM 5.16.1.2.1 at (1) (3-3-2025)] Another common CNC status is when the taxpayer does not respond, and the IRS decides not to pursue collection. These cases receive "CNC-unable to contact" status. [IRM 5.16.1.2.1 at (2) (3-3-2025)] Taxpayers who are in CNC status without an agreement with the IRS face uncertainty as the IRS can decide to pursue active collection at any time in the future. IRS procedures allow for "unable to locate" and "unable to contact" cases to systemically reactivate for collection when a new levy source appears, or a new address appears in IRS systems. [IRM 5.16.1.2 at (7) (3-3-2025)] The best method to avoid IRS collection enforcement activity (especially levies) requires working with the IRS to obtain the correct collection alternative, which may include CNC status.

After the taxpayer receives CNC status, they are likely to stay in this status for at least a year. The IRS can review CNC status annually through income reported on a tax return or through information statements (W-2s, 1099, etc.) received. [IRM 5.16.1.2.9 at (14) (3-3-2025)] If the income exceeds the taxpayer's proven necessary living expenses at the time CNC status was granted, the IRS may remove the account from CNC status and request that the taxpayer again prove her ability to pay.

If a taxpayer's financial status does not change, the IRS may continue to keep the taxpayer in CNC status until the collection statute of limitations expires. [IRM 5.16.1.2.9 at (14) (3-3-2025)] At the collection statute expiration date (CSED), the IRS will write-off any remaining balance owed on the CNC taxpayer.

Common Situations That Warrant CNC

Taxpayers with financial hardships may find themselves without the ability to meet necessary living expenses. Common scenarios that trigger CNC status are unemployment, underemployment, and other circumstances that render the taxpayer unable to earn sufficient income to pay living expenses. A taxpayer experiencing other hardships such as high medical expenses or other allowable necessary living expenses may warrant CNC if they are left with no income to make monthly payments. Taxpayers who have living expenses in excess of what the IRS Collection Financial Standards allow are not considered hardship cases that qualify for CNC status (i.e., high mortgage or car payments, other living expenses not allowed as necessary living expenses like private school tuition). [IRM 5.19.17.2.4 at (1) (3-15-2023)]

> **Pro Tip:** Taxpayers who qualify for CNC and have little or no equity in assets should also consider an Offer in Compromise to settle their taxes. Taxpayers who are in CNC would only have to offer their net realizable equity in assets (assuming they have no dissipated assets) to settle their tax bill.

CNC Terms

There are several other important terms involved in applying for CNC status:

1. *Requests to extend the collection statute of limitations*: the taxpayer will not be asked to extend the collection statute expiration date (CSED). Unlike a partial-pay installment agreement, the IRS does not have the authority to request an extension of the CSED. [IRM 5.14.2.2.3 (1-1-2016)]
2. *Penalties and interest continue to accrue*: the taxpayer will receive an annual notice of the balance owed, IRS Notice CP71A, which includes accrued penalties and interest owed on the balance. [IRM 21.3.1.6.34.1 (10-2-2023)]
3. *Tax lien filing*: IRS procedures require that the IRS make a lien determination and potentially file a Notice of Federal Tax Lien if the amount owed is greater than $10,000. [IRM 5.16.1.2 at (3) (3-3-2025)]
4. *CNC set-up fee*: there is no user fee for CNC.
5. *CNC default rules*: future balances owed will default to CNC status if the CNC determination is more than 12 months old. Taxpayers who have secured CNC status within the past 12 months and have a total assessed balance under $25,000 will generally retain their CNC status with an additional balance due return. [IRM 5.19.17.2.8 at (1) (7-5-2019)]
6. *Filing compliance*: generally, all tax returns need to be filed before CNC can be granted. [IRM 5.19.17.2 at (5) (3-15-2023)] However, for taxpayers with a hardship, the IRS must release a levy even if the taxpayer does not have all returns filed. The IRS has the discretion to place a taxpayer in final CNC hardship status when all returns are not filed if the non-filed years are more than six years old, the taxpayer does not have a filing requirement, or if the taxpayer is due a refund. [IRM 5.16.1.2.9 at (12) (3-3-2025)]
7. *Levy release*: levies are required to be released upon proof of hardship or a determination that a taxpayer qualifies for CNC. [IRM 5.16.1.2.9 at (10) (3-3-2025) and IRC §6343(e)]
8. *Confirmation letter*: taxpayer will receive IRS Letter 4223 or Letter 4624C, *Case Closed—Currently Not Collectible*, when the taxpayer has received hardship CNC status. [IRM 5.16.1.2.9 at (16) (3-3-2025) and IRM 5.19.17.2 at (7) (6-2-2023)]
9. *Passport restrictions*: the IRS will not certify CNC taxpayers as having seriously delinquent tax debt for purposes of passport restrictions. If the taxpayer has already been certified,

the IRS will reverse certification once CNC is established. [IRM 5.16.1.2.9 at (17) (3-3-2025)]

10. *Future refunds:* the IRS will continue to take any future refunds to pay the taxes owed.

11. *CNC status does not extend the CSED:* if the CSED expires on a tax year with a balance owed, the taxpayer's tax debt will be written off.

12. *Joint liabilities on separated taxpayers:* if joint taxpayers are separated, each taxpayer must qualify for CNC or face potential IRS collection enforcement. [IRM 5.19.17.2.10 (3-6-2020)]

Chapter 11.02: CNC Ability to Pay Analysis

Like ability to pay installment agreements (ATP IA), CNC requires that the taxpayer determine his ability to pay on the balances owed. The financial ability to pay analysis for CNC is similar to an ATP IA analysis. The only difference is that the taxpayer does not have monthly disposable income, after allowance of necessary living expenses. Similar to ATP IAs, for CNC status, the taxpayer's ability to pay is determined by two components:

1. how much he can pay with equity in assets, plus
2. how much he can pay with monthly payments to the IRS.

In the case of CNC status, the taxpayer typically has little ability to pay with equity in assets. The taxpayer also does not have the ability to make monthly payments based on the ability to pay analysis. In CNC monthly disposable income (MDI) determinations, the IRS only allows necessary living expenses, limited by IRS Collection Financial Standards, and expenses for the production of income, when computing MDI. IRS procedures allow CNC status if the taxpayer has $25 or less in MDI. [IRM 5.15.1.11 at (4b) (11-22-2021)]

CNC—Payment with Equity in Assets

Taxpayers who request CNC status are reviewed for any ability to pay with current assets. Taxpayers are asked to pay with current assets and/or to access equity in assets if this will not cause the taxpayer additional hardship. [IRM 5.16.1.2.9 at (1) (3-3-2025)] A hardship is not a mere inconvenience to the taxpayer. Hardship exists only if the taxpayer is unable to pay reasonable living expenses. If a taxpayer is unable to meet his current living expenses (i.e., MDI is $0), then the taxpayer is experiencing a hardship. In these cases, a taxpayer may be asked to pay down the tax owed with excess savings or other non-essential funds if that amount is not needed for future living expenses. However, the taxpayer will not be asked to incur additional monthly expenses that will increase hardship (i.e., borrow against a pension plan or home that would produce an additional monthly payment that the taxpayer cannot make). In practice, the IRS does not require the taxpayer to borrow against assets in a CNC if the additional loan payment would put the taxpayer at risk of not meeting monthly living expenses.

> **Example-** Brian owes the IRS $27,000 and is only able to find part-time work. When computing his ability to pay, he discovers that his monthly income is $2,000 a month, and

his necessary living expenses, limited by IRS Collection Financial Standards, is $3,200 a month. Brian's expenses exceed his income by $1,200 a month and Brian is using his $11,000 in savings to cover his living expenses each month. Brian has a home with $40,000 in equity. If he borrows against the equity, he will add to his monthly expenses (that he cannot already meet with his $2,000 in monthly income). The IRS will not want Brian to pay with his savings or borrow against the equity in his home because it would cause him an additional hardship.

CNC—Monthly Disposable Income Analysis

To qualify for CNC, a taxpayer's monthly disposable income (MDI) must be less than $25. [IRM 5.15.1.11 at (4b) (11-22-2021)] The MDI calculation for CNC is similar to the routine ATP IA. Taxpayers compute their average monthly income and expenses. Like the ATP analysis for routine IAs, the CNC ATP analysis only allows the taxpayer necessary living expenses and expenses necessary to produce income. Household living expenses are limited by IRS Collection Financial Standards. Taxpayers are also required to prove that their necessary living expenses are paid.

> **Pro Tip:** Many times, taxpayers in financial distress are not able to pay expenses that would be allowed as a necessary household living expense. For example, taxpayers may be in arrears with mortgage or car payments. In these cases, the IRS will limit the amount of expenses to only the paid expenses. This could change the taxpayer's ATP.

CNC Financial Analysis Illustration of Actual v. Allowable Necessary Living Expenses

The following two scenarios illustrate the ability to pay analysis when determining if the taxpayer qualifies for CNC. In this example, the taxpayer owes $50,000 (assessed balance), has 80 months until the CSED, does not have an ability to pay, and wants to request CNC status.

For each scenario, assume the taxpayer has $6,000 in average monthly revenue and the following actual and allowable expenses, and resulting MDI:

Income	Scenario 1	Scenario 2
Monthly average	$6,000	$6,000
Average Monthly Expenses	**Scenario 1**	**Scenario 2**
Actual	$6,800	$6,800
Necessary only, limited by IRS Collection Financial Standards	$5,700	$6,100
Monthly Disposable Income (MDI) (Income less expenses)	**Scenario 1**	**Scenario 2**
MDI – actual	($800)	($800)
MDI – necessary only, limited by IRS Collection Financial Standards	$300	($100)

In scenario 1, the taxpayer does not qualify for CNC despite having an inability to pay. The taxpayer's actual expenses result in negative MDI — and an inability to pay the IRS. However, in applying the IRS Collection Financial Standards, the taxpayer will pay $300 a month. The IRS will not accept CNC status because the actual expenses exceed the necessary business expenses allowed for the taxpayer according to limits set by IRS Collection Financial Standards (i.e., some actual expenses are not considered necessary and/or necessary expenses exceed the limits imposed by the Standards). In scenario 1, the taxpayer will have a $300 a month partial pay installment agreement. *Note:* $300 is a partial pay installment agreement because the taxpayer is projected not to be able to fully pay before the CSED expires in 80 months (i.e., 80 months at $300 a month payment is $24,000, which is less than the $50,000 amount owed).

In scenario 2, the taxpayer qualifies for CNC status. The taxpayer's MDI, using allowable expenses limited by IRS Collection Financial Standards, result in a negative MDI of $100.

Requesting CNC: Financial Disclosure to the IRS

In order to obtain CNC status with the IRS, the taxpayer must provide the IRS information and documents to prove financial status. Similar to an ATP IA, the taxpayer's financial disclosure may include a Collection Information Statement (Form 433-A or F) and supporting documentation.

Taxpayers with the following conditions may only have to provide limited information in situations where they do not owe a significant amount to the IRS:

- The taxpayer has a terminal illness or excessive medical bills.
- The taxpayer is incarcerated.
- The taxpayer's only source of income is Social Security, welfare, or unemployment.
- The taxpayer is unemployed with no source of income.

[IRM 5.16.1.2.9 at (6) (3-3-2025)]

> **Pro Tip:** The IRS does not publish the threshold of the amount of balances owed that will allow the taxpayer to provide limited financial disclosure. In practice, taxpayers who are unemployed and owe less than $10,000 need only provide an unemployment statement and financial information by phone to set up CNC status. Taxpayers should complete and be prepared with Form 433-A/F when contacting the IRS by phone to set up CNC status.

Termination of CNC Status

CNC status generally continues until the taxpayer's financial situation improves. Taxpayers who have changes in their financial situation can request a different agreement with the IRS based on their current and future ability to pay. The IRS may request that the taxpayer provide updated financial information to prove the ability to pay. Taxpayers whose income has increased past their reported allowable expenses could be subject to verification of their ability to pay. The IRS uses information statements (Forms W-2, 1099) as well as tax return information to monitor whether a taxpayer's income has increased and potentially no longer qualifies for CNC. [IRM 5.16.1.2.9 at (14) (3-3-2025)]

> **Pro Tip:** Taxpayers should quantify and report all of their necessary living expenses when requesting CNC status with the IRS. The IRS will "code" the taxpayer's CNC status with an annual total living expense amount that will be used to systemically remove the taxpayer from CNC status in the future. For example, if the taxpayer has $5,000 in monthly necessary living expenses ($60,000 annually), the IRS put hardship closing code "29" [IRM Exhibit 5.16.1-2] on the taxpayer's account indicating that the IRS will not systemically remove the taxpayer from CNC status until the taxpayer has reached over $60,000 in annual income. If the taxpayer provided a lesser amount (but enough to show that the taxpayer had MDI < $25), the taxpayer would set a lower threshold for removing CNC status.

Chapter 11.03: Steps to Request CNC

Similar to the ATP IA, CNC status is always secured with the IRS collection function. If the taxpayer is assigned to IRS collection, the taxpayer will secure the CNC agreement with the assigned collection function: either the Automated Collection System (i.e., IRS Campus Collection or "Service Center" collection) or local collection (the Collection Field function assignment to a revenue officer). If the taxpayer is in the IRS field collection "queue" awaiting assignment to an IRS revenue officer, the taxpayer must secure CNC with the revenue officer.

CNC status requests require the taxpayer to submit documents to show financial hardship. Taxpayers will need to complete the appropriate Collection Information Statements (Form 433-A or 433-F) to provide the IRS with detailed information about their assets, liabilities, income, and expenses. Depending on their circumstances, the IRS may request supporting information and documents to determine the taxpayer's ATP with equity in assets and MDI.

The taxpayer usually can provide the Collection Information Statement information by phone or by mail to the IRS. To expedite the CNC request, it is best to contact the IRS and provide all of the information by phone. The taxpayer can also fax the supporting documentation requested while on the phone. If the taxpayer cannot secure CNC on the phone with the available information, the IRS will provide a list of the information needed and a deadline to provide it to the IRS to avoid enforced collection.

> **Pro Tip:** It is essential that the taxpayer conduct their due diligence in determining the ability to pay according to IRS procedures. With the analysis in hand, any disagreements with the IRS can be isolated and immediately addressed. Taxpayers should also keep a full copy of all documents and representations made to the IRS in securing any IRS collection agreement.

Steps to Obtain CNC		
Steps		**Resources**
1	Compute ability to pay with equity in assets (voluntary lump sum payment) and MDI.	IRS collection templates – See **Appendix B**
2	Complete required Collection Information Statement.	IRS collection forms – See **Appendix C**
3	Gather and attach supporting documentation.	Required documentation – See **Chapter 9.05: ATP Financial Disclosure to the IRS**
4	Submit to IRS Collection (by phone or by mail).	Phone contacts for IRS collection – See **Chapter 1.05: Useful IRS Website Resources and Online Tools**
5	Resolve disputed issues and finalize agreement.	Appealing rejected CNC requests – See **Chapter 18: Collection Appeals Options**

Chapter 11.04: Appealing Rejected CNC Requests

The taxpayer has several avenues to request an appeal for a rejected CNC request. During collection appeals, the IRS generally suspends collection enforcement (liens and levies).

If a taxpayer's CNC request is rejected by the IRS, the taxpayer can first appeal the decision to the IRS collection employee's manager to reconsider the CNC request. The taxpayer will have the opportunity to present her position to the manager to contradict the facts considered by the manager. [IRM 5.19.8.4.16.4 at (2) (5-3-2023)] IRS procedures state that the manager will contact the taxpayer within 24 hours to informally discuss the case. However, in dealing with IRS ACS, it is common for the taxpayer not to be contacted within the window of 24 hours.

The IRS will contact the taxpayer/tax professional by phone from one of these locations:

Routing if the case is in IRS Collection: [IRM 5.19.8.4.16.3.1 (5-3-2023)]

If taxpayer is assigned to:	And Taxpayer Resides in:	Then Route to:
SB/SE (Files Schedule C, E, F or a business entity)	AL, AR, CT, DE, FL, LA, ME, MD, DC, MA, MS, NH, NJ, NC, NY, OK, PA, RI, SC, TN, VT, VA, International	Internal Revenue Service ACS Support, M/S 4-Q26.133 P.O. Box 42346 Philadelphia, PA 19101-2346

SB/SE (Files Schedule C, E, F or a business entity)	AK, AZ, CA, CO, GA, HI, ID, IL, IN, IA, KS, KY, MI, MN, MO, MT, NE, NV, NM, ND, OH, OR, SD, TX, UT, WA, WV, WI, WY	Internal Revenue Service ACS Support/CDP, Stop 813G 7940 Kentucky Dr. Florence, KY 41042
W&I (W-2 wage earners)	AK, AZ, CA, CO, HI, ID, IA, KS, MN, MO, MT, NE, NV, NM, ND, OK, OR, SD, TX, UT, WA, WY	Internal Revenue Service ACS Correspondence P.O. Box 24017, Stop 76100, Fresno, CA 93779-4017
W&I (W-2 wage earners)	AL, AR, CT, DE, FL, GA, IL, IN, KY, LA, ME, MD, DC, MA, MI, MS, NH, NJ, NY, NC, OH, PA, RI, SC, TN, VT, VA, WV, WI	Internal Revenue Service ACS Support/CDP , Stop P-4 5050 P.O. Box 219236 Kansas City, MO 64121-9236

Routing if the case is not yet assigned to IRS Collection:

If taxpayer is normally assigned to:	And Taxpayer Resides in:	Then Route to:
SB/SE (Files Schedule C, E, F or a business entity)	CT, ME, MA, NH, NY, RI, VT	Internal Revenue Service Stop 661 - TDA 1040 Waverly Avenue Holtsville, NY 11742
SB/SE (Files Schedule C, E, F or a business entity)	AL, AR, GA, IL, IN, IA, KS, KY, LA, MI, MN, MO, NE, NJ, ND, OH, OK, PA, SD, TN, TX, WV, WI, MS	Internal Revenue Service Stop 811 5333 Getwell Road Memphis, TN 38118
SB/SE (Files Schedule C, E, F or a business entity)	AK, AZ, CA, CO, HI, ID, MT, NV, NM, OR, UT, WA, WY	Internal Revenue Service M/S 5500 1973 Rulon White

		Blvd. Ogden, UT 84201
SB/SE (Files Schedule C, E, F or a business entity)	DE, FL, MD, DC, NC, SC, VA, International	Internal Revenue Service BLN 4N31.142 2970 Market St. Philadelphia, PA 19104
W&I (W-2 wage earners)	AK, AR, AZ, CO, CT, DE, HI, ID, IL, ME, MD, DC, MA, MT, NV, NH, NJ, NM, ND, OR, RI, SD, TN, UT, VT, WA, WI, WY	Internal Revenue Service Stop 832 310 Lowell Street Andover, MA 01810
W&I (W-2 wage earners)	AL, FL, GA, KY, LA, MS, NC, SC, TX, VA	Internal Revenue Service Stop 61 4800 Buford Highway Chamblee, GA 30341
W&I (W-2 wage earners)	AR, CA, IN, IA, KS, MI, MN, MO, NE, NY, OH, OK, PA, WV	Internal Revenue Service Stop P-4 5000 333 W. Pershing Road Kansas City, MO 64108-4302

IRS procedures are not clear whether the Collection Appeals Program (CAP) is available for rejected CNC requests. The IRS Internal Revenue Manual and the Form 9423, *Collection Appeal Request*, does not mention rejected CNC as one of the criteria for a CAP. [IRM 5.19.8.4.16.1 (8-5-2016)] However, the IRM also does not specifically exclude CNC rejections from this process. [IRM 5.19.8.4.16.2 (3-16-2018)] Ultimately, taxpayers without an agreement with the IRS, including a rejected CNC request, will have the ability to appeal through a CAP or a Collection Due Process hearing if the IRS moves to a lien filing or levy issuance or the taxpayer disagrees with an IRS proposal of an installment agreement.

If the IRS proceeds to file a lien or issue a levy notice, the taxpayer will have 30 days to request a formal Collection Due Process appeal. The CDP hearing can be used to both propose CNC status as well as argue a rejected CNC request. [IRC sections 6330 and 6320]

Taxpayers with hardships cannot ask the Taxpayer Advocate's office to intervene. [IRM 13.1.4.2.3.6 (1-3-2024)] Most collection determinations are reserved only for IRS collection functions (ACS or the CFf). The TAS can coordinate, recommend, and expedite a collection decision between the IRS and the taxpayer, especially when the taxpayer is in a hardship situation.

Chapter 11.05: Comprehensive Example

Example Brian and Jessica Andrews owe the IRS $40,000 for the tax years 2019 and 2020. Their assessed balance is $35,000 and the earliest CSED expiration is 90 months away. The Andrews have been experiencing financial hardship due to Brian's limited ability to work due to a medical condition. The taxpayer applies for CNC status on September 30, 2024.

The Andrews' financial information, ATP analysis, and CNC proposal to the IRS are as follows: (*Note:* This example uses the IRS expense standards for April 22, 2024- March 2025. For the most up-to-date expense standards, see the following: https://www.irs.gov/irm/part13/irm_13-001-004#idm140371124655360.)

To view more of this comprehensive example, see www.TaxProblemsHandbook.com and navigate to the **IRS Collection Solutions Handbook** tab to access the referenced item.

Chapter 12:

QUALIFY AND OBTAIN AN OFFER IN COMPROMISE FOR DOUBT AS TO COLLECTIBILITY (OIC-DATC)

This section covers how to qualify and obtain the IRS most common tax settlement program: the Offer in compromise for Doubt as to Collectibility (OIC-DATC).

Topic	Covers
Overview of the IRS OIC Program	The IRS OIC program, chances of an OIC, and reasons the IRS settles back taxes.
Types of OICs	The scope of the three types of OICs and when to use them.
OIC-DATC as a Hardship Option	Financial hardship conditions that warrant settlement of balances owed.
IRS OIC Terms and Personnel	The terms of an OIC and who to interact with at the IRS regarding an OIC.
IRS OIC Processing and Investigation Units	How the IRS processes and investigates an OIC.
Important Terms and Conditions for OICs	The detailed terms and conditions regarding an OIC.
Introduction to the Four Steps to Obtaining an OIC-DATC	Four steps of an OIC from due diligence and qualification through appeal.
Step 1A: Due Diligence and Qualification: Filing and Payment Compliance	How to determine if the taxpayer is in compliance for filing an OIC.
Step 1B: Due Diligence and Qualification: Analyzing Ability to Pay and OIC Qualification	How to determine if a taxpayer qualifies for an OIC, including computing the qualification and offer amount calculations.
Step 2: The OIC Application	How to apply for an OIC.
Step 3: The Offer Investigation	What to expect and how to respond during the OIC investigation.
Step 4: Finalize Terms and Complete Requirements	Post-investigation actions needed to finalize the OIC and maintain good standing.
OIC-DATC Example	Link to a comprehensive practical example of an OIC application.

Key Highlights:

- Taxpayers can settle their outstanding liability for less than the amount owed if they qualify for an OIC and are able to pay the offer amount. According to IRS data, few taxpayers actually receive an OIC.
- There are three types of OICs. However, the OIC–Doubt as to Collectibility is the most requested type of OIC.
- Taxpayers qualify for an OIC if they are unable to pay their outstanding balance in full (using net equity in assets and future monthly payments) before the collection statute of limitations expires.
- If a taxpayer qualifies for an OIC, she must compute how much she will need to offer and pay to settle her taxes.
- Most OICs usually take between 6-12 months to complete, from application through final approval from the IRS. Taxpayers can now initiate an OIC for Doubt as to Collectibility online in the Individual Online Account in the forms section.

Chapter 12.01: Overview of the IRS OIC Program

An offer in compromise ("OIC") is an agreement between a taxpayer and the government that settles a tax liability for less than the full amount owed. IRC §7122 and Treasury Regulation §301.7122-1 authorize the IRS to compromise tax liabilities.

There are four purposes for an OIC:

- Reach a resolution in the best interest of both the taxpayer and the government.
- Facilitate collection of taxes quickly and cost-efficiently.
- Collect revenue that may not otherwise be collectible.
- Allow taxpayers a fresh start.

Policy Statement P-5-100 (1-30-1992) says the IRS will accept an OIC when it is unlikely that the tax liability will be collected in full and the amount offered reasonably reflects collection potential. The IRS has the authority to create the administrative rules and procedures for taxpayers to compromise their liabilities. These rules and procedures are found in IRS forms, notices, announcements, and other materials. Most of the technical rules are found in the IRS Internal Revenue Manual (IRM), specifically in section 5.8 of the IRM. IRS personnel must follow these rules and apply them consistently when evaluating OICs.

Chapter 12.02: Types of OICs

There are three types of OICs:

- *OIC—Doubt as to Collectibility (OIC-DATC):* the taxpayer is unable to pay the balance owed in full, before the collection statute expires, with her net assets and future income.

- *OIC—Effective Tax Administration (ETA-OIC):* the taxpayer is able to pay the balance owed in full but requiring collection of the entire unpaid balance would cause the taxpayer economic hardship or would not be fair.
- *OIC—Doubt as to Liability (OIC-DATL):* the taxpayer disputes the amount of the liability owed.

The OIC-DATC is the most common OIC filed. The ETA-OIC can also be used in collection matters when the taxpayer is able to fully pay with assets and monthly payments, but special circumstances exist that cause the taxpayer hardship if the IRS collects the full amount owed. ETA-OICs are very rare. In the IRS FY2024, the IRS accepted only 293 ETA OICs. [IRS FOIA Response #2025-00032, October 2024] In the IRS FY2024, the IRS accepted only two OIC-DATL applications. [IRS FOIA Response #2025-00032, October 2024)]

The OIC-DATC is only available to taxpayers if they qualify. To qualify, the taxpayer must show the inability to fully pay the balance owed from net equity in assets and future income. [IRM 5.8.4.3.1 (4-30-2015)] To determine if a taxpayer qualifies, the taxpayer must compute his ability to pay using the OIC-DATC financial analysis rules.

An OIC-DATC presents a second hurdle after qualification: computing and paying the offer amount. The offer amount is equal to the net equity in assets plus a multiple of future monthly income. The multiple is determined by which OIC payment method is selected.

Within the OIC-DATC, a taxpayer may have special circumstances which warrant a lower offer amount (i.e., IRS agrees to accept less than the taxpayer's calculated reasonable collection potential). This type of OIC is called an "Offer in Compromise—Doubt as to Collectibility with Special Circumstances" (OIC-DATCSC). [IRM 5.8.4.2 (4-25-2025)] For example, a taxpayer may need to use assets, such as cash held in savings, to pay for a future medical treatment. In these cases, the taxpayer may request a lower offer amount based on these special circumstances. The factors used to determine an OIC-DATCSC are the same as used in determining an ETA-OIC. [IRM 5.8.11.3 at (3) (4-11-2024)] However, an OIC-DATCSC differs from an ETA offer because the taxpayer qualifies for an OIC-DATC — that is, he does not have the ability to pay the liability before the CSED expires. In ETA offers, the taxpayer does have the ability to pay the balance owed before the CSED expires, but for special circumstances, which have proven economic hardship or a public policy/equity basis for not paying the tax in full. Most OIC-DATCSC and ETA offers are considered due to an economic hardship that requires the taxpayer to use future assets to pay for special circumstances, such as an illness, and thus these assets are not available to pay the tax.

Chapter 12.03 OIC-DATC as a Hardship Option

The OIC program receives much publicity because it offers the potential to permanently settle a balance owed for less than the amount owed. However, the reality is that few taxpayers, in relation to the overall taxpayers who owe, are able to settle their taxes in this way.

In 2023, over 24 million taxpayers had a balance owed to the IRS. In 2024, approximately 26 million will owe the IRS back taxes. However, in 2024, only 33,591 applied for an OIC (all types of OICs). Out of these applicants, only 7,199 were accepted (21%). [IRS Data Books, 2010-2024, Tables 25 and 27]

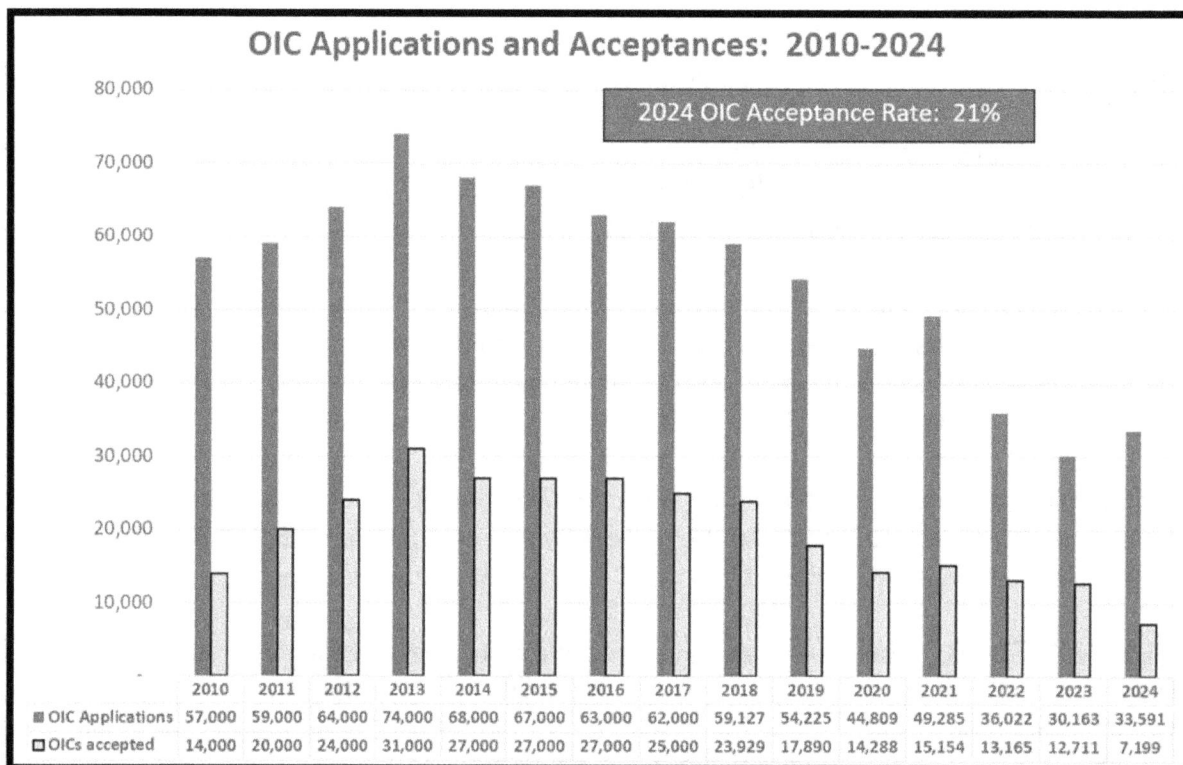

OIC Applications and Acceptances: 2010-2024

2024 OIC Acceptance Rate: 21%

	2010	2011	2012	2013	2014	2015	2016	2017	2018	2019	2020	2021	2022	2023	2024
OIC Applications	57,000	59,000	64,000	74,000	68,000	67,000	63,000	62,000	59,127	54,225	44,809	49,285	36,022	30,163	33,591
OICs accepted	14,000	20,000	24,000	31,000	27,000	27,000	27,000	25,000	23,929	17,890	14,288	15,154	13,165	12,711	7,199

There are two primary reasons for low OIC rates for tax debtors. First, in most circumstances, taxpayers may fully pay the IRS through an installment agreement and/or equity in assets. Second, if a taxpayer does qualify for an OIC-DATC, he is likely in financial distress and unable to afford to pay the offer amount. In both cases, the taxpayer must choose a different collection alternative with the IRS.

> **Pro Tip:** Taxpayers should always evaluate all collection alternatives before applying for an OIC. For example, if a taxpayer has significant equity in nonliquid assets, such as a home, the taxpayer may want to consider other hardship ability to pay agreements such as a PPIA or CNC.

Example- George owes the IRS $30,000 and does not have the ability to pay with monthly payments to the IRS (his computed monthly disposable income, limited by IRS collection financial standards, is $25 or less). He has $20,000 in net realizable equity in his home and is unable to borrow against it to pay his taxes. George qualifies for currently not collectible status and would not have to access the equity in his house to obtain CNC status. Assume George does not have any special circumstances to warrant a lower offer amount. If George wanted to apply for an OIC, he would have to offer, at a minimum, the net equity in his home, in the offer amount. Rather than offer the IRS $20,000 to settle his taxes, George may be in a better financial position to obtain CNC status in which he will not have to pay anything to the IRS. However, the IRS will still take George's future refunds until the tax is paid, or the CSED, whichever comes first.

Taxpayers who qualify for a partial pay installment agreement (PPIA) or CNC and have little/no assets should always consider an OIC-DATC as a collection alternative. In some cases, the taxpayer may have significant savings with an OIC.

Example- Tom has 100 months remaining on the collection statute for an outstanding balance of $80,000. Tom has no equity in assets and is able to pay the IRS $200 a month using IRS ability to pay rules with expenses limited by IRS Collection Financial Standards. Tom would qualify for both a partial pay installment agreement of $200 a month and an OIC-DATC.

Partial-Pay Installment Agreement Qualification	
Installment agreement factor	**Installment agreement**
Net equity in assets	No assets to pay the IRS.
Monthly disposable income	$200
Installment agreement – Amount to be paid before collection statute expires (100 months)	$200 × 100 months = $20,000
Total amount owed	$80,000
Fully paid before expiration of CSED?	No ($20,000 < $80,000)
Conclusion	Partial-pay installment agreement.

OIC-DATC Qualification		
OIC Factor	**Amount**	**Terms**
(1) Amount that could be paid with net equity in assets	$0	Taxpayer has no net equity.
(2) Amount that can be paid with future income (MDI × months remaining on CSED)	$200 × 100 months = $20,000	Taxpayer's MDI computed allowing only necessary living expenses. Household expenses limited by IRS Collection Financial Standards.
(3) Total amount that can be paid (1) + (2)	$0 + $20,000 = $20,000	The total amount that can be paid before the CSED expires.
(4) Total balance owed	$80,000	From example facts.
Qualify for OIC? Is total balance owed > total amount	Yes ($20,000 < $80,000)	The taxpayer qualifies because the IRS cannot collect the

that can be paid before CSED? (i.e., is (4) > (3))		amount in full before the expiration of the CSED.
OIC Offer amount	Net equity = $0, plus MDI × 12 months = $2,400 ($200 × 12 months) Offer amount = $2,400	Assumes NRE and MDI are the same for the qualification and offer amount computations (not likely). Assumes taxpayer chooses the lump-sum payment method that requires the taxpayer to offer the net equity in assets plus 12 months of MDI.

If Tom's financial condition does not change, he will pay $200 a month for 100 months, or $20,000. Tom does qualify for an OIC because he is not expected to be able to pay the IRS before the CSED expires. Tom's offer amount, using IRS rules for an OIC for a lump-sum payment method, is $2,400. Tom should consider an OIC if he can afford to pay the $2,400 offer amount and meet the other terms of the OIC. An OIC would net Tom projected savings of $17,600 ($20,000 in payments before the CSED expires versus a $2,400 offer amount in the OIC).

Taxpayers with temporary financial hardship (i.e., unemployment, underemployment, seasonal business) may not be good OIC-DATC candidates because it is projected that their income will return to normal. Business owners with temporary downturns in their circumstances also are not good OIC candidates if it is probable that their income will increase in the future. For example, many real estate brokers who suffered lower income during the housing crisis in 2008-2012 quickly recovered after the housing market returned to normal. These taxpayers did not make good OIC candidates because the IRS projected that their income would return when the housing market rebounded.

Good candidates for OICs include taxpayers who do not have the current ability to pay and whose future outlook is not likely to improve. These profiles include, but are not limited to, taxpayers who have

- Poor health.
- Long-term unemployment.
- Fixed income such as retirement.
- Low future earnings potential.

Taxpayers should explain their circumstances in OIC-DATC applications to help the IRS understand their future ability to pay using assets and income. Taxpayers should also provide supporting evidence that explains their long-term circumstances and justifies their computation of future income.

Chapter 12.04: IRS OIC Terms and Personnel

There are some important terms to understand when evaluating the offer in compromise collection alternative:

Term (acronym, if any)	Description
Ability to pay (ATP)	The amount a taxpayer can afford to pay the IRS on a balance owed based on net equity in assets and monthly disposable income.
Abuse of discretion	The primary basis of an appeal in IRS collection disputes. The IRS must follow the law and its collection rules and procedures. A taxpayer has a basis for appeal when the IRS abuses its discretion in applying the law and its procedures in a collection determination. Most IRS rules for collection are contained in the IRS's Internal Revenue Manual (IRM).
Asset/Equity table (AET)	IRS internal form that shows the IRS's computation of the taxpayer's ability to pay through net realizable equity in assets in an OIC.
Collateral agreement	A contract associated with an OIC that provides additional terms for the taxpayer when an OIC is approved. Can be used when there is a possibility of future income. Also commonly used to convince taxpayers to waive the benefit of future net operating or capital losses for future years.
Collection statute of limitations	Refers to the amount of time the IRS can collect on a balance owed. The collection statute expiration date (CSED) is ten years from the date the tax was assessed. It can be extended by several taxpayer or IRS actions, including the filing of an OIC.
Filing compliance	A taxpayer is "filing compliant" when he has filed all required returns. Filing compliance is required to enter into an IRS Collection agreement, including an OIC. Filing compliance generally refers to the filing of the current and past six years' returns according to IRS Policy Statement 5-133.
Financial disclosure	The process of disclosing financial information to the IRS for the purposes of collection. For an OIC, it is a Form 433-A(OIC) (individuals) and Form 433-B(OIC) (for businesses), plus supporting documentation.
Income/Expense table (IET)	IRS internal form that shows the IRS's computation of the taxpayer's ability to pay by making monthly installment agreement payments under an OIC.
IRS Centralized Offer in Compromise Unit (COIC)	IRS centralized OIC program units that process and investigate OICs. The two units are located in Memphis, TN and Holtville, NY.

IRS Collection Financial Standards	Used in determining a taxpayer's ability to pay, including the OIC collection alternative. The IRS allowable expense limitations limit the amount of housing/utilities, food/clothing/other expenses, and transportation costs that are allowed in determining MDI. These expenses also allow standard out-of-pocket medical expenses.
IRS Offer Examiner	The IRS person located in the COIC who investigates OIC applications. After the OIC is determined to be processible, the Offer Examiner investigates the taxpayer's personal and financial circumstances to determine if he qualifies for an OIC and the amount of the offer that is needed to settle the balance owed.
Monthly disposable income (MDI)	One of two components used to calculate a taxpayer's ability to pay. MDI is the amount of income remaining after necessary expenses have been paid. In the offer amount, the IRS provides additional allowances in computing MDI (as compared to MDI for OIC qualification).
Necessary living expenses	Household expenses for the health and welfare of the family and/or for the production of income that are allowed in determining monthly disposable income of a taxpayer in an ability to pay analysis. Some expenses are limited by IRS Collection Financial Standards (food/clothing, housing/utilities, transportation).
Net realizable equity in assets (NRE)	One of two components used to calculate a taxpayer's ability to pay. NRE is the calculation of the amount of equity available to pay toward outstanding liabilities. In an OIC, there are additional equity exclusions for the offer amount.
Payment compliance	A taxpayer is "payment compliant" when he has sufficient withholding and/or has made sufficient estimated tax payments so that he is not projected to owe when his current tax year return is filed. Payment compliance is required to enter into most IRS collection agreements, including an OIC.
Reasonable collection potential (RCP)	In an IRS OIC, this is the calculated amount of future income and equity in assets that the IRS can reasonably expect to receive if the taxes are settled. This is also referred to as the "offer amount" for an OIC.
Special Circumstances	Circumstances in which the taxpayer will require use of assets or future income that will allow for a lower offer amount in an OIC

Chapter 12.05: IRS OIC Processing and Investigation Units

The IRS processes and investigates OICs at its two centralized OIC units in Memphis, TN, and Brookhaven, NY. [IRM 5.8.1.14 (5-25-2023)] Almost any IRS unit is able to take receipt of an OIC, but all must be routed for processing through one of the COIC units. [IRM 5.8.1.14.1 (5-25-2023)] OICs are submitted to the appropriate COIC based on the taxpayer's state of residence:

COIC	States of residence
Mailing address: Memphis IRS Center COIC Unit P.O. Box 30803, AMC Memphis, TN 38130-0803 *Phone #:* 1-844-398-5025 (Hours: 8AM-5PM, CST) *Physical address:* Memphis Internal Revenue Service Center COIC Unit 5333 Getwell Rd. Stop 880 Memphis, TN 38118	AZ, CA, CO, HI, ID, KY, MS, NM, NV, OK, OR, TN, TX, UT, WA
Mailing address: Brookhaven IRS Center COIC Unit P.O. Box 9007 Holtsville, NY 11742-9007 *Phone #:* 1-844-805-4980 (Hours: 8AM-11PM, EST) *Physical address:* Brookhaven Internal Revenue Service Center COIC Unit 5000 Corporate Court Stop 680 Holtsville, NY 11742	AK, AL, AR, CT, DC, DE, FL, GA, IA, IL, IN, KS, LA, MA, MD, ME, MI, MN, MO, MT, NC, ND, NE, NH, NJ, NY, OH, PA, PR, RI, SC, SD, VA, VT, WI, WV, WY, or a foreign address

Investigation of OICs is usually completed by the COIC units. However, in certain circumstances, the IRS Collection Field Function (CFf) will conduct the investigation. Offer specialists within the CFf can conduct end-to-end offer investigations. IRS revenue officers (RO) can be involved in OICs to investigate the taxpayer's finances. The assistance of ROs is normally reserved for on-going business taxpayers and more complex taxpayer situations. For example, the offer examiner may request the RO to investigate asset values for a taxpayer who has an on-going business or for a high-debt taxpayer.

Revenue officers in the CFf who receive an OIC on an assigned case must provide input into the OIC investigation. They do so via Form 657, *Offer in Compromise Revenue Officer Report*. The RO can include additional information gathered during the field investigation that verifies or refutes amounts claimed by the taxpayer in his OIC application. [IRM 5.8.1.14.1 at (3) (5-25-2023)]

> **Pro Tip:** Taxpayers can usually expect to work directly with a COIC examiner in most OICs. OIC are rarely fully investigated outside of the COICs examiners. The COIC unit processes all OICs and fully works with all wage earner taxpayers and self-employed persons (generally with gross receipts under $500,000). Field OIC investigations are generally conducted for all business entity taxpayers, taxpayers with employees or unpaid payroll tax liabilities, international taxpayers, and taxpayers whose primary source of income is through a partnership or S corporation.

Chapter 12.06: Important Terms and Conditions for OICs

When evaluating an OIC, the taxpayer needs to consider the following important terms and conditions:

1. *The taxpayer must compromise all liabilities owed*: this includes all taxes for all years for the taxpayer. For example, a taxpayer may have income taxes, an individual shared responsibility payment liability, and assessed trust fund taxes (i.e., payroll, excise taxes) assessed against him. In an OIC, all taxes, penalties, and interest are compromised. [IRM 5.8.1.9 (5-25-2023)] An OIC will not compromise non-tax liabilities that are collected by the IRS (i.e., Treasury Offset Program collections). Non-title 26 (income tax) assessments for penalties for civil violations related to Reports of Foreign Bank and Financial Accounts (FBAR) are unable to be compromised under the OIC program. [IRM 5.8.1.11.6 (5-25-2023)]

2. *The taxpayer must stay in payment compliance during the offer period*: the IRS may return the OIC, without appeal rights, if the taxpayer does not remain in payment compliance (making sufficient withholding and estimated tax payments) while the offer is being investigated. [IRM 5.8.7.2.2.2 (4-24-2025)]

3. *The taxpayer cannot be in bankruptcy*: the IRS will not consider an OIC while a taxpayer is in bankruptcy. [IRM 5.8.2.4.1 (6-14-2024)]

4. *The taxpayer must wait for audit assessment and any innocent spouse determination*: for an OIC submitted solely for liabilities related to an audit or an underreporter notice (CP2000), the taxpayer must wait until the liability has been assessed prior to submitting the OIC. Open innocent spouse determinations need to be resolved before submitting an OIC. [IRM 5.8.4.22.1 (4-25-2025)]

5. *Payroll tax personal liability must be assessed*: Taxpayers who may be liable as a responsible person for the trust fund portion of outstanding payroll liabilities will not be eligible for an OIC until the trust fund recovery penalty investigation determination is complete. [IRM 5.8.4.21.1 (4-25-2025) and Form 656 instructions (4-2025)]

6. *The taxpayer must file and pay for next five years*: the taxpayer must remain in filing and payment compliance for the five years after the OIC is accepted or the OIC will default. [IRM 5.19.7.14.4.1 (12-9-2024) and IRM 5.19.7.14.4.2 (10-6-2022)] If the offer is defaulted, the taxpayer will be liable for the original debt, less payments, plus all accrued interest and penalties. Tax periods in which the CSED has expired will not be reinstated. [IRM 5.19.7.14.4.2 (10-6-2022)]

7. *Complete a processible application*: processible OIC applications include the Form 656, 433-A(OIC) and/or 433-B(OIC), the application fee, the required down payment, and supporting documentation. [IRM 5.8.2.8 (6-14-2024)] The taxpayer must have also filed all required tax returns and be current on estimated tax payments and/or withholding. If the offer is not processible, the IRS may request and provide the taxpayer a short period of time to cure any application deficiencies.

8. *A significant, nonrefundable down payment and/or periodic payments, and an application fee may be required:* unless the taxpayer qualifies for the low-income waiver, a separate check must be sent for the application fee ($205) and for the down payment. [IRM 5.8.1.13 (5-25-2023)] If the taxpayer selects the periodic payment, separate payments need to be made for each periodic payment.

9. *The taxpayer must cooperate in the OIC investigation*: requests for additional information requires a response from the taxpayer. If the taxpayer does not respond timely, the OIC application can be returned. [IRM 5.8.7.2.2.4 (4-24-2025)]

10. *IRS may file a Notice of Federal Tax Lien*: if the IRS has not done so already, the IRS may make a lien determination and file a Notice of Federal Tax Lien. [IRM 5.8.1.16 at (7) (5-25-2023)]

11. *The taxpayer must pay the offer amount*: for periodic payment OICs, the taxpayer must make all required payments while the offer is being investigated. After the OIC is accepted, the taxpayer must make all required offer payments. The IRS does allow the taxpayer to request a one-time extension on a required payment within a 24-month period (periodic payment OICs). However, all subsequent payments must be timely made. [IRM 5.8.4.24.1 (4-25-2025)]

12. *Penalties and interest accrue during offer period*: the failure-to-pay penalty and interest penalties continue to accrue while the OIC is investigated. If the OIC is accepted, the offer amount will settle penalties and interest, in addition to the taxes owed. [IRM 5.8.1.9.1 (4-20-2021)]

13. *The CSED is extended during offer period*: an OIC extends the CSED expiration date for the amount of time that the offer is investigated with the IRS (including appeals) plus 30 days. [Treasury Regulation §301.7122-1(i)(1)]

14. *The taxpayer must appeal any adverse determination within 30 days*: if the IRS rejects an OIC, the taxpayer has 30 days to appeal the rejection to the IRS Independent Office of Appeals. The IRS does not grant extensions to the 30-day requirement to appeal. [Treasury Regulation §301.7122-1(f)(5) and IRM 5.8.7.7.5 (4-24-2025)]

15. *OIC approvals are subject to public inspection*: members of the general public can view accepted OICs for one year after acceptance. Taxpayer information is redacted to protect the identity of taxpayers. [IRC §6103(k)(1), IRM 5.8.8.9 (11-6-2023), and IRS Form 15086] The request to review the public inspection file for an OIC is made on Form 15086, *Offer in Compromise Public Inspection File Request* (6-2024).

16. *Filing an OIC application may provide relief from IRS enforcement:* unless the taxpayer has filed an OIC solely to delay enforced collection, an OIC will stop levies and passport restrictions. [IRM 5.8.1.16 (5-25-2023)]

The IRS must also follow certain time limits to review and render a decision on an OIC application. According to IRC §7122, any offer-in-compromise submitted shall be deemed to be accepted if the offer is not rejected within 24 months after the date of the submission of the offer. This requirement dictates that the IRS complete the OIC determination before the expiration of the 24-month timeline. Failure to do so results in a deemed acceptance of the OIC by the IRS. In practice, the IRS rarely allows the OIC investigation and determination to approach the 24-month deadline. Most OIC determinations are made within 7-12 months after the offer is received by the IRS. In most instances, the 24-month requirement does not include any time that the OIC was in appeals. One exception involves OICs submitted during a Collection Due Process hearing. In a CDP hearing, the appeals officer provides the final rejection to the taxpayer and the time held by the appeals officer in a CDP is generally included in the 24-month timelines. [IRM 8.23.3.2.1 (8-21-2023)]

Chapter 12.07: Introduction to the Four Steps to Obtaining an OIC-DATC

There are four steps to obtaining an OIC-DATC.

Steps	Actions	Move to next step when:
#1: Due Diligence and Qualification	Three parts: #1: Filing required back tax returns and making required estimated tax payments and/or withholding adjustments. #2: Gathering and analyzing all relevant information, collection option alternatives, and whether the taxpayer qualifies for an OIC. #3: If the taxpayer qualifies, determining the offer amount and whether the taxpayer can meet the terms of the OIC. If the taxpayer is unable to pay the offer amount or meet the terms, he should select a more appropriate collection alternative.	√ In filing and payment compliance. √ Confirm taxpayer qualifies for OIC. √ Determine offer amount. √ Confirm ability to pay the offer amount and meet terms of OIC.
#2: Application	In this step, the taxpayer completes all of the required forms and attaches the required documentation to substantiate the OIC. The taxpayer must also pay the required application fee and down payment. The taxpayer should determine if he qualifies for a low-income waiver to be excluded	√ Application is complete, including required documentation. √ Application fee and OIC payment made. √ Low-income qualification determined. √ Application

	from the application fee and down payment.	package/fees submitted to proper COIC unit.
#3: Offer investigation	Once assigned to an offer examiner, the investigation is the longest part of the OIC process and can often last several months. It involves the interaction between the IRS and the taxpayer. To start this step, the IRS must first accept the OIC as processible, then proceed to determine the taxpayer's ability to pay. The IRS may request additional information from the taxpayer to which the taxpayer will need to respond timely in order to avoid a rejection due to non-response. In this step, the offer examiner and the taxpayer closely examine the financial situation of the taxpayer to determine an acceptable offer amount based on the taxpayer's reasonable collection potential. If the IRS and taxpayer cannot agree, the taxpayer will be offered an appeal. If an appeal is needed, the taxpayer will have to submit a timely petition and argue the merits of the case with the IRS appeals officer.	✓ All outstanding questions are answered. ✓ Qualification confirmed. ✓ Offer amount determined. ✓ Reject or accept determination. ✓ Appeal to IRS Independent Office of Appeals, if needed.
#4: Finalize terms and complete requirements	In the final step, the taxpayer and the IRS agree on terms and the offer amount. The taxpayer completes any appeal and makes the required payments timely to the IRS to complete the OIC. The taxpayer confirms that the balances owed are removed and any tax lien is released. The taxpayer files and pays timely for the next five years consistent with the terms of the OIC.	✓ IRS and taxpayer agree on terms. ✓ Taxpayer completes remaining payments and other terms of OIC. ✓ Balance owed and tax lien removed. ✓ Taxpayer remains in compliance for next five years.

The IRS determines if the application is processible within 24 hours of receipt. [IRM 5.8.2.4 at (2) (6-14-2024)] The offer investigation stage can begin immediately but is likely to take 2-5 months before the IRS can assign an offer examiner to begin investigation of the OIC application. The total investigation process typically takes 5-12 months, or longer during times where OIC applications are backlogged at the COIC units. If the taxpayer and the IRS cannot agree on the OIC after the initial investigation, the typical appeal can add eight months to the OIC process. [GAO Study, Opportunities Exist to Improve Monitoring and Transparency of Appeal Resolution Timeliness, GAO-18-659, Sept. 21, 2018]

> **Pro Tip:** Most OICs are completed within 6-12 months from application to approval. Taxpayers with more complex tax situations, higher debt taxpayers, and taxpayers with businesses can take between 9-14 months to complete. If the taxpayer requests an appeal due to a disagreement with the offer examiner, this process will generally add 4-8 months to the process.

Chapter 12.08: Step 1A: Due Diligence and Qualification: Filing and Payment Compliance

In the first step, the taxpayer completes any tax return filing and payment compliance prerequisites required. Before filing an OIC, the taxpayer must meet two important compliance requirements: filing and payment compliance.

The IRS requires that the taxpayer file all required tax returns and be up to date with estimated tax payments and/or withholding before accepting the OIC for investigation. Individual taxpayers need to have filed their current year return, plus the past six years in order to be "filing compliant." [IRM 5.8.2.4.1 at (2) (6-14-20242) and IRS Policy Statement 5-133 (8-6-2004)] Taxpayers who are not in filing compliance will have their OIC application returned. In these situations, the taxpayer's OIC application fee will be returned but the OIC down payment will not be returned – it will be applied to the outstanding liability. [IRM 5.8.2.4.1 at (1) (6-14-2024)]

> **Pro Tip:** The IRS only requires filing of returns for the past six years to be considered filing compliant. In most cases, the taxpayer should only file the past six years. However, some taxpayers should consider filing all past-due returns (even before six-year lookback period) if they would like to have all potential liabilities compromised. It is rare that the IRS will require an individual taxpayer to file prior to the six-year look back period. Taxpayers considering filing past the six-year lookback period need to carefully determine if they qualify for an OIC and can pay an offer amount to settle their liability. If the taxpayer cannot execute the OIC and has filed past the six-year lookback period, they may face a considerable amount owed that they could have avoided if they had followed the six-year rule.

To be payment compliant, the taxpayer must be up to date on all estimated tax payments and have the correct amount of federal income tax withheld so that he does not owe for the current tax year. For example, if the taxpayer has a projected balance due of $12,000 at the end of the current tax year, they would need to have timely made all required quarterly payments of $3,000 each quarter (or catch up missed quarters at the time of submitting the OIC) when submitting and during the offer investigation process. Failure to make required estimated payments or correct withholding may result in a returned OIC.

> **Pro Tip:** It is not only a requirement for the taxpayer to make required estimated tax payments, but it is usually in the taxpayer's best interest to do so prior to submitting the OIC for two reasons. First, it lowers the taxpayer's ability to pay because the taxpayer is allowed expenses for payment of taxes. Second, sufficient estimated tax payments reduce the chances of defaulting on an accepted OIC because the taxpayer will not owe when filing the next return.

After receipt of the OIC application, the IRS will research its records and determine if the taxpayer has made adequate estimated tax payments. If the IRS determines that the payments are not sufficient, they will ask the taxpayer to correct or explain why the taxpayer is not required to make estimated payments. Failure to correct or adequately explain will result in the OIC's return to the taxpayer. [IRM 5.8.3.8 (6-18-2024)]

The IRS will usually allow the taxpayer 15 days to make the requested estimated tax payments. [IRM 5.8.7.2.2.2 at (6) (4-24-2025)] If the payments are not made, the OIC is returned to the taxpayer. The IRS will retain the OIC application fee (assuming that the OIC was initially accepted as processible) and any OIC payments made will be applied to the balance owed.

Chapter 12.09: Step 1B: Due Diligence and Qualification: Analyzing Ability to Pay and OIC Qualification

After meeting the filing and payment compliance requirements, the taxpayer then analyzes, using relevant information, their ability to pay. If the taxpayer's calculated ability to pay concludes that the taxpayer cannot pay before the expiration of the CSED, the taxpayer qualifies for an OIC.

If the taxpayer does not qualify, they can consider the ETA-OIC or the OIC-DATCSC. However, if a taxpayer qualifies, there is an important next step: calculate how much to offer the IRS to settle the liability. This amount is referred to as the "offer amount" or "reasonable collection potential" of the taxpayer. If the taxpayer can pay the offer amount to settle the liability, the OIC is a viable collection alternative and should be pursued.

To qualify for an OIC-DATC, the taxpayer must be unable to pay the IRS with net realizable equity in assets (NRE) and monthly installment payments (MDI) before the collection statute of limitations expires. This process starts with the taxpayer gathering all relevant information to make the qualification determination.

Gather Required Information Needed to Analyze Ability to Pay

Taxpayers must analyze their personal and financial circumstances to determine their ability to pay. For an OIC, the taxpayer will need to gather the following information to determine the ability to pay and to qualify for an OIC.

Information category	Items needed	Time period
Personal information: household information	• Number in the family (i.e., dependents). • Ages of family members. • Location to apply IRS Collection Financial Standards. • Non-liable spouse information. • Shared expenses with non-liable persons.	As of date of application. Dependents from last year's tax return plus any changes.
Personal information: special circumstances	• Special future needs for assets and income (illness, unemployment, etc.).	As of date of application.
Financial information: assets and liabilities	• All assets and liabilities of the taxpayer.	As of date of application.
Financial information: household income	• All taxable and non-taxable sources of income.	The time period that best reflects the average future monthly income for the taxpayer. Normally: Wage earners: last 3 months. Self-employed: last 6-12 months.
Financial information: Necessary household living expenses and expenses necessary for production of income	• All necessary living expenses. • All expenses necessary for the production of income. • All other expenses that would be allowed. • Identify any shared expenses with non-liable persons.	The time period that best reflects the average household expenses for the taxpayer. Generally, the last 3-12 months.

Financial information: dissipated assets	• Any assets dissipated within the last three years. • Any assets transferred outside of the reach of the government to avoid collection.	Generally, past 3 years. The three years includes the year of application.
Tax information: amount owed, years owed, and CSEDs	For each year: • Balance owed. • CSED for each assessment.	Each year with a balance owed, at the time of the application.
Tax information: unfiled returns and unassessed amounts	• Unfiled returns for the current and past six years need to be filed prior to submitting an OIC. • All assessments related to compliance activity should generally be assessed prior to the OIC application (trust fund recovery penalty, audit results, and CP2000 results).	Unfiled: current and past six years. Compliance assessments must be assessed prior to filing the application.
Tax information: current payment compliance	• Current tax year tax projection. • Sufficient withholding and/or estimated tax payments to avoid balance owed for current year.	Current tax year.

Using the above information, the taxpayer can determine the ability to pay and to qualify for an OIC.

Determine OIC Qualification

Using the relevant financial information, the taxpayer can analyze the ability to pay. To qualify for an OIC-DATC, the taxpayer's ability to pay using assets and future income must be less than the total balance owed.

The qualification formula:

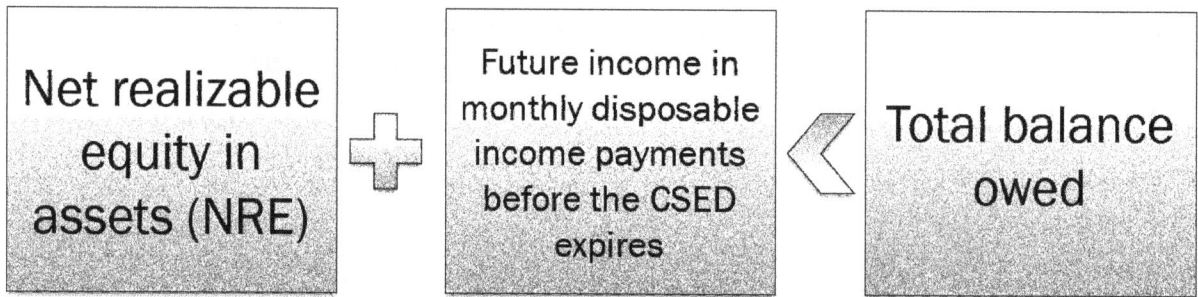

Taxpayers must compute their ability to pay as follows:

- Component #1: net realizable equity in assets (NRE) and
- Component #2: future monthly payments the IRS will receive before the collection statute of limitations expires.

If the NRE plus future income payments are less than the total balances owed, the taxpayer qualifies for an OIC-DATC.

Ability to Pay (Qualification) Component #1: NRE in Assets

The first component in determining qualification for an OIC-DATC is for the taxpayer to compute the net realizable equity in assets. The NRE in assets is equal to sum of the NRE equity in each asset. Each asset's NRE is equal to the fair market value of each asset at its quick sale value less any liabilities associated with the asset. Individual asset values cannot be less than zero. QSV is the value of the asset if it was disposed of within 90 days. The IRS has pre-set QSV percentages for most assets.

For QSV percentages for most assets, see **Chapter 9.06: Ability to Pay Component #1: Equity in Assets.**

> **Example- NRE Example.** A taxpayer has a home with a fair market value of $300,000, a QSV at 80% (IRS standard QSV for a home), and a mortgage of $200,000. The taxpayer has NRE in the home of $40,000 (($300,000 × 80%) = $240,000 QSV, less $200,000 debt, or $40,000).

For an OIC, all taxpayer assets must be included in NRE. This includes assets that are available to the taxpayer but are outside the reach of the government (i.e., foreign assets). The taxpayer may be required to include the value of assets transferred or disposed of prior to the offer submission in an acceptable offer amount. This includes assets that were transferred to third parties to avoid IRS collection and other dissipated assets. [IRM 5.8.4.3.1 (4-30-2015)]

For more on dissipated assets, see **Chapter 9.06: Ability to Pay Component #1: Equity in Assets.**

Example- Two months prior to submitting the OIC, the taxpayer cashed in a certificate of deposit for $50,000 to pay for his daughter's wedding and wedding present. The $50,000 would be included in the NRE in assets as a dissipated asset as it was sold within three years prior to the OIC application and was not used for necessary living expenses.

Pro Tip: OIC qualification and offer amount NRE calculations differ slightly – but their differences are important in determining if the OIC is a viable collection alternative. For example, determining NRE in cash and vehicles is different for the ability to pay determination (qualification for an OIC) and for the offer amount (reasonable collection potential). For OIC qualification calculations, the taxpayer is not allowed the $1,000 exclusion from cash in determining ability to pay. When the taxpayer computes the offer amount, the taxpayer can compute NRE in cash by also reducing the cash balance by $1,000 plus one month of necessary living expenses. For qualification of an OIC, the taxpayer is also not allowed the $3,450 exclusion to reduce the value of vehicles that would be allowed for purpose of computing the OIC offer amount.

For more on computing NRE in assets, see **Chapter 9.06: Ability to Pay Component #1: Equity in Assets.**

ATP (Qualification) Component #2: Future Monthly Payments

The second component in determining ability to pay is to determine how much the taxpayer could pay in monthly payments to the IRS before the expiration of the CSED. The taxpayer needs to compute his monthly disposable income (MDI) and the CSED(s) in order to be able to determine how much he can pay in monthly payments before the CSED(s) expire.

For more on computing MDI, see **Chapter 9.07: Ability to Pay Component #2: Monthly Disposable Income.**

Taxpayers can contact the IRS to determine the CSED date(s) for various tax years.

For more obtaining CSEDs, see **Chapter 1.12: Collection Statute of Limitations.**

Pro Tip: When calculating MDI for OIC qualification, taxpayers often erroneously allow the additional transportation operating expense for an older vehicle. An older vehicle is defined as a vehicle that is older than nine years, or has more than 125,000 miles. [IRM 5.8.5.22.3 at (6) (4-8-2024)] Older vehicles are allowed an additional $200 transportation operating expense for each qualified vehicle. However, this expense may only be allowed in computing the offer amount if the taxpayer makes a compelling case for higher operating expenses for qualification. Note that these additional allowances are not indicated on the OIC Form 433-A(OIC).

If the taxpayer only has a balance owed for one year and one assessment (i.e., he only has one CSED date), the taxpayer can take the number of months remaining before that CSED expires in computing the ability to pay with future income. However, taxpayers considering an OIC often owe for multiple years. If the taxpayer owes for multiple years, the calculation of how much the taxpayer can pay before the CSEDs expire becomes more difficult. The taxpayer will need to consider the payments that could be made before each CSED expires.

> **Example- Example of Ability to Pay with Future Income.** Taxpayer has MDI of $200 per month. The CSED is 100 months. The taxpayer's ability to pay with future income is $20,000 ($200 per month for 100 months).

> However, if the taxpayer owes for multiple years and/or has multiple CSEDs, the ability to pay with future payments may be different based on the CSED and amounts owed that are associated with each CSED.

> A sample calculation of ATP with future payments with multiple CSED/amounts owed appears below.

Year	Amount owed	Remaining months until CSED
2008	$75,000	10
2009	$25,000	45
2011	$2,000	60
Total owed	$102,000	

> Taxpayer has MDI of $200 a month. Taxpayer has the ability to pay as calculated below:

Year	# months on CSED	# of payment applied	ATP
2008	10	10	$2,000 (limited by 10 months remaining on CSED)
2009	45	35	$7,000 (limited by 35 remaining months on CSED)
2011	60	15	$2,000 (limited by amount owed)
		60 months	$11,000

> The taxpayer only has the ability to pay with future payments of $11,000. The CSEDs for 2008 and 2009 limit the amount that can be paid by the end of the CSED.

OIC Qualification: Comparing ATP to Tax Balances Owed

To qualify for an OIC-DATC, the taxpayer's ability to pay must be less than the tax owed. The ability to pay is made of two components: (NRE in all assets and future income payments that can be made before the CSED expires).

Example- Jane has the following tax debt situation:

- Owes $50,000.
- Has MDI of $200 a month.
- Has NRE in all assets of $5,000.
- Has 60 months remaining on the CSED.

Jane qualifies for an OIC because her ability to pay is less than the total balance owed:

Ability to pay	Amount
Component #1: NRE in all assets	$5,000
Component #2: MDI payments before expiration of the CSED	(60 × $200) = $12,000
Total ability to pay (Component #1 + Component #2)	$17,000
Balance owed	$50,000
Qualify? ATP < balance owed	Yes ($17,000 is less than balance owed of $50,000)

Qualify and Not Qualify Determination

If a taxpayer qualifies for an OIC-DATC, they would proceed to compute the offer amount that would be needed to settle the balance in full. If a taxpayer does not qualify for an OIC-DATC, they need to look for another collection alternative, such as an installment agreement, CNC, or an ETA-OIC.

IRS Discretion for an OIC-DATC

Treasury Regulation §301.7122-1(a) provides that the IRS may, at their discretion, compromise any liability. However, to apply the OIC program consistently and fairly, the IRS must develop rules in determining whether to compromise a liability.

In a case where the taxpayer qualifies for an OIC-DATC but a partial-pay installment agreement may collect a significant amount of the liability, the IRS states that it may use its discretion to reject the OIC-DATC. IRM 5.8.4.3 at (4) (4-25-2025) provides an example where the IRS may reject an OIC-DATC where a taxpayer qualifies for an OIC, but the IRS would project to receive a significant amount of the liability paid with a PPIA:

Example- IRM Example. The outstanding tax liability is $200,000 and the taxpayer submitted an offer in the amount of $36,000. The taxpayer is unable to fully pay the tax liability via an IA within the limits of the CSED. The taxpayer's RCP is $36,000 which is based solely on future income of $1,500 per month. Based on the calculation of RCP, the taxpayer's offer may be acceptable, yet there remains over nine years left on the CSED, so the government would potentially receive over $162,000 from a PPIA. In this instance, the fact that the government has the potential to receive an additional $126,000, which is substantially more than the monitoring costs incurred, provides that acceptance of the taxpayer's offer is not in the government's interest. The offer should be rejected on that basis, unless special circumstances are present which allow for acceptance under ETA or DATCSC.

Although these are rare instances, taxpayers should be aware that the IRS will use its discretion to protect the government's interest and reject an OIC when the taxpayer technically qualifies based on the ability to pay.

Computing the Offer Amount

The offer amount is defined as the reasonable collection potential (RCP) of the taxpayer.

The formula for RCP (offer amount) is as follows:

Step #2: OIC Offer Amount (Reasonable Collection Potential)

$$\text{Net realizable equity in assets, less exclusions} + \text{MDI (less allowances)} \times \text{Future Income Multiplier} = \text{Offer amount}$$

In addition to the computation of NRE in assets and MDI, the only difference in computing the ATP and RCP is that the RCP is equal to the taxpayer's MDI times a future income multiplier (not the number of months until the expiration of the CSED). In the ATP/qualification formula, the taxpayer would calculate ATP based on the remaining months until the expiration of the CSED. The future income multiplier is a set number of months of MDI to be included in an OIC. The number of months is determined by which OIC payment method is selected.

The two OIC payment methods are listed below with the number of months of MDI that is computed as part of the offer amount: [IRM 5.8.5.25 (9-24-2021)]

Payment method	# of months – future income multiplier	Payment terms	Advantages/disadvantages
Lump-sum	12 months (less if the time left on the CSED is	Taxpayer agrees to make a 20% down payment of the offer amount (unless low-income waiver applies).	Advantages • Lower offer amount when taxpayer has MDI. • No payments during offer investigation period.

	shorter than 12 months)	Remaining payment(s) must be made within five months of OIC acceptance.	Disadvantages • Requires 20% down payment unless qualifies for low-income waiver.
Periodic payment	24 months (less if the time left on the CSED is shorter than 24 months)	Taxpayer makes monthly scheduled payments over 24 months while the offer is being considered/after acceptance.	Advantages • Likely lower up-front payments. Disadvantages • Higher offer amount when taxpayer has MDI. • Possibly more out-of-pocket costs than lump-sum in long OIC investigation. • Payments must be made during OIC investigation.

Taxpayers do not have to make the down payment or periodic payments if they meet the low-income criteria. However, the time frame for paying the accepted offer amount will start on the date of written notice of acceptance. At that time, the taxpayer must begin making the payments in accordance with the terms of the accepted offer. [IRM 5.8.4.24 (4-25-2025)]

Example- Offer Amount Example. George has the following tax debt situation:

- Owes $50,000.
- Has MDI of $200 a month. (assume MDI for offer amount is the same as qualification – this is not likely)
- Has NRE in all assets of $5,000. (assume NRE for offer amount is the same as qualification – this is not likely)
- Has 60 months remaining on the CSED.

George qualifies for an OIC because his ability to pay is less than the total balance owed:

Ability to pay	Amount
Component #1: NRE in all assets	$5,000
Component #2: MDI payments before the expiration of the CSED	(60 × $200) = $12,000
Total ability to pay (Component #1 + Component #2)	$17,000
Balance owed	$50,000
Qualify? ATP < balance owed	Yes ($17,000 is less than balance owed of $50,000)

George's RCP or offer amount is as follows:

Reasonable collection potential	Lump-sum offer amount	Period payment offer amount
Component A: NRE in all assets (same as ATP amount)	$5,000	$5,000
Component B: MDI × future income multiplier • Lump-sum: 12 months • Periodic payment: 24 months	$200 × 12 months = $2,400	$200 × 24 months = $4,800
RCP (offer amount) (Component A + Component B)	$7,400	$9,800

The taxpayer is able to settle the $50,000 liability for $7,400 (lump-sum method) or $9,800 (periodic payment method), depending on which payment method is selected.

OIC Planning Considerations: Minimizing MDI and Imminent CSEDs

In some cases, the taxpayer may not qualify or the OIC offer amount may not be low enough to warrant the use of an OIC. In many cases, the taxpayer should resolve the tax debt situation with another collection alternative.

Taxpayers can sometimes reduce their ability to pay and offer amounts by taking advantage of expenses that the IRS allows to minimize MDI. Three common examples of allowable expenses appear below:

- *Vehicle payments*: a taxpayer with an older vehicle that has no monthly payment may acquire a needed vehicle that would lower his MDI.
- *Health insurance*: a taxpayer without health insurance should consider acquiring insurance. Besides being a good financial decision, health insurance is an allowable expense that reduces MDI; the taxpayer may choose to acquire insurance to lower MDI.
- *State/local tax installment agreement payments*: generally, the IRS will allow state and local tax installment payments if the taxpayer's state or local debt has been assessed and payment arrangements are made prior to the assessment of the federal tax debt. [IRM 5.8.5.22.4 at (7) (9-24-2021)] Taxpayers with both federal and state/local unfiled returns may want to file and establish the state/local debt and payments prior to the assessment of the federal debt in order to have this payment allowed as a necessary expense in computing MDI.

Adding these allowable expenses will reduce MDI and the offer amount if future income is a material part of the OIC.

It is never acceptable for the taxpayer to hide assets or income to qualify for an OIC.

Taxpayers with imminent CSEDs should closely consider whether an OIC is a correct option before applying. In some cases, it may be best for a hardship taxpayer to continue in CNC status or in a PPIA until the collection statute of limitations expires.

OIC-DATCSC: Special Circumstances That May Warrant a Lower Offer Amount

A taxpayer may have special circumstances that warrants a lower offer amount than the offer amount calculated based on the OIC payment method. In these cases, the taxpayer will submit an OIC—Doubt as to Collectibility with Special Circumstances (OIC-DATCSC).

The rules for applying "special circumstances" for an OIC-DATCSC are the same as ETA-OIC. The OIC-DATCSC requires that the taxpayer qualify for an OIC-DATC — that is, she does not have the ability to pay before the expiration of the CSED. In an ETA-OIC, taxpayers do have the ATP and do not qualify for an OIC-DATC. However, in both the OIC-DATCSC and the ETA-OIC, the taxpayer will compute an offer amount based on special circumstances. [IRM 5.8.4.2 (4-25-2025)]

OICs can be considered under DATCSC criteria when:

- The taxpayer cannot fully pay the tax due, and
- The taxpayer has proven special circumstances that warrant acceptance for less than the amount of the calculated RCP.

[IRM 5.8.4.2 at (3) (4-25-2025)]

The most likely special circumstance is economic hardship. To qualify for economic hardship, the taxpayer's financial condition must not allow her to meet basic necessary living expenses. Most economic hardship cases involve the taxpayer's need to use future assets to pay for well-documented expected future necessary living expenses.

The Internal Revenue Manual provides some factors to determine whether special circumstances exist:

- The taxpayer's age and employment status,
- Number, age, and health of the taxpayer's dependents,
- Cost of living in the area the taxpayer resides, and
- Any extraordinary circumstances such as special education expenses, a medical catastrophe, or natural disaster.

[IRM 5.8.11.3.1 at (5) (4-11-2024)]

The IRM dives further to explain how the IRS will make an economic hardship determination:

- The taxpayer is incapable of earning a living because of a long-term illness, medical condition or disability, and it is reasonably foreseeable that the financial resources will be exhausted providing for care and support during the course of the condition.
- The taxpayer may have a set monthly income and no other means of support and the income is exhausted each month in providing for the care of dependents.
- The taxpayer has assets but is unable to borrow against the equity in those assets, and liquidation to pay the outstanding tax liabilities would render the taxpayer unable to meet basic living expenses.

[IRM 5.8.11.3.1 at (6) (4-11-2024)]

The IRM also provides three practical examples on how economic hardship could be applied: [IRM 5.8.11.3.1 at (7) (4-11-2024)]

Example- Use of assets for future long-term medical care:

The taxpayer has assets sufficient to satisfy the tax liability and provides full time care and assistance to a dependent child, who has a serious long-term illness. It is expected that the taxpayer will need to use the equity in assets to provide for adequate basic living expenses and medical care for the child. The taxpayer's overall compliance history does not weigh against compromise.

Example- Use of permanent fixed income from a retirement plan asset:

The taxpayer is retired, and the only income is from a pension. The only asset is a retirement account and the funds in the account are sufficient to satisfy the liability. Liquidation of the retirement account would leave the taxpayer without adequate means to provide for basic living expenses. The taxpayer's overall compliance history does not weigh against compromise.

Example- Use of disability and fixed income:

The taxpayer is disabled and lives on a fixed income that will not, after allowance of adequate basic living expenses, permit full payment of the liability under an installment agreement. The taxpayer also owns a modest house that has been specially equipped to accommodate for a disability. The equity in the house is sufficient to permit payment of the liability owed. However, because of the disability and limited earning potential, the taxpayer is unable to obtain a mortgage or otherwise borrow against this equity. In addition, because the taxpayer's home has been specially equipped to accommodate the disability, forced sale of the taxpayer's residence would create severe adverse consequences for the taxpayer, making such a sale unlikely. The taxpayer's overall compliance history does not weigh against compromise.

These examples provide three very common situations that would warrant the taxpayer offering a lesser amount due to special circumstances. Taxpayers must compute the amount needed to cover the necessary living expenses. Often in these situations, taxpayers will require all or some of the equity in assets to fund future necessary living expenses based on their current financial condition. In many cases, taxpayers that qualify for an OIC-DATCSC with an economic hardship will qualify and obtain the CNC or PPIA collection alternative.

Step #1 Resources: ATP Section

For detailed information on calculating the taxpayer's ability to pay and reasonable collection potential for an OIC-DATC, see **Chapter 9: Determining Ability to Pay for IRS Collection Options**.

For information on completing the financial analysis for NRE, MDI, determining OIC-DATC qualification, and computing the offer amount, see **Chapter 9.06: Ability to Pay Component #1: Equity in Assets** and **Chapter 9.07: Ability to Pay Component #2: Monthly Disposable Income**.

For worksheets that can be used in the OIC financial analysis. refer to the **Appendix B**—and visit www.TaxProblemsHandbook.com under the **IRS Collection Solutions Handbook** tab for downloadable resources.

Title	Useful for:
OIC: Equity in Asset Summary for OIC Qualification Determination	Worksheet to value net equity in assets for purposes of determining if the taxpayer qualifies for an OIC-DATC.
Form 433-A(OIC): Equity in Asset Summary for Offer Amount Determination	Worksheet to compute net realizable equity in assets (for OIC-DATC offer amounts determination). Maps to Form 433-A(OIC).
Forms 433-A and 433-A(OIC): Net Business Income Analysis for Ability to Pay Calculation	Worksheet to determine the average net business income for ability to pay determinations for CNC, ATP IAs, and OIC-DATC. Maps to Forms 433-A and 433-A(OIC).
MDI Analysis Worksheet (for determining ability to pay for installment agreements, CNC, and OIC-DATC)	Worksheet to analyze the average monthly disposable income for ability to pay determinations for CNC, ATP IAs, and OIC-DATC.
Forms 433-A and 433-A(OIC) MDI Computation	Worksheet to determine final MDI for ability to pay determinations for CNC, ATP IAs, and OIC-DATC. Maps to Forms 433-A and 433-A(OIC).
Form 433-A(OIC): OIC Qualification and Offer Amount Computations	Worksheet to determine if the taxpayer qualifies for an OIC-DATC and to compute to offer amount. Maps to parts of Form 433-A(OIC) and Form 656.

Chapter 12.10: Step 2: The OIC Application.

After determining that the taxpayer qualifies for an OIC, calculate the offer amount, and determine that the taxpayer is able to pay the offer amount and meets all the other requirements to file an OIC. The next step is to complete the OIC application.

The application for an OIC-DATC is a Form 656, *Offer in Compromise*. The IRS provides Form 656-B, *Offer in Compromise* Booklet, which provides the Form 656 and the Forms 433 needed to file an OIC-DATC.

Initially Processible OIC Application

The goal of the OIC application is to provide the IRS with substantiation that the taxpayer qualifies for an OIC and can pay the proposed offer amount. For the IRS to consider an OIC, the OIC application must be "processible." Processible OICs have the minimum requirements necessary to proceed to the next step of the OIC process — investigation of the OIC.

OIC applications will be considered not processible if:

- *Bankruptcy*: the taxpayer is in an open bankruptcy proceeding.
- *The entire liability is still in question*: the taxpayer has an amended return or an OIC-DATL for the same liability in the OIC-DATC (it is best to wait until the liability in question is known).
- *Required fees and payments are not made*: the application fee and required down payment (lump-sum method) or first payment (periodic payment method) are not included with the application.
- *All liabilities are not assessed*: there is an unassessed liability due from a tax return or compliance activity, such as an audit or a trust fund recovery penalty.
- *Outstanding unfiled returns*: the taxpayer has unfiled tax returns. *Note*: If the taxpayer has filed within the past 60 days, she should provide a copy of the return with the application.

[IRM 5.8.2.4.1 (6-14-2024)]

The IRS can return the OIC application if any of the above conditions exist or required items are not included in the application. Not processible offers do not carry appeal rights and the taxpayer must resubmit the application with new documentation and new payments. If the OIC application is initially deemed to be not processible, the IRS will return the application fee. After the IRS deems the application to be initially processible, the IRS will keep the application fee even if the OIC application is returned during the investigation. With not processible OICs, the IRS will keep the down payment/first periodic payment and apply it to the taxpayer's liability owed unless the taxpayer's OIC is deemed not processible for bankruptcy, lack of application fee, no liabilities in question, unassessed liabilities, or expired CSEDs. [IRM 5.8.2.4.1 (6-14-2024)]

Required Supporting Information

The completed and signed <u>Form 656</u> is required for a taxpayer to request an OIC.

In addition, the OIC application booklet details the requirements and supporting documentation necessary to accompany the <u>Form 656</u>. The IRS requests the following documents with the <u>Form 656</u> and <u>433-A(OIC)</u> (Individuals):

- [ ] Copies of the most recent pay stub, earnings statement, etc., from each employer.
- [ ] Copies of the most recent statement for each investment and retirement account.
- [ ] Copies of all documents and records showing currently held digital assets.
- [ ] Copies of the most recent statement, etc., from all other sources of income such as pensions, Social Security, rental income, interest and dividends (including any received from a related partnership, corporation, LLC, LLP, etc.), court order for child support, alimony, royalties, agricultural subsidies, gambling income, oil credits, rent subsidies, sharing economy income from providing on-demand work, services or goods (e.g., Uber, Lyft, AirBnB, VRBO), income through digital platforms like an app or website, etc., and recurring capital gains from the sale of securities or other property such as digital assets.
- [ ] Copies of individual complete bank statements for the three most recent months. If you operate a business, copies of the six most recent complete statements for each business bank account.
- [ ] Completed Form 433-B (Collection Information Statement for Businesses) if you or your spouse have an interest in a business entity other than a sole-proprietorship.
- [ ] Copies of the most recent statement from lender(s) on loans such as mortgages, second mortgages, vehicles, etc., showing monthly payments, loan payoffs, and balances.
- [ ] List of Accounts Receivable or Notes Receivable, if applicable.
- [ ] Verification of delinquent State/Local Tax Liability showing total delinquent state/local taxes and amount of monthly payments, if applicable.
- [ ] Copies of court orders for child support/alimony payments claimed in monthly expense section.
- [ ] Copies of Trust documents if applicable per Section 9.
- [ ] Documentation to support any special circumstances described in the "Explanation of Circumstances" on Form 656, if applicable.
- [ ] Attach a Form 2848, *Power of Attorney and Declaration of Representative*, if you would like your attorney, CPA, or enrolled agent to represent you and you do not have a current form on file with the IRS. Ensure all years and forms involved in your offer are listed on Form 2848 and include the current tax year.
- [ ] Completed and signed current Form 656.

When <u>Form 433-B(OIC)</u> is required for business entity information, the IRS also requests the following:

- [ ] A current Profit and Loss statement covering at least the most recent 6–12 month period, if appropriate.
- [ ] Copies of the six most recent complete bank statements for each business account and copies of the three most recent statements for each investment account.
- [ ] If an asset is used as collateral on a loan, include copies of the most recent statement from lender(s) on loans, monthly payments, loan payoffs, and balances.
- [ ] Copies of the most recent statement of outstanding accounts and notes receivable.
- [ ] Copies of all documents and records showing currently held digital assets.
- [ ] Copies of the most recent statements from lenders on loans, mortgages (including second mortgages), monthly payments, loan payoffs, and balances.
- [ ] Copies of relevant supporting documentation of special circumstances described in the Section 3 on Form 656, if applicable.
- [ ] Attach a Form 2848, *Power of Attorney and Declaration of Representative*, if you would like your attorney, CPA, or enrolled agent to represent you and you do not have a current form on file with the IRS. Ensure all years and forms involved in your offer are listed on Form 2848 and include the current tax year.
- [ ] Completed and current signed Form 656.

The IRS will normally not reject the OIC application outright if all the listed items are not included. The IRS will usually allow 15-30 additional days for the taxpayer to provide any other information needed to consider the OIC. In addition, the offer examiner, during the offer investigation, may deem that the information submitted is not complete and later request additional documentation to support the OIC.

OIC Application Fee and the Low-Income Waiver

The OIC-DATC and ETA-OIC require a $205 application fee unless the taxpayer meets the low-income criteria. OICs submitted without the application fee are returned to the taxpayer. [IRM 5.8.2.4.1 at (1) (6-14-2024)] The down payment will not be returned with OICs returned for filing noncompliance, but the IRS will apply the down payment to the assessed liability. [IRM 5.8.2.4.1 at (2) (6-14-2024)] Taxpayers must submit a separate check for $205 for each OIC application. [Form 656B Instructions]

In order to meet the low-income waiver, the taxpayer's gross annual household income must be less than or equal to the following amounts:

Size of family unit	48 contiguous states, D.C., and U.S. Territories	Alaska	Hawaii
1	$37,650.00	$47,025.00	$43,275.00
2	$51,100.00	$63,850.00	$58,750.00
3	$64,550.00	$80,675.00	$74,225.00
4	$78,000.00	$97,500.00	$89,700.00
5	$91,450.00	$114,325.00	$105,175.00
6	$104,900.00	$131,150.00	$120,650.00
7	$118,350.00	$147,975.00	$136,125.00
8	$131,800.00	$164,800.00	$151,600.00
For each additional person, add	$13,450.00	$16,825.00	$15,475.00

The taxpayer must complete the low-income certification on Form 656, Section 1. The taxpayer's last year's tax return or current household income should be used to determine if she qualifies for the low-income waiver. [Form 656 and IRM 5.8.2.4.1 at (7) (6-14-2024)] Taxpayers who qualify for the low-income waiver also do not have to submit a down payment (lump-sum offer) or a monthly payment (periodic payment offer) with the OIC application or while the offer is being considered. If it is determined during the offer investigation that the taxpayer does not qualify for the low-income waiver, the taxpayer will be given the opportunity to amend the OIC and pay the application fee and required payments. Failure to do so will result in the OIC being returned to the taxpayer. [IRM 5.8.4.7 at (2d) (4-25-20245)]

Payment Terms

Form 656, Section 4, requires the taxpayer to choose the OIC payment terms.

Section 4	Payment Terms

Check only one of the payment options below to indicate how long it will take you to pay your offer in full. You must offer more than $0. The offer amount should be in whole dollars only.

Lump Sum

☐ **Check here if you will pay your offer in 5 or fewer payments within 5 or fewer months from the date of acceptance:**

Enclose a check for 20% of the offer amount (waived if you met the requirements for Low-Income Certification) and fill in the amount(s) of your future payment(s).

Total offer amount	-	20% initial payment	=	Remaining balance
$	-	$	=	$

You may pay the remaining balance in one payment after acceptance of the offer or up to five payments, but cannot exceed 5 months.

Amount of payment $	payable within		Month after acceptance
Amount of payment $	payable within		Months after acceptance
Amount of payment $	payable within		Months after acceptance
Amount of payment $	payable within		Months after acceptance
Amount of payment $	payable within		Months after acceptance

Periodic Payment

☐ **Check here if you will pay your offer in full in 6 to 24 months**

Enter the amount of your offer $ _____

Note: The total months may not exceed a total of 24. For example, if you are requesting your payments extend for 24 months then your first payment is considered to be month 1 and your last payment is considered month 24. There will be 22 payments between the first and last month.

Enclose a check for the first month's payment *(waived if you met the requirements for Low-Income Certification)*.

The first monthly payment of $ _____ is included with this offer then $ _____ will be paid on the *(pick number 1-28)* _____ day of each month thereafter for _____ months with a final payment of $ _____ to be paid on the _____ day of the _____ month.

You must continue to make these monthly payments while the IRS is considering the offer *(waived if you met the requirements for Low-Income Certification)*. **Failure to make regular monthly payments until you have received a final decision letter will cause your offer to be returned with no appeal rights. If you qualified under the Low-Income Certification and are not required to submit payments while the offer is under consideration, your first payment will be due 30 calendar days after acceptance of the offer, unless another date is agreed to in an amended offer.**

The taxpayer has two choices:

Option #1: Lump Sum Cash Method

This method requires the taxpayer to enclose a payment for 20% of the offer amount (waived if the low-income waiver applies) with the OIC application and pay the remaining OIC offer amount in five or fewer months after the OIC is accepted. For lump-sum case OICs, the taxpayer will not have to make payments during the OIC investigation period.

Option #2: Periodic Payment Method

This method requires that the taxpayer make periodic monthly payments to pay the offer in full during the OIC application and investigation period (unless the low-income wavier applies). The taxpayer must pay the offer in full in 6 to 24 months.

Taxpayers do not have to schedule equal monthly payments with either payment method. However, taxpayers are expected to pay the entire amount offered in as short a time as reasonably possible. [IRM 5.8.1.15.4 at (1) (4-20-2021)]

Taxpayers can later revise their OIC payment method with the IRS's offer examiner. But in order to do so, the taxpayer must submit the request in writing and submit any missing payments. [IRM 5.8.4.24.1 at (11) (4-25-2025)]

After investigation, many OICs require amendment to correct the offer amount. If the taxpayer and the IRS later agree to increase the offer amount, the taxpayer will need to revise/amend the OIC and submit the required payments. Taxpayers may amend the OIC periodic payment terms in accordance with the terms of the revised offer and continue to make the proposed installments during the evaluation of the OIC. [IRM 5.8.4.24.1 at (11) (4-25-2025)]

Designating Payments

Taxpayers can designate their lump-sum or monthly periodic payment to a specific tax year/period in Section 5 of the Form 656. [IRM 5.8.2.8.1 at (4) (6-14-2024)] Many taxpayers designate offer payments to the least imminent CSED year (usually the most current year filed) to reduce the time to collect in the event that the OIC is not accepted. If the taxpayer elects not to designate payments and the taxpayer's OIC is rejected or returned without refund of the down payment, the IRS automatically posts payments to the oldest collection statute year.

Section 5	Designation of Payment and Electronic Federal Tax Payment System (EFTPS)	

Designation of Payment

If you want your payment to be applied to a specific tax year and a specific tax debt, such as employment taxes or a Trust Fund Recovery Penalty,

tell us the tax period/quarter _____. If you are not specific with your designation we will apply any money you send to the government's best interest. If you want to designate any future payments not included with this Form 656 while the offer is pending [see section 7(j) below] with the IRS, you must include the specific tax year and type of tax at the time each payment is made. However, you cannot designate the application fee or any payment after the IRS accepts the offer.

Note: Payments submitted with your offer cannot be designated as estimated tax payments for a current or past tax year.

Electronic Federal Tax Payment System (EFTPS)

List offer payments made through Electronic Federal Tax Payment System (EFTPS) below.

Offer application fee	Date	Electronic funds transfer number *(15 digits)*
Offer payment	Date	Electronic funds transfer number *(15 digits)*

Note: Any Offer Application Fee or initial payment made electronically must be made the same date your offer is mailed.

Multiple Applications

The general rule is that there should be as many Forms 656 OIC applications as there are entities. A taxpayer with a married filing joint tax liability can file one OIC application. However, it is necessary to file more than one OIC application package (Form 656, 433, fees, and documents) if the taxpayer falls into the following situation:

- Taxpayer and spouse have separate liabilities.
- Taxpayer and her business have separate liabilities.

[IRM 5.8.4.7.3 (4-25-2025)]

It is important to notify the IRS of the need for multiple applications in these cases. For spouses with separate liabilities, the ability to pay and the offer amount will be based on their household finances. The offer amount is split between the two spouses when determining the married taxpayer's reasonable collection potential.

Example- This is a common example where multiple OIC applications are needed:

- Primary taxpayer owes for 2008 and 2009 as single.
- Secondary taxpayer owes for 2008 as married filing separately.
- Both owe for 2010 as joint filers.
- Primary taxpayer: 2008-2010.
- Secondary taxpayer: 2009-2010.
- The offer amount is $7,000.
- They are filing a lump-sum offer that requires a down payment of 20% ($1,400). The taxpayers do not qualify for the low-income waiver.

Two Forms 656 are needed. The primary taxpayer for the years 2008-2010 and the secondary taxpayer for the years 2008 and 2010. The offer amount, fees, and payments are determined as follows:

Married couple, with joint and separate debts

Family financials	Joint Liability	Primary Taxpayer: Separate liability	Secodnary Taxpayer: Separate liability
Liabilities owed: Years:	Owe $50,000 Year: 2010	Owe $5,000 Years: 2008 and 2009	Owe $3,000 Year: 2008
Lump sum offer		**Applications**	
amount= $7,000 20% down= $1,400	No Form 656 needed- each TP can cover debt owed in separate application	Separate Form 656 includes joint and ind debt Form 433A (joint information) Documentation (joint information) $186 user fee Offer Amount= (50%) $3,500 1st payment= (50%) $700	Separate Form 656 includes joint and ind debt Form 433A (joint information) Documentation (joint information) $186 user fee Offer Amount= (50%) $3,500 1st payment= (50%) $700
Does not qualify for low income waiver			

When a taxpayer is filing multiple OIC applications on related taxpayers, it is important to associate the OIC application packages to the offer amount. A cover letter should be included that indicates the number of applications and how the ability to pay and reasonable collection potential was determined.

There are many other instances where multiple OIC applications are required. Taxpayers with liabilities on multiple persons or entities are encouraged to review IRS guidance concerning multiple applications which is found in IRM 5.8.3.5 at (5) (6-18-2024).

OIC Application Checklist

To facilitate the offer investigation and acceptance, the taxpayer should provide a complete application that allows the IRS to determine the taxpayer's ability to pay (OIC qualification) and reasonable collection potential (offer amount). Use the following checklist to complete the OIC-DATC or OIC-DATCSC application.

OIC-DATC Application Checklist

Use this checklist to complete your OIC-DATC or OIC-DATCSC application:

✓	Application Document	Practice Tips
☐	Application cover letter	☐ Outline terms of the OIC and explain any special circumstances. ☐ Include the taxpayer's and third-party authorized (Power-of-attorney or Tax Information Authorization) information. ☐ Identify any years/taxes owed that were proposed/filed within the past 60 days or not yet recorded on IRS account transcript. ☐ Identify any associated OIC applications.
☐	Index of documents	☐ Provide an index of documents for later reference when talking with OIC examiner. ☐ Organize the documents in sections for later reference when dealing with the offer examiner by phone. ☐ Number each section and page.
☐	Third-party authorization	☐ Include a copy of the Form 2848, Power-of-attorney, or Form 8821, Tax Information Authorization that provides for a third-party to receive information/deal directly with the IRS
☐	Form 656 – OIC Application	All sections completed, including: ☐ Identify all taxes and years. ☐ Complete low-income certification, if applicable. ☐ Include reason for offer and explanation of special circumstances. ☐ Indicate payment method and terms. ☐ Designate payments and deposit, if applicable. ☐ Provide source of payments. ☐ Complete filing compliance requirements checklist. ☐ Complete payment compliance requirements checklist. ☐ Sign and date. ☐ Paid preparer/representative sign/date. ☐ Complete separate OIC application if taxpayer and spouse have separate liabilities or if taxpayer has separate business tax debt.
☐	OIC Application User Fee	☐ Separate check for $205. ☐ Made out to US Treasury. ☐ No fee if low-income certification applies.
☐	OIC down payment/first periodic payment	☐ Separate check for OIC down payment/periodic payment (20% down payment for OIC lump-sum offer or 1st payment for periodic payment offer). ☐ Made out to US Treasury. ☐ No down payment if low-income certification applies.
☐	Form(s) 433 A/B-OIC – Collection Information Statement(s)	☐ Form 433(A)-OIC: for individuals and self-employed. ☐ Form 433(B)-OIC: for corporations, partnerships, LLCs classified as a corporation, other LLCs. ☐ Sign/date Form(s) 433.
☐	Worksheet: offer qualification (ability to	☐ Summary of ability to pay (qualification).

	pay) and offer amount (reasonable collection potential) computation	☐	Summary of reasonable collection potential (offer amount).
		☐	Computation of MDI details and support for income/expense averaging methodology.
		☐	Special circumstances explained and exclusions from offer amount.
☐	Worksheet: net realizable equity in assets calculation	☐	List of assets at quick sale value, net of associated liabilities.
		☐	Exemptions and exclusions applied.
☐	Worksheet: monthly disposable income calculation	☐	Summary of income and expenses over averaging period(s).
		☐	Self-employed income/expenses for past 6-12 months, if applicable.
☐	Required documentation	☐	Copies ONLY – do not send originals.
		☐	Financial account statements, all accounts (ALL PAGES) for past 3 months (business accounts for past 6 months).
		☐	Copies of the most recent pay stub, earnings statement, etc., from each employer.
		☐	Copies of the most recent statement, etc., from all other sources of income such as pensions, Social Security, rental income, interest and dividends (including any received from a related partnership, corporation, LLC, LLP, etc.), court order for child support, alimony, and rent subsidies.
		☐	Copies of the most recent statement from lender(s) on loans such as mortgages, second mortgages, vehicles, etc., showing monthly payments, loan payoffs, and balances.
		☐	List of Notes Receivable, if applicable.
		☐	Verification of delinquent State/Local Tax Liability showing total delinquent state/local taxes and amount of monthly payments, if applicable.
		☐	Documentation to support any special circumstances described in the "Explanation of Circumstances" on Form 656, if applicable.
☐	Other supporting documentation	☐	Copies of all housing and utility expenses for averaging period.
		☐	Copies of medical bills paid for averaging period.
		☐	Copies of any expenses paid and documentation to warrant expenses that exceed the IRS Collection Financial Standards.
		☐	Court orders and/or agreements for any mandatory payments for child support, alimony, and other judgments.
		☐	Student loan statements and monthly payments made, if applicable.
		☐	Copies of any other necessary living expenses and expenses to produce income for averaging period.
		☐	Copies of any tax returns or assessment notices filed/received in the past 60 days.
☐	Copy/mailing of entire application	☐	Index the entire application for later reference.
		☐	Send to proper COIC Unit.
		☐	Keep complete copy for records and reference.

For the OIC-DATC Application Checklist, refer to the **Appendix B**—and visit www.TaxProblemsHandbook.com under the **IRS Collection Solutions Handbook** tab for downloadable resources.

Some documents listed above are optional but will facilitate the investigation. The taxpayer may want to provide a copy of her credit report(s) if her liability is greater than $100,000. When taxpayers owe over $100,000, IRS offer investigation procedures strongly suggest that the offer examiner check the taxpayer's financial history through credit reports. Credit reports may provide the offer examiner insight into items not disclosed in the OIC application, for example, dissipated assets.

Online OIC Application Submission

In 2025, individuals can use their IRS Online Account to initially submit an OIC. Form 656 is available in the "Forms" section of the Online Account. The workflow requires the user to determine their eligibility first before completing and submitting the form.

Filing using the Online Account form starts the OIC process.

> **Pro Tip**: it is still advisable to send an OIC application by certified mail to the IRS as the online application process is not streamlined and requires the taxpayer to submit documents by mail also.

IRS Receipt of the OIC Application

When the IRS receives a processible OIC application, the IRS OIC processing examiner will sign and date stamp the "IRS Received Date" on the Form 656. [IRM 5.8.2.4.1 at (9) (6-14-2024)] This date starts the time running on the IRS's two-year requirement to provide a written decision on the OIC.

Once the IRS receives the application and it is determined to be processible, the offer investigation process begins.

> **Pro Tip:** IRS COIC units have experienced delays in assigning the OIC application to an offer examiner after the application is received and deemed processible by the OIC processing examiner. It is not unusual for the IRS to send a letter acknowledging receipt of the OIC application by notifying the taxpayer that the IRS will not contact the taxpayer for five months. OICs sent to the Memphis OIC have traditionally experienced long delays between OIC application receipt and the offer examiner assignment investigation.

Chapter 12.11: Step 3: The Offer Investigation

OIC applications are generally investigated in the IRS Centralized OIC (COIC) units located at the IRS service centers in Memphis, TN, or in Holtsville, NY (Brookhaven).

For most individuals, including those taxpayers with a single proprietorship business, the COIC will conduct the investigation and determine qualification and the offer amount necessary to settle the liability. The person who conducts the OIC investigation is called an "offer examiner."

The offer investigation is the longest part of the OIC process, often taking several months from when the application is received to the final determination. OIC determinations may last several more months if the offer investigation determination results in a disagreement and a protest is filed with the IRS Independent Office of Appeals.

The Offer Investigation Process

The offer investigation process consists of five investigation steps:

1. *Initial qualification determination and perfection of the OIC application*: determining, based on financial information, if the taxpayer is able to fully pay the liability (i.e., ability

to pay > liability), and if there are any additional items that are needed for the application to proceed (estimated tax payments, withholding changes, omitted documentation, etc.).

2. *Background investigation*: review the taxpayer's application and supporting documents and compare against IRS sources of information.
3. *Preliminary determination*: analysis of ability to pay and reasonable collection potential.
4. *Requests for more information*: the offer examiner may request additional information before making a final determination.
5. *Final determination*: the acceptance or rejection of the OIC. This may include requiring the taxpayer to amend the original offer based on the offer examiner's findings of reasonable collection potential.

The offer examiner conducts all five investigation steps. However, if the COIC unit does not have enough resources or if the OIC application is complex, offer specialists located in the Collection Field function may be assigned to conduct or assist in the investigation.

If the OIC is filed when assigned to the CFf (a revenue officer), the RO will have input into the collectibility of the taxpayer. The RO will provide this input via Form 657, *Revenue Officer Report*.

Offer In Compromise - Revenue Officer Report

1. Taxpayer's name	2. Taxpayer's Identification Number (TIN)(s)

3. Taxpayer's Address *(Home or Business) (number, street, and room or suite no., city, state, ZIP code)*	4. Basis of offer *(check applicable box)*

4. Basis of offer *(check applicable box)*
- ☐ Doubt as to collectibility　　☐ Doubt as to liability
- ☐ Exceptional circumstances *(Effective Tax Administration)*

5. Amount of offer	6. Date offer received by IRS *(mmddyyyy)*

7. Submitted to Revenue Officer	☐ Yes ☐ No

8. Based on your investigation, do you believe the offer should be accepted?	☐ Yes ☐ No
9. Was the offer submitted to avoid, prevent, or stop field collection activity?	☐ Yes ☐ No
If yes, has this collection action been discussed with the taxpayer? *(explain in item 13 below)*	☐ Yes ☐ No

Any specific "solely to delay" issue as discussed in **IRM 5.8.3.13 and 5.8.4.20,** *Offer Submitted Solely to Delay Collection,* should be documented in item 13 below. The facts and circumstances supporting your decision to either suspend collection or not suspend collection should be clearly documented. An OIC is not considered submitted solely to delay collection based exclusively on the amount offered or an imminent CSED.

10. If taxpayer owes trust fund taxes or fuel excise taxes subject to the trust fund recovery penalty, has action relative to the trust fund recovery penalty or the personal liability for excise tax been taken? See IRM sections 5.1.24.5.8, 5.7.3, 5.7.4.9, and 5.8.4.22.1	☐ Yes ☐ No

(If no, check applicable box. IDRS should reflect appropriate ASEDR indicator)
☐ N/A　☐ below LEM　☐ other (explain in item 13 below)

a. Have the potential responsible parties been advised of the TFRP requirement?	☐ Yes ☐ No
b. Have all additional periods accrued since the TFRP recommendation been addressed?	☐ Yes ☐ No

Type of entity: *(Corp., LLC, SMO, partnership):* _____

TFRP DATL only:
Where is the TFRP file? *(location and date forwarded)*

11. Are all required returns filed? *(If no, please provide date(s) requested.)*	☐ Yes ☐ No
12. If the TP has an open filing requirement *(941, 940, etc.)* and is no longer required to file the return, have you closed all filing requirements as required by the IRM? *(If no, please explain why filing requirements were not closed)*	☐ Yes ☐ No ☐ N/A

13. State below any further information not clearly reflected in the offer in compromise and accompanying documents which should be considered when evaluating the offer. Please indicate any analysis of asset equity, monthly payment ability, and basis for determination. If the offer is from a business please indicate if assets have been viewed or would be necessary to view, i.e. TP operating out of their home or small office location *(ICS history should be documented with results)*. If known, please comment on whether or not in your opinion the county valuation is indicative of the true FMV of any real property owned by the TP and whether that value is reflected on the 433A/B *(OIC)*. Use an attachment if additional space is needed, or reference specific ICS history.

14. Signature of Revenue Officer	15. Telephone number	16. Date *(mmddyyyy)*
17. Approval of Group Manager *(required if solely to delay recommendation)*	18. Telephone number	19. Date *(mmddyyyy)*

Form **657** (Rev. 2-2015)　　Catalog Number 10445N　　publish.no.irs.gov　　Department of the Treasury - **Internal Revenue Service**

Local offer specialists generally get involved with an OIC application for the following taxpayer types:

- Corporations and partnerships.
- Estates and trusts.
- Incarcerated taxpayers.
- Businesses with employees.
- LLCs and LLPs.
- Sole proprietors with gross receipts over $500,000.
- International taxpayers.
- Individual taxpayers whose primary source of income is from a partnership.

Traditionally, taxpayers who owe less than $50,000 have a faster OIC investigation timeframe if they meet the following conditions:

- Are a wage earner or unemployed or have a small business with gross revenue under $500,000 (no business entities), and
- Have a household income under $100,000.

For these taxpayers, the IRS is able to accept more testimony by phone which results in faster determinations. In addition, IRS procedures do not require approved OICs for $50,000 or less in liability to be reviewed by IRS counsel attorneys before acceptance. [IRM 5.8.8.13 (11-6-2023)]

If not already filed, the IRS offer examiner will determine if a filing of a Notice of Federal Tax Lien is necessary. If the collection of the taxes appears to be in jeopardy (i.e., taxpayer is contemplating bankruptcy), the offer examiner is likely to pursue the filing of an NFTL. [IRM 5.8.4.7 at (2t) (2-10-2023)]

Initial Qualification and Offer Perfection

The assignment to the offer examiner may occur several months after the IRS has received the OIC application. Taxpayers are not required to provide updated financial information because of IRS processing delays in investigating the OIC. [IRM 5.8.5.3 (4-25-2025)]

Upon assignment of the OIC application, the offer examiner's (OE) first step is to redetermine if the taxpayer is in filing and payment compliance and analyze the financial information to see if the taxpayer is able to fully pay the liability owed with equity in assets and future installment payments (ability to pay determination).

The OE will again review the taxpayer's IRS account information and determine if the taxpayer is in filing and payment compliance. The taxpayer should have filed all required tax returns and have adequate withholding and/or be making estimated tax payments. The OE will determine if any related OICs should be filed as well (i.e., for spouse, business, etc.).

The OE will also review whether the taxpayer has made the required OIC payments. Taxpayers selecting the periodic payment method will be checked for all required payments. If applicable, the OE will determine if the taxpayer qualifies for the low-income waiver.

The OE will conduct a preliminary ability to pay calculation. If the taxpayer's ability to pay is greater than the taxes owed, and he does not indicate special circumstances, the OE will propose rejecting the OIC. The OE will call the taxpayer and send Letter 3499 requesting withdrawal of the OIC. The taxpayer is given 30 days to respond and provide additional evidence to refute the OE's determination.

The OE will also determine if the OIC was filed to delay the collection process. The IRS looks at several factors to determine if the taxpayer is filing the OIC to avoid IRS collection activity. Indicators that an OIC is being submitted to delay collection include the following:

- If a taxpayer submits an offer that is not materially different from a previous offer that was considered and rejected with appeal rights.
- If a taxpayer submits an offer that is not materially different from a previous offer that was considered and returned, and the cause of the OIC's return has not been addressed.
- If an IRS collection employee has contacted the taxpayer and determined that the next action necessary is to enforce collection through levy or seizure, and the taxpayer files a clearly frivolous offer that is considerably less than equity in assets and/or his ability to make future payments, and no special circumstances exist, and an IRS revenue officer determines that the current submission is to delay this enforcement action.

[IRM 5.8.4.7.1 (4-25-2025)]

IRM 5.8.4.7.1 (4-25-2025) contains many common examples of OICs submitted to delay collection. When the IRS determines that the OIC was submitted to delay collection, the OIC is returned and no formal appeal rights are offered. If the taxpayer so requests, he is given a chance to speak with the OE's manager to dispute the OE's determination.

Background Investigation

The OE will use both internal IRS research and other outside and third-party information to investigate the taxpayer's ability to pay. [IRM 5.8.5.3.1.1 (4-8-2024)] Some sources include:

- Prior tax returns inspected for financial inconsistencies.
- Prior wage and income transcripts reviewed for income, expenses, assets, and dissipated assets.
- Credit report review for all offers when tax owed is more than $100,000 (IRS has discretion to request a credit report for lower liabilities). [IRM 5.8.5.3.1.2 (4-8-2024)]
- State motor vehicle records.
- Real estate records and Google Maps to determine condition of real estate owned.

- LexisNexis and Accurint public records database for aliases, related business entities, UCC filings, properties, judgments, and vehicle registrations.
- Third-party verification of any questionable items.

The OE may review these outside sources and question any material discrepancies with the taxpayer's collection information statement and calculations of ability to pay and reasonable collection potential. The OE will provide the taxpayer an opportunity to explain any discrepancies and their impact on the OIC.

The OE will also investigate the finances of any non-liable persons (spouse, roommate, non-liable dependent, etc.) that are living in the taxpayer's household. The assets and income of a non-liable person are excluded from the computation of the taxpayer's ability to pay. However, the OE must determine the total household income in order to determine the allowable living expenses for the liable taxpayer. To gather information on non-liable persons, the IRS may use internal information such as tax return information and wage and income information returns (W-2s, 1099s, etc.) for such persons. [IRM 5.8.5.24 at (4) (9-24-2021)]

The OE will also have to determine how to allocate shared expenses. The taxpayer may be requested to provide information and agreements on how expenses are allocated with non-liable persons. If expenses are mingled, the taxpayer will be allowed to include expenses based on the percentage of household income. If the taxpayer has expenses that are separate from the non-liable person, the taxpayer will be allowed those expenses based on the amount paid. In either case, the taxpayer will not be allowed expenses in excess of the standards allowed unless the taxpayer has special circumstances that warrant deviation from the Collection Financial Standards. IRM 5.8.5.24 (9-24-2021) and 5.15.1.5 (11-22-2021) should be studied carefully for guidance on situations involving non-liable persons, including situations where separate OICs are filed for spouses with joint liabilities who are living apart or for community property state situations.

Collection Information Statements and related documentation submitted with an OIC should reflect current information as of the date of the OIC submission. The OE should make a determination based on the information submitted at the time of the OIC application. However, the OE may request additional documentation if all required information was not submitted with the OIC application. The OE may request that the taxpayer provide updated financial information to determine the taxpayer's ability to pay. If during the OIC investigation, the financial information becomes older than 12 months and it appears that a significant change has occurred, the OE may request updated financial information. [IRM 5.8.5.3 at (2) (9-24-2021)]

> **Pro Tip:** To expedite an OIC determination and limit the requests for additional information, it is important that the initial OIC application provide the OE with all of the required information, explanations and supporting documentation necessary to support the OIC ability to pay calculations. It is rare that OIC investigations last longer than 12 months. The taxpayer should be able to avoid having to "refresh" the OE with updated financial information if the original application presents a complete disclosure of the taxpayer's situation.

Preliminary Determination, Request for More Information, and Final Determination

The next step in the offer investigation is the preliminary determination of the OIC application. The OE will conclude the initial examination of the OIC application, the Form 433-A/B, the supporting documentation, and other evidence gathered to compute whether the taxpayer qualifies for an OIC (ability to pay calculation). If the taxpayer qualifies, the OE will determine the offer amount (reasonable collection potential calculation). The OE makes this determination using the IRS OIC financial analysis rules in IRM 5.8.5 and 5.15.1.

The OE will produce three calculations: [IRM 5.8.4.7 at (2i and 2j) (4-25-2025)]

Calculation #1: Future income — the Income/Expense Table ("IET")

The OE will compute the taxpayer's monthly disposable income and calculate how much can be paid before the CSED expires using the Income/Expense Table or "IET:"

TAXPAYER: _____

TIN/EIN: _____
Date: _____

INCOME/EXPENSE TABLE (IET) (Rev. 1-2014)

The Internal Revenue Service uses established National and Local standards for necessary living expenses when considering Offers in Compromise. Only necessary living expenses will be allowed. Other expenses, such as charitable contributions, education, credit cards, and voluntary retirement allotments are generally not considered as necessary living expenses.

Total Income		Necessary Living Expenses		
Source	Gross		Claimed	Allowed
20. Wages (T/P)		35. Food, Clothing, and Misc		
21. Wages (Spouse)		36. Housing and Utilities		
22. Interest - Dividend		37. Vehicle Ownership Costs		
23. Net Business Income		38. Vehicle Operating Costs		
24. Net Rental Income		39. Public Transportation		
25. Distributions		40. Health Insurance		
26. Pension/Soc. Sec. (TP)		41. Out of Pocket Health Care Costs		
27. Pension/Soc. Sec, (Spouse)		42. Court ordered payments		
28. Social Security (Taxpayer)		43. Child/dependent care		
29. Social Security (Spouse)		44. Life Insurance		
30. Child Support		45. Current Year Taxes (Income/FICA)		
31. Alimony		46. Secure Debts (Attach list)		
Other Income (Specify below)		47. Del. State or Local Taxes		
32.		48 Other Expenses (Attach list)		
33.		49. Total Living Expenses		
34. Total Income		50. Net Difference		

50.   Net difference times (a,b or c) = Amount that could be paid from future income:

Net difference =	Months	Amount that could be paid =

a) For cash offers, if the offer is payable in 5 or fewer installments within 5 months, project the payment by multiplying the **amount that could be paid** times 12 months or times the number of months remaining in the collection statute, whichever is shorter.

b) For cash offers, payable in 5 or fewer installments within 24 months or a periodic payment offer payable within 24 months project the payments by multiplying the **amount that could be paid** times 24 months or times the number of months remaining in the collection statute, whichever is shorter.

The total offer amount must be equal to, or greater than, the sum of the equity in assets and the amount that could be paid from future income unless special circumstance considerations have been approved.

NOTES:
Line 35 National Standard expenses: Maximum allowable by IRS National Expense Standard for food, housekeeping supplies, apparel and services, and personal care products, based upon the number of persons in the household.

Line 36 Housing & Utilities expenses: Housing and utility expenses are limited to standards established for the county of residence and the number of household members.

Line 37 & 38 Transportation expenses: Transportation expenses are limited to the standards established for zero, one or two vehicles, and to a maximum allowable amount for lease or purchase of one or two vehicles.

Months: The number of months shown may be greater than 24 months in order to determine the taxpayer's ability to fully pay the liability through an installment agreement.

Calculation #2: **Net realizable equity in assets — the Asset/Equity Table ("AET")**

The OE will compute the net realizable equity in assets and document this calculation in the Asset/Equity Table or "AET:"

Date:

TAXPAYER'S NAME: EIN/TIN:

ASSETS	Fair Market Value	Quick Sale Reduction Percentage	Quick Sale Value	Encumbrances or Exemptions	Net Realizable Equity
ASSET/EQUITY TABLE (AET) **(Rev. 3-2016)**					
1. Cash/Bank Accounts				$1,000.00	
2. Offer Deposit					
3. Loan Value Life Insurance					
4. Pensions / IRA/401(k)					
5. Real Estate					
6. Furniture/Personal Effects					
7. Vehicles					
8. Accounts Receivable					
9. Tools and/or Equipment					
Other -					
Future Income Value (see Income and Expense Table (IET) attached)					
TOTAL MINIMUM VALUE					

Item 1   Cash/Bank accounts has been reduced by $1,000. Net equity should not be less than -0-.
Item 6   IRC 6334(a)(2) allows an exemption of $9,120 for fuel, provisions, furniture and personal effects.
Item 7   Vehicle equity has been reduced by $3,450. Net equity should not be less than -0-.
Item 9   IRC 6334(a)(3) allows an exemption of $4,560 for tools of the trade.

REMARKS:

Calculation #3: The taxpayer's ability to pay and a recommendation by the OE. The OE adds the future income value from the IET to the AET to arrive at the taxpayer's ability to pay.

> **Example-** *Example of calculation #3 — The offer amount and the OE's recommendation.* In this case, the OE recommends that the offer amount be increased to the taxpayer's RCP:

Total Asset/Net Monthly Income Calculation

Entity TIN	Entity Type	Assets		Income Type Used	Income
###-##-####	Ind/Joint 1040	$4,109		Gross Monthly	$0
###-##-####	Sole Prop	$0		Net Monthly	$4,811
				Total Monthly Income =	$4,811
				Less Household expenses -	$4,282
	Total Assets:	$4,109		Total Net Monthly Income =	$529
				Months of Future Income x	12
				Total Monthly Income Recovered: +	$6,348
				Total Assets: +	$4,109
				Amount that could be paid: =	$10,457

Total Liability:	$255,300
Original Offer Amount:	$8,312

Recommendation: you will need to increase your offer. Based upon your financial information we determined that we cannot consider acceptance of less than $10,457 to resolve your case.

If the minimum combined IET and AET value is greater than the liability, the OE will determine that the taxpayer does not qualify for an OIC-DATC. The calculation will show that the taxpayer is able to pay the liability with the equity in assets and future income value on the IET calculated to the limits of the CSED.

However, if the taxpayer qualifies for an OIC-DATC, the IET and AET will reflect the reasonable collection potential. The total minimum value will reflect the terms of the OIC and the offer amount to be paid under the OIC. The future income on the IET will reflect the future income amount that would be collected under the lump-sum (12 months of net disposable income) or periodic payment (24 months of net disposable income) method.

In the preliminary determination or during the offer investigation, the OE will recommend one of the following:

- *Accept the OIC*: the offer amount is accepted by the IRS OE. [IRM 5.8.8.8 (11-6-2023)]
- *Modify/amend the OIC*: the OE determines that the taxpayer qualifies for an OIC, however the OE wants to modify the OIC. The modification could be to increase the offer amount or to secure a collateral agreement. In these cases, the OE will request that the taxpayer agree to amend the OIC before acceptance. [IRM 5.8.8.2 (11-6-2023)]
- *Terminate/return the OIC:* the taxpayer is not able to continue with the OIC because he broke the terms of the OIC (for example, by failure to provide information, inadequate or missing estimated tax payments or withholding changes, non-filing, file bankruptcy, taxpayer dies, or some other reason found in the IRM). [IRM 5.8.7.2.2 at (3) and (4) (4-25-2025)]

- *Withdraw the OIC*: it is mandatory for the taxpayer to withdraw the OIC if he is unable to correct an OIC insufficient down payment or subsequent required payments. The taxpayer may voluntarily withdraw if the taxpayer determines that he is unable to afford the offer amount. [IRM 5.8.7.4.2 (4-25-2025)]
- *Reject the OIC*: the OE determines that the taxpayer is able to fully pay the liability before the expiration of the CSED. [IRM 5.8.7.7 (4-25-2025)]
- *Send to the Collection Field function for further investigation*: the OE may determine that the taxpayer's finances need to be investigated further by a field specialist. This may occur if the taxpayer has complex business issues or if the IRS wants assurance that the taxpayer has fully and accurately disclosed all assets and sources of income. The IRS may also send an OIC case to Field Collection if the case has reasonable collectibility and enforcement should be pursued immediately. [IRM 5.8.7.10.4 (4-25-2025)]

For all adverse determinations, the OE will provide the taxpayer a chance to reply to the OE's recommendations. Only a rejected OIC may be further appealed to the IRS Independent Office of Appeals. OIC applications returned to the taxpayer do not have appeal rights. [IRM 5.8.7.2.2 at (2) (4-25-2025)]

The OE may also propose a "collateral agreement" as part of the OIC terms. [IRM 5.8.6.2 (6-25-2021)] A collateral agreement puts additional conditions on the OIC and may be used by the IRS if it is unsure of the taxpayer's future income or if the IRS wants to remove a future tax benefit as part of the condition of an OIC. [IRM 5.8.6.2.1 (10-19-2023)]

The most common collateral agreement is to ask the taxpayer to forego a future tax benefit, such as a net operating loss or capital loss carryforward. [IRM 5.8.6.2.3 (10-19-2023)]

If the IRS believes the taxpayer's current income is not at its full potential (prior income was higher and the IRS is concerned income will again increase after the offer is accepted), the IRS may require a collateral agreement to mitigate that risk. For example, if the taxpayer's current income is $20,000, the IRS may demand 10% of income in excess of $28,000, 15% of income in excess of $35,000, etc. Thus, the IRS shares any increase in income, but never more than the tax previously owed, including ongoing interest. [IRM 5.8.6.2.1.1 (10-19-2023)]

The IRS does not prefer collateral agreements and generally counteroffers to accept an increased offer amount without requiring a collateral agreement. It becomes an economic decision whether to accept the increased amount or a lower amount with a collateral agreement.

The IRS uses the Form 2261 series where there are Collateral Agreements for future income and other conditions such as net operating loss, capital loss, or basis reduction terms. [IRM 5.8.6.2.1.1 (10-19-2023)]

Form **2261-C** (Rev. January 2012)	Department of the Treasury — Internal Revenue Service **Collateral Agreement** Waiver of Net Operating Losses, Capital Losses, and Unused Business Credits

Name and Address of Taxpayer(s) and Corporations/Limited Liability Company	Social Security and Employer Identification Numbers

To: Commissioner of Internal Revenue

The taxpayer(s) identified above have submitted an offer dated __4/1/2019__ in the amount of $ __10,457.00__ to compromise unpaid tax liabilities plus interest, penalties, additions to tax, and additional amounts required by law (tax liability), for the taxable periods marked below: *(Please mark an "X" in the box for the correct description and fill-in the correct tax period(s), adding additional periods if needed.)*

[X] 1040/1120 Income Tax Year(s) __2007,2012,2013,2014,2015,2016,2017,2018__

[ ] 941 Employer's Quarterly Federal Tax Return - Quarterly Period(s) _____

[ ] 940 Employer's Annual Federal Unemployment (FUTA) Tax Return – Year(s) _____

[ ] Trust Fund Recovery Penalty as a responsible person of *(name of employer)* _____
for failure to pay withholding and Federal Insurance Contributions Act Taxes (Social Security taxes), for period(s) ending

[ ] Other Federal Tax(es) [specify type(s) and period(s)] _____

Note: If you need more space, use another sheet titled "Attachment to Form 2261-C Dated _____." Sign and date the attachment following the listing of the tax periods.

The purpose of this collateral agreement (hereinafter referred to as this agreement) is to provide additional consideration for acceptance of the offer in compromise described above. It is understood and agreed that for the purpose of computing the taxpayers' Federal income tax for all taxable years beginning after __December 31, 2018__ :

1. That the net operating losses sustained for the years _____ to _____ , inclusive, shall not be claimed as net operating loss deductions under the provisions of section 172 of the Internal Revenue Code.

2. That a partial net operating loss sustained for the years _____ to _____ , inclusive, shall only be claimed for the amount agreed to in this agreement. The amount agreed to that can be claimed as a net operating loss is _____ . As a result of this agreement, any losses that exceed this amount shall not be claimed as net operating loss deductions under the provisions of section 172 of the Internal Revenue Code.

3. That any net capital losses sustained for the years _prior_ to _2019_ , inclusive, shall not be claimed as carryovers or carrybacks under the provisions of section 1212 of the Internal Revenue Code.

4. That any unused business credits for the years _____ to _____ , inclusive, shall not be claimed as business credit carrybacks or carryovers under the provisions of Internal Revenue Code section 39 as applicable.

5. That the aggregate amount paid under the terms of the offer in compromise and taxes paid as the result of the waiver of the losses and credits involved in this agreement shall not exceed an amount equivalent to the liability covered by the offer plus statutory additions that would have become due in the absence of the compromise.

Catalog Number 18246Y	www.irs.gov	Form **2261-C** (Rev. 1-2012)

271

> **Pro Tip:** Collateral agreements are not preferred and are not often used by the IRS in OIC determinations. Taxpayers may want to offer a collateral agreement to gain OIC approval in situations where the OE believes the taxpayer's future income will be higher than the taxpayer's calculations.

During the offer investigation, the OE will arrive at a final determination. The determination can be to accept the offer, reject the offer, or modify/amend the offer. If the offer is accepted, the OE must get approval of the IRS Office of Chief Counsel (an IRS attorney) if the total liability is $50,000 or more. If approved, the OE will send the acceptance letter (IRS Letter 673) which will outline the terms of the agreement and next steps.

If the decision is to modify the OIC (usually to increase the offer amount), the OE can mark up the existing Form 656 or prepare an amended OIC with the modifications and ask the taxpayer to agree to the amended OIC terms. [IRM 5.8.8.3 (11-6-2023)] If the taxpayer agrees, the acceptance letter is sent to the taxpayer after the manager approves the OIC and any applicable IRS Counsel review is completed.

If the decision is to reject the OIC, the rejected OIC must undergo an independent review by an IRS OIC reviewer. If the reviewer concurs with the rejection, the rejection letter (usually IRS Letter 238) is sent to the taxpayer providing the taxpayer 30 days to appeal the OE decision. [Treasury Regulation §301.7122-1(f)(5)]

> **Pro Tip:** The primary reason for IRS rejection of an OIC is a dispute over the taxpayer's ability to pay and reasonable collection potential. Note that 11.3% of all OICs are appealed. [IRS Data Book, 2024, Table 29]

Common disputes include:

- Income averaging methods used, especially for self-employed individuals.
- Expense allowance above the standards.
- Valuation of an asset, including what is the quick sale value of the asset.
- Retired debt and impact on future income potential.
- Non-liable spouse calculations.
- Special circumstances and their impact on the offer amount.

The IRS can reject an OIC for public policy reasons or if the OIC is not in the best interests of the government. [IRM 5.8.7.7.2 (4-24-2025) and IRM 5.8.7.7.1 (4-24-2025)] Rejections for public policy reasons and not in the best interest of the government are rare and require special IRS management approval.

Appealing an OIC Rejection

If the taxpayer wants to contest the rejection, it is important for the taxpayer to request the appeal within the 30-day time limit. The IRS does not allow extensions to appeal on the final rejection letter. [IRM 5.8.7.7.5 (4-25-2025)] The OE will send the reasons for the offer rejection in the letter along with a copy of the IET and AET.

Taxpayers filing an appeal will use IRS Form 13711, *Request for Appeal of Offer in Compromise.* On the Form, the taxpayer should:

- List the disagreed items and the reason(s) for disagreement.
- List any facts supporting the taxpayer's position.
- List any law or authority on which the taxpayer is relying.
- Attach a copy of the rejected offer letter.
- Attach supporting documentation, if applicable.
- Be sure the form is signed by the taxpayer under penalties of perjury.

The appeals hearing will be held with an IRS appeals officer, who will take a fresh look at the case and the arguments made by the OE and the taxpayer. Appeals hearings for OIC matters only involve arguments claiming that the IRS has abused its discretion when applying the OIC procedural rules. Usually, the appeals hearing involves a dispute over the IRS's calculation of one of the components of the taxpayer's ability to pay (asset equity, income, allowable expenses). [IRM 8.23.3.2 (8-21-2023)]

> **Pro Tip:** Once the case is assigned to an appeals officer (AO), the AO should send the taxpayer an initial contact letter within 30 days. The AO will contact the taxpayer to set up either a phone or face-to-face conference. The taxpayer will be given the opportunity to request a face-to-face appeals conference. However, most OIC appeals are conducted by phone. The taxpayer is typically required to respond to the initial contact letter within 14 days. The appeals officer will appraise the facts, law and prospects of litigation, and may request additional information. The appeals officer is required to use sound judgment, see both sides of the issue(s), and be objective and impartial. The appeal officer will consider only disputed items. Any issues not previously addressed will not be considered in the appeal. [IRM 8.23.3.2 at (4) (8-21-2023)]

If the taxpayer agrees with the appeals officer's determination, an acceptance letter is issued with the terms and offer amount.

If the taxpayer disagrees with the appeals officer, the appeals officer will issue a rejection letter. When appeals upholds the IRS's rejection of the OIC, the only option for judicial review is if the taxpayer has filed the OIC as a result of a Collection Due Process hearing. If the OIC was initiated as part of a CDP hearing, the taxpayer can appeal the U.S. Tax Court on the grounds that the IRS "abused their discretion." [IRM 8.22.7.10.6.1 (9-23-2014)] Abuse of discretion considers "whether Appeal's factual and legal conclusions reached at a CDP hearing are reasonable, not whether they are best possible or indisputable." [IRM 8.22.4.2.1 at (2) (5-12-2022)] In short, the decision criteria are whether the IRS followed the rules in making the OIC determination.

> **Pro Tip:** Taxpayers may request Fast Track Mediation for an expedited review of a specific area of disagreement with the OE's ability to pay computation. FTM is not used very often by taxpayers and may not be used after the IRS OE issues a rejection letter. Taxpayers must request FTM through the OE or his manager and by filing a Form 13369, *Agreement to Mediate* (3-2022).

Requests for Reopening a Rejected OIC

Taxpayers who receive an IRS rejection letter must request an appeal within 30 days. If the taxpayer misses the deadline, the case cannot be reopened unless the taxpayer is able to show that she replied within the 30 days. Taxpayers who become incapacitated due to an emergency and are unable to respond within the 30-day period may request a reopening of their OIC. [IRM 5.8.7.7.7.1 (4-25-2025)] However, the IRS rarely allows a reopening and often requests the taxpayer to submit a new OIC application.

Returned OICs (not rejected ones) may be reopened by the IRS in certain circumstances. Taxpayers who have their offer returned because additional Forms 656 were needed (i.e., joint and separate liability scenarios) may take the steps needed to perfect the original OIC (submit additional Form 656 and application fee) and request that the returned offer be reconsidered. [IRM 5.8.7.3.3.3 (6-23-2022)] The IRS normally allows the taxpayer 30 days within which to perfect the offer.

An OIC that has been closed due to an IRS error may also be reopened. [IRM 5.8.7.4.2.1 (4-25-2025)]

24-Month Automatic Acceptance

IRC §7122(f) requires the IRS to make a determination on an OIC application within 24 months of the IRS received date (the date that the IRS receives the Form 656, deems the OIC as processable, and signs the Form 656). The 24-month rule is met if the offer is:

- Under judicial review.
- Withdrawn by the taxpayer.
- Returned to the taxpayer as not processible.
- Rejected by the IRS.
- Treated as withdrawn by the IRS due to the taxpayer's failure to make the second or later installment as required for a periodic payment OIC.

[IRM 5.8.7.3 (6-23-2022)]

The above actions are indicated as taken in an IRS letter to the taxpayer. In practice, the IRS rarely misses the 24-month determination window.

If the OIC originates from a CDP hearing, IRS appeals have the responsibility to make a determination within the 24-month period. [IRM 8.22.7.10.1.3 at (1) (8-26-2020)] Note that an amended Form 656 does not constitute a new offer and it does not impact the 24-month statute that started on the date the original offer was received. [IRM 8.22.7.10.1.3 at (3) (8-26-2020)]

Chapter 12.12: Step 4: Finalize Terms and Complete Requirements

Taxpayers with accepted OICs receive IRS Letter 673 (or equivalent letter). The letter will provide the final terms of the accepted OIC, including how to make required future payments.

The terms outlined in the letter include:

- *Payments*: complete offer conditions including instructions on making offer payments.
- *Five-year compliance requirement*: reminder to file and pay taxes owed for the next five years or default on the OIC.
- *Terms are final*: the taxpayer cannot contest the debt owed, in court, or otherwise. The IRS is also bound by the terms of the OIC. The IRS cannot reopen the OIC unless the documents provided were false, the taxpayer concealed assets, or a mutual mistake of a material fact was made that was sufficient to cause the offer agreement to be reopened. [IRM 5.8.9.2 (9-5-2024)]
- *Lien release*: any federal tax lien will be released after the final offer amount is paid. (The letter notes that if the final payment is by credit or debit card, it may take up to 120 days for a lien release — usually, liens are released within 30 days after final payment.) Normally, the IRS will release liens immediately if the taxpayer pays with a cashier check or money order. If payment is made by a personal check, the IRS will generally release the lien within 30 days.

Taxpayers will default on their OIC if they fail to:

- Fulfil the payment terms.
- Fulfil the terms of a related collateral agreement.
- Adhere to the compliance provisions (filing and payment obligations for the next five years).
- Return an erroneously issued refund.

Taxpayers will not default if they incur an unpaid individual shared responsibility payment liability. [IRM 5.19.7.14.4 (12-9-2024)] In addition, when one of the parties to the compromise fails to remain compliant with filing and payment terms, the offer is only defaulted as to the noncompliant spouse. [IRM 5.19.7.14.5 (7-9-2020)]

If the taxpayer is determined to be in default, the IRS will provide the taxpayer with the opportunity to correct the default by issuing the taxpayer a "potential default letter." If the taxpayer does not make the correction within the prescribed period allowed by the IRS, the IRS will default the OIC and reinstate unexpired prior removed liabilities to the taxpayer, less all payments and credits received. [IRM 5.19.7.15.1 (12-9-2024)]

> **Pro Tip:** In rare cases, taxpayers are able to "compromise a compromise" when the taxpayer is in default because she is unable to pay the balance of an accepted offer or meet the terms of any collateral agreement. In these cases, the IRS would apply the same rules as it would apply for determining OIC-DATCSC or ETA-OIC. The proposal would have to be made in writing (a letter) to the IRS. If the new terms are accepted, the IRS will adjust the terms and issue a new letter to the taxpayer (usually IRS Letter 1604).

One of the terms/conditions of an OIC prior to November 1, 2021, is that IRS would keep any refund, including interest, due to the taxpayer resulting from an overpayment of any tax or other liability, for tax periods extending through the calendar year in which the offer was accepted. This provision was deleted as of November 1, 2021.

Chapter 12.13: OIC-DATC Example

The following is an example of a self-employed taxpayer requesting an OIC-DATC. The example includes qualification and offer amount computations and the completed application. *Note:* The application date is April 30, 2024. This example uses the IRS Collection Standards and IRS OIC forms that are effective from April 22, 2024–March 2025. These standards and forms are updated annually in March/April. For the most up-to-date IRS Collection Standards, go to: https://www.irs.gov/businesses/small-businesses-self-employed/collection-financial-standards. For the most up-to-date Form 656-B, go to: https://www.irs.gov/pub/irs-pdf/f656b.pdf.

To view more of this comprehensive example, see www.TaxProblemsHandbook.com and navigate to the **IRS Collection Solutions Handbook** tab to access the referenced item.

Chapter 13:

OFFER IN COMPROMISE — EFFECTIVE TAX ADMINISTRATION (ETA-OIC)

This section covers how to qualify and obtain the little used tax settlement option for an ETA-OIC.

Topic	Covers
Overview of the Offer in Compromise—Effective Tax Administration	What is an ETA-OIC and how it can be used by a taxpayer to settle tax debts.
ETA for Economic Hardship	Conditions for qualifying for an ETA-OIC for financial hardship.
ETA for Public Policy or Equity Considerations	Conditions for qualifying for an ETA-OIC for public policy or equity consideration.
ETA-OIC Application	How to apply for an ETA-OIC.
ETA-OIC Investigation Process	The IRS investigation process and criteria for approving an ETA-OIC.
ETA-OIC Appeals	How to appeal an ETA-OIC.

Key Highlights:

- If a taxpayer does not qualify for an OIC-DATC, they may qualify for an Offer in compromise for Effective Tax Administration (ETA-OIC) if the taxpayer's liability is able to be collected in full, but collection would create an economic hardship or there is a compelling public policy or equity consideration that provides sufficient basis for compromise.
- ETA-OICs are very rare. However, most ETA-OICs are requested because of economic hardship. As an alternative, many taxpayers are provided other collection alternatives as a means to relief.
- The financial analysis and IRS offer investigation for an ETA-OIC is similar to that for an Offer in Compromise–Doubt as to Collectibility with Special Circumstances (OIC-DATCSC).
- Taxpayers who do not qualify for an OIC-DATC will have their OIC reviewed for ETA qualification.

Chapter 13.01: Overview of the Offer in Compromise — Effective Tax Administration

Taxpayers who do not qualify for an Offer in Compromise—Doubt as to Collectibility (OIC-DATC) because they have the means to pay the amount owed with equity in assets and future income may qualify for an Offer in compromise for Effective Tax Administration (ETA). ETA-OICs are for taxpayers who have special circumstances that warrant the IRS collecting less than the taxpayer's reasonable collection potential.

ETA offers are only available to taxpayers who do not qualify for an OIC-DATC or an OIC-Doubt as to Liability. [IRM 5.8.11.2 at (6) (4-11-2024)] That is, for an ETA offer, the taxpayer will be able to fully pay the liability before the collection statute expires and the liability in question is not in dispute.

ETA-OICs are very similar in process to OIC-DATCs with special circumstances (OIC-DATCSC). However, in an ETA-OIC, the taxpayer's initial ability to pay analysis shows that they have the ability to pay the liability in full (i.e., do not qualify for an OIC-DATCSC). [IRM 5.8.11.3 at (3) (4-11-2024)] All OIC-DATC applications that reveal that the taxpayer can fully pay before the collection statute expires (i.e., they do not qualify for an OIC-DATC) are reviewed to determine qualification for an ETA. [IRM 5.8.11.5 at (3) (4-11-2024)] In an ETA-OIC, the taxpayer can propose settlement of taxes when any of the following special circumstances that warrant the IRS accepting less than the full amount owed are present:

- *Economic hardship*: economic hardship occurs when a taxpayer is unable to pay reasonable basic living expenses. In these cases, the taxpayer will need future income and/or assets to meet basic living expenses, such as food/clothing/housing, or medical needs, dependent care, and a disability. [IRM 5.8.11.3.1 at (2) (4-11-2024)] ETA-OICs based on economic hardship are the most common form of ETA-OIC. Taxpayers who do not qualify for an OIC-DATC will have their OIC reviewed for circumstances justifying an ETA, especially for economic hardship. [IRM 5.8.11.5 at (3) (4-11-2024)]
- *Public policy or equity considerations*: these are non-hardship situations in which an acceptance of less than the full amount of liability would be fair, equitable and would promote effective tax administration for a compliant taxpayer. [IRM 5.8.11.3.2.1 (4-11-2024)] Public policy or equity ETA-OICs are extremely rare and require special approval for acceptance by the IRS because of tax administration policy considerations.

> **Pro Tip:** The IRS has discretionary authority, within its rules, to accept or deny an OIC. Most OICs are for DATC as these OICs clearly show that the taxpayer cannot pay the IRS before the statute of limitations to collect expires. However, in ETA-OICs, the taxpayer can pay in the future. As such, almost always, the ETA-OIC is not a practical remedy to settling back taxes because the IRS can use other collection alternatives in lieu of settling with an ETA-OIC. To this end, ETA-OICs are very rare and only taxpayers with exceptional circumstances should apply. In the IRS FY2024, the IRS accepted only 293 ETA-OICs. [IRS FOIA Response #2025-00032, October 2024]

Chapter 13.02: ETA for Economic Hardship

In an ETA-OIC for economic hardship, the taxpayer requests the IRS to settle the tax liability for less than the amount owed because he will need future income and/or assets to meet basic living expenses. [IRM 5.8.11.3.1 at (2) (4-11-2024)]

Basic living expenses are those expenses that provide for health, welfare, and the production of income of the taxpayer and the taxpayer's family. IRS Collection Financial Standards expense amounts are designed to provide guidance in determining a taxpayer's basic living expenses. If a taxpayer wants the IRS to allow an expense in excess of the standard, he must be prepared to provide evidence to support the deviation. For example, a disabled taxpayer that requires a special vehicle for transportation may be allowed a higher than standard vehicle ownership and operating costs each month because of the special features needed on his vehicle to accommodate the disability (i.e., wheelchair access, etc.). [IRM 5.8.11.3.1 at (4) (4-11-2024)]

In an ETA-OIC, the taxpayer does not meet the qualification for an OIC-DATC — that is, he is able to pay the tax with the equity in assets plus future monthly income before the collection statute expires. However, in an ETA-OIC, the taxpayer provides evidence that he will need the equity in the asset and/or the future income to meet expected necessary living expenses. [IRM 5.8.11.3.1 at (9) (4-11-2024)]

The IRS will consider other factors in addition to the economic hardship such as:

- The taxpayer's age and employment status,
- Number, age, and health of the taxpayer's dependents,
- Cost of living in the area in which the taxpayer resides, and
- Any extraordinary circumstances such as special education expenses, a medical catastrophe, or natural disaster.

   [IRM 5.8.11.3.1 at (5) (4-11-2024)]

The following are common scenarios for an ETA-OIC based on economic hardship:

- *Long-term illness or disability of taxpayer or dependent*: the medical condition or disability will require the taxpayer to exhaust assets and/or future income to pay for ongoing treatment, care, and support during the condition. For example, the taxpayer has equity in his home, but it will be needed to pay for future expenses for full-time medical care.
- *Fixed income*: the taxpayer's fixed income is exhausted each month in order to pay living expenses for the taxpayer and his dependents, and the taxpayer's financial condition will require him to access any equity in other assets to meet expenses (i.e., he will need to sell assets to meet the deficit each month in paying for necessary living expenses). As an example, a taxpayer's income leaves him $500 short each month in meeting necessary living expenses. The taxpayer must access his home equity indefinitely in order to meet the shortfall. The taxpayer may ultimately need to sell his home to meet necessary living expenses. In another case, a retired taxpayer has little income and her only asset is a retirement account. That account is needed to meet necessary living expenses. If the retirement account is liquidated to satisfy the tax liability, the liquidation would leave the taxpayer without adequate means to provide for basic living expenses.
- *Cannot access equity in assets*: taxpayer is unable to access equity or if he does access equity, it would cause him to be unable to meet necessary living expenses. For example, if a taxpayer sold his home and accessed the equity to pay the taxes, he would incur a higher monthly living cost (i.e., rent higher than mortgage) that would render him unable to meet living expenses.

Pro Tip: ETA-OICs are rare because the IRS can reject the OIC in favor of an installment agreement or CNC status. For example, if a taxpayer has sufficient equity to pay the liability but cannot pay the IRS a monthly amount in an installment agreement, the IRS will likely put the taxpayer in CNC status rather than allow an ETA-OIC. Under this scenario, if the taxpayer's circumstances were to change, the IRS may be able to collect on the debt in the future. This would not be the case if the IRS settles with an ETA-OIC.

[IRM 5.8.11.3.1 at (6) (4-11-2024)]

Determining the ETA-OIC Offer Amount for Economic Hardship

In economic hardship cases, an acceptable offer amount is determined by analyzing the financial information, supporting documentation, and the hardship that would be created if certain assets, or a portion of certain assets, were used to pay the liability. The taxpayer would need to determine how much equity in assets and/or future income will be needed to meet necessary living expenses without imposing an economic hardship on the taxpayer. [IRM 5.8.11.3.1 at (9) (4-11-2024)]

> **Example-** The IRS provides an example in the Internal Revenue Manual: [IRM 5.8.11.3.1 at (9) (4-11-2024)]
>
> The taxpayer was diagnosed with an illness that eventually will hinder any ability to work. Although currently employed, the taxpayer will soon be forced to quit his

job and would use personal funds for basic living expenses. The taxpayer owes $100,000 and has a reasonable collection potential of $150,000. An offer was submitted for $35,000. Through the investigation, it is determined that collecting more than $50,000 would cause an economic hardship for the taxpayer. A determination on economic hardship was made due to the fact the taxpayer's reasonable living expenses, including ongoing medical costs will exceed his income once the taxpayer is unemployed. The taxpayer is advised to raise the offer to $50,000 since it is the amount the Service can collect without creating an economic hardship.

In the IRS example, the taxpayer reduced the RCP (offer amount) by $115,000 because he needed these funds to meet basic living expenses. The taxpayer first determined his overall ability to pay and then reduced the amount by the funds needed to meet necessary living expenses. For this example, the taxpayer may have determined that he needed an extra $2,500 per month to pay for the 46 months remaining on the collection statute of limitations ($2,500 for 46 months = $115,000). If the taxpayer had an asset with equity of $150,000, the taxpayer would be claiming that he needed $115,000 of the equity to meet future medical and living expenses.

Taxpayers computing the ETA-OIC offer amount should start with the OIC-DATC computation to determine reasonable collection potential (RCP). [IRM 5.8.11.5.2 (4-11-2024)] The taxpayer would then make a calculation of the amount of net equity in assets and future income that would be needed to meet basic living expenses based on his economic hardship. [IRM 5.8.11.5.3 at (1) (4-11-2024)] This amount would be subtracted from the RCP to determine the ETA-OIC offer amount. Obviously, this projection will rely on many assumptions that must be supported in the OIC application.

There are many challenges in valuing the amount of future income/assets that will be needed for a taxpayer to meet future necessary living expenses. The taxpayer must initially provide a proposed offer amount. There can be much back-and-forth debate and negotiation between the offer examiner and the taxpayer about how much is needed to provide for the needs of the taxpayer. For this reason, the IRS often does not accept ETA-OICs. The taxpayer is often offered other options, such as currently not collectible or a small installment agreement, that will allow the taxpayer to meet basic living expenses. [IRM 5.8.11.3.1 at (10) (4-11-2024)]

Taxpayers who have a federal tax lien and need to access their equity in assets (i.e., their home or retirement savings) are the more likely candidates for an ETA-OIC for economic hardship. Taxpayers must provide a financial analysis of their economic hardship and future needs and be prepared to negotiate an acceptable offer amount with the IRS. Taxpayers may have to be persistent and advocate their ETA-OIC with IRS appeals in order to be successful in securing a settlement.

Chapter 13.03: ETA for Public Policy or Equity Considerations

The IRS generally settles balances owed because the taxpayer is unable to pay the balance owed before the collection statute expires (OIC-DATC) or if the taxpayer has special circumstances that create an economic hardship (OIC-DATCSC and the ETA-OIC for economic hardship). In all three of these situations, the taxpayers have an economic reason that they are unable to pay their balance owed.

An ETA for public policy/equity considerations are an exception to the traditional collection-related OIC. As such, the public policy/equity OIC is considered a non-economic hardship OICs (NEH-OIC). In NEH-OICs, the IRS is able to collect the balance in full through the taxpayer's equity in assets and/or future income — that is, she does not qualify for an OIC-DATC or an OIC–Doubt as to Collectibility for Special Circumstances (DATCSC). In a NEH-OIC, the IRS may accept an OIC to promote ETA where compelling public policy or equity considerations identified by the taxpayer provide a sufficient basis for accepting less than full payment. [IRM 5.8.11.3.2 at (2) (4-11-2024)] Taxpayers seeking a NEH-OIC must demonstrate that their circumstances are compelling enough to justify compromise. The IRS does not accept many NEH-OICs because, in such circumstances, taxpayers are asking for special treatment that is not openly offered to all taxpayers. [IRM 5.8.11.3.2 at (3) (4-11-2024)] The IRS is often reluctant to provide inequitable treatment among taxpayers.

Taxpayers requesting a NEH-OIC must have a good compliance history with the IRS. The IRS will also look at the taxpayer's compliance history in determining whether to accept an ETA-OIC. Taxpayer noncompliance will weigh against an ETA-OIC. For example, a taxpayer transferring assets to related parties at less than fair value to avoid paying taxes would weigh against the IRS acceptance of an ETA-OIC because to do otherwise would undermine tax administration. [IRM 5.8.11.3.2 at (5) (4-11-2024)] Taxpayers must be shown to have acted reasonably in the situation that gave rise to the liability.

The IRS will also be reluctant to provide a NEH-OIC to a taxpayer who will be put in a better position than she would have occupied had she timely met her obligation. Taxpayers who are involved with abusive tax transactions or tax shelters will not receive a NEH-OIC. [IRM 5.8.11.3.2 at (5) (4-11-2024)]

The IRS centralizes all NEH-OIC investigations in its NEH-ETA Group for consideration. The NEH-ETA group investigates NEH-OICs to ensure that the IRS is consistent in applying public policy and equity consideration criteria. [IRM 5.8.11.3.2 at (2) (4-11-2024)]

Examples of Public Policy/Equity Considerations

The IRS acceptance of NEH-OICs is very rare. In making a decision on a NEH-OIC, the IRS takes the approach that it does not want to undermine tax administration or set tax policy based on individual taxpayer circumstances. The IRS is reluctant to apply tax laws outside of the intent of

Congress, for example, where a taxpayer wishes to compromise a liability claiming unfair treatment of the tax laws.

The Internal Revenue Manual provides an example of a taxpayer perceived tax law inequity:

> The taxpayer argues that collection would be inequitable because the liability resulted from a discharge of indebtedness rather than from wages. Because Congress has clearly stated that a discharge of indebtedness results in taxable income to the taxpayer it would not promote ETA to compromise on these grounds. [IRM 5.8.11.3.2.1 at (11) (4-11-2024)]

In this case, the IRS would not compromise based on equity considerations. The taxpayer is clearly liable for taxes, penalties, or interest due to operation of law — that is, the cancellation of indebtedness is income as defined IRC §61(a)(12). If the IRS determined the law to be unfair and allowed the taxpayer relief from IRC §61(a)(12), it would undermine the will of Congress in imposing liability under those circumstances.

Another reason that the IRS may not allow an ETA-OIC based on public policy/equity is because the taxpayer may have other means to lower the balance owed. Taxpayers have the opportunity to contest penalties and interest owed if the IRS makes an error or unreasonably delays actions that cause the taxpayer to owe additional penalties and interest. [IRM 5.8.11.3.2.1 at (3) (4-11-2024)]

However, depending on the facts and circumstances, taxpayers may request an ETA-OIC on the following non-economic hardship grounds:

- *Owe because of criminal/fraudulent activity of another*: this is a common argument for taxpayers who owe back payroll tax liabilities where the claim is that they are the result of fraudulent actions by their payroll service provider. In such a case, the taxpayer will need to show that she acted reasonably in hiring, monitoring, and resolving issues related to unpaid payroll taxes that were outsourced to the provider. [IRM 5.8.11.3.2.1 at (5) (4-11-2024)]
- *Owe because taxpayer followed erroneous IRS advice*: a taxpayer followed the advice of an IRS employee and, as a result, owed additional taxes. For example, a taxpayer may have a NEH-OIC if the taxpayer owed additional taxes on an early distribution of an IRA because she relied on erroneous IRS advice. The taxpayer would have to show that the IRS informed the taxpayer that she had one year (instead of 60 days) to rollover her IRA, followed that advice and did the rollover within the year, but owed taxes nonetheless. In this case, because the tax liability in this example was caused by reliance on the Service's erroneous statement, and the taxpayer clearly could have avoided the liability had the Service given correct information, it is reasonable to conclude that collection in full would cause other taxpayers to question the fairness of the tax system. [IRM 5.8.11.3.2.1 at (3) (4-11-2024)]

NEH-OICs are unusual and require exceptional circumstances. The taxpayer has the burden to prove that collection of the tax in full would undermine public confidence that the tax laws are being administered in a fair and equitable manner. [IRM 5.8.11.3.2 at (4) (4-11-2024)]

Determining an acceptable offer amount for an ETA-OIC for public policy or equity considerations can be difficult. The IRS expects the taxpayer to offer an amount that is fair and equitable under the circumstances (not a nominal or token amount). For example, in order to determine the acceptable offer amount for an ETA-OIC based on public policy/equity or IRS error or delay, the taxpayer should propose an offer amount that would return the taxpayer to the same position as if the error/delay did not occur. [IRM 5.8.11.3.2.1 at (2) (4-11-2024)] The taxpayer will have to develop the facts and offer amount calculation and provide a justification for the amount offered. The taxpayer's financial condition may be a relevant consideration. [IRM 5.8.11.5.3.1 at (1b) (4-11-2024)]

Chapter 13.04: ETA-OIC Application

The ETA-OIC application process is similar to that for the OIC-DATC. The Form 656 application must be complete and include the required application fee and down payment. [IRM 5.8.11.4 at (3) (4-11-2024)]

Steps for an ETA-OIC

There are four steps to an ETA-OIC:

Step	Actions	Move to next step when:
#1: Due diligence and qualification	Five parts: #1: Complete filing and payment compliance. #2: Determine that the taxpayer qualifies for ETA for economic hardship or public policy/equity. Document the circumstances. #3: Gather and analyze all relevant information, collection option alternatives, and whether the taxpayer qualifies for an OIC. Compute the taxpayer's ability to pay under the OIC-DATC and confirm that the taxpayer does not qualify for an OIC-DATC. Consider if an OIC-DATCSC is more appropriate. #4: Determining special circumstances that warrant ETA qualification. Quantify the special circumstances, such as the	✓ Confirm taxpayer is filing and payment compliant. ✓ Confirm taxpayer qualifies for ETA. ✓ Confirm taxpayer does not qualify for OIC-DATC. ✓ Determine the offer amount. ✓ Confirm the taxpayer can pay offer amount.

	financial hardship, that will reduce the reasonable collection potential calculated for an OIC-DATC. #5: Compute the offer amount, delineate the special circumstances as follows: reasonable collection potential less the amount required due to special circumstances. If the taxpayer is unable to pay the offer amount or meet the terms, he should select a more appropriate collection alternative.	
#2: Application	In this step, the taxpayer completes all of the required forms and attaches the required documentation to substantiate the ETA-OIC. The taxpayer also provides the required application fee and down payment. The taxpayer will determine if he qualifies for a low-income waiver so as to be excluded from the application fee and down payment.	✓ Application is complete, including submission of required documentation and explanation of circumstances that warrant ETA. ✓ Application fee and OIC payment made. ✓ Low-income qualification determined. ✓ Application package/fees submitted to proper COIC unit.
#3: Offer investigation	The investigation is the longest part of the OIC process and can often last several months. It involves interaction between the IRS and the taxpayer. To begin this step, the IRS must first accept the OIC as processable, then proceed to determine the taxpayer's ability to pay (similar to that in an OIC-DATC). If the taxpayer is unable to pay the amount owed before the CSED expires, the offer will convert to an OIC-DATCSC. [IRM 5.8.11.5 at (2) (4-11-2024)] The IRS may request additional information from the taxpayer to which the taxpayer will need to respond timely to avoid a rejection due to non-response. In this step, the offer examiner closely	✓ All outstanding questions are answered. ✓ Qualification confirmed. ✓ Offer amount determined. ✓ Rejection or acceptance determination. ✓ Appeal to IRS Independent Office of Appeals, if needed.

	examines the financial situation of the taxpayer to determine an acceptable offer amount based on the taxpayer's reasonable collection potential, given the special circumstances. If the IRS and taxpayer are unable to agree, the taxpayer will be offered an appeal. If an appeal is needed, the taxpayer must submit a timely petition and argue the merits of the case with the IRS appeals officer.	
#4: Finalize terms and complete requirements	In the final step, the taxpayer and the IRS agree on the terms and offer amount. The taxpayer completes any appeal and makes the required payments to the IRS in a timely fashion to complete the OIC. The taxpayer confirms that the balances owed are removed and any tax lien is released. The taxpayer files and pays timely for the next five years consistent with the terms of the OIC.	✓ IRS and taxpayer agree on terms. ✓ Taxpayer completes remaining payments and other terms of OIC. ✓ Balance owed and tax lien removed. ✓ Taxpayer remains in compliance for next five years.

In an ETA-OIC, the taxpayer must compromise all liabilities (all years and all forms). If the ETA-OIC is for economic hardship, the taxpayer must show how he arrived at the offer amount. The taxpayer will detail his circumstances and explain how he needs to use equity in assets and/or future income to meet necessary living expenses. The taxpayer will calculate his ability to pay and reduce that amount by future projected living expense needs. This calculation should be provided in the OIC application.

In ETA-OICs, the taxpayer's offer amount must be $1 or more. Similar to the OIC-DATC, taxpayers must also be in compliance (filing and payment) before submitting the ETA-OIC.

ETA-OICs use the same application format as in an OIC-DATC — the Form 656. [IRM 5.8.11.4 at (2) (4-11-2024)] Taxpayers must complete Section 3 (or attach a separate statement) and document all special circumstances. All financial information must be provided to allow the IRS to evaluate the taxpayer's finances, ability to pay, and the reasonable collection potential (offer amount) given the special circumstances.

An offer requesting consideration under ETA must include all of the following:

- *Form 656,* Offer in Compromise.
- *A statement discussing the specific issue*(s) which would allow for acceptance of the offer.

- *Explanation of the special circumstances* and rationale for the acceptance of the calculated offer amount with documentation why some or all of the equity in assets is not included in the offer amount, how the offer amount is being funded, and any other pertinent information that describes how the amount offered was determined to be acceptable.
- *Financial statements,* <u>Forms 433-A(OIC),</u> *Collection Information Statement for Wage Earners and Self-Employed Individuals,* and <u>433-B(OIC),</u> *Collection Information Statement for Business.*
- *Appropriate supporting documentation* and verification, including supporting evidence and information on the taxpayer's situation (i.e., doctor's letter, copies of medical expenses, fixed income verification, etc.).

ETA-OIC Application Checklist

Use the following checklist to complete the ETA-OIC application.

ETA-OIC Application Checklist

Use this checklist to complete the ETA-OIC application:

✓	Application Document	Practice Tips
☐	Application cover letter	☐ Outline terms of the OIC and explain the special circumstances (economic hardship, public policy/equity consideration). ☐ Identify the taxpayer's third-party authorized (Power-of-attorney or Tax Information Authorization) information. ☐ Identify any years/taxes owed that were proposed/filed within the past 60 days. ☐ Identify any associated OIC applications.
☐	Index of documents	☐ Organize the documents in sections for later reference when dealing with the offer examiner by phone. ☐ Number each section and page.
☐	Third-party authorization	☐ Include a copy of the Form 2848, Power-of-attorney, or Form 8821, Tax Information Authorization that provides for a third-party to receive information/deal directly with the IRS.
☐	Form 656 – OIC Application	All sections completed, including: ☐ Identify all taxes and years. ☐ Complete Part 3 with ETA selected and reasons for ETA-OIC acceptance. ☐ Complete low-income certification, if applicable. ☐ Include detailed reason(s) and calculation of offer amount and explanation of special circumstances. ☐ Indicate payment method and terms. ☐ Designate payments and deposit, if applicable. ☐ Provide source of payments. ☐ Complete filing compliance requirements checklist. ☐ Complete payment compliance requirements checklist. ☐ Sign and date. ☐ Paid preparer/representative sign/date. ☐ Complete separate OIC application if taxpayer and spouse have separate liabilities or if taxpayer has separate business tax debt.
☐	OIC Application User Fee	☐ Separate check for $186. ☐ Made out to US Treasury. ☐ No fee if low-income certification applies.
☐	OIC down payment/first periodic payment	☐ Separate check for OIC down payment/periodic payment (20% down payment for OIC lump-sum offer or 1st payment for periodic payment offer). ☐ Made out to US Treasury. ☐ No down payment if low-income certification applies.

☐	Form(s) 433 A/B-OIC – Collection Information Statement(s)	☐	Form 433(A)-OIC: for individuals and self-employed.
		☐	Form 433(B)-OIC: for corporations, partnerships, LLCs classified as a corporation, other LLCs.
		☐	Sign/date Form(s) 433.
☐	Worksheet: offer qualification (ability to pay) and offer amount (reasonable collection potential) computation	☐	Summary of ability to pay (qualification).
		☐	Summary of reasonable collection potential (offer amount) considering the special circumstances.
		☐	Computation of MDI details and support for income/expense averaging methodology.
		☐	Special circumstances explained and how the exclusions from offer amount were computed.
☐	Worksheet: net realizable equity in assets calculation	☐	List of assets at quick sale value, net of associated liabilities.
		☐	Exemptions and exclusions applied.
☐	Worksheet: monthly disposable income calculation	☐	Summary of income and expenses over averaging period(s).
		☐	Self-employed income/expenses for past 6-12 months, if applicable.
☐	Required documentation	☐	Copies ONLY – do not send originals.
		☐	Third-party evidence to support special circumstances.
		☐	Financial account statements, all accounts (ALL PAGES) for past 3 months (business accounts for past 6 months).
		☐	Copies of the most recent pay stub, earnings statement, etc., from each employer.
		☐	Copies of the most recent statement, etc., from all other sources of income such as pensions, Social Security, rental income, interest and dividends (including any received from a related partnership, corporation, LLC, LLP, etc.), court order for child support, alimony, and rent subsidies.
		☐	Copies of the most recent statement from lender(s) on loans such as mortgages, second mortgages, vehicles, etc., showing monthly payments, loan payoffs, and balances.
		☐	List of notes receivable, if applicable.
		☐	Verification of delinquent State/Local Tax Liability showing total delinquent state/local taxes and amount of monthly payments, if applicable.
		☐	Documentation to support any special circumstances described in the "Explanation of Circumstances" on Form 656, if applicable.
☐	Other supporting documentation	☐	Copies of all housing and utility expenses for averaging period.
		☐	Copies of medical bills paid for averaging period.

		☐ Copies of any expenses paid and documentation to warrant expenses that exceed the IRS Collection Financial Standards.
		☐ Court orders and/or agreements for any mandatory payments for child support, alimony, and other judgments.
		☐ Student loan statements and monthly payments made, if applicable.
		☐ Copies of any other necessary living expenses and expenses to produce income for averaging period.
		☐ Copies of any tax returns or assessment notices filed/received in the past 60 days.
☐	Copy/mailing of entire application	☐ Index the entire application for later reference.
		☐ Send to proper COIC Unit.
		☐ Keep complete copy for records and reference.

For the ETA-OIC Application Checklist, refer to the **Appendix B**—and visit www.TaxProblemsHandbook.com under **the IRS Collection Solutions Handbook** tab for downloadable resources.

Taxpayers must pay the application fee and required down payment, depending on the type of payment method selected. Taxpayers who qualify for the low-income waiver will not have to pay the application fee or the down payment/periodic payment amounts. The fee is either refunded or applied against the amount of the offer if the offer is accepted to promote effective tax administration or accepted based on certain economic hardship criteria (special circumstances). [IRM 5.19.7.2.1.1 at (3) (7-9-2020)]

Taxpayers with incomplete applications will be given a short opportunity to perfect the application. However, taxpayers with unfiled returns will have the OIC application returned.

Chapter 13.05: ETA-OIC Investigation Process

The offer investigation process for an ETA-OIC is the same as for the OIC-DATC. The taxpayer's financial documents will be analyzed for the ability to pay. The offer examiner will determine the taxpayer's reasonable collection potential, given the special circumstances, to determine an acceptable offer amount.

NEH-OICs will require approval from the NEH-OIC Group. Taxpayers should expect all ETA-OIC applications to take at least six months to process (likely longer). Because ETA-OICs involve special circumstances, it is not uncommon for disputes to arise with the offer examiner. Taxpayers should be prepared to support and advocate for their special circumstances and resulting offer amount calculation with the IRS appeals officer in the IRS Independent Office of Appeals.

ETA-OIC Acceptance

Taxpayers receiving acceptance of their ETA-OIC will follow the same steps as for an OIC-DATC. All accepted ETA-OICs require approval from IRS Area Counsel where the amount of the assessed balance compromised is $50,000 or more. [IRM 5.8.11.7.2 at (2) (4-11-2024)]

Chapter 13.06: ETA-OIC Appeals

It is common in ETA-OICs for the taxpayer and the offer examiner to debate the proper offer amount. It is also common for an ETA-OIC to be rejected, requiring the taxpayer to appeal to the IRS Independent Office of Appeals who will take a fresh look at the taxpayer's circumstances. Taxpayers who receive a rejection letter from the IRS for an ETA-OIC will be offered the same appeal rights as given under an OIC-DATC.

The rejection letter will outline the offer examiner's rationale for not allowing the ETA-OIC. The offer examiner will also attach his calculation of the reasonable collection potential (the IET and AET forms) based on his interpretation of the facts and circumstances. Taxpayers are given 30 days (no extensions) to request an appeal. Taxpayers use Form 13711, *Request for Appeal of Offer in Compromise*, to outline their disagreements with the offer examiner's conclusion.

Taxpayers may appeal to the Tax Court if the ETA-OIC was filed in conjunction with a timely request for a Collection Due Process appeal. Otherwise, the decision of the IRS is final, and the taxpayer has no additional administrative appeal rights within the IRS.

For OIC appeals options, see **Chapter 18: Collection Appeals Options**.

Chapter 14:
REINSTATE/RENEGOTIATE A DEFAULTED OR TERMINATED IRS PAYMENT PLAN

This section covers how an IRS installment agreement falls into default and the taxpayer's options and steps to take to reinstate the agreement.

Topic	Covers
Overview of Defaulted and Terminated Installment Agreements	What defaults or terminates an IRS installment agreement and options after default.
Default Timeline and Reinstatement	Timing and notices when a taxpayer defaults on an installment agreement.
Renegotiating a New Collection Alternative	How to renegotiate a new IRS collection alternative after an IA default.
Appeals of Defaulted and Terminated Installment Agreements	How to appeal a defaulted IA.

Key Highlights:

- Taxpayers can default on an IRS payment plan if they miss payments or have new unpaid balances.
- Depending on their circumstances, taxpayers can reinstate their old agreement or renegotiate a new agreement if their financial circumstances change.
- Taxpayers who do not get into an agreement after default usually face IRS enforcement 90 days after the default notice is issued.

Chapter 14.01: Overview of Defaulted and Terminated Installment Agreements

In 2022, the IRS reported that 9% of all IRS payment plans defaulted. [TIGTA Report 2022-30-021, The Administration of Partial Payment Installment Agreements Needs Improvement, March 16, 2022] Taxpayers who default/terminate their IRS payment plan or "installment agreement" must reinstate the agreement, pay their balance in full, or renegotiate other collection alternatives to get back in good standing with the IRS and avoid enforced collection activity (i.e., liens, levies, passport restrictions).

Causes of Defaulted and Terminated Installment Agreements

There are five reasons the IRS terminates an installment agreement:

1. *Missed payments*: the taxpayer has missed two payments in a year (the IRS allows the taxpayer to miss one payment in a year without default on all payment plans except partial pay installment agreements).
2. *Owe more unpaid taxes*: the taxpayer files another return or has another balance that is owed (i.e., from an audit or CP2000 assessment) and does not pay the balance in full (including penalties and interest).
3. *Decline to respond*: the *IRS* asks the taxpayer to provide updated financial information and no information or incomplete information is provided (IRS terminates agreement).
4. *Does not adjust payments*: the taxpayer fails to pay a modified payment amount that he agreed to with the IRS and the IRS terminates the installment agreement.
5. *False information*: the taxpayer provided incorrect information that was the basis for the installment agreement.

   [IRM 5.14.11.3 at (1) (1-1-2015)]

Note: As part of the 2020 Taxpayer Relief Initiative due to the COVID-19 pandemic, the IRS automatically added certain new tax balances to existing installment agreements, for individual and out-of-business taxpayers. This taxpayer-friendly approach will occur instead of defaulting the agreement, which can complicate matters for those trying to pay their taxes.

Surprisingly, taxpayers with delinquent tax returns will not, on their own, cause a default on an installment agreement. [IRM 5.14.11.3 at (3) (1-1-2015)] Subsequent IRS enforcement (substitute for return filing) and posting of a new balance on the unfiled year will cause the default because the taxpayer now has a new assessment.

Affordable Care Act penalties also will not default an agreement. If the taxpayer has an Affordable Care Act (ACA or Obamacare) individual shared responsibility payment liability (ISRP) for not having adequate healthcare coverage and it generates an amount owed to the IRS, this will not on its own cause a default on the installment agreement. [IRM 5.14.11.3 at (1b) (1-1-2015)] Payment of unpaid ISRPs may be made through a voluntary payment, an installment agreement, or from future refunds. However, the taxpayer will default on an agreement if the taxpayer owes additional tax as a result of having to repay excess advanced premium tax credits used as a subsidy for marketplace coverage.

One Agreement Allowed

The IRS does not allow more than one collection arrangement per taxpayer. [IRM 5.14.1.4.2 at (2d) (12-23-2022)] For example, if the taxpayer is in an installment agreement for a year and then files and owes on the next year, the IRS will not give him a separate payment plan on the new return balance owed. The taxpayer should only have one agreement with the IRS and it must cover all balances owed.

In certain circumstances, the taxpayer may have an installment agreement related to a business that is separate from his individual payment plan. However, if the taxpayer consolidates the payment plan for multiple taxpayer identification numbers (TIN) into one payment plan, a new balance under any of the TINs will default the agreement. [IRM 5.14.1.4.2 at (2d) (12-23-2022)]

Chapter 14.02: Default Timeline and Reinstatement

When a taxpayer misses a payment, files another balance due return without payment, or fails to comply with the terms of the payment plan, the IRS ultimately sends one of two notices: CP523 or Letter 2975. This letter is sent certified to the taxpayer. [IRM 5.14.11.4 at (2) and (4) (1-1-2015)]

These notices do not terminate the agreement, but they do put the taxpayer on notice that he has 30 days within which to take action or the agreement will be terminated. [IRM 5.14.11.4 at (4) (1-1-2015)] Systemically, the IRS will not issue a levy until 90 days after the CP523/Letter 2975 date. [IRM 5.14.11.4 at (6) (1-1-2015)]

Within the 30 days following the CP523 notice, a taxpayer may reinstate the installment agreement to avoid IRS collection enforcement. However, the IRS has the discretion to request new financial information before reinstating the agreement; a decision as to reinstatement will depend on the taxpayer's circumstances. [IRM 5.14.11.5 (1-1-2015)]

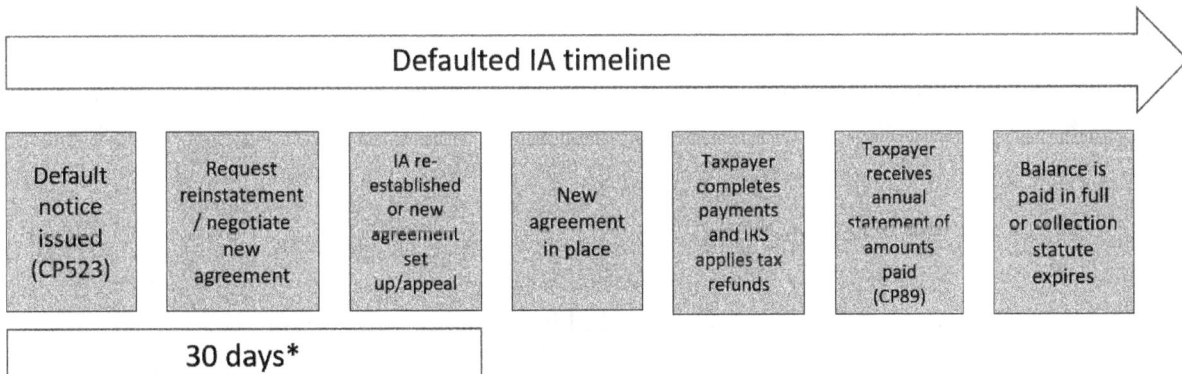

Defaulted IA timeline						
Default notice issued (CP523)	Request reinstatement / negotiate new agreement	IA re-established or new agreement set up/appeal	New agreement in place	Taxpayer completes payments and IRS applies tax refunds	Taxpayer receives annual statement of amounts paid (CP89)	Balance is paid in full or collection statute expires

30 days*

*if IRS terminates agreement and new agreement is not established, IRS can proceed with enforced collection 90 days after the CP523 date.

Routinely, the IRS allows two circumstances to be present before automatically agreeing to reinstate the payment plan:

1. The agreement defaulted because of a new tax liability and the new amount will be paid in two additional monthly payments, or

2. The taxpayer would qualify for a simple installment agreement (owes less than $50,000 and is able to pay before the CSED) AND the taxpayer has not defaulted on an installment agreement in the past 12 months.

   [IRM 5.14.11.5 at (2) (1-1-2015)]

In both circumstances, the IRS reserves the right to file a federal tax lien. [IRM 5.14.11.6 (1-1-2015)] However, in practice, the IRS will not file a lien (assuming one is not already filed) if the taxpayer qualifies and obtains a simple installment agreement.

The IRS charges a fee of $89 for reinstatement (low-income fee is $43 for non-direct debit agreements and $0 for low-income taxpayers with direct debit agreements). [IRM 5.14.1.2 at (10) (07-02-2024)] The IRS also allows taxpayers to revise/reinstate the agreement online for $10 (cannot reinstate or revise online for direct debit IAs). Fees will be reimbursed to low-income taxpayers after payments are completed.

Chapter 14.03: Renegotiating a New Collection Alternative

If the taxpayer does not qualify for the automatic criteria for reinstatement or the taxpayer needs different payment terms based on her financial situation, the IRS will require the financial information before setting up a new agreement. At that point, all potential collection alternatives will be evaluated based on the taxpayer's ability to pay.

If taxpayers are able to pay under the simple installment agreement terms, they may be able to provide limited financial information over the phone (usually employer and bank information) in order to reinstate the agreement. But if the taxpayer is unable to pay within the simple terms or owes more than $50,000, the IRS may want more detailed financial information if the taxpayer is not able to pay according to the full-pay non-streamlined installment agreement terms (owe between $50,000 and $250,000 and pay before the CSED). Taxpayers with over $50,000 owed will likely have a federal tax lien filed against them and be put in a payment plan based on their ability to pay.

If the taxpayer defaulted because of a new balance owed from a recently filed return, the IRS will also request the taxpayer to increase her withholding and/or make estimated tax payments if withholding/estimated tax payment noncompliance was the cause for the new balance.

Enforced Collection

If a taxpayer does not get back into good standing with the IRS within 90 days, she may face enforced IRS collection actions. If a lien had not been filed, the taxpayer may receive a tax lien filing if more than $10,000 is owed. [IRM 5.12.2.6 at (1) (10-14-2013)] The IRS will also look to employers, financial institutions, and other payers for payment in the form of a levy. If the taxpayer owes more than $64,000 (adjusted annually for inflation), the IRS will systemically start passport restriction proceedings with the State Department.

In most cases, it is practical for taxpayers to seek a new simple installment agreement to avoid financial disclosure and the filing of an NFTL. If the taxpayer is able to prove that she has adequate withholding and estimated tax payments in place to pay future tax filings (i.e., will not owe again) and agrees to direct debit payments, the IRS will often allow the taxpayer to reinstate the agreement.

Chapter 14.04: Appeals of Defaulted and Terminated Installment Agreements

Taxpayers often request that the defaulted or terminated installment agreement be reinstated on the same terms. However, the IRS may want a higher payment, direct debit payment, financial statement disclosure, or other terms that the taxpayer may disagree with.

If the taxpayer disagrees, she may request an informal review with the IRS collection manager. However, taxpayers may also request a Collection Appeal Program hearing (an informal hearing with an IRS appeals officer) within 30 days after receiving the CP523 notice. However, in order to take advantage of the CAP hearing, taxpayers will have to react quickly to attempt to reinstate the default agreement because the 30-day window expires 30 days after the date on the CP523 notice.

The taxpayer may have other appeals options after the IRS begins to enforce collection. For example, the taxpayer may have an opportunity for a Collection Due Process hearing if she receives a lien notice or another Final Notice of Intent to Levy. Practically, the taxpayer will need to evaluate the best appeals options, including manager review, if there is an issue with reinstating the defaulted installment agreement.

Chapter 15:
AVOID/RELEASE AN IRS WAGE GARNISHMENT AND LEVY

This section covers how the IRS enforces collection through a levy/garnishment and how to avoid/release a levy.

Topic	Covers
Overview of IRS Garnishments and Levies	The requirements for the IRS to issue a levy and how to prevent an IRS levy or garnishment.
Types of Levies	The common types of IRS levies and how they work.
IRS Levy Process	The IRS process and timing to enforce collection via a levy or garnishment.
Criteria for Releasing a Garnishment/Levy	Conditions in which the IRS will remove a levy.
Steps to Release a Garnishment/Levy	The process to release a levy.
Appealing Denied Levy Releases	How to appeal a denied levy release determination.

Key Highlights:

- If a taxpayer does not pay or enter into a collection alternative, the IRS may levy the taxpayer for payment. The IRS will identify levy sources through reported information returns (Forms W-2s, 1099s, 5498s, etc.) and information obtained from third parties.
- A garnishment or a levy is an IRS seizure of a taxpayer's income or assets to pay an outstanding tax liability.
- There are several types of IRS levies. Levies may be continuous or one-time depending on the source of income/asset being levied.
- Taxpayers can release a levy if they have a financial hardship or secure a collection alternative from the IRS.

Chapter 15.01: Overview of IRS Garnishments and Levies

A levy is a seizure of income or property to pay a tax debt. The most common form of a levy is a wage garnishment or bank levy.

Since 2012, levies have been on the decline. However, recent IRS enforcement measures have caused an uptick in levies issued for 2024 and beyond. [IRS Data Books, 2012-2024, Tables 25 and 27]

Number of IRS Levies: 2010-2024

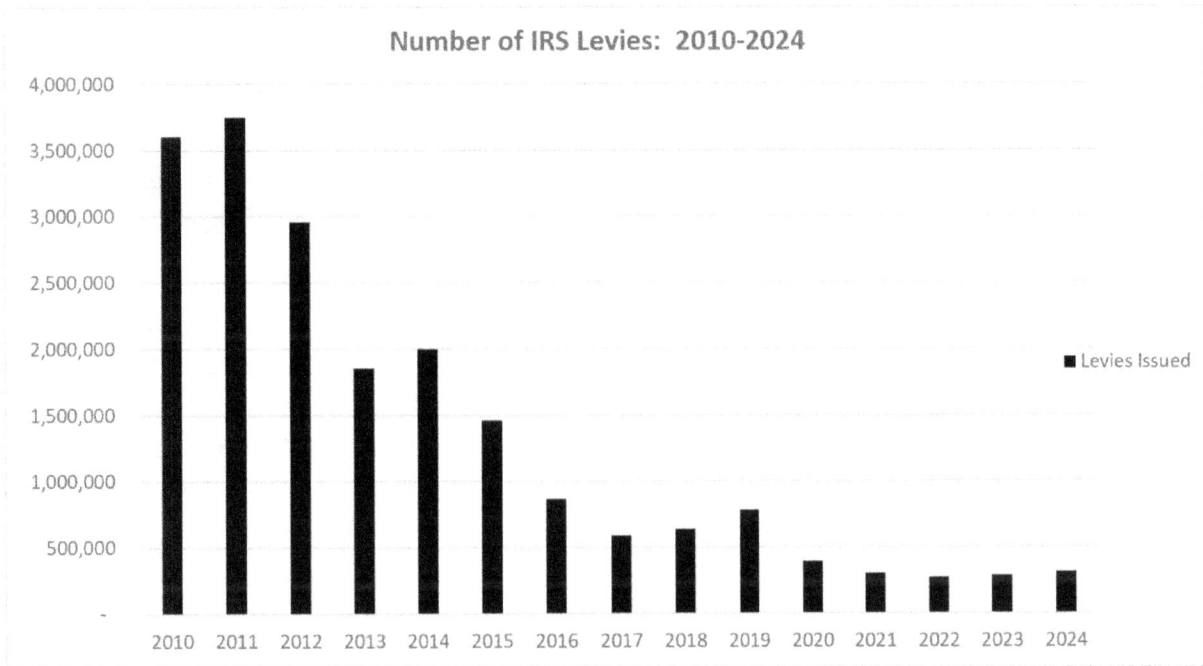

During the COVID-19 pandemic and IRS Taxpayer Relief Initiative changes, most IRS campus (Automated Collection System) levies ceased. However, IRS field collection has been active in issuing levies. The IRS restarted campus collection notices in October 2023. The IRS has restarted campus enforcement levies in the June 2025.

Requirements to Issue a Levy

If a taxpayer does not pay their tax balance, there are four actions that the IRS will take before a levy will be issued:

- Notice and demand for payment.
- Notice of intent to levy.
- Notice of a right to a Collection Due Process (CDP) hearing. [IRC §6330]
- Notice of third-party contact

[IRM 5.11.1.3.2 (04-03-2025)]

The IRC requires the IRS to provide taxpayers with notice of its intention to levy at least 30 calendar days before initiating the levy action. [IRC §6331(d)] This notice provides the taxpayer with the opportunity to appeal a levy action before it occurs.

The IRS issues a series of notices that complete the four requirements for a levy. IRS levies that originate from the IRS Automated Collection System (ACS) are usually generated after the IRS has sent all notices to the taxpayer.

IRS procedures used to require the IRS to "renotify" the taxpayer of the intent to levy if no action is on the account for 180 days before a new levy can be issued. However, in 2021, the IRS removed the 180-day requirement for revenue officer "manual levies." [IPU SB/SE-05-0221-0290 (2-22-2021)] IRS officials have stated that they intend to renotify taxpayers every 180 days despite the removal of the 180-day requirement from its procedures. Changes to IRM 5.11.1.3.2 at (2) indicate that the IRS will provide a renotification for ACS notices if the taxpayer has not received a prior notification in 1 year.

The IRS has followed a policy of notification prior to levying a taxpayer. In the past, if more than 180 days have elapsed since the last IRS Notice of Intent to Levy, the IRS may renotify the taxpayer of its intention to levy. Normally, if there is not an oral or written notification of intent to levy from the IRS within the past 180 days, the IRS may send another notice to the taxpayer before issuing a levy. The IRS is not required to provide a written re-warning but may provide oral warnings to the taxpayer and often follow up with a written warning notice.

> **Pro Tip:** In late 2023 and early 2024, the IRS restarted campus collection notices. For 2021 and earlier tax years, the IRS issued a "reminder" letter, Letter LT38, to renotify taxpayers about their balances owed and provide them an opportunity to pay or enter into a collection alternative to avoid future levies.

The IRS will levy up to the amount of tax owed for the tax period(s) subject to levy. Any tax may be collected by levy if the levy is made within ten years after the assessment of the tax, or any extensions of this ten-year period. [IRC §6502(a) and IRM 5.17.3.5.3 (1-7-2011)]

The most common levies are wage garnishments and bank levies. Social Security payments and state income tax refunds are commonly subject to levy. Note that many different types of income and property are subject to levy.

Property Exempt from Levy

There are many exceptions of property that is exempt from levy. Common exemptions include:

- Unemployment benefits.
- Workmen's compensation.
- Certain public assistance payments.

IRM 5.17.3.5.7 (1-7-2011) provides details of property that is exempt from levy.

Prevention of a Levy — The "Collection" Hold

Taxpayers are able to prevent a levy by paying their balance owed or entering into a collection alternative with the IRS before the levy is issued. Taxpayers facing a levy may ask the IRS for a "collection hold" to allow them time to pay or to secure a collection alternative. In practice, the IRS will normally grant one extension to allow the taxpayer to evaluate collection alternatives.

Taxpayers will be given a deadline to comply or face potential enforced collection, such as by imposition of a levy or lien. Based on their circumstances, taxpayers may receive additional time after the initial collection hold period to allow for certain actions to occur. Taxpayers often get multiple collection hold periods when the IRS is processing an original return that will eliminate the amount owed.

> **Pro Tip:** Taxpayers often use the 180-day extension to pay to avoid a levy and Notice of Federal Tax Lien. Taxpayers can use this collection alternative to actively pay down the balance and/or pay the balance in full. If the taxpayer cannot fully pay at the end of the 180 days, the taxpayer can enter into another appropriate collection alternative to avoid a levy.

Chapter 15.02: Type of Levies

The IRS has the capability to issue several types of levies targeting different assets or sources of income. However, all levies can be put into two categories: one-time levies and continuous levies.

One-Time Levies

Levies can be a one-time seizure. Bank, financial institution, and accounts receivable levies are one-time levies. The IRS will take the amount owed to the IRS that is in the account at the time the levy is issued; subsequent deposits into the account are not subject to the levy.

Continuous Levies

Levies may also be continuous, ending when the tax is paid or an agreement is set up with the IRS. Wage and state income tax refunds are continuous and remain until released or the amount of the levy is paid in full, or the collection statute of limitations expires. A continuous levy remains on the taxpayer's property or income until:

- It is released by the IRS,
- The tax debt is paid in full, or
- The collection statute expires.

[IRM 5.11.5.3 (12-22-2020)]

Common Levies

Below are the rules on the amounts levied and their duration, beginning with the most common levy types:

Levy type	Amount levied	Duration
Wage garnishment	Calculated amount based on taxpayer's exemptions and filing status.	Continuous
Banks and financial institutions	Amount in bank at time of levy up to the amount of the levy (freezes funds for 21 days after the levy is received prior to sending to the IRS).	One-time
Accounts receivable	Amount owed at time of levy; sent to the IRS according to the pay cycle of the payer.	One-time *Note:* Many payers treat erroneously treat accounts receivable levies as a continuous levy.
Social security	15% of proceeds (revenue officers can increase levy amount to 100% in egregious situations).	Continuous, and can remain in effect after the collection statute expires. *Note:* SSA payments are generally not subject to levy when the recipient's income is less than 250% of the poverty level. Social security disability income is excluded from levy. [TIGTA Report, Revenue Officer Levies of Social Security Benefits Indicate That Further Modification to Procedures is Warranted, June 30, 2016]
State income tax refund	100%	Continuous

Pro Tip: Many small business owners receive a continuous levy from the IRS. If the payments are not fixed and determinable, the levy should not be continuous. However, in practice, the IRS does not like to release continuous levies on independent contractors. Taxpayers must put pressure on the IRS by speaking with a manager or requesting a collection appeal to make the levy a "one-time" levy.

Wage Garnishment

A wage garnishment is a common form of IRS levy. A wage levy is sent to the taxpayer's current employer and attaches to the wages that the employer holds for payment to the employee. Wage levies are continuous – that is, they stay in place until the amount on the levy is paid or the IRS sends a levy release to the employer. [IRM 5.11.5.3 (12-22-2020)]

Regarding a wage levy, a portion of the taxpayer's wages is exempt from levy based on the taxpayer's marital status and number of exemptions. [IRC §6334(a)(9) and IRM 5.11.5.4 (12-22-2020)] Employers are responsible for properly calculating and remitting wage levy proceeds to the IRS. The IRS sends Publication 1494 with the Form 668-W, *Notice of Levy on Wages, Salary, and Other Income*, to assist employers in determining the amounts that are exempt from levy. [IRM 5.11.5.4.1 at (2) (12-22-2020)]

To help determine the exempt amount, a levy includes a Statement of Dependents and Filing Status. The employer gives this statement to the employee to complete and return within three days. If the employer does not receive the statement in three days, the exempt amount is computed as if the person is married filing separately with no dependents. Employers who ignore levies will be subject to stiff penalties. [IRC §6332(d) and IRM 5.17.4.12.3 (3-25-2022)]

The IRS does not mail the taxpayer a copy of a wage levy notice. The employer is responsible for giving the employee a copy of the levy when requesting the levy exemption amount. [IRM 5.11.2.2.7 (12-21-2020)]

State Income Tax Refund Levies

The IRS issues a state income tax refund (SITR) levy to collect on balances through its State Income Tax Levy Program (SITLP). Of the 42 states with income tax return filing requirements, 40 participate in the SITLP. [IRM 5.19.9.3 at (11) (6-23-2022) and TIGTA Report, The International Revenue Service Can More Effectively Address Noncompliance by Better Using and Controlling the Fed/State Program, August 29, 2018] A SITR levy can be avoided by entering into a payment agreement. [IRM 5.19.9.3.2 at (2) (10-20-2016)] However, currently not collectible status does not exclude the taxpayer from the SITR levy. [IRM 5.19.9.3.1 at (1) (10-20-2016)]

SITR levies do not require a Final Notice of Intent to Levy (L-1058/LT-11). The CP504 notice serves to warn taxpayers of the intent to levy through the SITR.

Per IRC §6330(f)(2), the taxpayer does not receive a Notice of Levy (Form 668) prior to the SITR levy. The CP92 notice is a "post-levy" notice informing the taxpayer of the refund levied and her right to appeal. The state also issues a letter informing the taxpayer of the levy. [IRM 5.19.9.3.4 (10-20-2016)] The CP92 provides the taxpayer with the opportunity to appeal the levy after the levy is made if that levy is the first levy made with respect to a particular tax and tax period. CP92s will not be issued if the taxpayer has received a prior opportunity to appeal via a different IRS letter. [IRM 5.19.9.3.4 at (7) (10-20-2016)] The amount levied is limited to the amount of tax owed on the levy notice.

Federal Payments Levies

The IRS may issue a continuous levy on certain federal payments (referred to as the Federal Payments Levy Program or "FPLP") in order to collect on back tax balances. [IRC §6331(h) and IRM 5.11.7.3.1.1 (7-1-2022)] The federal payment levy is most commonly attached to Social Security payments. Most FPLP levies garnish 15% of the specified payment. [IRM 5.11.7.3.1.1 at (2e) (7-1-2022)] FPLP levies are commonly issued against: SSA benefit payments (not SSI), federal employee retirement annuities, federal non-defense civilian contractor payments, federal employee salaries and travel payments, and Medicare provider and supplier payments. [IRM 5.11.7.3.1.1 at (2) (7-1-2022)]

An FPLP levy can be avoided by entering into an agreement with the IRS (i.e., obtaining an extension to fully pay, entering into an installment agreement, offer in compromise, or currently not collectible status). [IRM Exhibit 5.11.7-3] The CP90/CP91 notices indicate the time period to appeal the issuance of a levy. A CP90 is only issued if the taxpayer has not received a prior Notice of Intent to Levy on the same period/form. [IRM 5.11.7.3.4 at (2) (9-23-2016)] A CP91 for SSA levies will be reissued if 26 or more weeks have passed since a prior notice has been made to the taxpayer. [IRM 5.11.7.3.4 at (2) (9-23-2016)] The amount levied is limited to the amount of tax owed on the levy notice.

> **Pro Tip:** Social Security levies can continue past the collection statute expiration date. IRS CCA 202129006, released July 23, 2021, emphasized that Social Security income levy would continue after the collection statute runs due to the fact that the taxpayer has a fixed and determinable right to future payments on Social Security income at the time the levy arose. As a result, the levy is continuous even after the collection statute expires under Treasury Regulation §301.6331-1(a)(1). If the IRS starts to levy Social Security payments before the statute expires, the levy will continue until the amount is paid.

Bank Levies

A bank levy is a one-time levy. [IRM 5.11.4.6 at (1) (9-26-2014)] If such a levy is made, the financial institution is required to freeze the funds in the taxpayer's accounts up to the amount of the levy. [IRM 5.11.4.11 (9-26-2014)] Subsequent deposits are not subject to levy. Under IRC §6332(c), a bank must wait 21 calendar days after a levy is served before surrendering the funds in the account (including interest) held by the bank.

A levy served to a bank attaches to funds in any bank account in which the taxpayer has an unrestricted right to withdraw funds (signature authority) — even if multiple persons have signature authority for that bank account. [IRM 5.11.4.3 (9-26-2014)]

Bank levies are served to the financial institution on Form 668-A, *Notice of Levy*. For bank levies, the IRS will mail the taxpayer a copy of the notice (Form 8519 is used for this purpose) seven days after mailing it to the payer or financial institution. [IRM 5.19.4.3.10 at (4b) (2-18-2015)]

Chapter 15.03: IRS Levy Process

The IRS follows these steps before issuing a levy:

1. *Tax assessed*: taxpayer files a tax return and the tax is assessed. Alternatively, the IRS assesses additional tax due (i.e., through an audit or adjustment to the account, such as an amended return or a math error notice).
2. *Notice accessing tax and requesting payment*: the IRS issues the required notice and demand for payment (usually a CP14 notice for a filed tax return with an unpaid balance owed).
3. *More reminder notices*: the IRS sends other requests to pay (IRS notices CP501, CP503, and CP504) and the taxpayer fails to pay or enter into a collection alternative with the IRS.
4. *Send to IRS Collection for enforcement*: the IRS issues a Notice of Intent to Levy and offers a required Collection Due Process appeal (Letter LT 11 or L1058).
5. *Time expires and levy is issued*: with no resolution, the IRS issues a levy.

These steps are communicated to the taxpayer via a series of notices called the IRS collection notice stream.

If the taxpayer is assigned to a local revenue officer, the taxpayer has likely already been given the opportunity to pay through multiple IRS notices, including the CDP appeal rights notice. ROs will quickly issue a levy if the taxpayer has been warned of pending enforcement.

Collection Notice Stream

Prior to issuing a levy, the IRS will typically attempt to collect the unpaid balance by sending a series of notices to the taxpayer. The final notice (Final Notice of Intent to Levy or "FNIL" (Revenue Officer Letter 1058 or ACS Letter LT11)) satisfies the last requirement before a levy is issued. The notice prior to the Final Notice of Intent to Levy, the CP504 notice, serves to notify the taxpayer that the IRS has the ability to levy their state tax refund without sending a final notice.

Taxpayers filing on or before the April 15 annual deadline will normally receive their first demand for payment in the first week of June. If the taxpayer has no other compliance issues that warrant accelerated collection efforts, the IRS will issue the FNIL in early Fall. IRS ACS may issue a levy 30 days after the FNIL if the taxpayer has not made payment arrangements with the IRS.

The typical IRS automated levy process and timeline:

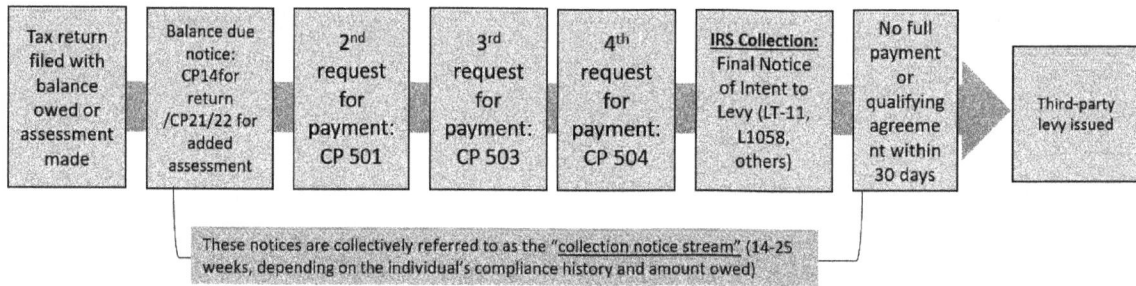

| Tax return filed with balance owed or assessment made | Balance due notice: CP14for return /CP21/22 for added assessment | 2nd request for payment: CP 501 | 3rd request for payment: CP 503 | 4th request for payment: CP 504 | IRS Collection: Final Notice of Intent to Levy (LT-11, L1058, others) | No full payment or qualifying agreement within 30 days | | Third-party levy issued |

These notices are collectively referred to as the "collection notice stream" (14-25 weeks, depending on the individual's compliance history and amount owed)

Chapter 15.04: Criteria for Releasing a Garnishment/Levy

The IRS will likely release a levy when any of the following conditions exist:

- The balance due is paid in full. The levy is released automatically, and the levy source should receive the levy release in 7-10 days. [IRM 5.19.4.4.10 at (9) (12-30-2024)]
- The taxpayer demonstrates financial hardship. [IRM 5.19.4.4.10 at (5j) (12-30-2024)]
- Releasing the levy will facilitate collection of the tax. [IRM 5.19.4.4.10 at (5i) (12-30-2024)]
- The IRS wrongly or erroneously issued a levy. [IRM 5.19.4.4.12 (3-4-2019)]
- The collection statute expiration date has passed. [IRM 5.19.4.4.10 at (5e) (12-30-2024)]
- The taxpayer files for bankruptcy. [IRM 5.19.4.4.10 at (5h) (12-30-2024)]
- The taxpayer files for an offer in compromise. [IRM 5.19.4.4.10 at (5g) (12-30-2024)]
- The taxpayer enters into an IRS collection agreement, including an installment agreement or short term payment plan with 180 (formerly extension of time to pay.) [IRM 5.19.4.4.10 at (5g) (12-30-2024)]

For most taxpayers, economic hardship and entering into a collection agreement are the best options for release of the levy.

Often taxpayers will argue that they no longer owe the liability. [IRM 5.19.4.4.10 at (5c) (12-30-2024)] For example, if the taxpayer's current year in-process refund will pay the balance owed, the IRS should release the refund with a copy of the return showing that the refund will pay the outstanding balance by refund offset.

For most, the solution is to get into one of the following IRS collection alternative arrangements as quickly as possible:

- Extension to pay.
- Installment agreement (i.e., payment plan).
- Currently not collectible status (CNC).
- Offer in compromise (OIC).

To get into a payment plan, CNC, an OIC, the taxpayer must be compliant. That is, he must have filed all required tax returns and have adequate current withholdings, federal tax deposits, and/or made estimated tax payments. The ETP does not require that the taxpayer be in filing compliance.

Hardship Levy Release

A taxpayer is able to attain release of a levy due to a documented economic hardship. [IRM 5.19.4.4.10 at (5j) (12-30-2024)] Economic hardship occurs when an individual taxpayer is unable to pay his or her reasonable basic living expenses.

Some examples of documented hardships include:

- Eviction notice.
- Utilities shut off notices.
- Unable to afford necessary and allowable living expenses (i.e., due to unemployment, etc.).
- Outstanding necessary medical expenses to continue treatment.

In cases of economic hardship, the IRS will release the levy even though the taxpayer is not compliant. The IRS may also partially release the levy if it is determined that only some of the levy proceeds are needed to relieve the economic hardship. Taxpayers with hardships are also encouraged to involve the Taxpayer Advocate's office to expedite the release of the levy.

The IRS uses Form 668-D, *Release of Levy/Release of Property from Levy*, to release a wage garnishment or other levy.

Chapter 15.05: Steps to Release a Garnishment/Levy

Taxpayers must work with the IRS collection function (ACS or revenue officer) that issued the levy to obtain a levy release. The steps in the process are as follows:

1. *Determine if the taxpayer is in filing and payment compliance.* if the taxpayer is not in an economic hardship, the taxpayer must correct filing and payment compliance issues.
2. *Evaluate which levy criteria is applicable.* economic hardship or a collection agreement is the most likely option. If the taxpayer is claiming economic hardship, she will need to document the hardship and contact the IRS for a levy release.
3. *Contact the IRS and obtain a collection alternative:* an extension to pay, payment plan, CNC, or file an OIC.
4. *After the collection alternative is reached or applied for, taxpayer should request the IRS to release the levy.* If needed, the taxpayer should request that the IRS expedite the release by faxing the release to the employer/payer. Have the employer/payer information available (contact person, fax, and phone number) so that the IRS is able to immediately fax over the levy release. [IRM 5.19.4.4.10 at (1) (12-30-2024)]

5. *Contact the levy source and confirm that the levy was released.* If not, recontact the IRS and have them resend the release.

It can take 30 days or more for a Social Security levy release. Taxpayers can ask the IRS to expedite SSA levy releases by faxing the levy release directly to the SSA. [IRM 5.19.4.4.10 at (1) (12-30-2024)]

Pro Tip: In many cases, the quickest method to obtain a levy release is to request an extension to full pay (short-term payment agreement up to 180 days). The IRS will often release a levy on a taxpayer with a prior clean compliance history who has entered into an ETP agreement. This will allow the taxpayer time to fully pay the liability or to enter into another collection alternative without a levy in place.

If a levy was issued in error, taxpayers should request that the IRS reimburse them for costs associated with an erroneous levy (i.e., erroneous bank levy that caused non-sufficient funds charges, etc.). Taxpayers will file Form 8546, *Claim for Reimbursement of Bank Charges*, to request reimbursement from fees as a result of an erroneous levy. [IRM 5.19.4.4.13 (12-12-2008)]

Chapter 15.06: Appealing Denied Levy Releases

Most levy release denials result from either a disagreement with the IRS on the terms of a requested collection alternative, such as the payment amount for an IRS installment agreement or CNC status, or economic hardship circumstances.

If the IRS will not release the levy, there are generally two appeal options:

- An informal conference with an IRS collection manager.
- An informal appeals conference with an IRS appeals officer under the Collection Appeals Program.

Most taxpayers want to resolve levy release disputes quickly. The quickest way is to resolve the dispute through an informal phone conference with an IRS collection manager. IRS procedures require the collection manager to contact the taxpayer within 24 hours. However, in practice, the manager rarely contacts back within 24 hours. This requires the taxpayer to follow up with the IRS to timely involve the manager. CAP hearings will generally take place within two weeks.

Taxpayers rarely qualify for a CDP hearing as requests for this formal appeals hearing must be made before the levy is issued. The taxpayer is given the opportunity to request a CDP after receiving an IRS notice that warns of the IRS intent to levy (IRS letters L1058, LT11, CP90). Taxpayers who miss the CDP deadline can request an Equivalent Hearing. State income tax levies and federal contractor levies are the exception to the CDP 30-day requirement. [IRM 5.1.9.3.1 at (4) (10-19-23)] A taxpayer can file a CDP hearing request for up to 30-days after the SITR levy (IRS notice CP92). The taxpayer can still qualify for an Equivalent hearing if she submits a written request (Form 12153) within one year of the date of the CDP levy notice. [IRM 8.22.4.3 at (2) (5-

12-2022)] Because CDP and EH take several months to complete, it makes them impractical as levy release appeals options.

> **Pro Tip:** the levy release denial appeals process clearly illustrates why it is best to practice levy avoidance. Most taxpayers obtain a levy release as a result of entering into a collection agreement with the IRS. If the taxpayer needs immediate relief from a levy without the ability to reach an agreement (i.e., they are not in filing compliance), there are few timely opportunities to argue the case.

Taxpayers facing economic hardships have another frequently used option if they have a hardship: they can ask the Taxpayer Advocate's office to intervene. If the taxpayer is experiencing a financial hardship, the Taxpayer Advocate can release a state income tax levy or a federal payment levy, such as a social security levy. However, the Taxpayer Advocate does not have the authority to release a wage or bank levy. Nevertheless, if the Taxpayer Advocate agrees that a financial hardship exists, the TAS case advocate will contact IRS Collection and request the levy release. Ultimately, IRS Collection has the final decision as to whether to release the levy. [IRM 13.1.4.2.3.15 (1-3-2024)]

Chapter 16:
AVOID/OBTAIN RELIEF FROM A FEDERAL TAX LIEN

This section covers how to avoid and obtain relief from a Notice of Federal Tax Lien (NFTL).

Topic	Covers
Overview of Tax Liens	The IRS lien filing criteria, the duration and scope of a tax lien, and how to obtain a payoff amount in order to pay the balance in full and obtain a lien release.
Lien Filing Procedures and Timing	IRS notices and procedures related to the filing of an NFTL.
Avoiding an NFTL	How to avoid an NFTL.
Lien Relief Options (Post-Filing of an NFTL)	How to obtain the appropriate lien relief, including: a lien release, lien withdrawal, lien subordination, or lien discharge.
Tax Lien — IRS Contacts, Forms, and Publications	The IRS's Centralized Lien Operation and forms and publications for assistance with lien relief from the IRS.

Key Highlights:

- A tax lien is the government's legal claim to a taxpayer's property for the amount of the unpaid balance.
- The IRS publicly notifies third parties of its interest in the taxpayer's property by filing a Notice of Federal Tax Lien (NFTL) to protect the government's interest in the taxpayer's property. The NFTL can adversely affect a taxpayer's credit and complicate financial transactions, such as a property sale.
- To avoid a tax lien, a taxpayer must timely obtain a qualifying collection alternative.
- Taxpayers with a Notice of Federal Tax Lien have two critical resources at the IRS for assistance: the Centralized Lien Operation (lien releases, other lien requests, and payoffs) and the local IRS Collection Advisory Group (answers lien questions and can expedite requests).

Chapter 16.01: Overview of Tax Liens

When a taxpayer fails to pay a tax liability, the government may use a lien to secure its legal claim to the taxpayer's property for the amount of the unpaid balance. Legally, a tax lien can arise when any person fails to pay the tax after the IRS makes a demand for payment. This is referred to a "silent or secret lien." [IRC §6321 and IRM 5.17.2.2 (3-19-2018)] In order to put other creditors and third parties on notice that the government has an interest in the taxpayer's property, the IRS may file a public "Notice of Federal Tax Lien." The NFTL publicly identifies that the IRS has a claim against the taxpayer's property. An NFTL is normally filed at the taxpayer's local courthouse and is a matter of public record. [See IRM Exhibit 5.12.7-2 for State and Territory Filing Locations] The NFTL is in effect until:

- The tax is paid in full. [IRM 5.12.3.3.1.1 (7-15-2015)]

- The liability is no longer due (i.e., the liability is satisfied by abatement or adjustment which can occur when the taxpayer files a return or contests liability and this reduces the amount owed to $0). [IRM 5.12.3.3.1.2 (7-15-2015)]

- The collection statute has expired. [IRM 5.12.3.3.2 (7-15-2015)]

- The taxpayer obtains an offer in compromise and pays the offer amount in full. [IRM 5.12.3.5.3 (7-15-2015)]

- The liability is discharged in bankruptcy. [IRM 5.9.17.18 at (2) (09-10-2024)]

- The taxpayer obtains a surety bond to secure payment of the debt (not common). [IRM 5.12.3.3.3 (7-15-2015)]

The IRS will also remove a lien when the lien was issued in error. [IRM 5.12.3.9 (7-15-2015)]

The federal tax lien attaches to all property and rights to property owned or acquired after the imposition of the lien by the taxpayer. This is a very broad concept and includes not only items which are typically thought of as property, i.e., tangible items and "things," but also to intangible items and "rights" (such as patents, copyrights, trademarks, etc.) which a taxpayer may have but are not necessarily marketable. [IRM 5.17.2.5 (3-19-2018)] Practically, when an NFTL is filed, a taxpayer must reveal the existence of the lien during property transactions. As a result of the existence of the lien, the taxpayer will likely have complications during property transactions, such as when trying to sell or transfer property, obtain a loan, or refinance loans.

Beginning in 2017, credit agencies do not report NFTLs on credit reports. However, lenders and other parties can access public records and lien databases to obtain information on taxpayers with NFTLs.

> **Pro Tip:** Because the NFTL is a matter of public record, taxpayers with an NFTL may be targets of tax scams and unwanted solicitation by companies stating that they are able to settle the tax debt.

IRS Lien Filing Criteria and Duration of a Tax Lien

Currently, the IRS will make a lien determination if the taxpayer owes more than $10,000. [IRM 5.12.2.6 at (1) (10-14-2013)] However, taxpayers who owe between $10,000-$50,000 may avoid an NFTL by timely executing a simple installment agreement (a payment plan stretching over 120 months or the remainder of the CSED, whichever is shorter).

A tax lien is in effect until the taxpayer satisfies the liability or the CSED expires (IRC §§6322 and 6502). In rare instances, the IRS may "reduce a lien to judgment" and extend the period to collect the outstanding liability. [IRM 25.3.5.2 (8-11-2022)] In order to reduce a lien to judgment, the IRS must involve the Department of Justice and file suit against the taxpayer. These suits are generally reserved for taxpayers who are uncooperative with the IRS and/or have assets that the IRS would like to seize to settle the liability. [IRM 34.6.2.1 (6-12-2012)] In 2024, the IRS only completed 71 property seizures. [IRS Data Book, 2024, Table 27]

If the CSED expires, the taxpayer will not receive a Release of Federal Tax Lien. [IRM 5.12.3.4.1.1 (7-15-2015)] The NFTL has an "expiration date" and will self-release 30 days after the date ten years after the assessment if the IRS does not refile the lien. [IRM 5.17.2.3.3 (1-8-2016)] The IRS may refile a tax lien if there is a new CSED date (an event occurs that extends the statute to collect). The Form 668(Y), *Notice of Federal Tax Lien*, lists the date that the lien self-releases in column (e). If the taxpayer pays or resolves the liability before this date, the taxpayer will receive a lien release within 30 days (up to 120 days if settled through an offer in compromise paid by debit/credit card). [IRM 5.12.3.3.1.1 (7-15-2015) and IRM 5.12.3.3.1.1.1 (07-15-2015)] If Form 668(Y) is not adequate to prove the lien has been released to an outside party, the taxpayer may request a certificate of release by contacting the IRS Centralized Lien Processing Unit at (800) 913-6050.

Obtaining a Payoff

Tax liens can be avoided by paying the balance in full. However, taxpayers will need to know the current balance owed to fully pay off the debt. The IRS can provide the current payoff amount and a payoff amount as of a certain future date upon request.

Prior to a lien filing, taxpayers can contact the IRS directly to obtain a "payoff calculator" for the total amount owed. Tax practitioners may contact the Practitioner Priority Service (PPS) hotline to obtain the payoff amounts. IRS PPS will only provide the payoff amount verbally.

> **Pro Tip:** In May 2021, the IRS began requiring only licensed tax professionals using Form 2848, *Power of Attorney*, to obtain taxpayer collection information on balance due accounts. This new restrictive policy continues to evolve, but tax professionals may want to use a Form 2848 to get detailed taxpayer collection information.

If an NFTL has already been filed, the taxpayer may contact the IRS Centralized Lien Operation or CLO and receive a payoff calculator in writing. The CLO can fax a payoff letter directly to the taxpayer or representative. The IRS CLO staff can assist with any lien-related questions and can resolve lien issues. The CLO can be reached at (800) 913-6050. The CLO line often has long hold times and taxpayers should call early to avoid these long wait times.

If needed, the IRS will send Letter 3640-B, *Taxpayer Lien Payoff Letter*, to the taxpayer with the details of the amounts owed. [IRM 5.12.3.17 (7-15-2015)]

> **Pro Tip:** IRS personnel will likely not be willing to fax the taxpayer or her tax representative the "payoff calculator." Taxpayers may ask for a letter or ask the representative to provide them detailed amounts for each year by phone. Taxpayers will have to write down the amounts if they need the information immediately. Taxpayers may also view their online account at irs.gov ("View your tax account") to obtain payoff balances. Taxpayers should not use IRS account transcripts to determine the payoff amounts because account transcripts may not include all accrued penalties and interest on the account. In the case of needing a written payoff amount related to a lien, the taxpayer should immediately contact the CLO and request Letter 3640 with the payoff amounts. The CLO will fax this letter to the taxpayer or their representative immediately.

Chapter 16.02: Lien Filing Procedures and Timing

Requirements for Filing an NFTL

There are three elements that must be present before a tax lien may be filed:

1. An IRS tax assessment creates a balance due,
2. The IRS sends a notice and demand for payment, such as a CP14 or an audit assessment (CP22), and
3. The taxpayer refuses or neglects to pay the amount due on the notice.

   [IRC §6321]

As soon as these requirements are met, a tax lien exists. However, if the tax lien is not publicly filed, the tax lien is referred to as a "silent lien" since it is not a matter of public record. As such, creditors are not put on notice that the IRS has an interest in the taxpayer's property.

To put third parties on notice, the IRS must file the lien publicly — this is the Notice of Federal Tax Lien (NFTL) — or IRS Form 668(Y). In practice, the IRS is not quick to file a public NFTL. The IRS gives the taxpayer several chances to pay and often allows months for payment before filing an NFTL. Lien determinations can be accelerated if the taxpayer is assigned to the Collection Field function (i.e., a local revenue officer) or if the taxpayer obtains a non-qualifying arrangement that requires a lien determination (i.e., owes more than $50,000, is in CNC status or partial pay installment agreement and owes greater than $10,000).

The IRS will not file an NFTL or take collection action if the taxpayer's balance owed is due to a shared responsibility payment. [IRM 5.12.2.3.1.1 (11-9-2015)]

The IRS will generally not file an NFTL if the aggregate unpaid balance of assessments is under $10,000. [IRM 5.12.2.6 at (1) (10-14-2013)]

Notice Stream and Timing of Filing of an NFTL

Most IRS collection accounts are assigned to the Automated Collection System (ACS). ACS will normally make a lien determination and file an NFTL after normal collection efforts are exhausted and no qualifying collection alternative has been secured by the taxpayer.

Normally, ACS will trigger the filing of an NFTL after a series of IRS collection letters have been sent (called the IRS collection "notice stream"). The notice stream is a series of IRS letters beginning with the balance due notice (i.e., IRS letter CP14) and continuing until the Final Notice of Intent to Levy (usually IRS Letter LT11 or Letter 1058 or its equivalent). Between the initial notice and the Final Notice, the taxpayer may receive other warning notices depending on the circumstances. These notices send increased warnings to the taxpayer to pay or to face potential collection enforcement, including the filing of an NFTL. After the taxpayer receives IRS notice CP504, they can be assigned to IRS Collection and an NFTL determination can be made at any time. Normally, ACS will make a lien determination if the taxpayer has not responded to the Final Notice of Intent to Levy and the balance meets the lien filing criteria.

> **Pro Tip:** IRS procedures provide guidance to collection officers (ACS and revenue officers) on making lien determinations. In practice, it is hard to predict when and if the ACS will trigger an NFTL filing, because the IRS does not appear to follow standard operating procedures on making lien determinations. Taxpayers should take a conservative approach, knowing that the IRS can file an NFTL if they owe more than $10,000 and have not secured a timely simple installment agreement that avoids the lien filing.

Revenue Officer Assignment

When collection accounts are assigned to the Collection Field function (CFf), an IRS revenue officer (RO) is required to make a lien determination within ten days of assignment. [IRM 5.12.2.3.2 (10-14-2013)] The RO will often give the taxpayer an opportunity to immediately pay. If the taxpayer does not satisfy the debt, the RO may quickly file an NFTL to protect the government's interest. Taxpayers who are assigned to a RO and wish to avoid an NFTL, should immediately pay the balance owed or request a simple installment agreement (if they qualify) when first contacted by the RO.

Filing of the NFTL and the Right to Appeal

The IRS issues Letter 3172, *Notice of Federal Tax Lien and Your Rights to a Hearing under IRC §6320*, when it files an NFTL. [IRM 5.12.1.13.1 (7-11-2018)] The taxpayer can contest an IRS lien determination (pre-filing or post-filing) by requesting a timely appeal.

The taxpayer may appeal a proposed lien determination or the filing of an NFTL with one or more of the three collection appeals options:

1. *Request a manager's conference (pre-filing and post-filing appeal)*: this is an informal conference held with an IRS manager to dispute a decision made by IRS collections. When a taxpayer appeals a lien action, a manager's conference must be held prior to requesting a Collection Appeals Program (CAP) hearing. [IRM 5.12.6.4.2 (1-19-2018)]
2. *Request a Collection Appeals Program hearing (pre-filing or post-filing appeal)*: taxpayers may request an informal appeal with IRS appeals on collection actions/decisions. Taxpayers are also able to request a CAP hearing when the IRS proposes filing an NFTL with a collection alternative. The IRS appeals officer's decision after a CAP hearing is final. Taxpayers request a CAP hearing by filing Form 9423, *Collection Appeal Request*. [IRM 5.12.6.4.2 (1-19-2018)]
3. *Request a Collection Due Process (CDP) or Equivalent Hearing (post-filing appeal)*: a CDP hearing may only be requested after a lien has been filed (IRS issues Letter 3172). [IRM 5.12.6.3.5 (1-19-2018)] The taxpayer will have 30 days after the filing of the NFTL to request a CDP. If the taxpayer misses the deadline, she may request an "Equivalent Hearing" (EH) if the request is made within one year of the NFTL filing. The appeals officer's decision after a CDP hearing may be appealed in U.S. Tax Court. Taxpayers request a CDP or EH with Form 12153, *Request for a Collection Due Process or Equivalent Hearing*. Taxpayers may also dispute the liability or offer a collection alternative in a CDP hearing which may provide relief from the NFTL.

The taxpayer can offer alternatives to the NFTL during these hearings. In a manager conference or CAP hearing, the taxpayer is only able to offer collection alternatives. However, in a CDP hearing, the taxpayer may propose other alternatives to resolving the debt, such as disputing the taxes or penalties.

> **Pro Tip:** If the taxpayer has had a prior opportunity to contest the taxes or penalties, the IRS will not normally allow the taxpayer a second opportunity in a CDP hearing. Taxpayers should be prepared to propose collection alternatives in all appeals cases where they are unable to contest the liability owed. Taxpayers can also request that the Taxpayer Advocate Service intervene if the taxpayer is suffering or about to suffer financial hardship because of the lien filing.

Disputing an NFTL

When it comes to tax lien filing, it is best to practice avoidance. Once the taxpayer receives IRS Letter 3172, the IRS has already filed an NFTL. Taxpayers sometimes attempt to argue that a lien should not be filed because it will affect their future earnings capability and may impede the collection of the liability. [IRM 5.17.2.8.7 (3-19-2018)] A taxpayer would need to provide the IRS with evidence that the lien will directly impact earnings. Taxpayers are rarely successful in removing liens with arguments that they will damage earning ability.

The NFTL can be removed by reducing the amount owed to $0 by successfully contesting the liability or by paying the balance owed. Taxpayers who want to contest the unpaid balance owed can do so using any of the appropriate methods.

- *Contest the original return liability*: file an amended return to correct the original return.
- *File an original tax return:* if the IRS filed and assessed a non-filed taxpayer, the taxpayer should file an original return to replace the substitute for return (SFR) filed by the IRS.
- *Contest the penalties owed*: taxpayer can ask for penalty abatement to reduce assessed penalties.
- *Contest an audit*: if the taxpayer owes the IRS as a result of an audit, the taxpayer may provide new information by requesting audit reconsideration.
- *Contest a CP2000 assessment*: if the taxpayer's liability originated from a CP2000 underreporter notice, the taxpayer may contest the assessment with a CP2000 reconsideration request.
- *Contest an erroneous assessment:* if the taxpayer owes the IRS as the result of an audit or an assessment of a trust fund recovery penalty, the taxpayer may contest the assessment with an Offer in Compromise—Doubt as to Liability.

Chapter 16.03: Avoiding an NFTL

If the taxpayer owes on an unpaid balance and cannot pay the amount in full, he can avoid an NFTL by timely obtaining an agreement in which the IRS does not require a lien determination. There are two collection alternative agreements which will not require the IRS to file an NFTL:

1. *Extension to pay agreement (ETP)*: a taxpayer can avoid a lien determination with the ACS by timely obtaining a short-term extension of 180 days to fully pay the amount owed. Revenue officers do not provide 180-day extensions to pay as a collection alternative. [IRM 5.19.4.5.3.1 at (5) (07-10-2023)]
2. *Guaranteed or simple installment agreement (GIA and SIA)*: a payment plan when the taxpayer's assessed balance is below $50,000 and he can pay within the CSED. It is important for the taxpayer to secure this agreement before an NFTL determination is made. [IRM 5.19.4.5.1.1 at (1) (12-2-2020)]

If completed timely, a combination of the ETP and the SIA can avoid an NFTL. When working with ACS, taxpayers can use the ETP agreement to provide up to 180 days to pay the assessed balance under $50,000 and obtain an SIA to avoid a lien filing.

If a taxpayer secures an extension to pay or guaranteed/simple agreement after the filing of an NFTL, the IRS will not release a tax lien. The taxpayer must pay the balance in full or seek other lien relief options such as a lien withdrawal. Beginning in 2011, the IRS will allow a compliant taxpayer a lien withdrawal if the taxpayer:

- Pays the balance owed to bring it under $25,000,
- Enters into a 60-month direct debit payment plan (or for the remainder of the CSED, whichever is shorter), and
- Makes three direct debit payments. After the third direct debit payment, the taxpayer may request a lien withdrawal through the IRS's Consolidated Advisory Group. [IRM 5.17.2.8.7.2 (12-12-2014)]

Chapter 16.04: Lien Relief Options (Post-Filing of an NFTL)

A taxpayer may quickly see if he has an NFTL filed on his account by reviewing his account transcripts or by calling the IRS.

An IRS account transcript will have a transaction code 582 "Notice of Federal Tax Lien filed" for each tax period in which a lien has been filed. The transcript will also note lien filing fees (TC 360) and the issuance of the Letter 3172 (TC 971 with description) as indicated below: [IRM 5.12.1.17 at (10) (7-11-2018)]

582	Lien placed on assets due to balance owed	03-08-2019	$0.00
360	Fees and other expenses for collection	04-01-2019	$6.00
971	Issued notice of lien filing and right to Collection Due Process hearing	03-14-2019	$0.00

After a NTFL is filed, the taxpayer has several relief options based on the circumstances:

- Lien release.
- Lien withdrawal.
- Lien subordination.
- Lien discharge.

The taxpayer needs to select the most appropriate relief based on the particular situation and needs.

Taxpayer needs to:	Lien relief option:	Request form:
Remove the lien from their property.	Lien release	No form — call, fax, or mail request by letter
Remove the Notice of Federal Tax Lien from public record and credit reports.	Lien withdrawal	Form 12277
Allow for new financing that will help pay the taxes owed such as a second mortgage, refinance, home equity, or debt consolidation loan.	Lien subordination	Form 14134
Sell property encumbered by a lien and/or pay tax debt with assets with the sale proceeds.	Lien discharge	Form 14135

Pro Tip: Most taxpayers and tax professionals can easily request a lien release or lien withdrawal. However, when requesting other forms of lien relief that are related to property transactions (subordination, discharge, and others), it is best to request assistance from real estate attorneys who have experience dealing with these matters with the IRS.

Lien Release

The lien release is the most common form of NFTL relief. A taxpayer will receive a lien release when the balance owed is fully satisfied by payment or other means (i.e., by lowering the liability or settlement).

What is it?	Form 668(Z) is the IRS's *Certificate of Release of Federal Tax Lien.* This Certificate releases the NFTL and removes the government's interest in the taxpayer's property.
Why is it needed?	To remove the government's interest in the taxpayer's property.
Application form	There is no application form for a Certificate of Lien Release. Taxpayers can contact the IRS's Centralized Lien Operations (CLO) directly by phone or by mail.
Timing	The IRS will automatically issue Form 668(Z) within 30 days after the taxpayer qualifies for the lien release.
Criteria for lien release	The IRS is required to issue a lien release within 30 days of the date on which: • The liability is satisfied (paid in full). • The liability is removed (amended return filed, audit reconsideration, etc.).

	<ul><li>The liability is legally unenforceable (such as when the liability is discharged in bankruptcy or the collection statute expires).</li><li>The IRS accepts a surety bond (for more on surety bonds, see the <u>Bureau of Fiscal Service website</u>.</li></ul>
Expedite process	The taxpayer can pay by certified or cashier's check to expedite relief. Taxpayers needing expedite releases in exchange for full payment should go to the local Taxpayer Assistance Center office. [<u>IRM 5.12.3.5.1</u> at (1) (07-15-2015)] The Taxpayer Advocate's office also has the authority to issue a lien release if the balance is paid in full and the taxpayer has a hardship situation. [<u>IRM 13.1.4.2.3.16</u> (1-3-2024)]
IRS contact	Contact the CLO directly. The CLO can fax lien releases directly to the taxpayer.
How to request	After the taxpayer meets the criteria to obtain a lien release: <ul><li>Call the CLO directly (800-913-6050) and request a copy of the lien release from the Centralized Lien Processing Unit. For other lien release requests, contact the IRS Consolidated Advisory Group.</li><li>There is no specific IRS lien release form.</li><li>The CLO can fax the Certificate of Lien Release immediately or mail it to the taxpayer.</li><li>If the IRS denies the request, follow up immediately with the local Collection Advisory Group or the Taxpayer Advocate office.</li></ul>
Assistance	<ul><li><u>Publication 1450</u>, *Instructions for Requesting a Certificate of Release of Federal Tax Lien*.</li><li>Centralized Lien Operation at 800-913-6050 (M-F, 8AM-5PM, local time).</li><li><u>Publication 4235</u> provides contact information for the local IRS Collection Advisory Group.</li></ul>

A Certificate of Lien Release normally takes a few weeks (but not more than 30 days) after the tax liability is paid in full by certified or cashier's check. If the taxpayer pays by credit or debit card, the lien release may take up to 120 days. [<u>IRM 5.12.3.3.1.1.1</u> (7-15-2015)] Paying by certified or cashier's check expedites the release. In some emergency situations, a local IRS office will issue a lien release immediately with proof of payment. [<u>IRM 5.12.3.5.1</u> (7-15-2015)]

Lien Withdrawal

Taxpayers often confuse a lien release with a lien withdrawal. The IRS grants a lien release only when the taxpayer satisfies the balance, or the collection of tax is no longer enforceable (if the collection statute expires, or the tax is removed). The IRS may grant lien withdrawal regardless of whether the tax has been paid in full. [IRM 5.12.9.2 at (3) (9-6-2019)] Both the lien release and the lien withdrawal are recorded locally at the county courthouse where the taxpayer resides. Lien withdrawals were particularly important to taxpayers prior to 2017 when NFTLs were reported on credit reports. A lien withdrawal would effectively remove the lien from the taxpayer's credit report. Starting in 2017, NFTLs no longer appear on credit reports. As such, many taxpayers do not see the need to request a lien withdrawal.

Taxpayers may request a lien withdrawal after receiving a Certificate of Release of Federal Tax Lien after fully satisfying the payment of their liability. Lien withdrawals are generally not provided if the taxpayer's liability self-released due to collection statute expiration or discharge in bankruptcy. [IRM 5.12.9.9 at (6) (9-6-2019)] Fully satisfied includes an accepted offer in compromise. [IRM 5.12.9.9 at (5) (9-6-2019)] If the taxpayer has received the Certificate of Release and has remained in filing and payment compliance, a written request using Form 12277, *Application for Withdrawal of Filed Form 668(Y), Notice of Federal Tax Lien*, can be made to the IRS Consolidated Advisory Group requesting the lien withdrawal. According to the instructions to Form 12277, the taxpayer should select the "best interest of the government" provision on the Form to withdraw the lien.

Taxpayers whose NFTL has self-released due to the expiration of the collection statute will generally not be able to obtain a lien withdrawal unless they have extenuating circumstances. [IRM 5.17.2.8.7.1 at (3) (3-19-2018)]

Lien withdrawal determinations are made by the IRS Consolidated Advisory Group. If the taxpayer is assigned to the Collection Field function, the revenue officer assigned to the taxpayer's account will make the determination.

What is it?	Form 10916(c), *Certificate of Withdrawal of Notice of Federal Tax Lien*. This Certificate withdraws the NFTL (Form 668(Y)).
Why is it needed?	To remove the public notice of an NFTL (*Note:* The taxpayer may still have a balance owed).
Application form	Form 12277, *Application for Withdrawal of Filed Form 668(Y), Notice of Federal Tax Lien*.
Timing	The IRS will issue Form 10916(c) to the recording office where the original NFTL was filed and provide a copy of the document to the taxpayer after the determination is made. Can take 90-120 days depending on the circumstances and reason for withdrawal.
Criteria for lien withdrawal	The IRS can grant a request for lien withdrawal under any of the following conditions: • Paid the tax in full. • Entered into a 60-month direct debit installment agreement if balance is below $25,000 (after three payments are made) (or expiration of the CSED, whichever is shorter).

	• Paid the full amount of an OIC. • Received an NFTL in error. • Proven to the IRS that withdrawal will facilitate the collection of the liability. • Received consent from the Taxpayer Advocate that it is in the best interests of the government to withdraw the NFTL (not common).
Expedite process	The taxpayer can pay by certified or cashier's check to expedite a lien release and subsequent lien withdrawal application. Taxpayers should contact their local Collection Advisory Group for expedite instructions.
IRS contact	Contact the IRS Consolidated Advisory Group directly. A message can be left at (859) 594-6090 or faxed at (844) 201-8392. See Publication 4235 for the contact information.
How to request	After taxpayer meets the conditions to obtain a lien withdrawal: [IRM 5.12.9.3 (10-14-2013)] • Prepare the lien withdrawal form and include supporting documents (Form 12277, *Application for Withdrawal of Filed Form 668(Y), Notice of Federal Tax Lien*). • Contact the IRS Consolidated Advisory Group and submit the lien withdrawal request. Obtain a time frame for completion and issuance of the Certificate. • Respond to the Advisory Group with any additional information requested. • If the IRS approves the withdrawal request, the IRS will issue a Certificate of Withdrawal. • If the IRS does not approve the request, follow up immediately with the Advisory Group manager and, if necessary, consider filing an appeal. (CAP hearing is available for lien withdrawal denials.)
Assistance	• IRS Consolidated Advisory Group at (859) 594-6090. • Centralized Lien Operation at 800-913-6050 (M-F, 8AM-5PM, local time). • Publication 4235 provides contact information for the local IRS Collection Advisory Group.

For routine lien withdrawals, taxpayers can contact the IRS Consolidated Advisory Group in Florence, KY. Taxpayers can leave a message and the IRS will return their phone call within 1-2 business days. Taxpayers can also contact the local IRS Collection Advisory Group to set expectations on lien withdrawal applications and determine the timing for approval in expedite situations. (*Note:* Most local offices require the taxpayer to leave a message.) The IRS is sometimes able to take an application for lien withdrawal by phone for taxpayers who have paid the balance in full or have set up a qualified installment agreement. (*Note:* This procedure may change as a result of the consolidation of all lien withdrawal requests by the IRS in Florence, KY.) The IRS will generally be quicker to grant lien withdrawal upon full payment of the balance due. For direct debit installment agreement lien withdrawal requests (where the taxpayer owes less than $25,000 and pays the balance within 60 months), the IRS will typically require three successful payments to clear before granting lien withdrawal.

Taxpayers will receive Form 10916(c), *Certificate of Withdrawal of Notice of Federal Tax Lien*. This Certificate withdraws the NFTL (Form 668(Y) will be issued when lien withdrawal is granted). [IRM 5.12.9.2 (9-6-2019)]

Lien Subordination

Taxpayers may need access to credit, equity, or to change loan terms to facilitate payment of the tax. However, lenders may not be willing to make any changes to financing if an NFTL has been filed. In these cases, the taxpayer would require lien subordination. Subordination is the act or process by which one person's rights or claims are moved voluntarily to a position ranked below those of other claimants. Subordination does not remove the lien but allows another lien to take priority over the federal tax lien. The IRS will only consider lien subordination if it is in the best interest of the government — that is, if the lien subordination facilitates the payment of tax. [IRM 5.17.2.8.6 (03-19-2018)]

Subordination is appropriate when this will aid in the collection of the tax. The IRS normally allows subordination in refinancing arrangements or the acquisition of second mortgages where the taxpayer will obtain proceeds from the refinance or second mortgage which will be put toward the tax owed or where the refinance or second mortgage allows the taxpayer to obtain new financing that will lower his interest rate and/or payments on that debt and thus allow the taxpayer to make a higher monthly payment to the IRS. [IRC §§6325(d)(1) and (d)(2)]

Taxpayers will use Form 14134, *Application for Certificate of Subordination of Federal Tax Lien*, to request lien subordination. Lien subordination requests are made to the IRS Consolidated Advisory Group.

Taxpayers must provide information on the loan, including lender information, property information, loan financing details, and copies of loan documents (appraisals, loan agreement, title report, closing statement, and the tax lien). [Publication 784]

What is it?	Form 669-D, *Certificate of Subordination of Property from Federal Tax Lien*. This Certificate subordinates the NFTL and allows the IRS claims to the taxpayer's property to move below a creditor in exchange for an increase in the collection of the back taxes owed.
Why is it needed?	To allow the taxpayer to refinance or access equity that will help pay or facilitate payment of the tax.

Application form	Form 14134, *Application for Certificate of Subordination of Federal Tax Lien.*
Timing	The IRS Advisory Group will notify the taxpayer of the decision and provide a projected date for mailing the certificate of subordination.
Criteria for lien subordination	The IRS can grant a request for lien subordination whenever this will facilitate the collection of the tax.
Expedite process	Taxpayers should contact their local Collection Advisory Group to get expedite instructions.
IRS contact	Contact the IRS Consolidated Advisory Group directly. Taxpayer can leave them a message at (859) 594-6090 or fax them at (844) 201-8392. [See Publication 4235 for the contact information]
How to request	When the taxpayer is applying for a loan and the lending institution requires lien subordination, the taxpayer will request subordination with the IRS as follows: • Prepare the lien subordination application and required documentation: Form 14134, *Application for Certificate of Subordination of a Federal Tax Lien.* • Contact the IRS Consolidated Advisory Group and submit the lien subordination request. Obtain a time frame for completion and issuance of the Certificate. • Respond to the Advisory Group with any additional information requested. • The IRS will issue a conditional commitment letter (Letter 4053) when the application is approved and there is a tentative agreement with the applicant. The IRS will issue the approval with the Form 669-D, *Certificate of Subordination of Federal Tax Lien,* after all requirements are met. • If the IRS does not approve the request, the taxpayer should contact the Collection Advisory Group manager and, if necessary, consider filing an appeal. (A CAP is also available.)
Assistance	• IRS Consolidated Advisory Group at (859) 594-6090. • Publication 784, *Instructions on How to Apply for a Certificate of Subordination of Federal Tax Lien.* • Centralized Lien Operation at 800-913-6050 (M-F, 8AM-5PM, local time) • Publication 4235 for contact information for the local IRS Collection Advisory Group.

In the subordination determination, the IRS will allow lien subordination if it is in the best interest of the government. [IRM 5.12.10.6.3 (9-30-2015)] This standard is met when the IRS will receive the proceeds from the new financing, or the lien subordination will enable the taxpayer to increase the monthly installment agreement payments.

For requests for lien subordination, the IRS will send the certificate of subordination when the taxpayer meets the conditions for the subordination (listed on the conditional commitment letter) and the government's interest in the property subject to the tax lien is satisfied.

If possible, taxpayers should consider sending the request for lien discharge or subordination to the IRS at least 45 days before the loan closing. [Publications 783 and 784] Doing so will allow sufficient time for review, determination, notification and the furnishing of any applicable documents by the transaction date. Taxpayers should contact the local IRS Collection Advisory Group directly to expedite the process.

> **Pro Tip**: lien subordinations are common for business that have to "factor" receivables with a financing company in order to improve their cash flow. The IRS commonly allows lien subordination to the factoring company if it will facilitate the collection of taxes.

Lien Discharge

A lien discharge removes the federal tax lien from specific property. Discharge allows the taxpayer to transfer the property to the new owner free of the lien. [IRM 5.12.10.2 (9-30-2015)] The IRS will typically only allow a lien discharge if the sale will benefit the IRS.

Per IRC §6325, a taxpayer can request a lien discharge under any one of the following five conditions: [IRM 5.12.10.3 at (2) (09-30-2015)]

IRC section	Discharge criteria
6325(b)(1)	*Property double the amount of liability:* the remaining property of the taxpayer has a fair market value that is double the sum of the amount of the federal tax lien plus other encumbrances that have priority over the federal tax lien. [IRM 5.12.10.3.1 (9-30-2015)]
6325(b)(2)(A)	*Part payment:* an amount not less than the value of the government's interest in the property is paid in partial satisfaction of the liability. To qualify, the taxpayer must be divested of all interest in the property after the transaction. [IRM 5.12.10.3.2 (09-30-2015)]
6325(b)(2)(B)	*No value:* it is determined that the interest of the United States in the property to be discharged from the lien has no value. To qualify, the

	taxpayer must be divested of all interest in the property after the transaction. [IRM 5.12.10.3.3 (09-30-2015)]
6325(b)(3)	*No value – short sale:* the proceeds of the sale are held as a fund subject to the liens and claims of the government in the same manner and priority as was the property that was discharged. To qualify, the taxpayer must be divested of all interest in the property after the transaction. [IRM 5.12.10.3.3.1 (09-30-2015)]
6325(b)(4)	*Right of substitution of value:* a third-party owner has the right to receive a certificate of discharge on any property subject to a federal tax lien if the third-party owner deposits an amount equal to the value of the government's interest in the property, as determined by the Service, or furnishes an acceptable bond in a like amount sufficient to cover the government's interest in the property. [IRM 5.12.10.3.5 (9-30-2015)]

Taxpayer should use Form 14135, *Application for Certificate of Discharge of Property from Federal Tax Lien*, to request a Certificate of Lien Discharge. In addition to the information in the application, the taxpayer will need to provide:

- A copy of the deed or title showing the legal description of the property (line 8 of Form 14135).
- Appraisal of the property (line 9 of Form 14135).
- One of the following: county valuation of the property, informal valuation of the property by a disinterested third party, proposed selling price if sold at auction (line 9 of Form 14135).
- Copy of the Notice of Federal Tax Lien(s) (line 10 of Form 14135).
- Copy of the sales contract or purchase agreement (line 11 of Form 14135).
- Copy of the current title report or a list of encumbrances that are senior to the Federal Tax Lien (line 12 of Form 14135).
- Copy of the proposed losing statement (HUD-1) or an itemized sheet of all proposed costs, commissions, and expenses associated with any transfer or sale associated with the property (line 13 of Form 14135).
- Additional information that is pertinent to the application such as pending litigation, unusual circumstances, etc. (line 14 of Form 14135).
- Escrow agreement for IRC §6325(b)(3) applicants (no value – short sale) (line 15 of Form 14135).

IRS Publication 783, *Instructions on How to Apply for Certificate of Discharge from Federal Tax Lien*, provides examples of each section of and how to complete the Form 14135.

What is it?	Form 669-B, *Certificate of Discharge of Property from Federal Tax Lien.* The certificate discharges the specific property from an NFTL and allows the taxpayer to transfer the property to the new owner free of the lien.
Why is it needed?	To remove a property from an NFTL.
Application form	Form 14135, *Application for Certificate of Discharge of Property from Federal Tax Lien.*
Timing	The IRS Collection Advisory Group Manager will notify the taxpayer of the decision and provide a projected date for mailing the certificate of discharge.
Criteria for lien discharge	The IRS will typically only allow a lien discharge if the sale will benefit the IRS.
Expedite process	Taxpayers should contact their local Collection Advisory Group to get expedite instructions.
IRS contact	Contact the IRS Consolidated Advisory Group directly. Taxpayer can leave them a message at (859) 594-6090 or fax them at (844) 201-8392. [See Publication 4235 for the contact information]
How to request	<ul><li>Determine lien discharge qualifications and applicable discharge criteria.</li><li>Prepare the lien discharge package (Form 14135, *Application for Certificate of Discharge of Property from Federal Tax Lien*, with all required documentation).</li><li>Contact the IRS Consolidated Advisory Group and submit the lien discharge request. Obtain a time frame for completion and issuance of the Certificate.</li><li>Respond to the Advisory Group with any additional information requested.</li><li>If the IRS approves the request, it issues a conditional commitment letter for a certificate of discharge.</li><li>Depending on the type of discharge requested, the taxpayer will receive a Certificate of Discharge when the conditions have been met.</li><li>If the IRS does not approve the request, the taxpayer should contact the Collection Advisory Group manager and, if necessary, consider filing an appeal. (A CAP is also available.)</li></ul>
Assistance	<ul><li>IRS Consolidated Advisory Group at (859) 594-6090.</li></ul>

	• Publication 783, *Instructions on How to Apply for Certificate of Discharge from Federal Tax Lien.* • Centralized Lien Operation at 800-913-6050 (M-F, 8AM-5PM, local time). • Publication 4235 for contact information for the local IRS Collection Advisory Group.

Depending on the type of discharge requested, the taxpayer will receive a Certificate of Discharge such as:

- Form 669-A, *Certificate of Discharge of Property from Federal Tax Lien Under Sec. 6325(b)(1) of the Internal Revenue Code*
- Form 669-B, *Certificate of Discharge of Property from Federal Tax Lien Under Sec. 6325(b)(2)(A) of the Internal Revenue Code*
- Form 669-C, *Certificate of Discharge of Property from Federal Tax Lien Under Sec. 6325(b)(2)(B) of the Internal Revenue Code*
- Form 669-H, *Certificate of Discharge of Property from Federal Tax Lien Under Sec. 6325(b)(3) of Internal Revenue Code*
- Form 669-G, *Certificate of Discharge of Property from Federal Tax Lien Sec. 6325(b)(4) of the Internal Revenue Code*

[IRM 5.12.10.3 (09-30-2015)]

The IRS requests that the taxpayer send the complete discharge application at least 45 days before the sale. In the case of a foreclosure, the IRS will send a conditional commitment letter for a certificate of discharge within 30 days of receiving a complete and approved application. [Publication 783]

The IRS Advisory Group processes lien relief applications on a first-in, first-out basis. In the case of a foreclosure or other urgent circumstance, the IRS will expedite the discharge application. [Publication 783]

Chapter 16.05: Tax Lien — IRS Contacts, Forms, and Publications

Centralized Lien Operation

The IRS has a Centralized Lien Operation (CLO) and local Collection Advisory Groups that assist with lien questions and lien relief options.

The CLO provides payoff information and lien releases and withdrawals after the liability has been satisfied (paid or no longer enforceable). Taxpayers needing a lien release can contact the CLO and receive the lien release Form 668(Z), *Certificate of Release of Federal Tax Lien.*

The CLO can be reached by phone, fax, or by mail:

Phone: (800) 913-6050, Monday-Friday, 8AM-5PM EST.
Fax: 855-390-3530

Address:

Centralized Lien Operation
PO Box 145595
Stop 8420G
Cincinnati, OH 45250-5595

IRS Consolidated Advisory Group Operation

The consolidated group processes requests for discharge, subordination, non-attachment, and withdrawal and can be reached by phone (leave a message), fax, or by mail:

Phone: (859) 594-6090 (leave a message)
Fax: (844) 201-8382

Address:

Advisory Consolidated Receipts
7940 Kentucky Drive
Stop 2850F
Florence, KY 41042

Local IRS Collection Advisory Group

The IRS's local Collection Advisory Groups are especially helpful when requesting expedited lien relief. Early contact with this Group can avoid confusion and expedite the approval of the application.

When contacting the local IRS Advisory Group, most taxpayers will have to leave a message and the IRS will contact the taxpayer in 1-2 business days.

Advisory Offices

To find the office serving your location, match the number for your State with the corresponding Advisory office in the table.

State	#
Alabama	9
Alaska	23
Arizona	1
Arkansas	20
California (North, Central)[1]	4
California (Central, South)[2]	3
California (South)[3]	2
Colorado	5
Connecticut	19
Delaware	18
District of Columbia	22
Florida (North)[4]	6
Florida (South)[5]	7
Georgia	8
Hawaii	3
Idaho	5
Illinois	21
Indiana	24
Iowa	11
Kansas	11
Kentucky	16
Louisiana	9
Maine	19
Maryland	22
Massachusetts	19
Michigan	10
Minnesota	11
Mississippi	9
Missouri	11

State	#
Montana	23
Nebraska	11
Nevada	1
New Hampshire	19
New Jersey	12
New Mexico	1
New York (NYC area)[6]	13
New York (All other areas)	14
North Carolina	15
North Dakota	11
Ohio	16
Oklahoma	17
Oregon	23
Pennsylvania	18
Rhode Island	19
South Carolina	15
South Dakota	11
Tennessee	20
Texas (North)[7]	17
Texas (South)[8]	21
Utah	5
Vermont	19
Virginia	22
Washington	23
West Virginia	16
Wisconsin	24
Wyoming	23
International[9]	7

[1] Including Monterey, San Benito, Merced, Madera Counties

[2] Including Los Angeles, San Luis Obispo, Fresno Counties

[3] Including Orange, San Bernardino, Inyo Counties

[4] Including Tallahassee, Jacksonville, Orlando, Tampa, St. Petersburg

[5] Including Miami, Ft. Lauderdale, Sarasota, Port St. Lucie

[6] Including Suffolk, Rockland, Westchester Counties

[7] Including Dallas, Ft. Worth, Abilene, Lubbock, Odessa, Tyler

[8] Including Houston, Austin, Beaumont, El Paso, Waco

[9] Including Puerto Rico, U.S. Possessions & Territories

#	Address	Phone/Fax
1	4041 N. Central Ave., Suite 112, MS 5021PHX, Phoenix, AZ 85012	Ph: 602-636-9358 Fx: 877-477-9225
2	24000 Avila Rd., MS 5905 Laguna Niguel, CA 92677	Ph: 949-575-6425 Fx: 877-477-9239
3	4041 N. Central Ave., Suite 112, MS 3890-LA, Phoenix, AZ 85012	Ph: 213-372-4545 Fx: 855-673-2055
4	1301 Clay St., Suite 1410S Oakland, CA 94612	Ph: 510-907-5173 Fx: 877-477-9228
5	1999 Broadway, MS 5021DEN Denver, CO 80202-2490	Ph: 303-603-4570 Fx: 877-477-9236
6	400 West Bay St., MS 5710 Jacksonville, FL 32202	Ph: 904-665-0832 Fx: 855-851-8234
7	1248 N. University Dr., MS 5780 Plantation, FL 33322	Ph: 954-991-4008 Fx: 855-851-8235
8	401 W. Peachtree St. NW, Room 900 MS 333-D Atlanta, GA 30308	Ph: 470-639-2495 Fx: 855-847-7741
9	1555 Poydras St., Suite 220-MS 65 New Orleans, LA 70112-3747	Ph: 504-202-9630 Fx: 877-477-9213
10	433 N. Summit St., Suite 220 Toledo, OH 43604-2638	Ph: 313-234-2398 Fx: 877-816-8631
11	30 E. 7th St., MS 5900 St. Paul, MN 55101-4940	Ph: 314-339-1604 Fx: 877-477-9247
12	4 Paragon Way, Suite 2 Freehold, NJ 07728	Ph: 973-921-4283 Fx: 877-477-8751
13	290 Broadway, MS 05-A New York, NY 10007	Ph: 212-436-1046 Fx: 877-477-8744
14	130 S Elmwood Ave., Suite 102 Buffalo, NY 14202	Ph: 518-242-5404 Fx: 855-687-2725
15	10715 David Taylor Dr., MS 25 Charlotte, NC 28262	Ph: 336-690-6095 Fx: 855-847-7742
16	550 Main St., Room 9010B Cincinnati, OH 45202	Ph: 513-975-6685 Fx: 855-807-0661
17	1100 Commerce Street Dallas, TX 75242-1027	Ph: 405-982-6604 Fx: 855-564-4242
18	1000 Liberty Ave., Room 701-A Pittsburgh, PA 15222	Ph: 412-404-9700 Fx: 877-477-8750
19	380 Westminster St., 4th floor Providence, RI 02903	Ph: 617-316-2608 Fx: 877-477-8740
20	801 Broadway, MS 53 Nashville, TN 37203	Ph: 615-250-5306 Fx: 877-477-9209
21	1919 Smith St., MS 5021 HOU Houston, TX 77002	Ph: 713-209-4399 Fx: 877-477-9214
22	400 N. 8th St., Room 898, Box 75 Richmond, VA 23219	Ph: 804-916-8039 Fx: 855-851-8233
23	915 2nd Ave., MS W245 Seattle, WA 98174	Ph: 206-946-3080 Fx: 877-477-9227
24	211 W. Wisconsin Ave., MS 5303MIL Milwaukee, WI 53203	Ph: 414-231-2121 Fx: 877-477-9261

Local Collection Advisory Group contact information can be found in IRS <u>Publication 4235</u>.

Lien Forms and Publications

IRS <u>Publication 4235</u> provides taxpayers with information on who to contact for specific information lien relief options:

Topic	Instructions, Forms, or Additional Information*	Office to Contact
General question about a Notice of Federal Tax Lien	IRS website: Understanding a Federal Tax Lien	**Centralized Lien Operation** P.O. Box 145595, Stop 8420G Cincinnati, OH 45250-5595 Phone: 800-913-6050 Outside the U.S.: 859-320-3526 Fax: 855-390-3530
Getting a lien release or lien payoff balance	Publication 1450, Instructions for Requesting a Certificate of **Release** of Federal Tax Lien	
Selling or transferring property subject to the lien	Publication 783, How to Apply for a Certificate of **Discharge** of Property From Federal Tax Lien	**Advisory Consolidated Receipts** 7940 Kentucky Drive, Stop 2850A Florence, KY 41042-2915 Phone: 859-594-6090 Fax: 844-201-8382
Borrowing or refinancing using property subject to the lien	Publication 784, How to Prepare an Application for a Certificate of **Subordination** of Federal Tax Lien	
Borrowing to purchase property when taxes are owed	Publication 785, **Purchase Money Mortgages** and Subordination of Federal Tax Lien	
Clarifying who the lien is against or what lien attaches	Publication 1024, How to Prepare an Application for a Certificate of Non-Attachment of Federal Tax Lien	
Withdrawing the notice of lien from the public record	Form 12277, Application for **Withdrawal** of Filed Form 668(Y), Notice of Federal Tax Lien	
Foreclosure — Non-Judicial sale notices**	Publication 786, Instructions for Preparing a Notice of **Non-Judicial Sale** and Application for Consent to Sale	
Foreclosure — General questions and Redeeming Property	IRS website: Understanding a Federal Tax Lien Publication 487, How to Prepare an Application Requesting the U.S. Release Its Right to Redeem Property Secured by a Federal Tax Lien	Advisory office for state where the notice of lien is filed (see page 2)
General question about lien on deceased taxpayer	IRS website: Deceased Person	Advisory office for state where the notice of lien is filed (see page 2)
Form 706 Tax Liens and IRC 2056A QDOT Collateral	IRS website: Frequently Asked Questions on Estate Taxes	**Estate Tax Advisory Group** 55 South Market St., MS 5350 San Jose, CA 95113 Phone: (669) 229-1504 Fax: (877) 477-9243
Making a claim for refund; Question on issues not shown	Publication 594, The IRS Collection Process	Advisory office for state where the taxpayer resides (see page 2)

Chapter 17:
PASSPORT RESTRICTIONS ON SERIOUSLY DELINQUENT TAX DEBT

This section discusses how to avoid and remove passport restrictions when the taxpayer has seriously delinquent tax debt (SDTD).

Topic	Covers
Overview of Passport Restrictions	Conditions in which the IRS will certify the taxpayer as having seriously delinquent tax debt (SDTD) and therefore subject to passport restrictions.
Seriously Delinquent Tax Debt (SDTD) Certification Process	The process and criteria the IRS uses to certify a taxpayer as having SDTD for passport restrictions.
SDTD Decertification — Removal of Passport Restrictions	How to decertify from having SDTD.
Expedited Decertification Procedures	The criteria and how to request expedited decertification to remove passport restrictions.
IRS Contacts	IRS phone contacts to receive passport restriction assistance.

Key Highlights:

- Taxpayers who owe more than $64,000 (adjusted annually for inflation) and who do not meet one of the exclusions for seriously delinquent tax debt face passport restrictions.
- Taxpayers can remove passport restrictions by paying the full amount of the tax or by entering into a qualified collection alternative with the IRS.
- After the IRS has certified the taxpayer as having seriously delinquent tax debt, taxpayers cannot remove the passport restrictions by simply paying the balance to bring it under $64,000. The taxpayer must also address the remaining balance by obtaining a qualified collection alternative before the passport restrictions will be removed.

Chapter 17.01: Overview of Passport Restrictions

In 2015, Congress passed the Fixing America's Surface Transportation Act (FAST Act) [Pub. L. No. 114-94, section 32101(e), 129 Stat. 1311, 1732 (2015)], which allows the Department of State (DOS) to deny a passport application and to revoke or limit a passport if the IRS certifies a taxpayer as having seriously delinquent tax debt (SDTD).

The IRS's role is to certify taxpayers who have "seriously delinquent tax debt." The IRS is required to notify the DOS of taxpayers certified as owing SDTD. [IRM 5.19.25.2 (8-12-2020)] The DOS's role is to deny their passport application or renewal. If the SDTD taxpayer currently has a valid passport, the DOS may revoke the passport or limit the ability to travel outside the United States. Whether a passport will be revoked or limited is left solely to the discretion of the DOS. [IRM 5.19.25.2 (8-12-2020)]

IRC §7345(b) defines a seriously delinquent tax debt as an "unpaid, legally enforceable federal tax liability of an individual," which:

1. Has been assessed,
2. Is greater than $64,000 (assessed amount only, indexed annually for inflation), and
3. Meets either of the following criteria:

   - a notice of lien has been filed under IRC §6323 and the Collection Due Process (CDP) hearing rights under IRC §6320 have been exhausted or lapsed, [IRM 5.19.25.3 (1-24-2024)] or
   - a levy has been made under IRC §6331. [IRM 5.19.25.3 (1-24-2024)]

The dollar threshold for SDTD is adjusted annually for inflation in the Revenue Procedure released each November which updates the inflation adjustments. Revenue Procedure 2024-40, section 3.60, provides the updated SDTD amount for 2025.

A seriously delinquent tax debt includes assessed penalties and interest but does not include accrued interest and penalties. [IRM 5.19.25.3 at (2) (1-24-2024)] It also does not include non-tax debts, such as Affordable Care Act assessments, criminal restitution assessments, child support obligations, and Foreign Bank and Financial Reporting (FBAR) penalties. [IRM 5.19.25.3 at (3) (1-24-2024)]

By law, certain situations are excluded from certification as SDTD:

- Debts timely paid through an installment agreement (IA) or offer in compromise (OIC).
- Where collection is suspended because the taxpayer requested a CDP hearing, or a CDP hearing is pending.
- Where collection is suspended because the taxpayer has requested relief from joint liability (i.e., innocent spouse relief).

  [IRM 5.19.25.4 (1-24-2024)]

The IRS also has significant discretion to exclude cases from passport certification. Additional exclusions include:

- Debt determined to be in currently not collectible (CNC) status due to hardship.
- Debt that resulted from identity theft.

- Debt of taxpayers in a disaster zone.
- Debt of a taxpayer in bankruptcy.
- Debt of a deceased taxpayer.
- Debts included in a pending offer in compromise or pending installment agreement.
- Debt for which there is a pending claim and the resulting adjustment is expected to result in no balance due.

[IRM 5.19.25.5 (1-24-2024)]

An extension to pay agreement does not qualify the debt from decertification. [IRM 5.19.25.4 at (1a) (1-24-2024)] In addition, once certified, a taxpayer cannot decertify the debt by solely paying down the balance to bring it under $64,000. [IRM 5.19.25.3 at (2) (1-24-2024)] The taxpayer must meet one of the statutory or discretionary exclusions.

If the taxpayer is able to get adjustments to reduce the balance below the SDTD threshold ($64,000), the IRS may grant decertification. This can occur as a result of penalty abatement or a return correction or adjustment. The Internal Revenue Manual provides the following example:

The taxpayer has a liability of $66,000 for tax period 2015 due to an SFR (IRS filed a return for the taxpayer) assessment. The taxpayer's seriously delinquent tax debt is certified and a Notice CP508C is issued. The taxpayer is in the process of renewing a U.S. Passport with the Department of State. The taxpayer files a return for tax period 2015 which reduces the tax debt to $30,000. Once the taxpayer's return for 2015 is processed and posted, the taxpayer will be eligible for decertification.

[IRM 5.19.25.10 at (4e) (1-24-2024)]

However, certain other adjustments will not decertify the taxpayer. According to the Internal Revenue Manual, taxpayers granted reasonable-cause penalty abatement that reduces the assessed balance below the SDTD threshold will receive decertification. [IRM 5.19.25.10 at (4e) (1-24-2024)]

The IRS will reverse a certification if the taxpayer meets either a statutory or discretionary exclusion. The IRS began taking steps to certify qualifying taxpayers for passport revocation/denial on January 22, 2018. [IRS News Release IR-2019-23, February 27, 2019]

Chapter 17.02: Seriously Delinquent Tax Debt (SDTD) Certification Process

A taxpayer with a seriously delinquent tax debt is generally someone who owes the IRS more than $64,000 in back taxes, penalties and interest for which the IRS has filed a Notice of Federal Tax Lien and the period to challenge it has expired or the IRS has issued a levy. Each week, IRS systems scan for taxpayers meeting SDTD criteria. If the criteria are met, the IRS system generates the certification notice and DOS notification.

When the IRS certifies a taxpayer to the DOS as owing a seriously delinquent tax debt, the taxpayer receives a Notice CP508C, *Passport Denied or Revoked Due to Serious Tax Delinquency*, from the IRS. [IRM 5.19.25.7 at (2) (1-24-2024)] The IRS will send written notice by regular mail to the taxpayer's last known address.

Note: The taxpayer's authorized third party (Power of Attorney authorized by Form 2848 or third party authorized under a Form 8821) will not receive a copy of this notice.

> **Pro Tip:** Taxpayers living overseas who owe back taxes should make sure the IRS has their current mailing address. They should also monitor their mail. The taxpayer should also not rely on third parties (POAs or authorized third parties) because authorized third parties do not receive IRS notice CP508C.

When the Letter CP508C is sent to the taxpayer, the DOS is also notified that the taxpayer has SDTD.

Generally, the State Department will not issue passports to taxpayers after receiving their delinquent debt certification from the IRS. However, before denying a passport renewal or new passport application, the DOS will hold the taxpayer's application for 90 days to allow him to:

- Resolve any erroneous certification issues,
- Make full payment of the tax debt, or
- Enter a satisfactory payment arrangement with the IRS.

[IRM 5.19.25.9 (1-24-2024)]

The DOS will notify the taxpayer in writing If the taxpayer's passport application is denied or revoked.

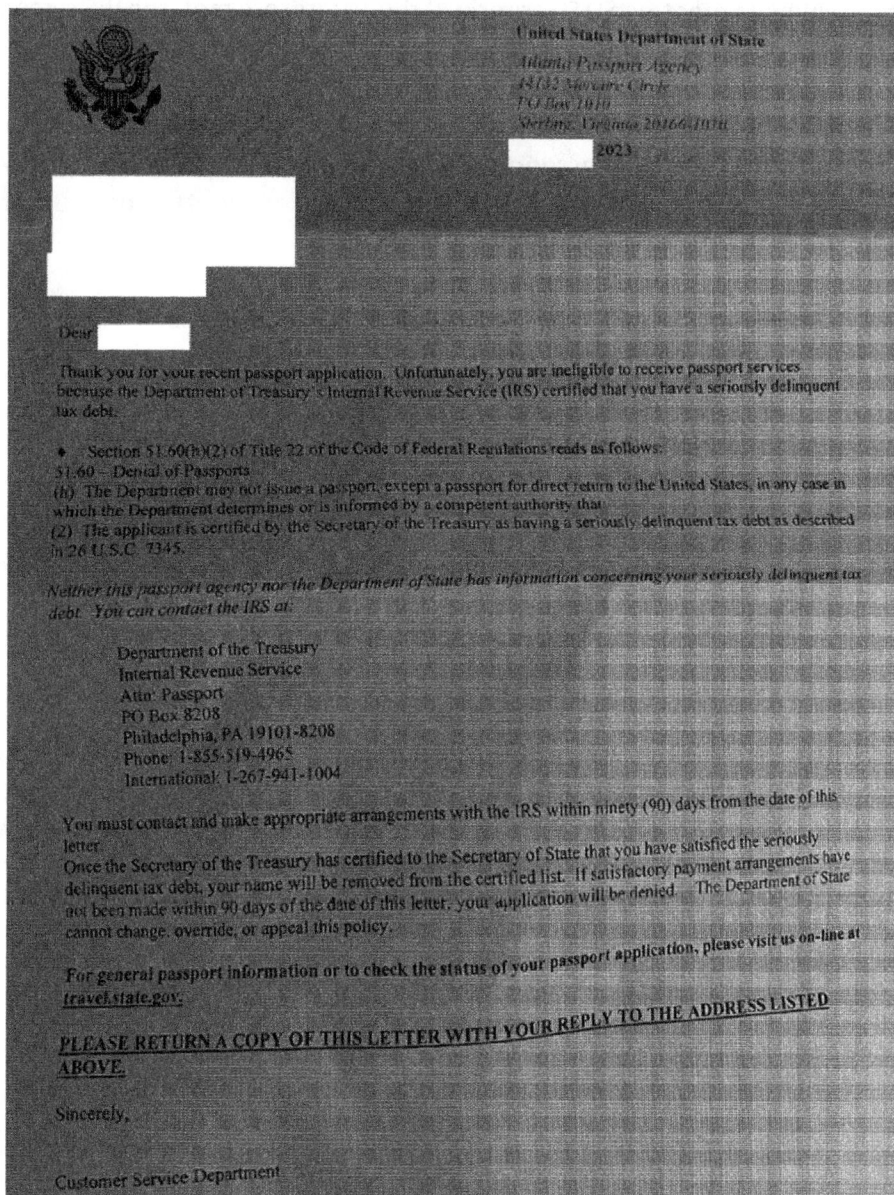

United States Department of State
Atlanta Passport Agency
4*?(?2 Mercure Circle
P.O. Box 7070
Sterling, Virginia 20166-0000

2023

Dear

Thank you for your recent passport application. Unfortunately, you are ineligible to receive passport services because the Department of Treasury's Internal Revenue Service (IRS) certified that you have a seriously delinquent tax debt.

- Section 51.60(h)(2) of Title 22 of the Code of Federal Regulations reads as follows:

51.60 – Denial of Passports
(h) The Department may not issue a passport, except a passport for direct return to the United States, in any case in which the Department determines or is informed by a competent authority that:
(2) The applicant is certified by the Secretary of the Treasury as having a seriously delinquent tax debt as described in 26 U.S.C. 7345.

Neither this passport agency nor the Department of State has information concerning your seriously delinquent tax debt. You can contact the IRS at:

Department of the Treasury
Internal Revenue Service
Attn: Passport
PO Box 8208
Philadelphia, PA 19101-8208
Phone: 1-855-519-4965
International: 1-267-941-1004

You must contact and make appropriate arrangements with the IRS within ninety (90) days from the date of this letter.

Once the Secretary of the Treasury has certified to the Secretary of State that you have satisfied the seriously delinquent tax debt, your name will be removed from the certified list. If satisfactory payment arrangements have not been made within 90 days of the date of this letter, your application will be denied. The Department of State cannot change, override, or appeal this policy.

For general passport information or to check the status of your passport application, please visit us on-line at travel.state.gov.

PLEASE RETURN A COPY OF THIS LETTER WITH YOUR REPLY TO THE ADDRESS LISTED ABOVE.

Sincerely,

Customer Service Department

Beginning in July 2019, IRS procedures state that the IRS may request the U.S. Department of State to consider revoking a U.S. passport of a certified individual. Prior to this request to the State Department, the IRS will issue Letter 6152, *Notice of Intent to Request U.S. Department of State Revoke Your Passport*, advising the taxpayer of the IRS's intent, and allowing the taxpayer 30 days (90 days if outside the U.S.) to contact the IRS to resolve the tax liability. [IRM 5.19.25.11.2 (1-24-2024)] If the IRS makes a recommendation for passport revocation, the taxpayer is not eligible for expedited decertification if needed. [IRM 5.19.25.11.2 at (1) (1-24-2024)] The most likely situation that would warrant the IRS to request revocation would likely come from an IRS field collection revenue officer. [IRM 5.19.25.11.2 at (2) (1-24-2024)]

The guidance states that the IRS will consider asking the U.S. Department of State to revoke a passport under the following circumstances:

- To protect the integrity of the legislation (such as when a taxpayer obtains a decertification based on a promise to pay and fails to act as agreed).
- If revocation is needed to encourage payment of the tax by incentivizing taxpayers with offshore activities or interests to resolve their liabilities.
- In other instances where the facts and circumstances indicate that revocation would facilitate the payment of tax.

Taxpayers can see if they have passport restrictions by reviewing their IRS account transcripts. If the taxpayer has been certified as having SDTD, they will see a TC 971 with the description "Passport certified seriously delinquent tax debt." [IRM 5.19.25.7 at (1) (1-24-2024)]

| 971 | Passport certified seriously delinquent tax debt | 04-01-2019 | $0.00 |

There is no administrative appeal, claim process, or administrative hearing that can be filed with the IRS if the taxpayer believes that a certification is erroneous. After the IRS notifies a taxpayer of certification, the taxpayer may bring a civil action against the United States in the U.S. Tax Court or a U.S. District Court. If the court determines that the certification is erroneous or if the IRS failed to decertify the taxpayer when the certification should have been reversed, it can order the certification reversed. [IRM 5.19.25.13 (8-12-2020)] Although the IRS does not allow an administrative appeal for certification, taxpayers are likely to be in the midst of a dispute involving a collection alternative or the liability itself which would allow them an administrative appeal.

Chapter 17.03: SDTD Decertification — Removal of Passport Restrictions

Once the taxpayer meets a criterion for decertification (i.e., the debt is fully paid or is subject to a statutory or discretionary exclusion), the taxpayer's debt is decertified with the DOS.

The IRS will reverse the SDTD certification within 30 days of the date the tax debt is resolved and provide notification to the State Department as soon as practicable. The taxpayer will receive IRS notice CP508R, *Reversal of Notice of Certification of Your Seriously Delinquent Federal Tax Debt to the State Department*, when the tax debt is decertified from being SDTD. [IRM 5.19.25.10 (1-24-2024)]

Chapter 17.04: Expedited Decertification Procedures

Taxpayers can qualify for expedited decertification. Domestic taxpayers can request expedited decertification if all of the following conditions are present:

- A certified taxpayer gets in good standing with the IRS on their debt and is eligible for decertification (they paid the tax or met a statutory or discretionary exclusion),
- The taxpayer states that foreign travel is scheduled within 45 days or less, and
- The taxpayer has a pending application for a passport or renewal, has received notification that their passport application was denied or revoked by the Department of State (DOS), and provides a copy of the passport denial letter issued by the DOS within the past 90 days.

International taxpayers residing outside of the United States can request expedited decertification. They must meet one of the statutory or discretionary exclusions from certification and self-identify that they have an urgent need for decertification (travel, use of passport). They do not need to provide proof of travel or a denial letter issued by the DOS.

[IRM 5.19.25.10.1 at (2) (1-24-2024)]

The IRS normally has up to 30 days to decertify the taxpayer with the DOS. After the decertification is sent to the DOS, they should remove passport restrictions. However, a taxpayer who lives abroad or plans foreign travel within 45 days and has a passport application or renewal pending can request expedited decertification.

If the taxpayer has plans for foreign travel within 45 days or lives abroad, has a passport application or renewal pending (and provides the passport application number), the taxpayer should request that the IRS expedite the certification by completing Form 14794, *Expedited Passport Decertification*, and submit it to the IRS SB/SE Passport Analyst. The standard 30-day decertification time is reduced by 14-21 days from the receipt of Form 14794. [IRM 5.19.25.10.1 (1-24-2024)] The IRS website provides updates on the decertification expedite process.

The taxpayer should contact the IRS Taxpayer Advocate Service if there are issues related to obtaining an expedited decertification.

> **Pro Tip:** In practice, expedited decertification is rarely completed in 14-21 days. Taxpayers should be in an agreement or full-pay their tax prior to requesting decertification to eliminate many of the issues regarding decertification. Also, the rules for expedited decertification change frequently. Taxpayers should visit IRS.gov or contact the IRS's Philadelphia Call Center for the latest procedures for expediting decertification.

Chapter 17.05: IRS Contacts

Passport certification questions are answered at the IRS's Philadelphia Call Center. This call center can be reached at: 855-519-4965 (domestic calls) or 267-941-1004 (International calls). [IRM 5.19.25.12 (1-24-2024)] Expedite decertification requests can also be made to IRS Collection or to the IRS Taxpayer Advocate Service.

Chapter 18:
COLLECTION APPEALS OPTIONS

This section discusses taxpayers' options and the process to appeal adverse collection determinations.

Topic	Covers
Collection Appeals Options	The appeals options when disputing an adverse IRS collection determination.
Manager Review and Taxpayer Advocate Intervention	When and how to use the quick, informal appeals process through an IRS manager and the Taxpayer Advocate.
Collection Appeals Program	When and how to use the informal Collection Appeals Program.
The Collection Due Process (CDP) Hearing and the Equivalent Hearing (EH)	When and how to use the more formal Collection Due Process or Equivalent Hearing.
Offer in Compromise (OIC) Appeals	When and how to appeal an OIC adverse determination.
IRS Contacts	IRS appeals contacts to obtain the status of a collection appeals case.

Key Highlights:

- Most adverse collection actions can be appealed within the IRS, but the type of hearing and the rules governing the appeal vary depending on the type of collection issue.
- There are five options for collection appeal within the IRS. The most common appeal is to request an informal review with an IRS collection manager.
- If the taxpayer is facing economic harm resulting from a collection enforcement action, the taxpayer may ask the Taxpayer Advocate to intervene.

Chapter 18.01: Collection Appeals Options

The role of the IRS Independent Office of Appeals in collection matters is to resolve collection disputes. Taxpayers wishing to obtain a collection alternative may appeal denial determinations from IRS collection personnel. Taxpayers facing adverse collection activity (liens and levies) may also appeal the action.

Certain collection appeals can offer the opportunity for the taxpayer to have the IRS review the accuracy of the taxes and penalties owed. This can help the taxpayer more effectively contest the amounts owed, including penalties.

Appeals is an independent function within the IRS. Collection appeals are usually completed by phone with IRS appeals officers. [IRM 8.22.4.5 (8-26-2020)] Appeals follow a judicial approach — that is, appeals officers do not raise new issues. Material new issues are generally forwarded back to IRS Collection for investigation. The appeals officer mainly looks at the collection case to see if the IRS followed the procedural rules (i.e., did they "abuse their discretion"). [IRM 8.22.4.2.1 (5-12-2022)]

Most collection disputes are resolved by requesting a manager review. IRS collection managers can take a quick, fresh look at the dispute and potentially propose a solution for the taxpayer. As such, the IRS manager should always be the first step of any appeal in a collection dispute. It is important for taxpayers to provide a collection solution that aligns with IRS collection rules when appealing.

There are five IRS collection appeals options. Taxpayers should select the applicable option. Note that they may take advantage of multiple options in certain circumstances.

- *Manager review:* an informal review of the facts and circumstances and discussion of proposed solutions and actions with an IRS collection manager.
- *Collection Appeals Program hearing (CAP):* a hearing with an appeals officer with the IRS Independent Office of Appeals in which the determination is final. All collection alternatives, except the OIC, may be argued in a CAP hearing.
- *Collection Due Process (CDP) or Equivalent Hearing (EH):* a CDP hearing is with an appeals officer with the IRS Independent Office of Appeals in which the determination is subject to review by the U.S. Tax Court. The EH is not subject to judicial review. The CDP and EH are triggered by lien and levy actions. A CDP hearing and the EH also allow the taxpayer to argue the validity of the liability owed.
- *IRS appeals hearing for an OIC rejection:* a hearing with an appeals officer with the IRS Independent Office of Appeals for a dispute related to a rejected offer in compromise application. This hearing is subject to judicial review only if the taxpayer filed the OIC application as part of a collection alternative proposed for a Collection Due Process hearing. [IRM 8.23.1.4 at (5) (8-23-2021)]
- *Taxpayer Advocate Service:* an emergency request for the Taxpayer Advocate to intervene and provide assistance to a taxpayer who is experiencing an adverse collection action that will or is causing economic harm.

Appeal option	IRS Collection Compliance Function: IRS Manager	IRS Office of Appeals: Collection Appeals Program (CAP) hearing	Collection Due Process (CDP) hearing	OIC Appeal	Taxpayer Advocate
Summary of the Five Collection Appeals Options					
Scope of issues addressed	Can be used for all collection determinations; required prior to requesting a CAP hearing on a lien, levy, or seizure.	All collection determinations (except OIC determinations); cannot contest liability or penalties.	Lien filing. Final Notice of Intent to Levy Notice of Levy on State Tax Refund (post-levy).	OIC rejection.	Economic harm due to adverse collection action (usually a systemic levy).
Form of request	Oral.	Oral, Form 9423.	Form 12153.	Form 13711.	Form 911.
Timing of request	Immediate request upon adverse decision.	• Within 30 days of an IA rejection or termination. • Within 2 days after manager conference on lien or levy action.	Within 30 days of Notice of Federal Tax Lien (NFTL) or Final Notice of Intent to Levy (FNIL).	Within 30 days of OIC rejection determination.	Immediate request upon hardship.
Timing of hearing	Within two days of request.	5-15 days from request.	Eight to 12 weeks from request, accelerated for certain issues (penalty abatement).	6-10 weeks from request.	5 business days after request.
Judicial review	No	No	Yes	No (yes, if OIC filed in a CDP hearing)	No
Extend CSED?	No	No	Yes	Yes, within OIC CSED rules.	Yes
Other	Often requested when client is in CFf.	Cannot challenge liability/penalties. Must request manager conference first before CAP request (exception: installment agreements).	Can offer collection alternatives, challenge liability and penalties.	If OIC submitted during CDP, can appeal denial to Tax Court.	Will not intervene on compliance issues – only hardship issues.

Chapter 18.02: Manager Review and Taxpayer Advocate Intervention

A taxpayer's first course of action in resolving collection disputes with the IRS is to speak to the IRS employee's manager. Manager conferences are quick and informal and can provide a good second look into resolving the collection issue. In fact, before a taxpayer requests a CAP appeal, they must discuss the problem with the Collection manager (there is an exception for installment agreement rejections and terminations). [IRM 5.19.8.2 at (5) (3-16-2018)] Taxpayers or representatives who make themselves unavailable to the manager for the mandatory discussion will not be entitled to a CAP appeal unless it is apparent that the IRS manager did not offer a "reasonable" opportunity for such discussion to occur. [IRM 8.24.1.3 at (10) (9-8-2021)]

The Taxpayer Advocate Service (TAS) can also help in collection disputes, especially when the taxpayer is facing economic harm from a levy or when the IRS does not respond to requests for appeal. However, the TAS does not have the ability to alter collection agreements or release a lien or levy (*Note:* The TAS can release a systemic levy due to hardship, i.e., a state income tax levy). [IRM 13.1.4.2.3.15 (1-3-2024) and IRM 13.1.4.2.3.16 (1-3-2024)] TAS must work directly with IRS collection to facilitate relief.

Chapter 18.03: Collection Appeals Program

The Collection Appeals Program is designed as a quicker, more formal independent review of a taxpayer's collection dispute. As such, a Collection Appeals Program (CAP) hearing can be used in almost all collection disputes, for example:

- Before or after the IRS files a Notice of Federal Tax Lien (NFTL).
- Before or after the IRS levies or seizes property.
- When the IRS denies a request for a lien-related certificate (such as a certificate of subordination or discharge) or a request for an NFTL withdrawal.
- When the IRS rejects a taxpayer's request for an installment agreement (IA).
- When the IRS rejects a taxpayer's proposed modification to an existing IA.
- When the IRS proposes or completes a modification or termination of an existing IA.
- When the IRS denies a taxpayer's request to return levied property.

   [IRM 8.24.1.3 at (2) (9-28-2021)]

Some collection disputes require the taxpayer to first attempt to address the issue with IRS collection before request a CAP hearing. If the taxpayer wants to request a CAP hearing to appeal a lien, levy, or seizure action, the IRS requires the taxpayer to first request a conference with a collection manager. Taxpayers are not required to have a manager conference for installment agreement issues. However, it is highly recommended that the taxpayer takes advantage of the opportunity to resolve their collection issue with the manager. If an agreement cannot be reached with the collection manager or if the taxpayer does not get a response from the collection manager, the taxpayer should reaffirm their request for a CAP hearing within two business days. [IRM 5.19.8.4.16.4 at (6) (5-3-2023)]

Requesting a CAP Hearing

Taxpayers may call or write the IRS to request a CAP hearing. To request by phone (the most common method), the taxpayer should call the number on the last notice received. The request is simple: inform the IRS employee that you are requesting a Collection Appeals Program hearing and explain the collection action you are appealing (lien, levy, installment agreement rejection, etc.). [IRM 5.19.8.4.16.4 at (2) (5-3-2023)] The employee will forward the case first to an IRS manager who is required to contact the taxpayer within two business days. [IRM 5.1.9.4.2 at (1) (8-30-2018)] If a resolution is not reached with the IRS manager, the manager will immediately forward the case to the IRS Independent Office of Appeals. [IRM 5.19.8.4.16.4 at (5) (5-3-2023)]

Taxpayers can also complete Form 9423, *Collection Appeal Request*, to document their disagreement(s) and request a CAP hearing. Taxpayers should send the request by contacting the IRS collection function and faxing the form directly to them or by mailing it to the address on their last notice. Taxpayers usually make the request by phone or fax the Form 9423 as most CAP requests involve an urgent need to resolve a collection agreement.

> **Pro Tip:** IRS employees often do not contact taxpayers back for the required manager conference or CAP hearing within the required time frames. Taxpayers should document that they did not receive a manager conference on the Form 9423 and proceed to request the CAP hearing. Taxpayers may also have to follow up multiple times to obtain a CAP appeal if the IRS neglects to contact the taxpayer. If the taxpayer gets no answer from the IRS, they should immediately contact the Taxpayer Advocate with concerns.

CAP Process and Timelines

The CAP process from beginning to end is usually less than three weeks.

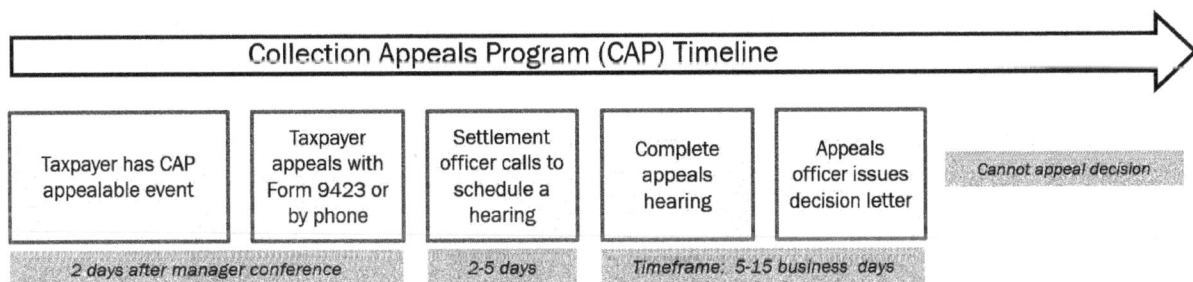

Normally, all IRS collection enforcement actions cease while CAP hearings are pending. However, if the IRS determines that the taxpayer is trying to delay collection actions, the IRS can proceed with collection actions during the CAP process.

Appeals' CAP hearing decision is limited to sustaining Collection or otherwise directing Collection to take the appropriate corrective action (i.e., release levy). [IRM 8.24.1.3.8 at (13) (08-20-2024)]

Exclusions from CAP

There are several situations in which a taxpayer may not request a CAP hearing. These include situations in which the IRS has a separate appeals process in place:

- Pre or post assessment of Trust Fund Recovery Penalties.
- Rejection of Offer in Compromise.
- Penalty appeals.
- Jeopardy levies.
- Audit reconsideration.
- Claims for refund or abatement.
- Original requests for return of levied property.

  [IRM 8.24.1.3 (9-28-2021)]

Taxpayers often wish to argue the validity of the tax and penalties owed in a CAP hearing. However, CAP cannot be used to determine a taxpayer's liability including reopening examinations, CP2000 assessments, or claims for refund. Examination reconsiderations and claims are appealable under their own appeals procedures.

When to Use a CAP

Taxpayers may have the ability to request a CAP and/or CDP/EH. CAP hearings have advantages and disadvantages.

Advantages of a CAP:

- *Collection actions are suspended*: if the CAP is to dispute a pending lien or levy, the IRS will usually suspend these actions while the taxpayer's appeal is being considered.
- *Can be used for most collection disagreements*: includes liens, levies, and terms of installment agreements.
- *No deadline to request*: there is no deadline for requesting a CAP hearing except for installment agreement issues and after a Notice of Seizure is received (ten days – see Form 9423)
- *Quick resolution*: hearing is typically held quickly (in two to five days). However, the manager conference is still the quickest method to get an independent IRS review.
- *Collection statute is not extended*: unlike the CDP hearing, a CAP does not extend the time period for the IRS to collect (i.e., the CSED or collection statute expiration date).
- *Can be used to prevent a lien*: unlike CDP hearings in which a lien is already filed, a CAP is available *before* a tax lien is filed and can be used to propose a collection alternative that will avoid the lien filing.

Disadvantages of a CAP:

- *May not release an existing levy immediately*: the taxpayer may have to wait two to three weeks before the appeal decision. Taxpayers with a levy in place may suffer economic harm during the time period while awaiting the appeals decision.
- *IRS often ignores CAP requests:* IRS employees often miss timelines for contacting taxpayers. As a result, CAP hearings may require multiple requests or intervention by the TAS to expedite the hearing.
- *Limited scope:* CAP hearings only address the collection agreement dispute. Taxpayers cannot dispute the correctness of the amount owed. Penalties can also not be disputed in a CAP.
- *Decision is final:* a CAP is less formal, and the determinations cannot be challenged in court.

Chapter 18.04: The Collection Due Process (CDP) Hearing and the Equivalent Hearing (EH)

The Collection Due Process (CDP) hearing enables a taxpayer to specifically appeal two collection enforcement actions: the filing of a Notice of Federal Tax Lien (NFTL) and a Notice of Intent to Levy. [IRM 8.22.4.2.2 at (2) and (3) (8-26-2020)] Taxpayers must timely file for a CDP hearing. That is, they must request the hearing within 30 days of receipt of the NFTL or a Notice of Intent to Levy. If they miss the time frame to file, they can request an Equivalent Hearing (EH) but the hearing must be requested within one year of the lien or levy notice. The CDP and EH are very similar except that an EH is not subject to judicial review.

Specifically, the following collection enforcement actions/letters start the time frame to request a CDP hearing:

- Notice of Federal Tax Lien Filing and Your Right to a Hearing (IRS Letter 3172 and Form 668(Y)).
- Notice of Intent to Levy and Notice of Your Right to a Hearing (usually IRS Letter 1058 or LT11).
- Notice of Levy on Your State Tax Refund (IRS Letter CP92).
- Notice of Disqualified Employment Tax Levy (post-levy notice) (IRS Letter LT73 or Letter 1058E).
- Notice of Federal Contractor Levy (post-levy notice) (IRS Letter 1058-F).
- Notice for Federal Payment Levy Program (IRS Letter CP90).
- Notice of Jeopardy Levy and Right to Appeal (IRS Letter 2439).
- IRS Notices LT 73 and LT 75 (business tax levies)

[IRM 5.19.8.3 (8-5-2016) and IRM 8.22.4.2.2 at (1) (8-26-2020)]

The CDP Request must be made within 30 days of the NFTL or levy notice. An EH must be made within one year after the levy notice or NFTL. Taxpayers should use Form 12153, *Request for a Collection Due Process or Equivalent Hearing*. The taxpayer must file the request for the appeal with the office initiating the action (the address shown on the lien or levy notice). [IRM 5.19.8.4.2 at (7) (5-3-2023)] She may mail or fax the Form 12153 to the address shown on the last notice or call the phone number on the notice. To prove that the CDP request was timely made, taxpayers should always send the request for a CDP hearing by certified mail to the address on the lien or levy notice.

Taxpayers requesting a CDP/EH hearing must propose a solution. In a CDP/EH hearing, a taxpayer can propose many different solutions. These include suggesting:

- Collection alternatives such as an installment agreement, offer in compromise or currently not collectible status.
- Correction of IRS errors, such as premature lien filing or procedural issues.
- Lien relief options, such as subordination or discharge of a federal tax lien.
- Spousal defenses, such as innocent spouse.
- Economic hardship, such as not being able to meet basic living expenses.
- Contesting the tax liability, but only if the taxpayer did not receive a statutory notice of deficiency or did not have an opportunity to dispute the tax liability. IRM 8.22.8.3 at (8) and (9) (8-26-2020) provides specific examples of letters and actions that constitute prior opportunity to contest the liability.
- Penalty abatement.

CDP/EH Process and Timelines

A CDP or EH can take several months to complete. The IRS does not have a strict time frame for completion because the collection statute of limitations is extended during the time period that the taxpayer is involved with a CDP appeal. [IRM 8.22.4.2.3 (5-12-2022)] However, for an EH, the collection statute is not extended. The process and time frames for a CDP/EH are as follows:

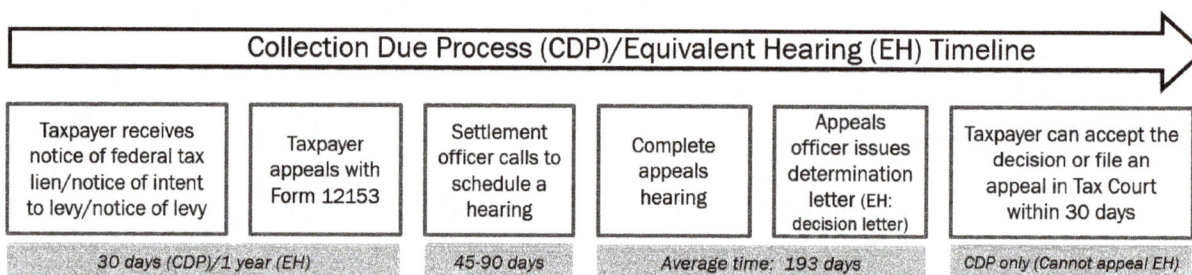

In the CDP/EH, the appeals officer will verify that legal and procedural requirements have been met. The appeals officer will do a comprehensive review to determine if the IRS has followed its procedural rules:

Per IRM 8.22.5.4.2 (8-31-2020), the preliminary procedural review is as follows:

Requirement	Description
Collection's Administrative Procedures	All applicable procedures in IRM Part 5 and the Treasury Regulations relating to the filing of the NFTL or the issuance of the notice of intent to levy were followed.
Valid Assessment	A valid assessment was made for each tax and period on the CDP notice and the liability is correct.
Notice and Demand	Notice of tax due and demand for payment (notice and demand) was issued to the taxpayer's last known address.
Balance Due	There was a balance due when the CDP levy notice was issued or when the NFTL was requested.
Verification of Certain Penalties	Verify written supervisory approval of certain penalties was received. See IRM 8.22.5.4.2.1.7.
CDP Notice Properly Issued	If a taxpayer disputes the timeliness determination, verify a CDP lien or levy notice was properly issued to the taxpayer • Notice of Intent to Levy: IRC 6330(a)(1) and IRC 6331(d)(1) (except for jeopardy levies) • Notice of Federal Tax Lien: IRC 6320(a)(1)

The appeals officer will then consider the taxpayer's collection alternative and/or challenge to the liability. The appeals officer will document the determination on Letter 3193, *Notice of Determination*. Equivalent Hearings will receive the less formal Decision Letter. [IRM Exhibit 8.22.4-2] The taxpayer may seek judicial review of the CDP Notice of Determination by filing a petition in the U.S. Tax Court within 30 days. [IRC §6330 and IRM 8.22.4.2.2 at (13) (8-26-2020)] The taxpayer may withdraw from a CDP hearing at any time by filing Form 12256, *Withdrawal of Request for Collection Due Process or Equivalent Hearing*. [IRM Exhibit 8.22.4-2] The appeals officer may request that the taxpayer withdraw when agreement is reached on a collection alternative or reduction in amount owed (i.e., penalty abatement).

Suspension of Collection Enforcement During a CDP/EH

A CDP or EH is an appeal option for an NFTL filing and a Notice of Intent to Levy. However, for NFTL filings, the CDP or EH is applicable only after the NFTL is filed. Taxpayers should consider using a CAP hearing and/or entering into a collection alternative that may preclude a lien determination in order to avoid an NFTL.

A CDP or EH request can stop levy actions. If the taxpayer files a timely request for a CDP hearing during the levy notice period, levy actions for the tax periods pertaining to the CDP notice must be suspended during the appeal period and while any court proceedings are pending with the following exceptions:

- Jeopardy levy situations.
- Levies on state income tax refunds.
- Levies served on federal contractors.
- Disqualified employment tax levies.

  [IRM 5.1.9.3.5.1 (08-30-2018)]

- Levy action is generally suspended on:

- Tax periods not subject to the CDP levy hearing, unless all pre-levy notifications have been met.
- Tax periods subject to an equivalent hearing.
- Periods subject to a CDP NFTL hearing.

However, the IRS may take levy action if:

- Collection is at risk (i.e., if the taxpayer is dissipating or transferring assets, pyramiding additional liabilities, etc.).
- Taxpayer raises only frivolous issues.
- Taxpayer is requesting an installment agreement or offer in compromise solely to delay the collection process.

When to Use a CDP or EH

Unlike CAP hearings, a CDP/EH provides a taxpayer with the ability to resolve balances owed with more than just a collection alternative. Taxpayers may effectively use a CDP or EH to obtain complicated collection alternatives to challenge the amount owed. Timely CDP hearings allow the taxpayer to freeze levy activity while proposing an alternative or to request penalty abatement or raise other challenges to a balance owed.

Advantages of CDP/EH:

- *More formal and appealable:* a CDP and EH provide the taxpayer with a clear written determination by the IRS. The taxpayer can challenge the appeals officer's decision in a CDP in U.S. Tax Court.
- *Broad scope:* the taxpayer is not limited to simply offering a collection alternative. The CDP or EH will offer the taxpayer an opportunity to contest the liability if he has not been given a prior forum to do so. Taxpayers may also raise other issues/solutions such as innocent spouse and penalty abatement.

  [IRM 8.22.4.2.2 (8-26-2020)]

Disadvantages of CDP/EH:

- *Does not stop an NFTL if the lien has already been filed:* a CDP/EH is not available until after an NFTL is filed. Therefore, a CDP or EH cannot be used to prevent an NFTL.
- *Collection period is extended:* a CDP (not an EH) extends the collection statute from the request date to the date of final determination. Taxpayers that do not want to extend imminent CSEDs may want to consider using an EH instead of a CDP.
- *Long duration to complete:* the CDP and EH can take months to complete.

Chapter 18.05: Offer in Compromise (OIC) Appeals

Taxpayers may obtain a collection appeal for rejected offer in compromise (OIC) for Doubt as to Collectibility (DATC), Doubt as to Collectibility–Special Circumstances (DATC-SC), and for Effective Tax Administration (ETA). Only a rejection can be appealed. No appeal for is available for an OIC withdrawal, termination, or return.

IRS appeals officers review OIC rejections related to collection matters (i.e., OICs for DATC, DATC-SC, and ETA). The appeals officer will review the OIC to determine if the offer examiner abused his discretion, that is, determining whether the offer examiner properly follow the IRS's rules for qualification for an OIC (ability to pay) and the calculation of the offer amount (reasonable collection potential). Appeals officers can evaluate new information presented by the taxpayer but will not re-examine agreed items previously addressed during the OIC investigation. The taxpayer will not be asked to provide updated financial information if the financial information provided in less than 12 months old from the date it was received in appeals. [IRM 8.23.3.4 at (7) (8-21-2023)]

Per Treasury Regulation §301.7122-1(f)(5), the taxpayer has 30 days from the date on the rejection letter to appeal a rejected OIC. The IRS does not allow extensions to appeal on the final rejection letter.

Reasons for Rejection

The most common rejection for an OIC occurs when the IRS determines that the taxpayer has the ability to pay more than the offer amount. Common disputes often involve income and expense averages and allowances, asset valuations, and dissipated assets.

An OIC may also be rejected for other reasons:

- *Noncompliant taxpayer*: OIC rejected because of a taxpayer's egregious compliance history such as filing frivolous returns or related company return non-filing.

Not in best interest of the government: taxpayer qualifies for an OIC-DATC but can pay substantially more via an installment agreement before the collection statute expires as opposed to the calculated offer amount.

The IRS may reject an OIC because acceptance might be detrimental to the interests of fair tax administration, even though it is shown conclusively that the amount offered is greater than could be collected by any other means. [IRS Policy Statement 5-89 (7-26-1960) and IRM 5.8.7.7.2 (04-24-2025)]

  [IRM 5.8.7.7.1 at (3) (04-24-2025)]

Rejection due to "not in the best interests of the government" and "public policy" reasons are rare. In most circumstances, the taxpayer will raise the ability to pay, specifically the following issues:

- Income averaging methods, especially for self-employed individuals.
- Expenses above the standards.
- Valuation of an asset, including quick sale value percentages.
- Retired debt and impact on future income potential.
- Non-liable spouse calculations.
- Extenuating circumstances (DATC-SC and ETA considerations).

When the IRS rejects an OIC-DATC, the offer examiner will send the Income/Expense Table (IET) and the Asset/Equity Table (AET) that shows the IRS's calculation and interpretation of the taxpayer's ability to pay. The IET and AET provide the government's basis for rejection.

Taxpayers must complete Form 13711, *Request for Appeal of Offer in Compromise,* and list their disagreements, attaching all additional supporting documentation. The appeal should start with a brief explanation of why the taxpayer disagrees with the IRS's determination. The taxpayer should specifically address each disputed item on the IET and AET. The taxpayer should also include any supporting authority for his position. If the offer was based on Special Circumstances or Effective Tax Administration, the taxpayer should include an explanation as to why he disagrees with the IRS's determination.

Taxpayers should also include a copy of the rejected offer letter.

Taxpayers may want to discuss any potential bankruptcy filing with the offer examiner or IRS appeals officer when arguing what is the taxpayer's reasonable collection potential (offer amount). IRS offer examiners and appeals officers will consider the taxes that may be dischargeable and determine the RCP during a bankruptcy proceeding. Taxpayers should raise this argument during the OIC investigation and appeals process as an effective means of reducing the offer amount. [IRM 8.23.3.4.2.3 at (2) (8-21-2023)]

IRS Appeals has the final determination on an OIC except when an OIC is filed as part of a Collection Due Process hearing (CDP). CDP determinations are subject to judicial review. Taxpayers and tax pros should look to submit OICs through a CDP in order to have the ability for a court review of an IRS determination.

OIC Appeals Timeline

Taxpayers need to appeal the OIC rejection within 30 days of the rejection letter. Appeal requests outside of the 30-day time frame will be rejected and the taxpayer will need to need to reapply (with a new application and new user fee/payments) to have an OIC considered. [IRM 5.8.7.7.5 (6-23-2022)]

```
┌──────────────────────────────────────────────────────────────────────────────────┐
│           Offer in Compromise Appeal (OIC) Timeline                         ──────▶ │
└──────────────────────────────────────────────────────────────────────────────────┘
```

Taxpayer's OIC is rejected	Taxpayer appeals with Form 13711	Settlement officer schedules hearing (Letter 5564)	Complete appeals hearing	Appeals officer issues determination letter	Taxpayer can accept the decision or, if OIC filed during CDP, appeal in Tax Court within 30 days

30 days after rejection letter	*Ave: 61 days*	*Average time: 179 days*

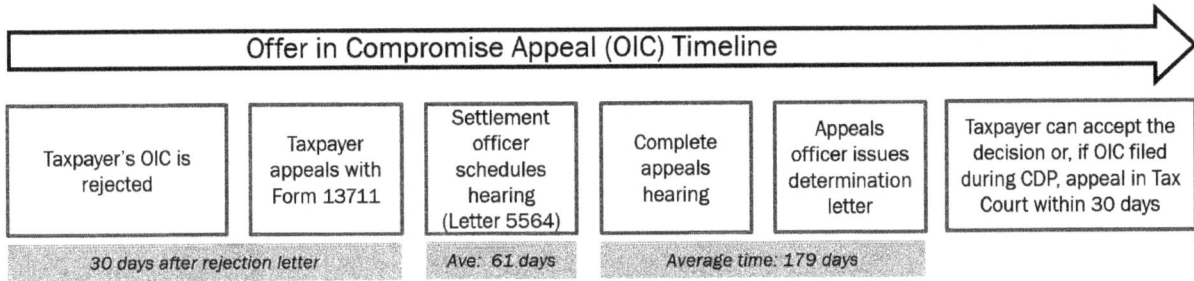

If Appeals sustains the rejected OIC, the taxpayer is unable to appeal to the Tax Court unless the OIC was filed in relation to a Collection Due Process hearing request. [U.S. v. Asemani, No. 04-4144 (U.S. Ct. App. 3d Cir., January 6, 2006)]

Chapter 18.06: IRS Contacts

IRS collection appeals may take place at various IRS campuses (i.e., "service centers") and field offices. Automated Collection System CDP cases are generally received and processed in the four ACS Support sites. The SB/SE sites are Philadelphia and Cincinnati. The W&I sites are Kansas City and Fresno. [IRM 5.19.8.4.2 at (1) (5-3-2023)] CAP hearings can be assigned to Service Center appeals sites. Collection Field function assigned cases are usually directed to local IRS appeals offices.

Once the appeals request is received, the appeals officer will contact the taxpayer by phone and/or mail to schedule the appeals conference. Taxpayers may follow up on appeals assignments by calling the Appeals Customer Service line at (559) 233-1267. [IRM 5.19.8.4.9.1 at (5) (5-3-2023)] The taxpayer can leave a message with the Appeals Customer Service line and, if the appeals case is assigned to an appeals officer, the IRS will respond back in 24-48 hours with the appeals officer's contact information.

Appendix A:
IRS EXPENSE ALLOWANCES AND COLLECTION FINANCIAL STANDARDS

IRS expense allowances and collection financial standards are used to determine a taxpayer's ability to pay.

Topic	Covers
Overview of Allowable Living Expenses	IRS expense limitation rules used to determine the taxpayer's ability to pay when obtaining an IRS ability to pay collection agreement.
Expenses Subject to the IRS Collection Financial Standards	The four categories of expenses limited/allowed under the IRS Collection Financial Standards.
IRS Collection Financial Standards: Food, Clothing, and Other Expenses	The national standard allowed for food, clothing and other miscellaneous expenses used in determining a taxpayer's ability to pay.
IRS Collection Financial Standards: Transportation Costs	The local standard allowed for vehicle ownership, operating expenses, and public transportation used in determining a taxpayer's ability to pay.
IRS Collection Financial Standards: Out-of-Pocket Medical Expenses	The national standard for out-of-pocket medical expenses allowed in determining a taxpayer's ability to pay.
IRS Collection Financial Standards: Housing/Utilities Standards	The local standard allowed for housing and utility expenses used in determining a taxpayer's ability to pay.
Housing and Utilities Standards for Each State and Territory/County	URLs for the housing/utilities standards allowed based on where the taxpayer resides.

Key Highlights:

- In determining ability to pay agreements (CNC, ATP IAs, OICs), certain taxpayer allowable living expenses are limited by the IRS Collection Financial Standards.
- The Collection Financial Standards limit the amount of necessary living expenses in four areas: food, clothing, and other; housing/utilities; transportation; and out-of-pocket medical expenses. The IRS standards are used as a guideline; taxpayers can be allowed reasonable exceptions to the standards if the expenses paid are for the health and welfare of the family and/or the production of income.

- The Collection Financial Standards are updated annually. The IRS generally releases these yearly updates in March/April, and the new amounts are effective immediately. The April 21, 2025, standards update included cost increases in the standard expenses allowed.
- In addition to the four categories of expenses limited by the IRS Collection Financial Standards, taxpayers are also allowed the amount that they pay for other necessary living expenses and potentially, other conditional expenses, in determining their ability to pay.

Appendix A.01: Overview of Allowable Living Expenses

The IRS sets limits or provides a standard amount allowed for certain allowable living expenses (ALEs) that individual taxpayers can incur when determining their ability to pay (ATP). These limits are referred to as the IRS's Collection Financial Standards (CFS).

The CFS provide a guideline for expenses allowed in determining a taxpayer's ability to pay. Taxpayers can exceed the CFS if the standard amount is inadequate to provide for the taxpayer's basic living expenses. Taxpayers must provide substantiation to IRS collection personnel before an amount higher than the standard will be considered. [IRM 5.19.13.3.2.2 at (3) (6-6-2019)]

The IRS applies the CFS in the following ability to pay agreements:

- Currently not collectible status
- Ability to pay installment agreements (i.e., taxpayer is not requesting a guaranteed, simple, or a full-pay non-streamlined installment agreement)
- Offer in Compromise—Doubt as to Collectibility and Effective Tax Administration agreements

The IRS generally allows reasonable taxpayer living expenses to exceed the CFS if the taxpayer is going to pay within six years or the collection statute of limitations, whichever is shorter. [IRM 5.19.13.3.5 (7-22-2016)] These agreements are referred to as "conditional installment agreements" or "six-year installment agreements." If the taxpayer's ability to pay shows that she cannot fully pay within six years, the amounts allowed for one or more conditional expense items may be reduced so that the liability can be fully paid within six years, if the taxpayer concurs. [IRM 5.19.13.3.5 at (1d) (7-22-2016)]

> **Pro Tip:** The new full-pay non-streamlined installment agreement (NSIA), which allows taxpayers to pay balances owed between $50,000 and $250,000 through their CSED, will remove the need for most routine ATP and conditional IAs. The NSIA will allow the taxpayer to pay on likely longer terms (through the end of the CSED) and not limit the taxpayer to paying within six years. Full-pay NSIAs do not require financial disclosure and use of CFS in determining the payment amount.

The IRS updates the CFP annually in March/April and publishes these updates on its website.

> **Pro Tip:** The IRS rarely requests substantiation of a taxpayer's expenses if the taxpayer can pay within six years or the collection statute, whichever is less, unless the taxpayer has defaulted on past agreements or has a history of filing and not paying.

The CFS only apply to individual taxpayers and not to business entities. Taxpayers who file a Form 1040, Schedule C, *Profit and Loss from Business*, or Schedule E, *Supplemental Income and Loss*, or Schedule F, *Profit or Loss from Farming*, do not have expense standards related to computing their net business income. Business taxpayers compute their income by using actual monthly business income and out-of-pocket expenses to produce income. As such, "living" expense standards do not apply. Individual taxpayers with businesses cannot use non-cash expenses such as depreciation or amortization in computing their net business income. [IRM 5.19.13.3.1 at (11) (08-14-2023)]

> **Pro Tip:** Although the CFS do not apply in determining business income, taxpayers who file Schedule C business returns are allowed to use the expense standards to determine their person/individual household ability to pay. Taxpayers who have mixed person/business expenses (i.e., personal and business use of a vehicle, office in the home, etc.) must adjust their personal expenses so that they do not "double-dip" by using the same expense for both personal and business. For example, if a vehicle is used for business and personal use, the taxpayer will determine the total cost of ownership and operating expenses for the vehicle and deduct the amount already claimed by the business from the personal expenses allowed in determining the household ability to pay.

CFS are not available for international taxpayers or taxpayers in the U.S. Territories, with the exception of housing and utilities in Puerto Rico. In the absence of standardized figures for foreign countries, a fair and consistent approach should be applied to what is allowed as living expenses for these taxpayers. These taxpayers' submission of living expenses is generally accepted, provided they appear reasonable. [IRM 5.19.13.3.2.2 at (4) (6-6-2019)]

In addition to the four categories of living expenses subject to CFS, the IRS also allows actual expenses for other necessary expenses (i.e., taxes paid, health insurance, term life insurance, mandatory retirement, etc.) and other conditional expenses (i.e., alimony, child support, childcare, legal fees, etc.). [IRM 5.19.13.3.2 at (1) (08-14-2023)]

Appendix A.02: Expenses Subject to the IRS Collection Financial Standards

There are four categories of expenses that are subject to CFS.

Expense category	Type of standard	How determined
Food, clothing, and other	Standard amount allowed.	Based on number of dependents in family.
Housing and Utilities	Limited to amount paid up to standard allowed.	Two factors: • number of dependents in family • Location (state/county)
Transportation: • Ownership costs • Operating costs • Public transportation	Ownership: limited to amount paid up to the standard amount. Operating costs: standard allowed. Public transportation: standard amount allowed.	Ownership: • Up to two vehicles. Operating costs: • Up to two vehicles. • Based on location. Public transportation costs: • National allowance.
Out-of-pocket medical	Standard amount allowed but does not provide a limit (taxpayer can claim additional expenses by providing proof of additional expenses paid).	• Standard based on age. • Actual based on qualified amounts paid.

Taxpayers can exceed the standard if they can show that the standard amount is inadequate to meet their living expenses or expenses necessary to produce income. Some common situations that call for a deviation from the standard are as follows:

- *Food, clothing, and other expenses*: a taxpayer who incurs additional food costs for a special diet related to a medical condition.
- *Transportation operating costs*: where a taxpayer has a long-distance commute for work, the IRS can allow a larger operating cost or larger than normal repair bills for an older vehicle with no monthly payment.

- *Transportation ownership costs*: payment for a special vehicle needed to transport a handicapped person in the household.
- *Housing/utilities*: special housing to accommodate a taxpayer with disabilities. [IRM 5.15.1.2 at (15) (11-22-2021)]

Appendix A.03: IRS Collection Financial Standards: Food, Clothing, and Other Expenses

Taxpayers are allowed the total National Standards monthly amount computed for their family size, with no need to show amounts actually spent. [IRM 5.19.13.3.2.3 at (3) (08-14-2023)] Substantiation is only required if the taxpayer claims more than the national standards amounts and consideration is being given to allowing the additional expense. If the amount claimed is more than the total allowed by the National Standards for food, housekeeping supplies, apparel and services, and personal care products and services, the taxpayer must provide documentation to substantiate that those expenses are necessary living expenses. [IRM 5.19.13.3.2.3 at (3) and (4) (08-14-2023)] Deviations from the standard amount are not allowed for miscellaneous expenses. Generally, the total number of persons attributed to a taxpayer for purposes of the National Standards should be the same as those allowed as exemptions on the taxpayer's most recent year income tax return.

Food, Clothing, and Other Expenses				
Expense	One Person	Two Persons	Three Persons	Four Persons
Food (1)	$497	$863	$1,068	$1,255
Housekeeping supplies (2)	$45	$75	$82	$91
Apparel & services (3)	$93	$181	$188	$276
Personal care products & services (4)	$50	$91	$94	$117
Miscellaneous (5)	$154	$271	$321	$390
Total	$839	$1,481	$1,753	$2,129
More than four persons			**Additional Persons Amount**	
For each additional person, add to four-person total allowance:			$394	

Note: The standards listed are as of 4/21/2025 and are likely effective until April 2026. The standards change each March/April and are listed on the:
https://www.irs.gov/businesses/small-businesses-self-employed/national-standards-food-clothing-and-other-items

Many expenses are included in the food, clothing and miscellaneous categories:

1. Food includes food at home and food away from home. Food at home refers to the total expenditures for food from grocery stores or other food stores. It excludes the purchase

of nonfood items. Food away from home includes all meals and snacks, including tips, at fast-food, take-out, delivery and full-service restaurants, etc.

2. Housekeeping supplies includes laundry and cleaning supplies, stationery supplies, postage, delivery services, miscellaneous household products, and lawn and garden supplies.
3. Apparel and services include clothing, footwear, material, patterns and notions for making clothes, alterations and repairs, clothing rental, clothing storage, dry cleaning and laundry that is sent out, watches, jewelry and repairs to watches and jewelry.
4. Personal care products and services includes products for hair, oral hygiene products, shaving needs, cosmetics and bath products, electric personal care appliances, and other personal care products.
5. The miscellaneous allowance is for expenses taxpayers may incur that are not included in any other allowable living expense category, or for any portion of expenses that exceed the Collection Financial Standards and are not allowed under a deviation. Taxpayers can use the miscellaneous allowance to pay for expenses that exceed the standards, or for other expenses such as credit card payments, bank fees and charges, reading material and school supplies.

[IRM 5.19.13.3.2.3 at (1) (08-14-2023)]

Appendix A.04: IRS Collection Financial Standards: Transportation Costs

There are three standards for transportation:

1. *Ownership costs*: the ownership costs provide a monthly allowance for the lease or purchase of up to two automobiles. This a national standard. A single taxpayer is normally allowed one automobile. For each automobile, taxpayers will be allowed the lesser of:

    * the monthly payment on the lease or car loan, or
    * the ownership costs standard allowed.

    [IRM 5.19.13.3.2.5.2 at (6) (4-3-2020)]

If a taxpayer has no lease or car loan payment, the amount allowed for ownership costs will be $0.

Allowable Ownership Costs		
	One Car	**Two Cars**
National	$662	$1,324

Note: The standards listed are as of 4/21/2025 and are likely effective until April 2026. The standards change each March/April and are listed on the:
https://www.irs.gov/businesses/small-businesses-self-employed/local-standards-transportation

2. *Operating costs*: a taxpayer is allowed operating costs, based on the regional and metropolitan area in which they reside. For each automobile, taxpayers will be allowed the lesser of:

- the amount actually spent monthly in operating costs, or
- the operating costs standard amount allowed.

[IRM 5.19.13.3.2.5.2 at (6) (4-3-2020)]

> **Pro Tip:** In practice, the IRS routinely allows the standard operating cost allowance. Only in incidents where the taxpayer has expenses above the standard will he need to provide documentation as to actual operating costs.

Operating costs include:

- Insurance,
- Registration fees and inspections,
- Normal maintenance and repairs,
- Fuel,
- Parking, and
- Tolls.

[IRM 5.19.13.3.2.5.2 at (3) (4-3-2020)]

Operating Costs (see the transportation census region/MSA for the applicable location)		
	One Car	**Two Cars**
Northeast Region	$302	$604
Boston	$338	$676
New York	$401	$802
Philadelphia	$300	$600
Midwest Region	$259	$518
Chicago	$296	$592
Cleveland	$259	$518
Detroit	$365	$730
Minneapolis-St. Paul	$284	$568
St. Louis	$232	$464
South Region	$281	$562
Atlanta	$320	$640
Baltimore	$306	$612
Dallas-Ft. Worth	$320	$640
Houston	$359	$718
Miami	$400	$800
Tampa	$335	$670

Washington, D.C.	$295	$590
West Region	$297	$594
Anchorage	$219	$438
Denver	$337	$674
Honolulu	$252	$504
Los Angeles	$353	$706
Phoenix	$358	$716
San Diego	$335	$670
San Francisco	$362	$724
Seattle	$270	$540

Note: The standards listed are as of 4/21/2025 and are likely effective until April 2026. The standards change each March/April and are listed on the: https://www.irs.gov/businesses/small-businesses-self-employed/local-standards-transportation

Transportation Census Regions/Metropolitan Statistical Areas (MSAs) for Determining Location: The transportation operating cost table lists the states that comprise each Census Region and MSA. If the taxpayer does not reside in an MSA, the regional standard should be used.

Northeast Census Region: Maine, New Hampshire, Vermont, Massachusetts, Rhode Island, Connecticut, Pennsylvania, New York, New Jersey.

MSA	Counties
Boston	in MA: Essex, Middlesex, Norfolk, Plymouth, Suffolk
	in NH: Rockingham, Strafford
New York	in NY: Bronx, Kings, Nassau, New York, Putnam, Queens, Richmond, Rockland, Suffolk, Westchester
	in NJ: Bergen, Essex, Hudson, Hunterdon, Middlesex, Monmouth, Morris, Ocean, Passaic, Somerset, Sussex, Union
Philadelphia	in PA: Bucks, Chester, Delaware, Montgomery, Philadelphia
	in NJ: Burlington, Camden, Gloucester, Salem
	in DE: New Castle
	in MD: Cecil

Midwest Census Region: North Dakota, South Dakota, Nebraska, Kansas, Missouri, Illinois, Indiana, Ohio, Michigan, Wisconsin, Minnesota, Iowa.

MSA	Counties (unless otherwise specified)
Chicago	in IL: Cook, DeKalb, DuPage, Grundy, Kane, Kendall, Lake, McHenry, Will
	in IN: Jasper, Lake, Newton, Porter
	in WI: Kenosha
Cleveland	in OH: Ashtabula, Cuyahoga, Geauga, Lake, Lorain, Medina
Detroit	in MI: Lapeer, Livingston, Macomb, Oakland, St. Clair, Wayne

Minneapolis-St. Paul	in MN: Anoka, Carver, Chisago, Dakota, Hennepin, Isanti, Le Sueur, Mille Lacs, Ramsey, Scott, Sherburne, Washington, Wright
	in WI: Pierce, St. Croix
St. Louis	in MO: Franklin, Jefferson, Lincoln, St. Charles, St. Louis county, Warren, St. Louis city, Crawford
	in IL: Bond, Calhoun, Clinton, Jersey, Macoupin, Madison, Monroe, St. Clair

South Census Region: Texas, Oklahoma, Arkansas, Louisiana, Mississippi, Tennessee, Kentucky, West Virginia, Virginia, Maryland, District of Columbia, Delaware, North Carolina, South Carolina, Georgia, Florida, Alabama.

MSA	Counties (unless otherwise specified)
Atlanta	in GA: Barrow, Bartow, Butts, Carroll, Cherokee, Clayton, Cobb, Coweta, Dawson, DeKalb, Douglas, Fayette, Forsyth, Fulton, Gwinnett, Haralson, Heard, Henry, Jasper, Lumpkin, Meriwether, Morgan, Newton, Paulding, Pickens, Pike, Rockdale, Spalding, Walton
Baltimore	in MD: Anne Arundel, Baltimore county, Carroll, Harford, Howard, Queen Anne's, Baltimore city
Dallas-Ft. Worth	in TX: Collin, Dallas, Denton, Ellis, Hunt, Johnson, Kaufman, Parker, Rockwall, Tarrant, Wise
Houston	in TX: Austin, Brazoria, Chambers, Fort Bend, Galveston, Harris, Liberty, Montgomery, San Jacinto, Waller
Miami	in FL: Broward, Miami-Dade, Palm Beach
Tampa	in FL: Hernando, Hillsborough, Pasco, Pinellas
Washington, D.C.	in DC: District of Columbia
	in MD: Charles, Frederick, Montgomery, Prince George
	in VA: Arlington, Clarke, Culpeper, Fairfax county, Fauquier, Loudoun, Prince William, Rappahannock, Spotsylvania, Stafford, Warren, Alexandria city, Fairfax city, Falls Church city, Fredericksburg city, Manassas city, Manassas Park city
	in WV: Jefferson

West Census Region: New Mexico, Arizona, Colorado, Wyoming, Montana, Nevada, Utah, Washington, Oregon, Idaho, California, Alaska, Hawaii.

MSA	Counties (unless otherwise specified)
Anchorage	in AK: Anchorage, Matanuska-Susitna
Denver	in CO: Adams, Arapahoe, Broomfield, Clear Creek, Denver, Douglas, Elbert, Gilpin, Jefferson, Park
Honolulu	in HI: Honolulu
Los Angeles	in CA: Los Angeles, Orange
Phoenix	in AZ: Maricopa, Pinal

San Diego	in CA: San Diego
San Francisco	in CA: Alameda, Contra Costa, Marin, San Francisco, San Mateo
Seattle	in WA: King, Pierce, Snohomish

3. *Public transportation costs*: there is a single nationwide allowance for public transportation — mass transit fares for a train, bus, taxi, ferry, etc. [IRM 5.19.13.3.2.5.2 at (4) (4-3-2020)] Taxpayers with no vehicle are allowed the standard amount monthly, per household, the amount spent will not be subject to scrutiny.

If a taxpayer owns a vehicle and uses public transportation, expenses may be allowed for both, provided they are needed for the health and welfare of the taxpayer or family, or to produce income. However, the expenses allowed would be actual expenses incurred for ownership costs, operating costs and public transportation, or the standard amounts, whichever is less. [IRM 5.19.13.3.2.5.2 at (10) (4-3-2020)]

Public Transportation	
National	$244

Note: The standards listed are current as of 4/21/2025 and are likely effective until April 2026. The standards change each March/April and are listed on the:

https://www.irs.gov/businesses/small-businesses-self-employed/local-standards-transportation

If the amount claimed for Ownership Costs, Operating Costs or Public Transportation is more than the total allowed by the transportation standards, the taxpayer must provide documentation to substantiate that those expenses are necessary living expenses. [IRM 5.19.13.3.2.5.2 at (7) and (12) (4-3-2020)]

Appendix A.05: IRS Collection Financial Standards: Out-of-Pocket Medical Expenses

Taxpayers and their dependents are allowed the standard amount monthly for out-of-pocket medical expenses on a per person basis, without questioning the amounts actually spent. [IRM 5.19.13.3.2.4 at (4) (6-10-2015)] If the amount claimed is more than the total allowed by the health care standards, the taxpayer must provide documentation to substantiate that those expenses are necessary living expenses. [IRM 5.19.13.3.2.4 at (6) and (7) (6-10-2015)] Generally, the number of persons allowed should be the same as those allowed as exemptions on the taxpayer's most recent year income tax return. [IRM 5.19.13.3.2.2 at (2) (6-6-2019)]

Out-of-Pocket Medical Expenses	
Age	Out of Pocket Costs
Under 65	$84
65 and Older	$149

Note: The standards listed are as of 4/21/2025 and are likely effective until April 2026. The standards change each March/April and are listed on the: https://www.irs.gov/businesses/small-businesses-self-employed/national-standards-out-of-pocket-health-care

Expenses for out-of-pocket health care expenses include medical services, prescription drugs, and medical supplies (e.g., eyeglasses, contact lenses, etc.). Elective procedures such as plastic surgery or elective dental work are generally not allowed. [IRM 5.19.13.3.2.4 at (3) (6-10-2015)]

These amounts do not include health insurance premiums paid. Health insurance premiums are allowed in full as a separate necessary expense.

Appendix A.06: IRS Collection Financial Standards: Housing/Utilities Standards

Taxpayers are allowed up to the local standards monthly amount for housing and utilities for their family size and location. The taxpayer must have paid these expenses for them to be allowed. If the amount claimed is more than the total allowed by the local standards for housing and utilities, the taxpayer must provide documentation to substantiate that those expenses are necessary living expenses. Deviations from the standard amount are not allowed for housing/utilities expenses except in the case of conditional installment agreements (six-year payment plans based on actual expenses).

The standard for a particular county and family size includes both housing and utilities allowed for a taxpayer's primary place of residence. Housing and utilities standards are also provided for Puerto Rico.

Housing and utilities standards include expenses paid.

Housing expenses include:

- Monthly rent or mortgage payment,
- Property taxes,
- Homeowner's or renter's insurance,
- Necessary maintenance and repairs, and
- Homeowner dues and condominium fees.

  [IRM 5.19.13.3.2.5.1 at (2) (11-25-2014)]

Utility expenses include:

- Gas,
- Electricity,

- Water,
- Fuel oil, coal, bottled gas,
- Trash and garbage collection,
- Wood and other fuels,
- Septic cleaning,
- Telephone,
- Cell phone,
- Internet services, and
- Cable television.

[IRM 5.19.13.3.2.5.1 at (3) (11-25-2014)]

The tables include five categories — for households with one, two, three, four, and five or more persons.

Generally, the total number of persons allowed under the National Standards should be the same as those allowed as exemptions on the taxpayer's most recent year income tax return. [IRM 5.19.13.3.2.2 at (2) (6-6-2019)]

> **Example 3-49** A family of four in Autauga County, Alabama, is entitled to housing and utility expenses up to $2,149 (limitation under the Standard). The taxpayer can accumulate all expenses paid each month for mortgage or rent, property taxes, interest, insurance, maintenance, repairs, gas, electric, water, heating oil, garbage collection, residential telephone service, cell phone service, cable television, and Internet service. However, unless the taxpayer is requesting a conditional installment agreement (i.e., a six-year payment plan that fully pays the balance owed in the six years), the taxpayer will be limited to the standard amount.

State of Alabama Housing/utility standards by county:

County	2025 Published ALE Housing Expense for a Family of 1	2025 Published ALE Housing Expense for a Family of 2	2025 Published ALE Housing Expense for a Family of 3	2025 Published ALE Housing Expense for a Family of 4	2025 Published ALE Housing Expense for a Family of 5
Autauga County	$1,533	$1,800	$1,897	$2,115	$2,149

Housing/Utility Standards: County with Lowest/Highest Allowance (*Family of Four*)			
State/Territory	# of Counties	Allowance	
		Lowest	Highest
Alabama	67	$1,613 (Coosa)	$2,441 (Shelby)
Alaska	30	$1,092 (Kusilvak)	$3,423 (Sitka City and Borough)

Arizona	15	$1,694 (Greenlee)	$2,688 (Maricopa)
Arkansas	75	$1,511 (Nevada)	$2,381 (Benton)
California	58	$2,137 (Modoc)	$5,953 (Marin)
Colorado	64	$1,713 (Baca)	$3,685 (Douglas)
Connecticut	9	$2,733 (Northeastern CT Planning Region)	$4,482 (Western CT Planning Region)
Delaware	3	$2,414 (Sussex)	$2,716 (New Castle)
District of Columbia	1	$3,949 (n/a)	$3,949 (n/a)
Florida	67	$1,785 (Dixie)	$4,237 (Monroe)
Georgia	159	$1,512 (Quitman)	$3,320 (Forsyth)
Hawaii	5	$2,915 (Hawaii)	$3,949 (Honolulu)
Idaho	44	$1,854 (Gooding)	$2,823 (Blaine)
Illinois	102	$1,617 (Pulaski)	$3,230 (Lake)
Indiana	92	$1,646 (Fayette)	$2,919 (Hamilton)
Iowa	99	$1,707 (Montgomery)	$2,985 (Dallas)
Kansas	105	$1,646 (Comache and Osborne)	$3,062 (Johnson)
Kentucky	120	$1,477 (Menifee)	$2,930 (Oldham)
Louisiana	64	$1,571 (Tensas)	$2,873 (Plaquemines)
Maine	16	$1,792 (Aroostook)	$2,925 (Cumberland)
Maryland	24	$1,845 (Alleghany)	$3,820 (Howard)
Massachusetts	14	$2,536 (Berkshire)	$4,531 (Nantucket)
Michigan	83	$1,658 (Iosco)	$2,956 (Washtenaw)
Minnesota	87	$1,807 (Pipestone)	$3,364 (Carver)
Mississippi	82	$1,536 (Holmes)	$2,591 (Issaquena)
Missouri	115	$1,570 (Hickory)	$2,764 (Platte)
Montana	56	$1,511 (Prairie)	$2,999 (Gallatin)
Nebraska	93	$1,523 (Garden)	$2,837 (Sarpy)
Nevada	17	$1,864 (Mineral)	$2,854 (Washoe)
New Hampshire	10	$2,175 (Coos)	$3,472 (Rockingham)
New Jersey	21	$2,633 (Cumberland)	$4,500 (Bergen)
New Mexico	33	$1,482 (Quay)	$2,963 (Los Alamos)
New York	62	$1,824 (Chautauqua)	$5,484 (New York)
North Carolina	100	$1,667 (Graham)	$2,997 (Orange)
North Dakota	53	$1, 793 (Eddy)	$2,699 (Billings)
Ohio	88	$1,689 (Crawford)	$3,348 (Delaware)

Oklahoma	77	$1,597 (Cimarron)	$2,461 (McClain)
Oregon	36	$1,879 (Harney)	$3,319 (Clackamas)
Pennsylvania	67	$1,662 (Forest)	$3,609 (Chester)
Puerto Rico	78	$1,104 (Maricao)	$2,209 (Guaynabo)
Rhode Island	5	$2,909 (Providence)	$3,531 (Newport)
South Carolina	46	$1,602 (Marion)	$2,940 (Charleston)
South Dakota	66	$1,433 (Oglala Lakota)	$2,679 (Lincoln)
Tennessee	95	$1,597 (Van Buren)	$3,473 (Williamson)
Texas	254	$1,543 (Collingsworth)	$3,657 (Crockett)
Utah	29	$1,829 (Emery)	$3,734 (Summit)
Vermont	14	$2,179 (Essex)	$3,102 (Chittenden)
Virginia	134	$1,571 (Buena Vista)	$5,278 (Falls Church)
Washington	39	$1,871 (Ferry)	$4,107 (King)
West Virginia	55	$1,270 (Gilmer)	$2,503 (Jefferson)
Wisconsin	72	$1,821 (Langlade)	$3,017 (Dane)
Wyoming	23	$1,840 (Washakie)	$3,758 (Teton)
TOTAL	3,222	Lowest in U.S. (excluding Puerto Rico): $1,092 (Kusilvak, Alaska)	Highest in U.S. (excluding Puerto Rico): $5,953 (Marin, California)

Note: The standards listed are as of 4/21/2025 and are likely effective until April 2026. The standards change each March and are listed on the: https://www.irs.gov/businesses/small-businesses-self-employed/local-standards-housing-and-utilities

Appendix A.07: Housing and Utilities Standards for Each State and Territory/County

The standards change each March/April and are listed on the IRS website at https://www.irs.gov/businesses/small-businesses-self-employed/collection-financial-standards

Local Standards: Housing and Utilities

Help   News   English ⌄   Charities & Nonprofits   Tax Pros

File   Pay   Refunds   Credits & Deductions   Forms & Instructions   Search

Home / File / Businesses and Self-Employed / Small Business and Self-Employed / Local Standards: Housing and Utilities

Local Standards: Housing and Utilities

Individuals

Businesses and Self-Employed

Business Tax Account

Small Business and Self-Employed

Employer ID Numbers

Business Taxes

Reporting Information Returns

Self-Employed

Starting a Business

Operating a Business

Closing a Business

Industries/Professions

Small Business Events

Online Learning

Large Business

Disclaimer: IRS Collection Financial Standards are intended for use in calculating repayment of delinquent taxes. These Standards are effective on April 22, 2024 for purposes of federal tax administration only. Expense information for use in bankruptcy calculations can be found on the website for the U.S. Trustee Program ⌕.

Download the housing and utilities standards [PDF] in PDF format for printing. Please note that the standard amounts change, so if you elect to print them, check back periodically to assure you have the latest version.

Please be advised that the housing and utilities document is 116 printed pages.

Please choose a state or territory.

Alabama
Alaska
Arizona
Arkansas
California
Colorado
Connecticut
Delaware
District of Columbia
Florida
Georgia
Hawaii
Idaho
Illinois
Indiana
Iowa
Kansas
Kentucky

Related Topics

- Collection Financial Standards
- Local Standards: Transportation
- National Standards: Food, Clothing and Other Items
- National Standards: Out-of-Pocket Health Care
- Tools

Appendix B:
IRS COLLECTION TEMPLATES LINKS (WORKSHEETS, CHECKLISTS, ETC.)

Title	Useful for:
Form 433-A: Equity in Asset Summary (for CNC and Installment Agreements)	Worksheet to determine ability to pay with net equity in assets for CNC status or an ATP IA. Maps to Form 433-A.
OIC: Equity in Asset Summary for OIC Qualification Determination	Worksheet to value net equity in assets for purposes of determining if the taxpayer qualifies for an OIC-DATC.
Form 433-A(OIC): Equity in Asset Summary for Offer Amount Determination	Worksheet to compute net realizable equity in assets (for OIC-DATC offer amounts determination). Maps to Form 433-A(OIC).
Forms 433-A and 433-A(OIC): Net Business Income Analysis for Ability to Pay Calculation	Worksheet to determine the average net business income for ability to pay determinations for CNC, ATP IAs, and OIC-DATC. Maps to Forms 433-A and 433-A(OIC)).
MDI Analysis Worksheet (for determining ability to pay for installment agreements, CNC, and OIC-DATC)	Worksheet to analyze the average monthly disposable income for ability to pay determinations for CNC, ATP IAs, and OIC-DATC.
Forms 433-A and 433-A(OIC) MDI Computation	Worksheet to determine final MDI for ability to pay determinations for CNC, ATP IAs, and OIC-DATC. Maps to Forms 433-A and 433-A(OIC)).
Form 433-A(OIC): OIC Qualification and Offer Amount Computations	Worksheet to determine if the taxpayer qualifies for an OIC-DATC and to compute the offer amount. Maps to parts of Form 433-A(OIC) and Form 656.
Collection Issue Resolution Checklist	Checklist of sequence of eight steps to be taken to resolve a taxpayer's collection and related issues.
Taxpayer Information Task List — IRS Collection Issue	List of information needed to address a collection issue.
IRS Account Research Worksheet — Collection Issue (contact by phone/in person)	Obtain a tax history and IRS transcripts/records needed to address a collection issue.

Request to Designate Payment	Provide instructions to the IRS when designating a payment to a specific year/form/tax/amount.
OIC-DATC Application Checklist	Checklist and sequence of items to include in an OIC-DATC application.
ETA-OIC Application Checklist	Checklist and sequence of items to include in an ETA OIC application.

For more details on this topic, visit www.TaxProblemsHandbook.com and navigate to the **IRS Collection Solutions Handbook** tab to access the referenced item.

Appendix C:
IRS COLLECTION FORMS

The IRS website (IRS.gov) contains useful forms such as those listed below.

Form	Title	Useful for:	Links on IRS.gov
433-A	*Collection Information Statement for Wage Earners and Self-Employed Individuals*	Financial disclosure to IRS for ability to pay agreements for CNC or installment agreements (individuals and Schedule C taxpayers).	https://www.irs.gov/pub/irs-pdf/f433a.pdf
433-B	*Collection Information Statement for Businesses*	Financial disclosure to IRS for ability to pay agreements for CNC or installment agreements (business entities).	https://www.irs.gov/pub/irs-pdf/f433b.pdf
433-D	*Installment Agreement*	Installment agreement request form for direct debit agreements and 84-month agreements.	https://www.irs.gov/pub/irs-pdf/f433d.pdf
433-F	*Collection Information Statement*	Financial disclosure to IRS for ability to pay agreements for CNC or installment agreements (individual wage earners).	https://www.irs.gov/pub/irs-pdf/f433f.pdf
433-H	*Installment Agreement Request and Collection Information Statement*	Installment agreement request form and financial disclosure form for individual wage earners who cannot pay within 72 months or owe more than $50,000.	https://www.irs.gov/pub/irs-access/f433h_accessible.pdf

656-B	*Offer in Compromise Booklet*	File an Offer in Compromise for Doubt as to Collectibility or for Effective Tax Administration Contains: Forms 433-A(OIC), 433-B(OIC), and Form 656.	https://www.irs.gov/pub/irs-pdf/f656b.pdf
1127	*Application for Extension of Time for Payment of Tax Due to Undue Hardship*	Apply for six-month extension to pay with waiver of failure to pay penalty (18 months for deficiency assessment).	https://www.irs.gov/pub/irs-pdf/f1127.pdf
2159	*Payroll Deduction Agreement*	Set up installment agreement payments through a deduction from employee's payroll.	https://www.irs.gov/pub/irs-pdf/f2159.pdf
9423	*Collection Appeal Request*	Request for a Collection Appeals Program hearing.	https://www.irs.gov/pub/irs-pdf/f9423.pdf
9465	*Installment Agreement Request*	Request for a simple installment agreement (guaranteed or simple), either by direct debit or by check.	https://www.irs.gov/pub/irs-pdf/f9465.pdf
12153	*Request for a Collection Due Process or Equivalent Hearing*	Request for a Collection Due Process or Equivalent hearing as a result of a lien or levy notice.	https://www.irs.gov/pub/irs-pdf/f12153.pdf
12277	*Application for Withdrawal of Filed Form 668(Y), Notice of Federal Tax Lien*	Request lien withdrawal.	https://www.irs.gov/pub/irs-pdf/f12277.pdf

13711	*Request for Appeal of Offer in Compromise*	Request for appeal of an adverse OIC determination with the IRS Office of Appeals.	https://www.irs.gov/pub/irs-pdf/f13711.pdf
13844	*Application for Reduced User Fee for Installment Agreements*	Request to lower installment agreement set-up fee based on low-income criteria.	https://www.irs.gov/pub/irs-pdf/f13844.pdf
14134	*Application for Certificate of Subordination of Federal Tax Lien*	Request lien subordination.	https://www.irs.gov/pub/irs-pdf/f14134.pdf
14135	*Application for Certificate of Discharge of Property from Federal Tax Lien*	Request lien discharge.	https://www.irs.gov/pub/irs-pdf/f14134.pdf

Appendix D:
COMMON IRS NOTICES AND TAXPAYER NOTIFICATIONS

For more details on this topic, visit www.TaxProblemsHandbook.com and navigate to the **IRS Collection Solutions Handbook** tab to access the referenced item.

Notice #	Title	Used for:
CP14	*Balance Due for Year*	First balance due notice.
CP14i	*Balance Due: Installment Agreement Set-up*	Taxpayer with a balance due owed on a filed return in which a payment plan was requested and granted.
CP90	*Intent to Levy and Notice of Right to Hearing*	Notice of Intent to levy on a federal payment.
CP91	*Final Notice Before Levy on Social Security Benefits*	Notice of intent to seize 15% of social security benefits.
CP92	*Notice of Levy on Your State Tax Refund — Notice of Your Right to a Hearing*	Notification of state income tax levy.
CP501	*Balance Due Notice*	Second balance due notice (first notice was CP14).
CP503	*Second Reminder: Balance Due Notice*	Third balance due notice (prior notice was CP501).
CP504	*Notice of Intent to Levy*	Fourth balance due notice; notice of intent to levy state income tax refund.
CP508C	*Notice of Certification of Your Seriously Delinquent Federal Tax Debt to the State Department*	Notify taxpayer that they are subject to passport restrictions on past-due tax debt owed.
CP508R	*Reversal of Notice of Certification of Your Seriously Delinquent Federal Tax Debt to the State Department*	Notify taxpayer that he or she is in good standing and not subject to passport restrictions.
CP521	*Monthly Installment Agreement Reminder*	Notify taxpayer of monthly installment agreement payment due (with payment voucher).
CP522	*IRS Partial Pay Installment Agreement—Two-year review*	Notice requiring taxpayer to provide new financial information related to a partial pay installment agreement (as required by law). Taxpayer directed to

		call IRS at 800-831-0273 (taxpayer will be given an extension number on the CP522).
CP523	*Notice of Intent to Levy and Intent to Terminate Your Installment Agreement*	Notify taxpayer that he/she is in default of the installment agreement.
Form 8519	*Taxpayer Copy of Notice of Levy*	Notify taxpayer that a bank/financial institution levy was issued for collection of back balances owed.
Letter LT11/L1058	*Final Notice of Intent to Levy (LT11: Automated Collection System; L1058: Collection Field Function)*	Notify taxpayer that he or she is subject to levy in 30 days and he/she has a right to request a Collection Due Process Hearing within 30 days.
Letter LT16	*Account Has Been Assigned for Collection Enforcement*	Notifies taxpayer that he/she is assigned to IRS collection for enforcement (lien and levy).
Letter LT38	*Reminder: You Have a Balance Due; IRS Has Ways to Help You*	IRS reminder notice sent in 2024 to taxpayers who owe in years prior to 2022. The notice provides years and amounts owed, with information and links to collection alternatives.
Letter 3172	*Notice of Federal Tax Lien and Right to a Hearing under IRC §6320*	Notifies taxpayer that a Notice of Federal Tax Lien has been filed and he/she has a right to request a Collection Due Process hearing within 30 days.
CP89	*Annual Installment Agreement Notice*	Annual notice for those in an installment agreement that shows amounts paid and balances owed.
CP71 Series	*Annual Notice*	Annual installment agreement reminder for taxpayers in CNC or assigned to collection.
CP40	*Taxpayer Account Assigned to a Private Debt Collection Agency*	Taxpayer's account has been assigned to PDC. Further notices and contacts for collection will be made by one of the PDCs.
Letter 725	*Meeting Scheduled with Taxpayer*	Revenue officer meeting request/confirmation.
Form 9297	*Summary of Taxpayer Contact*	Revenue officer request and deadline for information.
PDC Letter	*Private Debt Collection Letter*	Letter from the PDC that notifies taxpayer that he/she is assigned to a Private Debt Collection agency.

Appendix E:
IRS COLLECTION PUBLICATIONS

The IRS website (IRS.gov) contains useful publications such as those listed below.

Publication	Title	Link on IRS.gov
Pub. 594	*The IRS Collection Process*	https://www.irs.gov/pub/irs-pdf/p594.pdf
Notice 746	*Information about Your Notice, Penalty and Interest*	https://www.irs.gov/pub/irs-pdf/n746.pdf
Pub. 783	*How to Apply for Certificate of Discharge from Federal Tax Lien*	https://www.irs.gov/pub/irs-pdf/p783.pdf
Pub. 784	*How to Apply for a Certificate of Subordination of Federal Tax Lien*	https://www.irs.gov/pub/irs-pdf/p784.pdf
Pub. 1024	*How to Apply for a Certificate of Non-Attachment of Federal Tax Lien*	https://www.irs.gov/pub/irs-pdf/p1024.pdf
Pub. 1450	*Instructions for Requesting a Certificate of Release of Federal Tax Lien*	https://www.irs.gov/pub/irs-pdf/p1450.pdf
Pub. 1468	*Guidelines for Processing Notice of Federal Tax Lien Documents*	https://www.irs.gov/pub/irs-pdf/p1468.pdf
Pub. 1660	*Collection Appeal Rights*	https://www.irs.gov/pub/irs-pdf/p1660.pdf
Pub. 1854	*How to Prepare a Collection Information Statement (Form 433-A)*	https://www.irs.gov/pub/irs-pdf/p1854.pdf
Pub. 4235	*Collection Advisory Offices Contact Information*	https://www.irs.gov/pub/irs-pdf/p4235.pdf
Pub. 4518	*What You Can Expect When the IRS Assigns Your Account to a Private Collection Agency*	https://www.irs.gov/pub/irs-pdf/p4518.pdf
Pub. 5059	*How to Prepare a Collection Information Statement (Form 433-B)*	https://www.irs.gov/pub/irs-pdf/p5059.pdf
Form 9465 Instructions	*Instructions for Form 9465*	https://www.irs.gov/pub/irs-pdf/i9465.pdf

Appendix F: Index

www.ingramcontent.com/pod-product-compliance
Lightning Source LLC
Chambersburg PA
CBHW081457200326
41518CB00015B/2290